THE ECONOMIES OF CHINA AND INDIA
Cooperation and Conflict

Volume 2: Competitiveness, External Cooperation Strategy and Income Distribution: Changes in China

THE ECONOMIES OF CHINA AND INDIA
Cooperation and Conflict

Volume 2: Competitiveness, External Cooperation Strategy and Income Distribution: Changes in China

Editors

Manmohan Agarwal

Centre for Development Studies, India & Research and Information Systems for Developing Countries, India

Jing Wang

University of Western Ontario, Canada

John Whalley

University of Western Ontario, Canada & Centre for International Governance Innovation (CIGI), Canada & National Bureau of Economic Research (NBER), USA

World Scientific

NEW JERSEY • LONDON • SINGAPORE • BEIJING • SHANGHAI • HONG KONG • TAIPEI • CHENNAI • TOKYO

Published by

World Scientific Publishing Co. Pte. Ltd.

5 Toh Tuck Link, Singapore 596224

USA office: 27 Warren Street, Suite 401-402, Hackensack, NJ 07601

UK office: 57 Shelton Street, Covent Garden, London WC2H 9HE

Library of Congress Cataloging-in-Publication Data

Names: Whalley, John, editor. | Agarwal, Manmohan, editor. | Wang, Jing, 1974 April 21– editor.

Title: The economies of China and India : cooperation and conflict / editor-in-chief, John Walley; [edited by] Manmohan Agarwal (Centre for Development Studies, India & Research and Information Systems for Developing Countries, India), Jing Wang (University of Western Ontario, Canada)

Description: New Jersey : World Scientific, [2016] Contents: Volume 1. China and India: The International Context and Economic Growth, Manufacturing Performance and Rural Development -- Volume 2. Competitiveness, External Cooperation Strategy, and Income Distribution: Changes in China -- Volume 3. Economic Growth, Employment and Inclusivity: The International Environment.

Identifiers: LCCN 2016006686| ISBN 9789813100398 (hbk : set : alk. paper) | ISBN 9789813100534 (hbk : vol 3 : alk. paper) | ISBN 9789813100527 (hbk : vol 2 : alk. paper) | ISBN 9789813100510 (hbk : vol 1 : alk. paper)

Subjects: LCSH: Economic development--China. | Economic development--India. | China--Economic conditions--1949– | India--Economic conditions--1947– | China--Economic policy--1949– | India--Economic policy--1947– | China--Foreign economic relations. | India--Foreign economic relations.

Classification: LCC HC427.95 .E34135 2016 | DDC 330.951--dc23

LC record available at https://lccn.loc.gov/2016006686

British Library Cataloguing-in-Publication Data

A catalogue record for this book is available from the British Library.

Desk Editors: Herbert Moses/Yu Shan Tay

Typeset by Stallion Press
Email: enquiries@stallionpress.com

Printed in Singapore

Contents

Acknowledgment

The editors would like to acknowledge the support of the China Policy and Research Group (CPRG) at the University of Western Ontario (Canada) for the participation of Chinese researchers in the project. CPRG acknowledges supports from the Ontario Research Fund and Centre for International Governance Innovation (CIGI, Canada). The editors thank the staff at World Scientific Publishing, Herbert Moses, Xiao Qi, R. Raghavarshini, as well as Zvi Ruder for logistical and moral support. Editor Manmohan Agarwal also would like to thank the participants of seminars at the Centre for Development Studies Kerala where some of the papers were presented for helpful comments.

About the Editors

John Whalley is the Professor of Economics and Co-Director of the Centre for the Study of International Economic Relations at Western University; Research Associate at the National Bureau of Economic Research (NBER); Coordinator of Global Economy Group at the CESifo; and Distinguished Fellow at the Centre for Global Governance Innovation (CIGI). Professor Whalley is ranked No.1 in Canada among publishing economists in the RePEc rankings. He won the Hellmuth Prize for Achievement in Research, and also is 2012 Killam Prize Winner.

Manmohan Agarwal is the Reserve Bank Chair at the Centre for Development Studies at Thiruvananthapuram, Kerala, India. Earlier he had retired as a professor from Jawaharlal Nehru University, New Delhi, India where he taught for almost thirty years. Subsequently, he was a senior fellow at the Centre for International Governance Innovation (CIGI) at Waterloo Canada where he worked on issues of the world economy including the G20 and South-South cooperation. He is also a Senior Fellow at Research and Information Systems for Developing Countries, New Delhi and an adjunct senior fellow with the Institute of Chinese Studies. He also worked for a number of years at the World Bank and the International Monetary Fund. His research has been mainly in the area of International Economics and Development Economics.

Jing Wang is currently both the coordinator and research associate of the Centre for the Study of International Economic Relations at Western University. She was a Postdoctoral Associate in Department of Economics at Western University for years, and also held positions of associate research fellow in the Institute of Quantitative & Technical Economics at Chinese Academy of Social Sciences and editor of the Journal of Quantitative & Technical Economics.

List of Contributors

Hejing Chen
Department of Economics, Western University, Canada

Min Du
China Population & Development Research Center, China

Shuangyan Gong
China Population & Development Research Center, China

Qing Guo
Economics School, Shandong University of Finance and Economics, China

Tingting He
School of Economics and Business Administration, Beijing Normal University, China

Chunding Li
Institute of World Economics and Politics, Chinese Academy of Social Sciences, China Department of Economics, Western University, Canada

Yongchao Li
Economics School, Shandong University of Finance and Economics, China

Dongmei Liu
China Population & Development Research Center, China

Hongyan Liu
China Population & Development Research Center, China

Weili Liu
College of Economics, Shenzhen University, China

Risheng Mao
Institute of World Economics & Politics, Chinese Academy of Social Sciences, China

Dana Medianu
Department of Economics, Western University, Canada

Keting Shen
Department of Economics, Western University, Canada
School of Economics, Zhejiang Gongshang University, China

Yi Shi
China Population & Development Research Center, China

Jin Song
Department of Economic Development, Institute of World Economics and Politics, Chinese Academy of Social Sciences, China

Hui Wan
China Population & Development Research Center, China

Jing Wang
Department of Economics, Western University, Canada

Jun Wang
School of Management, Shandong University, China

John Whalley
Department of Economics, Western University, Canada
Centre for International Governance Innovation (CIGI), Canada
National Bureau of Economic Research (NBER), USA

Juan Yang
School of Economics and Business Administration, Beijing Normal University, China

Dan Zhou
Beijing University of Agriculture, China
Institute of World Economics and Politics, Chinese Academy of Social Sciences, China

Introduction

Jing Wang

China's remarkable rapid GDP growth in the recent decades made a "growth miracle", while exports of labor-intensive products and investments in infrastructures and real estates have contributed the most to this miracle. However, with the world economy experiencing profound adjustments since the onset of the 2008 Global Financial Crisis, China's unbalanced rapid GDP growth also has been interrupted and China's economy entered into a so-called "New Normal" stage. China's annual GDP growth rates were 9.5%, 7.7%, 7.7%, 7.3%, and 6.9% in 2011–2015 respectively (Statistical Communiqué of the People's Republic of China on the 2015 National Economic and Social Development, National Bureau of Statistics of China, February 29, 2016). The "New Normal" means that China's economy will not put high GDP growth as the first priority. While ensuring a medium–high growth rate of GDP, China will put more importance on economic structure improvement and upgrading, and on transformation of growth driven forces from input and investment to innovation.

Though China's GDP growth has slowed gradually (except year 2010 due to the huge stimulate pack) after the 2008 crisis, it remains more rapid than other major economies of the world. From international experiences, it is inevitable that GDP growth slows down after continuous high growth over a relatively long period. There are only 13 economies over the world which maintained 7% plus growth for 25 consecutive years since the World War II, amongst only Taiwan maintained 7% plus in the fourth decade and others all experienced slowing down growth since the third decade. China has entered its fourth decade of high growth and it is increasingly difficult to grow rapidly from a larger base.

The shifting gear of China's economy from the previous high speed to a medium-to-high speed growth was caused by domestic and international factors together. Domestically, China's economy encountered growing downward pressures in recent years, which included weakening comparative advantage of labor resource, increasing factor costs, aging, sluggish investment growth, and lack of drivers of consumption. Externally, international markets showed no sign of major revival and global economy is still seeking for new driving forces.

China's excessively rapid economic growth has covered or even worsened some problems of its out-of-balance economic structures. These include relatively slower growth of per capita annual disposable income, huge urban–rural and regional differences, vanishing demographic dividend, increasing pressures on industrial structure upgrading and optimizing, sluggish resident consumption, unsustainable exports pattern, the inefficient pattern of growth, environmental degradation and pollution, mounting pressure on prices, and entrenched structural and institutional obstacles.

No matter China chooses to or has to change its economic development pattern, it experienced significant changes in recent years.

China's services sector grew more rapidly than industry since 2012 and the gap was widening over time. The shares of value added of services sector in GDP increased steadily, with 44.3% in 2011 and 50.5% in 2015. Whereas the shares of value added of industry in GDP decreased over time, losing a leading position to the services since 2013 (data from the Statistical Communiqué of the People's Republic of China on the 2015 National Economic and Social Development, National Bureau of Statistics of China, February 29, 2016). Under such situation, China adopted more new approaches to accelerate its industrial transition and upgrade.

China government has stressed the importance of industrial transition and upgrade for decades. Recent policies have focused on phasing out obsolete capacities, resolving the overcapacity, and promoting the transition from "Made in China" to "created in China" and to "intelligent manufacturing in China". China's State Council has unveiled a national plan, dubbed "Made in China 2025" in May 2015, focusing on promoting manufacturing. "Made in China 2025" is the first 10-year action plan designed to transform China from a manufacturing giant into a world manufacturing power. The "Made in China 2025" has clear principles, goals, tools, and sector focus.

China's foreign trade had grown at two-digit speed before the 2008 financial crisis and experienced negative growth in 2009. Except the rebounce in 2010, the growth rates of China's foreign trade decreased year by year. China's exports dropped 2.9% and imports were down 14.1% in 2015. According to monthly trade data from the General Administration of Customs of China, the downward trends of 2015 have continued and even worsened. Meanwhile, China's trade structure has changed significantly. Shares of processing trade for both exports and imports have dropped quickly over the last decade, and the shares of primary products in exports have decreased.

To cope with the exceptionally complex and severe circumstances both domestically and internationally, China actively participated in bilateral and regional trade negotiations, and made special efforts in fostering new advantages of international cooperation and competition.

One emphasis of China's efforts is to promote trade and economic cooperation with countries involved in the "Belt and Road" initiative (the Silk Road Economic Belt and the 21st Century Maritime Silk Road). The focus of the "belt and Road" initiatives is the creation of an economic land belt that includes countries on the original Silk Road through Central Asia, West Asia, the Middle East, and Europe, as well as a maritime road that links China's port facilities with the African coast. With redirecting China's domestic overcapacity and capital for regional infrastructure development, China could improve trade and financial relationship with countries involved. Maybe a "Belt and Road" free trade zone in the future is not impossible. The launch of Asian Infrastructure Investment Bank (AIIB) could provide financing support to the "Belt and Road" initiatives.

Another emphasis is China's free trade zone strategy, which includes the promotion of regional economy integration outside China and setting up free trade zones inside China. China has concluded 14 free trade agreements with 22 countries and economies including the ASEAN, Chill, Australia, New Zealand, Singapore, and Hong Kong (China). China also participated in negotiations on Regional Comprehensive Economic Partnership (RCEP) and China–Japan–Korea free trade agreement. China started the trial of Shanghai Pilot Free Trade Zone in 2013 and has set up other three free trade zones in China afterwards. These free trade zones aim to promote liberalization on the capital account and trade facilitation.

Given all the issues and new policy responses inside and outside China, the prospects of China economy in mid-term and long term caused heated discussion. This book seeks to provide information on industry, trade and investment negotiation, labor market, income distribution, welfare, and environment and analyze the realities and challenges China's economy faces.

The first section of the book deals with the competitiveness of China's industry. The paper by Wang and Whalley (WW) explored if the Chinese markets for manufactured products are more competitive than in the US by comparing China–US industrial concentration ratios. The authors presented estimates of 4- and 8-firm concentration ratios by industry and in weighted average form for the manufacturing sector for Chinese enterprises for 2002 and 2007. Their results showed that China–US ratios are approximately 0.5 for both 4- and 8-firm concentration ratios. Also in China, industrial concentration declined significantly over the period 2002–2007, while estimates for the US pointed slightly increasing over time. Thus, the authors argued that markets for Chinese manufactured products are considerably more competitive than that in the US, which is opposite to the view of highly concentrated Chinese domestic market and non-market economy of China in China's World Trade Organization (WTO) accession terms.

Nested Constant Elasticity of Substitution (CES) production functions over multiple inputs have been widely used in the CGE-based policy modeling literature; however, lack of reliable estimates of substitution elasticities for nested structures has been acknowledged for a long time. This is especially true for the Chinese case. Driven by the distinct characteristics of the China economy, Shen and Whalley (SW) explored a three-factor two-level aggregate production function with inputs capital (K), labor (L), and energy (E) and presented estimates of substitution elasticities of normalized nested CES aggregate production functions for China with different nested structures of input factors capital, labor (or human capital adjusted labor), and energy using normalized data for the period 1979–2006. They used grid search-based nonlinear estimation procedures and found the substitution elasticities they estimated are all positive. For the widely used $(K, L)\ E$ structure, they found that the substitution elasticities between capital and labor for China are below unity. When human capital adjusted labor was used as input instead of unadjusted raw labor, estimates of substitution elasticities between capital and labor became lower. SW compared their estimates with existing literature and found that that their estimates of substitution elasticities for all three different nested structures of two-level CES production functions for China, no matter using labor with or without human capital adjusted, all have satisfactory and relatively high values of goodness-of-fit with comparatively higher standard errors. They argued that the $(E, L)\ K$ structure seems more appropriate for the Chinese economy.

Wang and Whalley (WW1) reported comparisons of firm concentration ratios for value-added in manufactured products for China, the US, and the UK. They calculated 5- and 15-firm concentration ratios in manufacturing for the UK and China for 2003 and 2004 using the similar method they used for both the US and China for 2002 and 2007 in Chapter 1. These in turn differ in date and firm level and so only US–China and UK–China pairwise comparisons are possible rather than direct three way comparisons. Estimates showed that comparable concentration ratios are approximately one half in China compared to the US and approximately three quarters in China compared to the UK. Additional calculations pointed to the robustness of their findings.

The paper by Liu analyzed the quality of China's imported and exported products by measuring quality ladders and quality ranking using a modified quality ladder model and both the enterprise database and the customs data. The empirical study supported that the quality of intermediate goods is higher than the quality of final goods China exported. The author argued that processing trade in China can increase export, upgrade quality, and increase wage. The author also calculated total factor productivity (TFP) with Chinese data 2002–2006 and estimate the impact of quality ladder and quality ranking on productivity, skill intensity, and capital intensity. The findings indicated quality upgrading is necessary to developing countries for export success, upgrade technology, and economic development.

The second section of the book discusses China's external cooperation strategy. Bilateral investment treaties (BITs) and double tax treaties (DTTs) are the two most widely used types of international agreements for both protecting foreign investors and providing such investment non-discriminatory treatment and from double taxation. Chen, Li, and Whalley (CLW) examined the impact of both China's BITs and DTTs simultaneously on China's bilateral foreign direct investment (FDI) inflows and outflows. They briefly reviewed the development of word BITs, DTTs and FDI flows, and China's case since the 1980s. They conducted panel data fixed effect analyses for both gravity and CMM models. They created a weighted measure of BITs to reflect the relative importance of different states as the FDI source, and then performed empirical research using China's bilateral FDI flow data. They found that cumulative number of BITs China signed had a positive but minor impact on both China's FDI inflows and outflows. The effect of a dummy BIT was always significant and positive for China's FDI inflows, while negative but not always significant for China's FDI outflows. They argued that BITs and DTTs served more to promote China's FDI inflows than FDI outflows.

Large prospective trade deals including Transatlantic Trade and Investment Partnership (TTIP) and Trans-Pacific Partnership (TPP) have been widely referred as the "mega deal". Li, Wang, and Whalley (LWW) explored a possible description of trade mega deal and argued that the phenomenon of mega deal was much broader than just these two. They then calculated the trade volume coverage and trade barrier coverage for potential mega deals, including both deals from which China for now is excluded and the (possible) mega deals that China could become involved with over the next decade. Their calculations showed that if all possible mega deals concluded the incremental trade coverages were large, especially for China. They also employed a 13-country Armington type global general equilibrium model and the simulation results showed that almost all mega deal member countries would gain and nearly all mega deal non-member countries would lose in terms of welfare and trade. They argued that where mega deals to be concluded, the pressures on those countries or blocs who were not parties to conclude their own deals would grow. Also they argued that China more so than any other larger country or entity would see itself as driven into its own mega trade deals by the need to compete in the system.

China is seen from outside as having a large State Owned Enterprise (SOE) sector, and large SOEs are seen as having a protected monopoly position in domestic Chinese markets. Thus, the trade arrangements involving SOEs become a key element in trade negotiations raised by China's trading partners. Chen and Whalley (CW) discussed some of the key sub-issues potentially arising with SOEs in China's trade negotiations. These included arrangements for SOEs under China's antitrust laws as well as the operation of these arrangements in practice via case law; the potential increase in Chinese coverage of the WTO government procurement code were Chinese SOEs to be included under it; the implications of changing relative size of the SOE and private sectors in China for the "non-market" economy designation China consented to upon WTO accession; and claimed subsidization of SOEs through various devices. They argued that cross sub-issue bargaining could be a possible resolution for China regarding these sub-issues.

After the 2008 financial crisis, the BRICS countries (Brazil, China, India, Russia, and South Africa) have speeded up economic cooperation and reached a series of consensus in promoting trade liberalization and facilitation. The paper by Zhou measured the bilateral trade cost elasticity between the BRICS countries from 2000 to 2010 using translog gravity model. As trade cost-cutting measure has heterogeneous impact on different participation among these countries, it is important to measure the different impact of trade costs reduction on the trade volume of different countries. The results showed that the trade cost elasticities of BRICS vary within a wide range between [0.48, 245]. Russia's average trade cost elasticity is the highest (36.66), followed by South Africa (29.31) and China at the lowest (1.84). The author argued that the results implied that China stands first in the open degree among the BRICS, and there would be little potential for China to expand export by reducing trade costs.

The third section of the book deals with China's labor market and income distribution issues. Mao and Whalley (MW) investigated the impacts of Renminbi (RMB) real exchange rate movements on China's employment and wage rates with highlighting ownership structure of manufacturing industries. They used a panel dataset covering 456 four-digit industries over the period 2001–2009 and investigated the effects of exchange rate movements on labor market behavior taking into account trends of RMB real exchange rate changes by industry before and after the reform of RMB exchange rate regime in July 2005. Instead of using an aggregate RMB real effective exchange rate, they constructed industry specific real effective exchange rates for 163 three-digit industries. With controlling other factors, their empirical results showed that RMB real exchange rate movements have significant effects on both wage rates and net employment. Their estimation results indicated that labor market for private enterprises is less responsive to exchange rate fluctuations than that for SOEs, and exchange rate movements generated larger effects on the labor market activity of SOEs and FIEs than private firms.

China's rural to urban labor migration had reached 274 million in 2014; however, it has suffered from severe market segmentation generated by Chinese hukou registration system. Paper by Song discussed China's hukou-based labor market segmentation, and analyzed the impacts of hukou reform on labor market.

Migrant workers have consequently faced the discriminated wage income, unequal job opportunity, and limited access to social security and public service. The author showed the situation of such discriminations over time using comparable data from multiple sources. The author also stressed the problem of migrants' absence in pension contribution and benefits under current scheme design. The author evaluated the impact of reforms on hukou taken by local and central Chinese government since the 1990s on labor market. The author argued that these reforms have caused noticeable change to Chinese labor market and migration behavior. Hukou restriction across cities has shown a clear hierarchy feature; segmentation across provinces has been enhanced by hukou uniform reform; and the resident certificate system that has been gradually set up promotes migrants to live stably at one destination.

It is a stylized fact that education plays a quite important role to individuals' income, and individuals' education is largely dependent on their parental socio-economic status. To examine the impact of family background on their children's educational attainment in China, Yang, and He (YH) examined the causal effect of China's intergenerational mobility in education by employing COX proportional model with using the Cultural Revolution as an instrument variable and data from the Chinese Household Income Project 2002 urban survey. The data shows that education of the cohort that was affected by the Cultural Revolution is 2.5 years less than that of cohorts that were not affected by the Cultural Revolution. Their empirical results showed that the Cultural Revolution does interrupt a generation's education and the affected cohort's education is 0.242 year less than the unaffected group. Also father's education does have an impact on children's education, especially for girls and the impacts for boys are insignificant. The hazard ratio for children not attending higher education will decrease 30.45% with one year's increase of father's schooling, while it may reduce 54.25% for girls.

The last section of this book gives a touch on China's health care in extremely poor area, transportation market, and water availability. Paper by Du *et al.* (DLWGLS) summarized the effect of maternal healthcare project conducted by the United Nations Fund for Population Activities (UNFPA) and the China Family Planning Association in an extremely poor and remote area in 2011 and 2015. Their survey on education, first marriage age, first birth age, household income, and transportation conditions in sample villages in 2011 revealed a shocking picture. By identifying support targets precisely and diverting resources to the poorest areas, developing community level service network, and carrying out publicity, mobilization and support activities relating to maternal healthcare, the survey in 2015 showed that the project has effectively improved the accessibility of healthcare service in mountainous communities, significantly strengthened the maternal healthcare knowledge gained by peasant households, and significantly improved the proportion of women receiving maternal services in this area.

Paper by Guo and Li (GL) discussed the introduction of competition in Chinese railways by analyzing intermodal competition in China. Time series regression results showed that competition between railways and highway in short-distance market focusing on both price and network construction. In medium- distance market, competition between railway and civil aviation focused on mainly price. And railways and civil aviation concentrated on competition via price and speed in long-distance market.

China's rapid growth over the last 20 years or more has been obtained with relatively little increase in the physical volume of water, this may against the typical opinion that China's water problems is severe and water availability could threaten the sustainability of China's future growth. Medianu and Whalley (MW1) used a growth accounting approach to investigate both the contribution played in the past by water availability in constraining China's growth performance, and what would be involved in the future. They used a modified version of Solow growth accounting in which water in efficiency units enters the production technology, and investment in water management assets raises efficiency of water use. Their counterfactual experiments suggested that water affects China's growth rates and will affect growth in the future but at uncertain rates. They argued that the degree depends on the elasticity of substitution between non-water capital and water in efficiency units and on the size of investments in water assets.

Part I

Competitiveness

Chapter 1

Are Chinese Markets for Manufactured Products More Competitive than in the US?: A Comparison of China–US Industrial Concentration Ratios*

Jun Wang

School of Management, Shandong University
wangjunsdu@163.com

John Whalley

Department of Economics, Western University
Centre for International Governance Innovation (CIGI)
National Bureau of Economic Research (NBER)
jwhalley@uwo.ca

Abstract: We present estimates of 4- and 8-firm concentration ratios by industry and in weighted average form for the manufacturing sector for Chinese enterprises for 2002 and 2007. These are then compared to available estimates for the same years and industrial classification for the US. These comparisons clearly point in

*We are grateful to the Ontario Research Fund, Centre for International Governance Innovation (CIGI) and the Shandong University Independent Innovation Fund (IFYT12060) for support.

the direction of China having sharply lower concentration ratios, in the order of one half of the US for 4-firm ratios. One possible implication is that markets for Chinese manufactured products are considerably more competitive than in the US.

In this chapter, we present estimates of 4- and 8-firm concentration ratios by industry and in weighted average form for the manufacturing sector for Chinese enterprises for 2002 and 2007. These are then compared to available estimates for the same years and industrial classification for the US. These comparisons clearly point in the direction of China having sharply lower concentration ratios, in the order of one half of the US for 4-firm ratios. One possible implication is that markets for Chinese manufactured products are considerably more competitive than in the US.

For our central comparisons we use data from the Chinese National Bureau of Statistics (NBS) and the US Census Bureau (CB). Our calculations for China are made for the same individual industrial categories and years used in the US CB data, and so we can draw country comparisons between concentration ratios organized on the same industrial classification. These groupings not only differ a little from those used in other US studies (Pryor, 2001, 2002), but also allow weighted average concentration ratios for both countries to be calculated using value added by industry as weights.

For 4-firm concentration ratios, the weighted average for Chinese manufacturing enterprises in 2002 is in the range of 0.2 and around 0.15 in 2007, approximately half of what is reported in CB data for the US. China–US ratio comparisons are a little larger than one half for 8-firm concentration ratios. The ratio estimates reported here also suggest that in China industrial concentration is declining significantly over the period 2002–2007, while estimates for the US point in the direction of slightly increasing ratios over time. All these suggests that relative competitiveness in manufactures between the US and China are diverging rather than converging. We also report on supplementary calculations of concentration ratios from other sources, which while not so directly comparable, also point in the same general direction.

Several qualifications are in order for interpreting these calculations. First, the data we use only relate to the manufacturing sector in China and the US and thus exclude critical service sectors such as banking, telecoms and transportation where there is extensive presence of large state-owned monopoly enterprises in China. The relative concentration estimates for the whole economy could be much closer where non-manufacturing sectors are able to be included. In addition, it is not possible from available data to separate out individual categories of enterprises, which could also affect the calculations. For instance, foreign-owned enterprises producing exclusively for export are included in these estimates for China, and thus concentration ratios include both foreign and domestic economic activities. Finally, the Chinese economy is widely thought to be considerably more regionally fragmented than the more regionally integrated US economy. Thus, in any individual regional economy there could be less competition in the Chinese economy than in the US economy, even though the aggregate economy wide concentration ratios suggest the opposite.

1 Data and Methods of Calculation

1.1 Chinese data

We use Chinese data from three separate sources to calculate individual concentration ratios for manufacturing industries, which we then aggregate using industry value-added weights. Since we use US concentration ratio estimates from United States CB data for comparative purposes, we restrict Chinese data to the same years as available in US data, and also place Chinese data onto the same industrial classification as US CB data.

To do this we use concordances between the North American Industry Classification System (NAICS), the National Industry Classification for China (GB)[1] and the International Standard Industry Classification (ISIC). We report Chinese industrial concentration ratios for the same ISIC classification as in the US CB data.

1.1.1 *Data Sources*

The first Chinese source is the China Industrial Enterprises data from the Chinese NBS for 2002 and 2007. It covers all state-owned enterprises (SOEs), and those non-SOEs with annual sales of 5 million RMB (Chinese currency) or more. The data contain firm identification information and their operation and performance information, including both sales and value added.

1.1.2 *Data Adjustments*

To improve the accuracy of the data, we have deleted some observations which seemed potentially unreliable based on the following criteria: (1) We delete observations where key indicators are missing (number of employees, total assets or net fixed assets, etc.). (2) Following Jefferson *et al.* (2008), we delete observations where the numbers of employees are less than eight because they are likely

[1] The National Industry Classification for China is used by the NBS, which is abbreviated as GB/T4754-2002. Here we use GB to represent this abbreviation.

individually owned firms without a reliable accounting system. (3) Following Bai *et al.* (2009), we also delete observations with a ratio of profit either below a 0.1% level or above a 99.9% level. (4) If total assets are less than current assets and the net value of fixed assets we drop the observations. And if accumulated depreciation is less than the current depreciation, we also drop the observations. (5) We delete observations that for which paid-up capital is less than or equal to 0 and delete observations with reported sales below 5 million RMB.

1.1.3 *Calculation of Concentration Ratios*

Using the modified Chinese data, we calculate the concentration ratios of three-digit GB industries and then transfer these concentration ratios to corresponding ISIC categories. We use a three-step procedure to calculate weighted average aggregate concentration ratios for the whole manufacturing sector for China for comparison purposes to US data.

We first calculate each enterprise's share of total manufacturing industry value added in each industry in each year, S_{it}^{j}, i.e.

$$S_{it}^{j} = VA_{it}/X_{jt}, \quad i = 1, \ldots, m; \quad j = 1, \ldots, r; \quad t = 2002, 2007 \qquad (1)$$

where VA_{it} is the value added of enterprise i in year t and X_{jt} is industry j's value added in year t. m and r are separately the number of enterprises in industry j and the number of industries.

We then calculate n-firm concentration ratios for industry j as

$$CR_{nj} = \sum_{j} \max_{n} S_{it}^{j}. \qquad (2)$$

In our later tables we concentrate on 4- and 8-firm concentration ratios.

The Chinese NBS publish a "National Industry Classification Comment" which contains a correspondence table between GB (2002) and ISIC (Rev. 3). The correspondence between GB and ISIC codes is not one to one; rather one GB code corresponds to several ISIC codes and one ISIC code corresponds to several GB codes. In order to make them match, we assume that the number of ISIC codes corresponding GB code j is Q. We denote the value added of industry j with GB code j as X_j and the n-firm concentration ratios as CR_{nj}. If we split industry j into Q-unit same size sub-industries, then the value added and concentration ratio of each sub-industry separately are X_j/Q and CR_{nj}.

Under this treatment, each ISIC industry corresponds to a group including several sub-industries on a GB classification. Meanwhile, one sub-industry for GB corresponds to one industry for ISIC. This allows us to calculate the weighted average concentration ratio using the value added of each sub-industry for each group as the corresponding concentration ratio using three-digit ISIC codes.

Using a weighted average method, we calculate the concentration ratios for two-digit ISIC codes and then for the whole of the manufacturing industry. For each year we weight industries by their value added for the corresponding year. These results are reported in Table 1.

1.2 US data

For the US, we use manufacturing industry concentration ratios from the Economic Census conducted by the US CB from which they calculate weighted concentration ratios. We adjust their data to correspond to the same ISIC codes as the Chinese data. The original data are published as concentration ratios for three-digit to six-digit NAICS codes for 2002 and 2007. We use concentration ratios for five-digit NAICS codes to calculate US concentration ratios comparable to those for China. The United Nations Statistics Division issues a correspondence table between ISIC (Rev. 3.1) and NAICS (2002). We first use this correspondence to transfer concentration ratios for five-digit NAICS categories to corresponding ISIC categories.

Using this correspondence, we find that each three-digit ISIC code corresponds to a group including several five-digit NAICS codes. We calculate the weighted average concentration ratio for each group as the corresponding concentration ratio using three-digit ISIC codes. Following the calculation of Chinese ratios, we also calculate the concentration ratios for two-digit ISIC codes and the whole manufacturing industry for the US as a weighted average where industry value added are weights. These results are reported in Table 1.

2 US–Chinese Industrial Concentration Comparisons

Table 1 reports our central estimates of market concentration ratios for the Chinese and US manufacturing sectors for 2002 and 2007 for both 4- and 8-firm ISIC categories. These estimates show considerably lower concentration ratios in China for both years, and also for both 4- and 8-firm calculations. Ratios of comparable US to China concentration ratios (reported in Table 2) increase from 1.75 to 2.37 between 2002 and 2007 for 4-firm ISIC categories aggregated by value added. For 8-firm ISIC categories, aggregated ratios increase in relative terms from 1.56 to 2.17 between 2002 and 2007. For the large majority of industries the concentration ratios for China substantially exceed those for the US, with the maximum divergence being for the 4-firm ISIC comparison for 2002 for office, accounting and computing machinery. From these estimates, an inference would seem to be that Chinese markets for manufacturing goods are significantly more competitive than US markets, and

Table 1. Manufacturing concentration ratio of the US and China in 2002 and 2007 (%).

	US				China			
Industry	**2002 4-firm**	**2002 8-firm**	**2007 4-firm**	**2007 8-firm**	**2002 4-firm**	**2002 8-firm**	**2007 4-firm**	**2007 8-firm**
Total manufacturing	**36.5**	**47.6**	**36.8**	**48.9**	**20.8**	**30.5**	**15.5**	**22.5**
Food products and beverages	43.2	57.5	43.7	57.3	18.5	27.1	14.0	20.2
Tobacco products	89.5	95.8	92.5	97.1	30.3	44.8	34.6	53.4
Textiles	27.3	36.6	30.0	39.5	9.5	13.6	11.1	14.0
Wearing apparel; dressing and dyeing of fur	24.0	30.9	18.2	27.2	7.7	11.6	5.1	7.9
Tanning and dressing of leather; manufacture of luggage, handbags, saddlery, harness and footwear	14.9	22.1	15.9	23.3	21.5	27.8	10.8	14.6
Wood and of products of wood and cork, except furniture; manufacture of articles of straw and plaiting materials	18.9	26.5	19.2	26.1	14.7	22.3	8.5	12.5
Paper and paper products	35.2	47.7	35.2	49.0	14.4	21.5	14.3	20.6
Publishing, printing and reproduction of recorded media	13.4	19.5	15.5	21.3	11.0	17.2	7.2	11.4
Coke, refined petroleum products and nuclear fuel	37.3	54.2	39.5	65.1	35.3	57.2	24.6	36.4
Chemicals and chemical products	39.8	52.9	43.2	57.1	15.7	22.7	14.1	19.9
Rubber and plastics products	30.2	40.1	30.0	39.7	18.1	28.3	13.7	20.5
Other non-metallic mineral products	34.0	46.6	34.6	46.8	9.4	13.8	6.2	9.4
Basic metals	28.4	40.1	36.9	49.1	31.9	46.0	19.1	28.2
Fabricated metal products, except machinery and equipment	14.0	20.1	14.7	20.5	14.2	21.5	10.8	15.6

(*Continued*)

Table 1. (*Continued*)

Industry	US 2002 4-firm	US 2002 8-firm	US 2007 4-firm	US 2007 8-firm	China 2002 4-firm	China 2002 8-firm	China 2007 4-firm	China 2007 8-firm
Machinery and equipment n.e.c.	36.3	48.0	36.4	47.4	15.3	22.7	16.3	23.0
Office, accounting and computing machinery	46.8	61.1	56.6	64.5	12.8	20.5	18.5	28.0
Electrical machinery and apparatus n.e.c.	32.8	42.1	27.9	38.0	37.9	55.5	10.5	15.4
Radio, television and communication equipment and apparatus	45.8	54.7	45.1	55.6	22.0	32.1	19.5	27.8
Medical, precision and optical instruments, watches and clocks	23.4	32.6	21.6	32.7	31.7	44.9	23.7	33.2
Motor vehicles, trailers and semi-trailers	63.8	74.2	57.5	68.3	26.2	37.5	15.3	23.5
Other transport equipment	39.7	51.0	39.7	50.5	26.8	41.5	19.9	29.9
Furniture; manufacturing n.e.c.	23.6	31.3	24.4	32.7	18.6	26.8	9.7	14.5

Note: We use the ISIC as the industrial classification standard and value added as weights.
Source: Author calculations.

the difference in domestic competitive concentration is increasing rather than decreasing.

3 Supportive Supplementary Calculations and Estimates

We also report some supplementary Chinese calculations of concentration ratios and, for the US, secondary estimates of concentration ratios that together provide the same general picture that we suggest for our main China–US comparison above. These are not on a strictly comparable industrial classification basis and the years differ slightly from one another. We use Chinese data from two separate sources to calculate individual industrial concentration ratios for sales for 24 Chinese industries, which we then aggregate using industry sales as weights. We make no

Table 2. Manufacturing concentration ratio comparison (US/China) in 2002 and 2007.

ISIC code	Industry	2002 4-firm	2002 8-firm	2007 4-firm	2007 8-firm
	Total manufacturing	**1.75**	**1.56**	**2.37**	**2.17**
15	Food products and beverages	2.34	2.12	3.12	2.84
16	Tobacco products	2.95	2.14	2.67	1.82
17	Textiles	2.87	2.69	2.70	2.82
18	Wearing apparel; dressing and dyeing of fur	3.12	2.66	3.57	3.44
19	Tanning and dressing of leather; manufacture of luggage, handbags, saddlery, harness and footwear	0.69	0.79	1.47	1.60
20	Wood and of products of wood and cork, except furniture; manufacture of articles of straw and plaiting materials	1.29	1.19	2.26	2.09
21	Paper and paper products	2.44	2.22	2.46	2.38
22	Publishing, printing and reproduction of recorded media	1.22	1.13	2.15	1.87
23	Coke, refined petroleum products and nuclear fuel	1.06	0.95	1.61	1.79
24	Chemicals and chemical products	2.54	2.33	3.06	2.87
25	Rubber and plastics products	1.67	1.42	2.19	1.94
26	Other non-metallic mineral products	3.62	3.38	5.58	4.98
27	Basic metals	0.89	0.87	1.93	1.74
28	Fabricated metal products, except machinery and equipment	0.99	0.93	1.36	1.31
29	Machinery and equipment n.e.c.	2.37	2.11	2.23	2.06
30	Office, accounting and computing machinery	3.66	2.98	3.06	2.30
31	Electrical machinery and apparatus n.e.c.	0.87	0.76	2.66	2.47
32	Radio, television and communication equipment and apparatus	2.08	1.70	2.31	2.00
33	Medical, precision and optical instruments, watches and clocks	0.74	0.73	0.91	0.98
34	Motor vehicles, trailers and semi-trailers	2.44	1.98	3.76	2.91
35	Other transport equipment	1.48	1.23	1.99	1.69
36	Furniture; manufacturing n.e.c.	1.27	1.17	2.52	2.26

Note: The numbers before 15 in the industrial classification are for ISIC codes for non-manufacturing industries.
Source: Author calculations.

original calculation of US concentration ratios for comparative purposes, but instead rely on secondary sources (Pryor, 2001) for supplementary US concentration ratio estimates.

The main Chinese source for these supplementary calculations is data compiled by an industrial trade association in China, *China Enterprise Confederation/China Enterprise Directors Association.* This is a non-state organization of which enterprises in China are members. Every year it conducts a survey among its members. In the survey it asks for data on a range of items, including name of the enterprise, sales income, profit and assets. It then tabulates this information which is then published in an annual publication for the top 500 Chinese companies. It unfortunately does this with gaps so that only an incomplete picture of industrial activity can be obtained in certain years. We have been able to purchase missing data for individual years over the period 2000–2010, but the only item for which a complete series for all years is available for all 500 top firms is "sales income". "Sales income" equates with revenue from sales by the enterprise during the year and differs from the value added used in our central comparison.

The industrial classification on which this data is available is for the 24 manufacturing industries listed in Table 3. Data is also available on the same classification of individual industries for total sales reported in the Chinese Statistical Yearbook, our second supplementary data source. We allocate sales income data for individual enterprise to the 24 manufacturing industry categories using judgment, given that some of the enterprises are multi-product enterprises.

Having identified sales income by the enterprise for the top 500 Chinese firms, we then use data by industry from the China Statistical Yearbook on total sales for the whole industry on the same 24 industry classification.[2]

Having allocated enterprise shares of sales to the 24 manufacturing industry groups using a best judgment procedure where multi-product enterprises are involved, we then calculate concentration ratios for each industry for the same 4- and 8-firm cases as above.

Where substantial concentration ratios occur (such as in petroleum processing in 2004) and there is not a minimum of either the four (or) eight enterprises required for the concentration ratios in the corresponding industrial classification, then the industry values are not defined. This explains the blanks in Table 3 (such as CR_4 under foods, 2004).

As a China–US comparison, Table 4 reports Pryor's (2002) estimates of US concentration ratios for 1992 and 1997 using value added as weights to aggregate concentration ratios. These stand in similar relation to the supplementary Chinese concentration ratios in Table 3 as in our main comparative estimates in Table 1. Estimates for China are approximately one half of those for the US and the difference between the US and Chinese ratios increases over time.

[2]The NBS of China publishes aggregate data by industry in the China Statistical Yearbook each year. They also can be checked through their website. The website address is http://www.stats.gov.cn/tjsj/ndsj/.

Table 3. Supplementary estimates of market concentration ratio for Chinese manufacturing industries (%).

GB Code	Industry	CR_n	2002	2003	2004	2005	2006	2007
	Total manufacturing	**4**	**22.0**	**22.9**	**18.1**	**19.4**	**19.5**	**18.6**
		8	**27.0**	**28.7**	**28.2**	**24.4**	**25.0**	**23.4**
13	Processing of Food from Agricultural Products	4	4.6	4.4	16.0	14.7	13.9	13.4
		8			18.6	17.6	16.6	17.1
14	Foods	4	13.8	13.6	9.9	10.9	17.1	16.0
		8	21.3			18.2	23.8	22.4
15	Beverages	4	14.9	15.5	15.2	14.2	13.7	13.7
		8	20.8					
16	Tobacco	4	32.0	28.2	29.6	36.1	39.4	39.4
		8	41.4	39.8	44.3	54.1	57.8	59.2
17	Textile	4	4.1	6.4	7.0	6.2	6.3	6.4
		8	6.0	8.4		9.5		9.5
18	Textile Wearing Apparel, Footwear and Caps	4		6.9	8.0	8.6	8.2	7.6
22	Paper and Paper Products	4						6.1
25	Processing of Petroleum, Coking, Processing of Nuclear Fuel	4	77.1	73.3		68.3	70.3	67.8
		8						
26	Raw Chemical Materials and Chemical Products	4	5.0	4.5	4.6	4.2	3.8	6.5
		8	7.0	6.5	6.5	6.1	5.8	8.7
27	Medicines	4	29.5	30.5	28.4	18.1	18.4	12.8
		8	42.3	42.1	38.8	27.3	26.7	
28	Chemical Fibers	4	15.2	16.4	18.0	16.4	17.0	17.2
29	Rubber and Plastics	4	3.8	3.8	4.1	4.2	4.7	4.6
		8		6.4				
31	Non-metallic Mineral	4		2.6	5.1	5.5	5.0	5.5
		8						
32	Mining, Smelting and Pressing of Ferrous Metals	4	20.3	23.2	21.5	18.0	15.7	14.7
		8	28.7	32.0	29.0	25.9	23.8	23.3
33	Smelting and Pressing of Non-ferrous Metals	4	13.7	14.5	15.1	13.2	14.1	12.5
		8	18.8	18.7	19.8	18.5	20.4	16.9
34	Metal Products	4	25.4	26.8	27.4	26.5	26.5	25.0
35	General Purpose Machinery	4		3.1	3.0	5.2		
		8		4.9				
36	Special Purpose Machinery	4	14.3	13.0	13.1	7.9	11.0	7.7
		8	20.3	18.0	18.1	12.2	16.1	11.8
37	Transport Equipment	4	33.6	30.5	26.9	25.9	24.0	22.8
		8	45.9	40.5	38.3	36.9	35.7	33.9

(*Continued*)

Table 3. (*Continued*)

GB Code	Industry	CR_n	2002	2003	2004	2005	2006	2007
39	Electrical Machinery and	4	29.9	23.5	22.4	19.0	13.5	12.0
	Equipment	8	39.9	31.9	28.8	24.8	20.8	17.0
40	Communication Equipment,	4	15.1	9.3	8.6	10.2	10.2	12.6
	Computers and Other Electronic Equipment	8	22.1	13.7	13.1	14.4	15.4	18.0
44	Production and Supply of	4	30.4	76.7	55.2	48.7	48.6	49.2
	Electric Power and Heat Power	8	34.3	84.1	64.2	56.0	55.2	56.5

Note: The numbers before 13 in the industrial classification are for GB codes for non-manufacturing industries. We use industrial sales as weights to calculate the total manufacturing. We report the concentration ratios for 2002–2007 for the 9 column limit of the table and report those for 2001, 2008–2010 as online appendix.
Source: Author calculations.

Table 4. Pryor's (2002) estimates of US manufacturing concentration ratio in 1992 and 1997.

SIC code	Industry	1992 4-firm	1992 8-firm	1997 4-firm	1997 8-firm
	Total manufacturing	**39.4**	**51.5**	**42.0**	**53.7**
20	Food and kindred products	48.1	61.1	42.6	52.0
21	Tobacco manufacturing	83.7	90.0	89.0	90.4
22	Textile mill products	36.0	50.4	37.3	52.8
23	Apparel and other textile products	29.4	39.6	25.7	35.6
24	Lumber and wood products	21.7	30.1	22.1	30.0
25	Furniture and fixtures	28.0	38.3	28.5	39.8
26	Paper and allied products	37.0	53.9	39.5	56.5
27	Printing and publishing	21.9	31.1	21.8	32.6
28	Chemicals and allied products	38.4	53.0	39.3	53.2
29	Petroleum and coal products	30.7	48.7	29.6	48.1
30	Rubber and misc. plastic products	21.5	30.1	20.8	29.4
31	Leather and leather products	44.1	60.5	48.6	64.2
32	Stone, glass, clay products	37.9	49.8	37.2	49.0
33	Primary metal industries	36.5	53.1	35.9	52.1
34	Fabricated metal products	25.4	33.6	26.2	36.4
35	Machinery except electrical	32.3	43.2	32.8	46.2
36	Electric, electronic equipment	42.7	56.1	49.1	60.3
37	Transportation equipment	67.0	78.4	72.7	83.3
38	Instruments, related products	37.3	50.6	53.7	63.9
39	Miscellaneous manufacturing	26.4	36.2	34.4	42.0

Note: The numbers before 20 in the industrial classification are for SIC codes for non-manufacturing industries. Pryor (2002) uses SIC as the industrial classification standard, and value added as weights.
Source: Pryor (2002).

4 Concluding Remarks

In China's World Trade Organization (WTO) accession terms, China agreed to being classified as a non-market economy, thus affecting China's situation with respect to anti-dumping duties in OECD export markets. The basis for the non-market claim was in part the preponderance of SOEs in China's manufacturing sector at the time and the belief that they dominated Chinese domestic markets which were viewed as highly concentrated. The calculations we report of relative concentration ratios between China and US point in the opposite direction of China having a more competitive manufacturing sector than the US and hence, if anything, China now having more claim that they have evolved from the non-market economy status of a decade ago. Our calculations challenge this still wildly held perception, but this claim is subject to the qualifications set out in the introduction.

References

Bai, C.-E., L. Jianyong, and T. Zhigang (2009), How Does Privatization Work in China? *Journal of Comparative Economics*, 37(3), 453–470.

China Enterprise Confederation/China Enterprise Directors Association 2001–2010. Top 500 Enterprises of China (Online). Available from: http://www.cec1979.org.cn/c500/chinese/.

Chinese National Bureau of Statistics (NBS) 2001–2007. Chinese Statistical Yearbooks. China Statistics Press (Online). Available from: http://www.stats.gov.cn/tjsj/ndsj/.

Chinese National Bureau of Statistics (NBS) 2002. *National Industry Classification Comment*. China Statistics Press.

Chinese National Bureau of Statistics (NBS) 2002 and 2007. China Industrial Enterprises data.

Jefferson, G.H., T. Rawski, and Y. Zhang (2008), Productivity Growth and Convergence across China's Industrial Economy, *Journal of Chinese Economics and Business Studies,* 6(2), 121–140.

Pryor, F.L. (2001), New Trends in U.S. Industrial Concentration. *Review of Industrial Organization,* 18(3), 301–326.

Pryor, F.L. (2002), New Trends in U.S. Industrial Concentration, 1992–1997, *Review of Industrial Organization,* 20(2), 183–185.

United Nations Statistics Division (2002), Correspondence between NAICS 2002 (US) and ISIC Rev.3.1 (Online). Available from: http://unstats.un.org/unsd/cr/registry/regso.asp?Ci=29&Lg=1

US Census Bureau 2002 and 2007. Concentration Ratios (Online). Available from: http://www.census.gov/econ/concentration.html.

Chapter 2

Capital–Labor–Energy Substitution in Nested CES Production Functions for China*

Keting Shen

Department of Economics, Western University, Canada
School of Economics, Zhejiang Gongshang University, China

John Whalley

Department of Economics,
Western University, Canada
Centre for International Governance Innovation (CIGI), Canada
National Bureau of Economic Research (NBER), USA
jwhalley@uwo.ca

Abstract: In the CGE-based policy modeling literature, especially recent literature on policy modeling for global climate change, nested Constant Elasticity of Substitution (CES) production functions over multiple inputs have been widely used. Although lack of reliable estimates of substitution elasticities for nested structures has been acknowledged for a long time, the problem has not yet been solved satisfactorily. This is especially the situation for the Chinese case for which modeling work has global implications. This chapter reports estimates of substitution elasticities for normalized nested CES aggregate production functions for China with different nested structures of input factors: capital, labor with or without human capital adjustment, and energy using data for the period 1979–2006.

*We are grateful to the Ontario Research Fund (ORF) for financial support, to seminar participants at UWO for comments, and to Aaron Gertz and Chunbing Xing for interactions.

We adopt grid search-based nonlinear optimization techniques for estimation. The results show that all the substitution elasticities we estimate are positive. For the widely used $(K, L)E$ structure, we find that the substitution elasticity between capital and labor for China is below unity. When human capital adjusted labor is used as input instead of unadjusted raw labor, estimates of substitution elasticity between capital and labor become lower. By considering the significance of estimates, our results suggest that the $(E, L)K$ structure seems more appropriate for the Chinese economy.

1 Introduction

This chapter presents estimates of substitution elasticities of normalized nested Constant Elasticity of Substitution (CES) aggregate production functions for China with different nested structures using grid search-based nonlinear estimation procedures and a time series data set for the period 1979–2006. These estimates are motivated mainly by the following concerns: (1) That the substitution elasticity between energy and capital (or labor) for China is central to analyses of the impacts of emission reduction initiatives; (2) That an aggregate capital–labor substitution elasticity greater than one can be used directly to explain China's declining labor share in GDP (where labor is the slower growing factor); (3) That aggregate substitution elasticities between capital and labor for China are dependent on whether or not the labor is adjusted by human capital; and (4) Whether normalization of production function or sample data is important in parameter estimation. The special focus on China is motivated in part by a relative lack of estimates in the literature, and also by the distinct characteristics of the Chinese case. For example, the high growth rate which makes newly produced capital a larger fraction of the capital stock at any point in time. If substitution for existing capital by labor or energy is more difficult, this would suggest higher estimated elasticities for China.

Elasticities of substitution in CES production functions are of great importance for CGE-based policy modeling, since the results of counterfactual policy analyses and the comparative static behavior of these models can be highly sensitive to the values used for elasticity parameters. For example, Jacoby *et al.* (2006) find that the elasticity of substitution between energy and value added (the capital–labor composite) is the key parameter in the MIT EPPA model and significantly affects the costs of a "Kyoto forever" scenario for the US economy. Okagawa and Ban (2008) estimate nested CES production functions using panel data for OECD countries and suggest that compared with their new estimates, conventional parameter values could overestimate the necessary carbon price by 44%. Burniaux and Martins (2012) show that increasing the substitution elasticity between energy and value added (inter-factor elasticity) induces higher carbon leakage, especially when the joint sensitivity to both inter-factor and inter-fuel elasticities of substitution are considered.

Although lack of reliable estimates of substitution elasticities has been acknowledged for a long time, the problem has not yet been solved satisfactorily (Dawkins *et al.*, 2001). Burniaux *et al.* (1992) survey earlier literature on the estimation of substitution elasticities between capital, labor and energy. They conclude that most of the estimates of substitution elasticities between capital and labor lie within the range of 0.5–1.5. Recent empirical evidence suggests that a CES aggregate production function should generally have a below unity substitution elasticity between capital and labor (see Chirinko, 2008; Klump *et al.*, 2011, for example). Surveys of CGE-based climate policy modeling show that different quantitative models may differ significantly both in structures of production functions and values of substitution elasticities (see Table 1 in Van der Werf, 2008, for example). There are also long-standing controversies on capital–energy substitutability or complementarity (see Solow, 1987; and Thompson and Taylor, 1995, for example), and the capital-skill complementarity hypothesis formalized firstly by Griliches (1969). For China, low estimates such as these are potentially inconsistent with the conventional understanding of the mechanism that leads to a falling share of the slower growing factor, labor.

In this chapter, we report estimates of substitution elasticities of nested CES aggregate production functions for China with different nested structures of input

Table 1. Estimates of substitution elasticities for two-level normalized CES production functions of China.

Nest structure	Estimate of σ with $\nu = 1$	Std. error of σ	R^2	Estimate of σ without $\nu = 1$	Std. error of σ	Est. of ν	Std. error of ν	R^2
K, HL	0.5565	0.6095	0.9989	0.5562	0.4968	1.0828	0.2626	0.9989
$(K, HL)E$	0.6648	1.1727		0.9670	2.6916			
K, E	0.5829	0.4099	0.9989	0.6553	0.6044	1.0655	0.2943	0.9989
$(K, E)HL$	0.6091	0.7827		0.5980	0.6350			
E, HL	0.9113	2.4950	0.9989	0.8113	1.9676	1.0367	0.3037	0.9989
$(E, HL)K$	0.5755	0.1578		0.6014	0.2713			
K, L	0.7418	1.1275	0.9989	0.7072	1.4294	1.0238	1.0121	0.9989
$(K, L)E$	0.5059	1.0382		0.6373	1.5392			
K, E	0.5312	0.5756	0.9989	0.4356	0.6190	0.8635	0.9174	0.9989
$(K, E)L$	0.8691	1.5440		0.7833	7.0084			
E, L	2.8637	22.2009	0.9989	1.6949	9.5032	0.9577	0.9077	0.9989
$(E, L)K$	0.6057	0.1819		0.5680	0.9647			

Source: Authors' estimates.

factors capital, labor (or human capital adjusted labor), and energy using normalized data for the period 1979–2006. We use grid search-based nonlinear estimation techniques. Our results show that all the substitution elasticities we estimate are positive. For the widely used $(K, L)E$ structure, we find that the substitution elasticities between capital and labor for China are below unity. When human capital adjusted labor is used as input instead of unadjusted raw labor, estimates of substitution elasticities between capital and labor become lower. By considering the significance of estimates, our results suggest that the $(E, L)K$ structure seems more appropriate for the Chinese economy.

Although China is often included in much of the recent literature of CGE-based climate policy modeling, the lack of reliable estimates of substitution elasticities for China is a special problem. Su *et al.* (2011) is the most closely related empirical study for China we have found in literature. Su *et al.* (2011) estimate elasticities of substitution for a two-level nested CES aggregate production function of capital, labor and energy for China with a dataset from 1953 to 2006 (one of the two sub-samples is the market-period 1979–2006) using nonlinear estimation methods development by Mishra (2006). Our estimates go beyond those in Su *et al.*'s study in the following areas: (1) That by using normalized CES production functions and grid search-based optimization methods, the standard errors of our estimates are comparatively lower; (2) That by considering the significance of estimates, our results suggest a statistically significant nested structure $(E, L)K$ while their estimates show that all three nested structures are insignificant; (3) That by using labor with or without human capital adjustment, our results provide more comprehensive estimates of substitution elasticity between capital and labor.

The rest of the chapter is organized as follows. We first introduce the specification of nested CES production functions and dataset we use in estimating substitution elasticities of nested CES functions in Section 2. The empirical results are presented in Section 3, and we also make a comparison with results in recent literature in this section. Finally, we offer a conclusion in Section 4.

2 Specification of Nested CES Functions and Data Sets

We consider a three-factor two-level aggregate production function with inputs capital (K), labor (L) and energy (E). The first level of the two-level CES function is given by a CES function of K and L

$$X = B[\beta K^{-\rho} + (1-\beta)L^{-\rho}]^{-\frac{1}{\rho}}. \tag{1}$$

Then this first level CES function is nested into the second level function of X and E

$$Y = A[\alpha X^{-\theta} + (1-\alpha)E^{-\theta}]^{-\frac{1}{\theta}}. \tag{2}$$

Substituting Equation (1) into (2) yields the two-level CES function

$$Y = A\left[\alpha\left(B[\beta K^{-\rho} + (1-\beta)L^{-\rho}]^{-\frac{1}{\rho}}\right)^{-\theta} + (1-\alpha)E^{-\theta}\right]^{-\frac{1}{\theta}}. \quad (3)$$

Equation (3) gives out one of the three nested structures of the three-factor two-level CES production function of capital (K), labor (L) and energy (E). We denote it as $(K, L)E$.

Accordingly, we can express the other two nested structures of the three-factor two-level CES production function as $(K, E)L$ and $(E, L)K$

$$Y = A\left[\alpha\left(B[\beta K^{-\rho} + (1-\beta)E^{-\rho}]^{-\frac{1}{\rho}}\right)^{-\theta} + (1-\alpha)L^{-\theta}\right]^{-\frac{1}{\theta}}, \quad (4)$$

$$Y = A\left[\alpha\left(B[\beta E^{-\rho} + (1-\beta)L^{-\rho}]^{-\frac{1}{\rho}}\right)^{-\theta} + (1-\alpha)K^{-\theta}\right]^{-\frac{1}{\theta}}. \quad (5)$$

Although the estimation of the parameters may seem straightforward, there are some problems that need to be addressed further before we have reliable estimates of substitution elasticities for China. Estimating substitution elasticities by using the Kmenta approximation or restricted translog functions has been proved unsuitable when an underlying CES function different from the Cobb–Douglas form is used (Thursby and Lovell, 1978; Henningsen and Henningsen, 2011). To overcome the issues related to the Kmenta approximation without having to use cumbersome nonlinear estimation procedures, researchers have tried to estimate a system of linear equations derived from the first order conditions of cost minimization. However, this approach usually requires comprehensive price data, which in most cases is difficult to obtain and may lead to additional measurement error (Koesler and Schymura, 2012).

Results based on nonlinear optimization techniques in many cases seem problematic due to convergence problems and yield unstable estimates (Henningsen and Henningsen, 2012). Furthermore, almost all of the recent literature using nonlinear estimation techniques is usually based on un-normalized CES functions. Since there are different measures for input factors capital, labor, and energy (capital in constant 2005 PPP dollars, labor in persons and energy in million tonnes oil equivalent, for example), we can find that with un-normalized CES functions, that merely a change of measure (change to constant 1995 PPP dollars, for example) may lead to quite different substitution elasticity estimates (see Klump *et al.*, 2011 for a recent survey of the discussion). Last but not least, estimates of substitution elasticities obtained by simply pooling all data across different regions may miss possible differences on substitution elasticities across countries (see Duffy and Papageorgiou, 2000; Klump *et al.*, 2011 for discussion on related issues).

In order to eliminate potential impacts for substitution elasticity estimates that different measures of input factors may have, we should normalize Equations (3)–(5) before estimation. Here we normalize these two-level CES functions by utilizing the normalization procedure introduced by La Grandville (1989) and advanced by Klump and De La Grandville (2000) and Klump and Preissler (2000).

We firstly define a baseline or reference point (Y_0, K_0, L_0, E_0). Assume all the three factor markets are competitive, by defining baseline factor shares $\pi_0 = \frac{r_0 K_0}{Y_0}$ and $\pi_0' = \frac{p_0^X X_0}{Y_0}$, let $B = X_0[\pi_0 K_0^\rho + (1-\pi_0)L_0^\rho]^{-\frac{1}{\rho}}$, $A = Y_0[\pi_0' X_0^\theta + (1-\pi_0') E_0^\theta]^{-\frac{1}{\theta}}$, $\beta = \frac{\pi_0 K_0^\rho}{\pi_0 K_0^\rho + (1-\pi_0)L_0^\rho}$ and $\alpha = \frac{\pi_0' X_0^\theta}{\pi_0' X_0^\theta + (1-\pi_0')E_0^\theta}$, we can rewrite Equation (3) as

$$Y = Y_0 \left[\pi_0' \left(\pi_0 \left(\frac{K}{K_0} \right)^{-\rho} + (1-\pi_0) \left(\frac{L}{L_0} \right)^{-\rho} \right)^{\frac{\theta}{\rho}} + (1-\pi_0') \left(\frac{E}{E_0} \right)^{-\theta} \right]^{-\frac{1}{\theta}}. \tag{6}$$

By allowing for Hicks-neutral technological change in production function, Equation (6) can be expressed as

$$\frac{Y}{Y_0} = \xi e^{\lambda t} \left[\pi_0' \left(\pi_0 \left(\frac{K}{K_0} \right)^{-\rho} + (1-\pi_0) \left(\frac{L}{L_0} \right)^{-\rho} \right)^{\frac{\theta}{\rho}} + (1-\pi_0') \left(\frac{E}{E_0} \right)^{-\theta} \right]^{-\frac{1}{\theta}}. \tag{7}$$

By further considering parameter for returns to scale v, we have

$$\frac{Y}{Y_0} = \xi e^{\lambda t} \left[\pi_0' \left(\pi_0 \left(\frac{K}{K_0} \right)^{-\rho} + (1-\pi_0) \left(\frac{L}{L_0} \right)^{-\rho} \right)^{\frac{\theta}{\rho}} + (1-\pi_0') \left(\frac{E}{E_0} \right)^{-\theta} \right]^{-\frac{v}{\theta}}. \tag{8}$$

In addition to considering raw (unadjusted) labor (L) as input in our nested CES specifications as Equations (6) and (7), we also examine whether labor input adjusted for human capital accumulation might change the results:

$$\frac{Y}{Y_0} = \xi e^{\lambda t} \left[\pi_0' \left(\pi_0 \left(\frac{K}{K_0} \right)^{-\rho} + (1-\pi_0) \left(\frac{HL}{HL_0} \right)^{-\rho} \right)^{\frac{\theta}{\rho}} + (1-\pi_0') \left(\frac{E}{E_0} \right)^{-\theta} \right]^{-\frac{1}{\theta}}, \tag{9}$$

$$\frac{Y}{Y_0} = \xi e^{\lambda t} \left[\pi_0' \left(\pi_0 \left(\frac{K}{K_0} \right)^{-\rho} + (1-\pi_0) \left(\frac{HL}{HL_0} \right)^{-\rho} \right)^{\frac{\theta}{\rho}} + (1-\pi_0') \left(\frac{E}{E_0} \right)^{-\theta} \right]^{-\frac{v}{\theta}}, \tag{10}$$

where *HL* denotes human capital or "quality" adjusted labor.

The motivation for including human capital or "quality" adjusted labor in these production functions comes primarily from Romer (1986) and Lucas (1988), who both place emphasis on the importance of human capital in accounting for economic growth. Previous empirical studies of economic growth across countries have revealed that production function parameter estimates can change significantly by using some form of human capital adjusted labor as input, see Mankiw *et al.* (1992) and Caselli *et al.* (1996), for example. Duffy and Papageorgiou (2000) have a short survey on earlier literature and makes an explicit comparison on substitution elasticity estimates for an aggregate CES production function with capital and labor.

Equations (7)–(10) present four different specifications of the nested CES structure $(K, L)E$. Correspondingly, we can also use similar specifications to Equations (7)–(10) for the other two nested structures of the three-factor two-level CES production function $(K, E)L$ and $(E, L)K$.

The data set used in this chapter combine time series from three different sources. The first is Extended Penn World Tables (EPWT) version 4.0 (Marquetti and Foley, 2011). We extract from the EPWT data set output Y_t (Real GDP in chain indexed 2005 PPP dollars), capital stock K_t (net fixed standardized capital stock in 2005 PPP dollars) and labor employed L_t (number of employed workers in persons). The second is the 2012 BP Statistical Review of World Energy. We get from this statistical report data on primary energy consumption E_t (expressed in million tonnes oil equivalent). The reason why we use EPWT and BP Statistical Review of World Energy data here instead of data from National Bureau of Statistics of China is mainly for comparison of results with other studies.

To construct data on human capital, we use Barro and Lee (2011) estimates of the average years of schooling in the population over 15 years old (Barro and Lee v.1.2). Following Caselli (2005), we define human capital as $H_t = e^{\varphi(s_t)}$. The human capital or "quality" adjusted labor can then be expressed as

$$HL_t = H_t \cdot L_t = e^{\varphi(s_t)} L_t. \tag{11}$$

We assume the Mincerian return rate of education is 10%, i.e. $\varphi(s_t) = 0.1 \cdot s_t$. Here, s_t is the average years of schooling at time t. Barro and Lee's (2011) data set of average years of schooling s_t is available in every five years from 1950 to 2010. Since s_t changes slowly over time, we treat s_t as invariant before new data is available.

Since different measures of input factors may have different potential impacts on substitution elasticity estimates, we normalize all the time series of Y, K, L and E with data of the baseline or reference point. For consistency and reliability, we set the geometric average of series as their corresponding reference point (see Klump *et al.*, 2007 for a short discussion of the choice of reference point).

3 Empirical Results

Nested CES functions are nonlinear in parameters and the substitution elasticities cannot be easily estimated using standard nonlinear estimation techniques. Results based on the nonlinear optimization techniques in many cases may seem problematic due to tricky implementation and convergence problems and yield unstable estimates (Henningsen and Henningsen, 2012).

Markandya and Pedroso-Galinato (2007) estimate multi-level CES production functions by a nonlinear estimation method in the STATA program which uses an iterative procedure to find the parameter values in the relationship that cause the sum of squared residuals (SSR) to be minimized. It starts with approximate guesses of the parameter values and computes the SSR. The iteration process continues until it finds final convergence where changes slightly in any direction for the parameter values would cause the SSR to increase. Mishra (2006) tests five different optimization methods including Rosenbrock–quasi-Newton (RQN), differential evolution (DE) and repulsive particle swarm (RPS) methods by simulating data generated from two-level CES production functions. He finds that two global optimization methods, DE and RPS, perform better than other more popularly used methods of nonlinear regression. Su *et al.* (2011) estimate substitution elasticities of two-level CES production functions for China using Mishra's (2006) method. In order to improve further the accuracy of estimation, they perform a nonlinear regression fitting process after applying Mishra's method and make use of the estimated results as the initial values of the fitting regression.

Henningsen and Henningsen (2011) develop an *R*-package micEconCES to estimate the CES function directly using different nonlinear optimization algorithms. As a further explanation of their package, Henningsen and Henningsen (2012) distinguish three factors that often cause severe problems when estimating CES functions by nonlinear optimization algorithms and the corresponding methods for alleviating or solving these problems: (i) removing discontinuities by using limits, (ii) removing rounding errors by using local linear approximations, and (iii) overcoming problems with an ill-behaved objective function by using a grid search procedure. Their package also includes three global optimization methods, namely, the Nelder–Mead routines (NM), the Simulated Annealing algorithm (SANN) and the DE algorithm. Koesler and Schymura (2012) estimate three-level CES production functions using the nonlinear estimation procedures based on micEconCES. Their findings show that compared to standard linear estimation using the Kmenta approximations, nonlinear estimation techniques perform significantly better.

We adopt grid search-based nonlinear estimation procedures in this chapter by using the *R*-package micEconCES. In contrast to the methods used by Koesler and Schymura (2012), we firstly run different nonlinear optimization algorithms in micEconCES and derive intervals for the two substitution elasticities due to these different estimates, then set intervals two or three times larger than those estimated in previous steps and perform grid search procedures. Finally we recalculate results using those different nonlinear optimization algorithms with values of substitution elasticities derived from grid search as starting points, and find the best fitting estimates.

Recent literature estimates nested CES production functions at both an aggregate and sectoral level with different data sets and estimation techniques. For example, Kemfert (1998) estimates the substitution elasticity of all three different nested structures for CES functions of capital, labor and energy using the nonlinear estimation techniques in Shazam for aggregate German industry and seven industrial sectors, and finds that CES production functions with a *(KE)–L* nesting structure describe Germany's aggregate industry production behavior the best, while a *(KL)−E* structure fits the sectoral data better. Van der Werf (2008) estimates the parameters of the two-level CES production functions of capital, labor and energy using a system of equations derived from the first order conditions for cost minimization with two-digit industry level data from 12 OECD countries. The findings show that the *(KL)–E* structure fits the data the best and estimates of substitution elasticities are usually considerably lower than one. Okagawa and Ban (2008) estimate parameters of two-level nested CES functions with the same technique as Van der Werf (2008), using panel data on 14 countries with 19 industries for the period 1995–2004 drawn from a dataset compiled by the EU–KLEMS project of EU. They find higher values of substitution elasticities closely related to energy inputs for energy-intensive industries and lower values for other industries compared to the values often used in existing models. Su *et al.* (2011) estimate substitution elasticities for a two-level nested CES aggregate production function of capital, labor and energy for China with a dataset from 1953 to 2006 (one of the two sub-samples is the market-period 1979–2006). Their results suggest that all the three nested structures fit the data almost equally well, but statistically insignificant.

Our estimates of substitution elasticities for all the three different nested structures of the two-level CES production functions for China both with human capital adjusted labor and raw (or unadjusted) labor are shown in Table 1. The results show that all the estimates of substitution elasticities for three different nested structures of the two-level CES production functions for China, no matter using labor with or without human capital adjusted, almost have the same goodness of fit, with a R^2 round to 0.9989. These results are similar to Su *et al.*'s (2011) estimates which have a R^2 round to 0.9997, while different to Kemfert's (1998) for German economy which have a R^2 round to 0.9997, 0.786, and 0.9986 for $(KE)L$, $(KL)E$ and $(EL)K$ structure, respectively.

Our estimates have comparatively higher standard errors (while lower than those of Su *et al.*'s results), which means that the estimates may have high variances, and may be mainly due to the comparatively small sample size. An alternative choice to alleviate the problem of high variation is to pool together provincial data. However, estimates of substitution elasticities obtained by simply pooling together all data across different regions may also miss possible differences on substitution elasticities across regions, especially when we consider about significant regional disparities on production technology in different part of China. We suggest that a sample of selected provinces with less regional disparities may be used to some extent to avoid this problem. Nevertheless, by considering the significance of the estimates, our results suggest that the $(E, L)K$ structure seems more appropriate for the Chinese economy. This finding is quite different to Su *et al.* (2011), and also different to Kemfert (1998) for German economy.

We can also see from Table 1 that when human capital adjusted labor HL is used as input instead of raw (or unadjusted) labor L, estimates of substitution elasticities between capital and labor become lower. For example, results in Table 1 show that with constant returns to scale $\nu = 1$, σ between $K - HL$ is 0.5565, while σ between $K - L$ it is 0.7418; with variant returns to scale $\nu \gtreqless 1$, σ between $K - HL$ is 0.5562, while σ between $K - L$ it is 0.7072. We can find similar relationship between $(KE) - HL$ vs. $(KE) - L$, and $E - HL$ vs. $E - L$. These results seems consistent with Griliches's (1969) hypothesis on capital-skill complementarity. See also Duffy and Papageorgiou's (2000) estimates with a cross-country datasets. Although Duffy and Papageorgiou (2000) give out estimates of substitution elasticities between capital and labor that are greater than one, we find that their results with human capital adjusted labor HL are also lower than those with raw or unadjusted labor L.

Another interesting finding from our estimates is that the estimates of substitution elasticities between capital and labor may systematically lower than one. Note that we have an estimate of σ between $K - L$ equals to 0.7072, close to Su *et al.*'s (2011) estimate of 0.7676. Our results may add new evidence to the recent literature arguing that a CES aggregate production function should generally have a below unity substitution elasticity between capital and labor. However, estimates of substitution elasticity between capital and labor lower than one for China are potentially inconsistent with the conventional understanding of the mechanism that leads to a falling share in GDP of the slower growing factor, labor, of the Chinese economy. This finding may suggest that we have to find alternative mechanisms to explain the falling labor share in GDP for China.

4 Conclusion

In the CGE-based policy modeling literature, especially recent literature on policy modeling for global climate change, nested CES production functions over multiple inputs have been widely used. Although lack of reliable estimates of substitution elasticities for nested structures has been acknowledged for a long time, the problem has not yet been solved satisfactorily. This is especially the situation for the Chinese case for which modeling work has global implications.

In this chapter, we report estimates of substitution elasticities of normalized nested CES aggregate production functions for China with input factors capital, labor (with raw or unadjusted labor and human capital adjusted labor), and energy. In order to have a direct comparison with existing literature, we use a data set for the period 1979–2006. We adopt grid search-based nonlinear optimization techniques using R-package micEconCES for estimation.

Our results show that estimates of substitution elasticities for all three different nested structures of two-level CES production functions for China, no matter using labor with or without human capital adjusted, all have satisfactory goodness of fit with relatively high R^2 values. The estimates of substitution elasticities have comparatively higher standard errors, which mean that the estimates may have high variations. Nevertheless, our estimates are a necessary response to a relative lack of estimates for substitution elasticities for China in existing literature. Notably, by considering the significance of estimates, our results suggest that the $(E, L)K$ structure seems more appropriate for the Chinese economy.

Our estimates address several problems occurred in existing literature estimating substitution elasticities for China, and also provide evidence on the difference of substitution elasticities between physical capital and labor with or without human capital adjustment. Our finding that the substitution elasticity between capital and labor for China below unity may also call into question some earlier literature explaining the falling labor share in GDP with a substitution elasticity above one.

References

Barro, R. and J. Lee (2010), A New Data Set of Educational Attainment in the World, 1950–2010, *NBER Working Paper No. 15902* (Updated November 2011).

Burniaux, J., J.P. Martin, G. Nicoletti, and J.O. Martins (1992), GREEN A Multi-Sector, Multi-Region General Equilibrium Model for Quantifying the Costs of Curbing CO2 Emissions: A Technical Manual, OECD Economics Department, *Working Papers No. 116.*

Burniaux, J. and J.O. Martins (2012), Carbon Leakages: A General Equilibrium View, *Econ Theory*, 49, 473–495.

Caselli, F. (2005), Accounting for Income Differences Across Countries, in P. Aghion and S. Durlauf (Eds): *Chapter 9 in the Handbook of Economic Growth* Vol. 1A, North Holland.

Caselli, F., G. Esquivel and F. Lefort (1996), Reopening the Convergence Debate: A New Look at Cross-Country Growth Empirics, *Journal of Economic Growth*, 1(3), 363–389.

Chirinko, R.S. (2008), σ: The Long and Short of It, *Journal of Macroeconomics*, 30(2), 671–686.

Dawkins, C., T.N. Srinivasan, J. Whalley, and J.J. Heckman (2001), *Calibration, in Handbook of Econometrics*. Vol. 5, Chapter 58, pp. 3653–3703.

Duffy, J. and C. Papageorgiou (2000), A Cross-Country Empirical Investigation of the Aggregate Production Function Specification, *Journal of Economic Growth*, 5(1), 87–120.

Griliches, Z. (1969), Capital-Skill Complementarity, *The Review of Economics and Statistics*, 51(4), 465–468.

Henningsen A. and G. Henningsen (2011), Econometric Estimation of the Constant Elasticity of Substitution Function in R: Package micEconCES, *FOI Working Paper 2011 / 9.*

Henningsen A. and G. Henningsen (2012), On estimation of the CES production function — Revisited, *Economics Letters*, 115, 67–69.

Jacoby, H.D., J.M. Reilly, J.R. Mcfarland, and S. Paltsev (2006), Technology and Technical Change in the MIT EPPA Model, *Energy Economics*, 28, 610–631.

Kemfert, C., (1998), Estimated Substitution Elasticities of a Nested CES Production Function Approach for Germany, *Energy Economics*, 20, 249–264.

Klump, R. and O. De La Grandville (2000), Economic Growth and the Elasticity of Substitution: Two Theorems and Some Suggestions, *American Economic Review*, 90(1), 282–291.

Klump, R. and H. Preissler (2000), CES Production Functions and Economic Growth, *The Scandinavian Journal of Economics*, 102(1), 41–56.

Klump, R., P. McAdam, and A. Willman (2007), Factor Substitution and Factor-Augmenting Technical Progress in the United States: a Normalized Supply-Side System Approach, *The Review of Economics and Statistics*, 89(1), 183–192.

Klump, R., P. McAdam, and A. Willman (2011), The Normalized CES Production Function, Theory and Empirics, European Central Bank, *Working Paper Series No. 1294.*

Koesler, S. and M. Schymura (2012), Substitution Elasticities in a CES Production Framework: An Empirical Analysis on the Basis of Non-Linear Least Squares Estimations, *ZEW Discussion Paper No. 12-007.*

La Grandville, O. De (1989), In Quest of the Slutzky Diamond, *American Economic Review*, 79, 468–481.

Lucas, R.E. (1988), On the Mechanics of Economic Development, *Journal of Monetary Economics*, 22, 3–42.

Mankiw, N.G., D. Romer, and D.N. Weil (1992), A Contribution to the Empirics of Economic Growth, *Quarterly Journal of Economics*, 107, 407–437.

Markandya, A. and S. Pedroso-Galinato (2007), How Substitutable Is Natural Capital? *Environmental and Resource Economics*, 37(1), 297–312.

Marquetti A. and D. Foley (2011), Extended Penn World Tables Version 4.0, last updated in August 2011.

Mishra, S. (2006), A Note on Numerical Estimation of Sato's Two-Level CES Production Function, Social Science Research Network.

Okagawa, A. and K. Ban (2008), Estimation of Substitution Elasticities for CGE Models, *Discussion Papers in Economics and Business, No. 08-16*.

Romer, P.M. (1986), Increasing Returns and Long-Run Growth, *Journal of Political Economy*, 94, 1002–1037.

Solow, J.L. (1987), The Capital-Energy Complementarity Debate Revisited, *American Economic Review*, 77, 605–614.

Su, X., W. Zhou, K. Nakagami, H. Ren and H. Mu (2011), Capital Stock–Labor–Energy Substitution and Production Efficiency Study for China, Energy *Economics*, 34(4), 1208–1213.

Thompson, P. and T. Taylor (1995), The capital-energy substitutability debate: A New Look, *Review of Economics & Statistics*, 77, 565–569.

Thursby, J.G. and C.K. Lovell (1978), In Investigation of the Kmenta Approximation to the CES Function, *International Economic Review*, 19(2), 363–377.

Van der Werf, E. (2008), Production Functions for Climate Policy Modeling: An Empirical Analysis, *Energy Economics*, 30, 2964–2979.

Chapter 3

China–UK–US Differences in Industrial Products Concentration*

Jun Wang

School of Management, Shandong University
wangjunsdu@163.com

John Whalley

Department of Economics, Western University, Canada
Centre for International Governance Innovation (CIGI), Canada
National Bureau of Economic Research (NBER), USA
jwhalley@uwo.ca

Abstract: This chapter reports 4- and 8-firm concentration ratios in manufacturing for both the US and China for similar years (2002, 2007) and 5- and 15-firm concentration ratios for the UK and China for 2003 and 2004. These comparisons reflect the use of detailed enterprise level data from the Chinese National Bureau of Statistics arranged so as to be compatible in comparison with available estimates for the US and the UK. These in turn differ in date and firm level and so only US–China and UK–China pairwise comparisons are possible rather than direct three way comparisons. Estimates show that comparable concentration ratios are approximately one half in China compared to the US and approximately three quarters in China compared to the UK. These calculations suggest systemic difference in concentration ratios between China and OECD economies.

*We are grateful to the Ontario Research Fund, CIGI and the Shandong University Independent Innovation Fund (IFYT12060) for support.

1 Introduction

This chapter reports on comparisons of firm concentration ratios for value-added in manufactured products for China, the US and the UK. Estimates are in pairwise form that allow for comparisons between countries based on the same sub-sectorial classifications and the same pairwise years but are not the basis for a full three way comparisons. Estimates for the US and the UK are given from published reports and hence the industrial classifications used and years of these data are given. Data for China are from detailed enterprise surveys conducted by the National Bureau of Statistics (NBS) and these are used to separately construct concentration ratios for China for similar years and classifications to available US and UK estimates.

These data show that for similar 4- and 8-firm concentration ratios for the US and China ratios in China are approximately one half of those in the US, a result also reported on in Wang and Whalley (2014). Moreover, as Wang and Whalley also note, ratios over time appear to be falling in China while slightly rising in the US. But a similar, if less stark, picture also emerges for the China–UK comparisons which are for different years and different classification from the US–China comparison. The overall picture points to a possible systemic difference between China and the OECD economies both in terms of concentration ratios and their evolution. The implication seemingly is that Chinese markets for industrial manufactured products are more competitive than those both in the US and even possibly the OECD more broadly.

One possible explanation for these findings is enterprise reform over the last 15 years in China which has allowed entry of large number of smaller enterprises than is the characteristic of more mature OECD markets. We note the relative absence in the data of large Chinese state-owned enterprise (SOE) in banking, petroleum processing and distribution, and non-manufacturing more generally and other qualifications to this interpretation of these relative concentration ratio data.

We then analyze the significance of various factors that potentially influence for these differences. One is the use of consistent cross country weights to produce aggregate measures of concentration. In sensitivity analysis, we alternately apply both US and Chinese value-added weights and UK and Chinese weights by industry to both US and Chinese and UK and Chinese data and calculate the impacts for the years of comparable data in pairwise comparisons. Since differences in sub-industry size across countries are reflected in the different countries weights, we also construct indices of similarity and difference in industrial concentration by sub-industry by comparing sub-industry 4- and 8-firm concentration ratios to mean concentration ratios for the year in similar pairwise comparisons. The same relationship to the mean for an industry in both countries in a pairwise comparisons we score as a +ve. Dissimilarities we score as a −ve. We then sum the +ves and −ves across industries and take a predominantly positive summed index as an indicator of similarity, and hence little impact of differences in industrial structure by country on the differences in concentration ratios across countries. Finally, we separately construct concentration ratios for China for the two sub enterprise groups of SOEs and other enterprises (or non-state enterprise, POE) in making comparisons so as to isolate the influenced state owned enterprises (SOEs).

These additional calculations point to the robustness of the finding of significant differences in the Chinese–US and Chinese–UK pairwise comparisons of concentration ratios with them persisting through the sensitivity analyses we perform. Both the UK and the US continue to show significant differences from China and more concentration ratios than in Chinese data. Differences in SOE concentration are higher for China than for the UK and US. These later comparisons again potentially point to a systemic difference for China relative to the OECD economies in industrial concentration, rather than a difference localized to only pairwise comparisons between particular economies.

2 Data Sources

2.1 Chinese data

We use Chinese data NBS to calculate individual concentration ratios for manufacturing industries, which we then aggregate to manufacturing industry concentration ratios using industry value-added as weights. Since we use US concentration ratio estimates from United States Census Bureau data and UK concentration ratios from Mahajan (2005, 2006) for comparative purposes, we restrict Chinese data to the same years as used in other country estimates, and also separately place Chinese data onto the same industrial classification as US and UK data.

To do this, we use available correspondences between the North American Industry Classification System (NAICS), the National Industry Classification for China (GB)[1] and the International Standard Industry Classification (ISIC). We report Chinese industrial concentration ratios for the same ISIC classification as in the US CB and the Mahajan (2005, 2006) classification in UK data.

The Chinese data source is China Industrial Enterprises data from the NBS of China for 2002, 2003, 2004, and 2007. This data covers all SOEs, and those non-SOEs with annual sales of five million RMB (Chinese currency) or more. The data contain firm identification information, and their operation and performance information, including both sales and value-added.

[1] The National Industry Classification for China is used by the NBS, which is abbreviated as GB/T4754-2002. Here we use GB to represent this abbreviation.

To remove inaccuracies in the data, we have deleted some observations which seemed potentially unreliable based on the following criteria: (1) We first delete observations where key indicators are missing (number of employees, total assets or net fixed assets, etc.); (2) Following Jefferson *et al.* (2008), we then delete observations where the number of employees is less than eight because they are likely individually owned firms without a reliable accounting system; (3) Following Bai *et al.* (2009), we also delete observations with a ratio of profit either below a 0.1% level or above a 99.9% level; (4) If total assets are less than current assets and the net value of fixed assets we also drop the observation. And if accumulated depreciation is less than current depreciation, we also drop the observation; (5) We delete observations for which paid-up capital is less than or equal to 0 and delete observations with reported sales below 5 million RMB.

Using the modified Chinese data, we have calculated the concentration ratios of three-digit GB industries in China and then transferred these concentration ratios to the corresponding industrial categories used in both US and UK analysis. We use the a three-step procedure to calculate weighted average aggregate concentration ratios for the whole manufacturing sector for China for comparative purposes to US and UK estimates (Pryor, 2001, 2002).

We first calculate each enterprise's share of total manufacturing industry value-added in each industry in each year, S_{it}^{j}, i.e.

$$S_{it}^{j} = VA_{it}/X_{jt}, \quad i = 1, \ldots, i \cdots m; \quad j = 1, \ldots, j, \ldots, r; \quad t = 2002, 2007, \tag{1}$$

where VA_{it} is the value-added of enterprise i in year t and X_{jt} is industry j's value-added in year t. m and r are separately the number of enterprises in industry j and the number of industries.

We can then calculate n-firm concentration ratios for industry j as

$$CR_{nj} = \sum_{j} \max_{n} S_{it}^{j}. \tag{2}$$

The Chinese NBS publishes a "National Industry Classification Comment" which contains a correspondence table between GB (2002) and ISIC (Rev. 3) which can be used to match Chinese data to a comparable classification to that in US data. The correspondence between GB and ISIC codes is not one to one; rather one GB code corresponds to several ISIC codes and one ISIC code can correspond to several GB codes. In order to match them, it is assumed that the number of ISIC codes corresponding to GB code j is Q. We denote the value-added of industry j with GB code j as X_j and the n-firm concentration ratios as CR_{nj}. If we split industry j into Q-unit same size sub-industries, then the value-added and concentration ratio of each sub-industry separately are X_j/Q and CR_{nj}.

Under this treatment, each ISIC industry corresponds to a group including several sub-industries on a GB classification. Meanwhile, one sub-industry for GB corresponds to one industry for ISIC. This allow us to calculate the weighted average concentration for each group ratio using the value-added of each sub-industry as the corresponding concentration ratio and using three-digit ISIC codes.

Using a weighted average method, we can calculate the concentration ratios for two-digit ISIC codes and then for the whole of the manufacturing industry. For each year we weight industries by their value-added for the corresponding year.

For comparison with US concentration ratios, we calculate 4- and 8-firm manufacturing industry concentration ratios for China for 2002 and 2007. These are reported in Table 1. For comparison with UK concentration ratios, we calculate 5 and 15 firm manufacturing industry concentration ratios for China for 2003 and 2004. These are reported in Table 5.

Following the same method as above, we also separately calculate the Chinese SOE sector and POE sector manufacturing industry concentration ratios for 4 and 8 firms for 2002 and 2007 for comparison purpose with the US. These are separately reported in Tables 2 and 3.

We also calculate the Chinese SOE sector and POE sector manufacturing industry concentration ratios for 5 and 15 firms for 2003 and 2004 for comparison with the UK. These are separately reported in Tables 6 and 7. For the code-19-industry for the SOE sector, we cannot calculate the concentration ratio because there are less than 5 firms in this industry. We mark the corresponding entry as "n/a" in the relevant tables.

2.2 US data and concentration ratios

For the purposes of comparison between Chinese and US concentration ratios, we use manufacturing industry concentration ratios from the Economic Census conducted by the US Census Bureau from which they calculate weighted average concentration ratios.[2] We adjust their data to correspond to the same ISIC codes as the Chinese data. The original data are published as concentration ratios for three-digit to six-digit NAICS code for 2002 and 2007. We use concentration ratios for five-digit NAICS codes to calculate US concentration ratios comparable to those for China. The United Nations Statistics Division issues a correspondence table between ISIC (Rev. 3) and NAICS (2002).[3] We use this correspondence to transfer concentration ratios for five-digit NAICS categories to corresponding ISIC categories.

[2] http://www.census.gov/econ/concentration.html.

[3] http://unstats.un.org/unsd/cr/registry/regso.asp?Ci=28&Lg=1&Co=&T=0&p=5.

Table 1. Manufacturing concentration ratio (ISIC Classification) comparisons between US and China in 2002 and 2007 (%).

ISIC code	Industry	US				China				Ratio Comparison (US/China)			
		2002 4-firm	2002 8-firm	2007 4-firm	2007 8-firm	2002 4-firm	2002 8-firm	2007 4-firm	2007 8-firm	2002 4-firm	2002 8-firm	2007 4-firm	2007 8-firm
	Total manufacturing A	**36.5**	**47.6**	**36.8**	**48.9**	**20.8**	**30.5**	**15.5**	**22.5**	**1.75**	**1.56**	**2.37**	**2.17**
	Total manufacturing B	**38.4**	**49.1**	**38.5**	**49.8**	**20.4**	**30.3**	**15.2**	**22.2**	**1.88**	**1.62**	**2.53**	**2.24**
15	Food products and beverages	43.2	57.5	43.7	57.3	18.5	27.1	14	20.2	2.34	2.12	3.12	2.84
16	Tobacco products	89.5	95.8	92.5	97.1	30.3	44.8	34.6	53.4	2.95	2.14	2.67	1.82
17	Textiles	27.3	36.6	30	39.5	9.5	13.6	11.1	14	2.87	2.69	2.70	2.82
18	Wearing apparel; dressing and dyeing of fur	24	30.9	18.2	27.2	7.7	11.6	5.1	7.9	3.12	2.66	3.57	3.44
19	Tanning and dressing of leather; manufacture of luggage, handbags, saddlery, harness and footwear	14.9	22.1	15.9	23.3	21.5	27.8	10.8	14.6	**0.69**	**0.79**	1.47	1.60
20	Wood and of products of wood and cork, except furniture; manufacture of articles of straw and plaiting materials	18.9	26.5	19.2	26.1	14.7	22.3	8.5	12.5	1.29	1.19	2.26	2.09
21	Paper and paper products	35.2	47.7	35.2	49	14.4	21.5	14.3	20.6	2.44	2.22	2.46	2.38
22	Publishing, printing and reproduction of recorded media	13.4	19.5	15.5	21.3	11	17.2	7.2	11.4	1.22	1.13	2.15	1.87
23	Coke, refined petroleum products and nuclear fuel	37.3	54.2	39.5	65.1	35.3	57.2	24.6	36.4	1.06	**0.95**	1.61	1.79
24	Chemicals and chemical products	39.8	52.9	43.2	57.1	15.7	22.7	14.1	19.9	2.54	2.33	3.06	2.87
25	Rubber and plastics products	30.2	40.1	30	39.7	18.1	28.3	13.7	20.5	1.67	1.42	2.19	1.94
26	Other non-metallic mineral products	34	46.6	34.6	46.8	9.4	13.8	6.2	9.4	3.62	3.38	5.58	4.98

27	Basic metals	28.4	40.1	36.9	49.1	31.9	46	19.1	28.2	**0.89**	**0.87**	1.93	1.74
28	Fabricated metal products, except machinery and equipment	14	20.1	14.7	20.5	14.2	21.5	10.8	15.6	**0.99**	**0.93**	1.36	1.31
29	Machinery and equipment n.e.c.	36.3	48	36.4	47.4	15.3	22.7	16.3	23	2.37	2.11	2.23	2.06
30	Office, accounting and computing machinery	46.8	61.1	56.6	64.5	12.8	20.5	18.5	28	3.66	2.98	3.06	2.30
31	Electrical machinery and apparatus n.e.c.	32.8	42.1	27.9	38	37.9	55.5	10.5	15.4	**0.87**	**0.76**	2.66	2.47
32	Radio, television and communication equipment and apparatus	45.8	54.7	45.1	55.6	22	32.1	19.5	27.8	2.08	1.70	2.31	2.00
33	Medical, precision and optical instruments, watches and clocks	23.4	32.6	21.6	32.7	31.7	44.9	23.7	33.2	**0.74**	**0.73**	**0.91**	**0.98**
34	Motor vehicles, trailers and semi-trailers	63.8	74.2	57.5	68.3	26.2	37.5	15.3	23.5	2.44	1.98	3.76	2.91
35	Other transport equipment	39.7	51	39.7	50.5	26.8	41.5	19.9	29.9	1.48	1.23	1.99	1.69
36	Furniture; manufacturing n.e.c.	23.6	31.3	24.4	32.7	18.6	26.8	9.7	14.5	1.27	1.17	2.52	2.26

Notes: We use value-added as weights. The numbers before 15 in the industrial classification are for ISIC codes for non-manufacturing industries. For Total manufacturing A, we use their owns value-added for US and China as the weight to calculate the total manufacturing concentration ratios. For Total manufacturing B, we use US value-added as weights to calculate total manufacturing concentration ratio for China and use Chinese value-added as weights to calculate total manufacturing concentration ratio for US.

Table 2. Manufacturing concentration ratio (ISIC classification) comparisons between US and China SOE sector in 2002 and 2007 (%).

ISIC code	Industry	US				China SOE Sector				Ratio Comparison (US/China)			
		2002 4-firm	2002 8-firm	2007 4-firm	2007 8-firm	2002 4-firm	2002 8-firm	2007 4-firm	2007 8-firm	2002 4-firm	2002 8-firm	2007 4-firm	2007 8-firm
	Total manufacturing	**36.5**	**47.6**	**36.8**	**48.9**	**38.4**	**54.1**	**40.0**	**56.0**	**0.95**	**0.88**	**0.92**	**0.87**
15	Food products and beverages	43.2	57.5	43.7	57.3	40.9	54.5	55.8	68.6	1.06	1.06	**0.78**	**0.84**
16	Tobacco products	89.5	95.8	92.5	97.1	30.4	44.9	34.7	53.4	2.94	2.13	2.67	1.82
17	Textiles	27.3	36.6	30	39.5	21.0	29.0	38.4	53.3	1.30	1.26	**0.78**	**0.74**
18	Wearing apparel; dressing and dyeing of fur	24	30.9	18.2	27.2	31.6	42.1	39.1	49.2	**0.76**	**0.73**	**0.47**	**0.55**
19	Tanning and dressing of leather; manufacture of luggage, handbags, saddlery, harness and footwear	14.9	22.1	15.9	23.3	88.2	90.1	87.7	93.6	**0.17**	**0.25**	**0.18**	**0.25**
20	Wood and of products of wood and cork, except furniture; manufacture of articles of straw and plaiting materials	18.9	26.5	19.2	26.1	35.0	49.6	40.8	53.7	**0.54**	**0.53**	**0.47**	**0.49**
21	Paper and paper products	35.2	47.7	35.2	49	29.6	46.4	46.5	64.2	1.19	1.03	**0.76**	**0.76**
22	Publishing, printing and reproduction of recorded media	13.4	19.5	15.5	21.3	26.1	39.6	31.3	43.8	**0.51**	**0.49**	**0.50**	**0.49**
23	Coke, refined petroleum products and nuclear fuel	37.3	54.2	39.5	65.1	39.7	64.5	41.8	60.6	**0.94**	**0.84**	**0.94**	1.07
24	Chemicals and chemical products	39.8	52.9	43.2	57.1	34.5	47.6	35.1	49.4	1.15	1.11	1.23	1.16
25	Rubber and plastics products	30.2	40.1	30	39.7	59.4	78.5	63.4	81.0	**0.51**	**0.51**	**0.47**	**0.49**
26	Other non-metallic mineral products	34	46.6	34.6	46.8	22.5	33.2	25.0	37.1	1.51	1.40	1.38	1.26

27	Basic metals	28.4	40.1	36.9	49.1	42.9	60.8	41.6	58.3	**0.66**	**0.66**	**0.89**	**0.84**
28	Fabricated metal products, except machinery and equipment	14	20.1	14.7	20.5	44.9	59.7	44.7	61.2	**0.31**	**0.34**	**0.33**	**0.33**
29	Machinery and equipment n.e.c.	36.3	48	36.4	47.4	37.4	52.3	45.4	59.8	**0.97**	**0.92**	**0.80**	**0.79**
30	Office, accounting and computing machinery	46.8	61.1	56.6	64.5	40.3	54.6	72.1	82.7	1.16	1.12	**0.79**	**0.78**
31	Electrical machinery and apparatus n.e.c.	32.8	42.1	27.9	38	81.3	81.3	51.2	67.3	**0.40**	**0.52**	**0.54**	**0.56**
32	Radio, television and communication equipment and apparatus	45.8	54.7	45.1	55.6	53.5	67.6	61.0	73.0	**0.86**	**0.81**	**0.74**	**0.76**
33	Medical, precision and optical instruments, watches and clocks	23.4	32.6	21.6	32.7	57.5	73.5	48.4	63.8	**0.41**	**0.44**	**0.45**	**0.51**
34	Motor vehicles, trailers and semi-trailers	63.8	74.2	57.5	68.3	41.5	56.5	31.0	46.7	1.54	1.31	1.85	1.46
35	Other transport equipment	39.7	51	39.7	50.5	45.8	66.0	32.6	46.6	**0.87**	**0.77**	1.22	1.08
36	Furniture; manufacturing n.e.c.	23.6	31.3	24.4	32.7	57.5	68	41.6	60.9	**0.41**	**0.46**	**0.59**	**0.54**

Note: We use value-added as weights. The numbers before 15 in the industrial classification are for ISIC codes for non-manufacturing industries.

Table 3. Manufacturing concentration ratio (ISIC Classification) comparisons between US and China SOE sector in 2002 and 2007 (%).

ISIC code	Industry	US				China POE Sector				Ratio Comparison (US/China)			
		2002 4-firm	2002 8-firm	2007 4-firm	2007 8-firm	2002 4-firm	2002 8-firm	2007 4-firm	2007 8-firm	2002 4-firm	2002 8-firm	2007 4-firm	2007 8-firm
	Total manufacturing	**36.5**	**47.6**	**36.8**	**48.9**	**18.0**	**26.3**	**13.0**	**18.6**	**2.03**	**1.81**	**2.83**	**2.63**
15	Food products and beverages	43.2	57.5	43.7	57.3	18.0	27.0	12.2	18.4	2.40	2.13	3.58	3.11
16	Tobacco products	89.5	95.8	92.5	97.1	60.8	73.0	44.9	44.9	1.47	1.31	2.06	2.16
17	Textiles	27.3	36.6	30	39.5	10.3	14.9	11.4	14.3	2.65	2.46	2.63	2.76
18	Wearing apparel; dressing and dyeing of fur	24	30.9	18.2	27.2	7.9	12.0	5.2	8.0	3.04	2.58	3.50	3.40
19	Tanning and dressing of leather; manufacture of luggage, handbags, saddlery, harness and footwear	14.9	22.1	15.9	23.3	18.9	25.2	9.0	12.9	**0.79**	**0.88**	1.77	1.81
20	Wood and of products of wood and cork, except furniture; manufacture of articles of straw and plaiting materials	18.9	26.5	19.2	26.1	16.5	24.6	8.8	13.0	1.15	1.08	2.18	2.01
21	Paper and paper products	35.2	47.7	35.2	49	16.2	24.1	15.1	20.9	2.17	1.98	2.33	2.34
22	Publishing, printing and reproduction of recorded media	13.4	19.5	15.5	21.3	11.5	17.8	5.8	10.0	1.17	1.10	2.67	2.13
23	Coke, refined petroleum products and nuclear fuel	37.3	54.2	39.5	65.1	36.8	52.4	9.3	16.4	1.01	1.03	4.25	3.97
24	Chemicals and chemical products	39.8	52.9	43.2	57.1	14.0	21.0	13.1	18.5	2.84	2.52	3.30	3.09
25	Rubber and plastics products	30.2	40.1	30	39.7	19.7	29.2	14.0	20.8	1.53	1.37	2.14	1.91
26	Other non-metallic mineral products	34	46.6	34.6	46.8	10.3	15.0	6.3	9.5	3.30	3.11	5.49	4.93

27	Basic metals	28.4	40.1	36.9	49.1	22.3	31.4	14.3	21.4	1.27	1.28	2.58	2.29
28	Fabricated metal products, except machinery and equipment	14	20.1	14.7	20.5	13.8	20.9	9.9	14.1	1.01	**0.96**	1.48	1.45
29	Machinery and equipment n.e.c.	36.3	48	36.4	47.4	15.1	22.9	15.3	21.1	2.40	2.10	2.38	2.25
30	Office, accounting and computing machinery	46.8	61.1	56.6	64.5	14.9	23.3	19.4	29.1	3.14	2.62	2.92	2.22
31	Electrical machinery and apparatus n.e.c.	32.8	42.1	27.9	38	45.1	53.7	10.2	14.9	**0.73**	**0.78**	2.74	2.55
32	Radio, television and communication equipment and apparatus	45.8	54.7	45.1	55.6	23.8	34.5	20.4	28.4	1.92	1.59	2.21	1.96
33	Medical, precision and optical instruments, watches and clocks	23.4	32.6	21.6	32.7	35.4	50.9	26.4	35.9	**0.66**	**0.64**	**0.82**	**0.91**
34	Motor vehicles, trailers and semi-trailers	63.8	74.2	57.5	68.3	18.0	23.9	10.4	13.9	3.54	3.10	5.53	4.91
35	Other transport equipment	39.7	51	39.7	50.5	23.6	35.2	22.6	31.0	1.68	1.45	1.76	1.63
36	Furniture; manufacturing n.e.c.	23.6	31.3	24.4	32.7	17.4	25.2	9.4	14.1	1.36	1.24	2.60	2.32

Note: We use value-added as weights. The numbers before 15 in the industrial classification are for ISIC codes for non-manufacturing industries.

Table 4. Manufacturing concentration ratio (ISIC Classification) similarity comparisons between US and China SOE sector in 2002 and 2007.

ISIC code	Industry	Whole Sector 2002 4-firm	Whole Sector 2002 8-firm	Whole Sector 2007 4-firm	Whole Sector 2007 8-firm	SOE Sector 2002 4-firm	SOE Sector 2002 8-firm	SOE Sector 2007 4-firm	SOE Sector 2007 8-firm	POE Sector 2002 4-firm	POE Sector 2002 8-firm	POE Sector 2007 4-firm	POE Sector 2007 8-firm
15	Food products and beverages	–	–	–	–	+	+	+	+	+	+	–	–
16	Tobacco products	+	+	+	+	–	–	–	–	+	+	+	+
17	Textiles	+	+	+	+	+	+	+	+	+	+	+	+
18	Wearing apparel; dressing and dyeing of fur	+	+	+	+	+	+	+	+	+	+	+	+
19	Tanning and dressing of leather; manufacture of luggage, handbags, saddlery, harness and footwear	–	+	+	+	–	–	–	–	–	+	+	+
20	Wood and of products of wood and cork, except furniture; manufacture of articles of straw and plaiting materials	+	+	+	+	+	+	–	+	+	+	+	+
21	Paper and paper products	+	–	+	–	+	–	–	+	+	–	–	+
22	Publishing, printing and reproduction of recorded media	+	+	+	+	+	+	+	+	+	+	+	+
23	Coke, refined petroleum products and nuclear fuel	+	+	+	+	+	+	+	+	+	+	–	–
24	Chemicals and chemical products	–	–	–	–	–	–	–	–	–	–	+	–
25	Rubber and plastics products	+	+	+	+	–	–	–	–	–	–	–	–
26	Other non-metallic mineral products	+	+	+	+	+	+	+	+	+	+	+	+
27	Basic metals	–	–	+	+	–	–	+	+	–	–	+	+

28	Fabricated metal products, except machinery and equipment	+	+	+	+	−	−	−	−	+	+	+	+
29	Machinery and equipment n.e.c.	+	−	−	−	+	−	−	−	+	−	−	−
30	Office, accounting and computing machinery	−	−	+	+	+	+	+	+	−	−	+	+
31	Electrical machinery and apparatus n.e.c.	−	−	+	+	−	−	−	−	−	−	+	+
32	Radio, television and communication equipment and apparatus	+	+	+	+	+	+	+	+	+	+	+	+
33	Medical, precision and optical instruments, watches and clocks	−	−	−	−	−	−	−	−	−	−	−	−
34	Motor vehicles, trailers and semi-trailers	+	+	−	+	+	+	−	−	+	−	−	−
35	Other transport equipment	+	+	+	+	+	+	−	−	+	+	+	+
36	Furniture; manufacturing n.e.c.	+	+	+	+	−	−	−	−	+	+	+	+
	Number of Plus	15	14	17	17	13	11	9	11	15	13	15	15
	Number of minus	7	8	5	5	9	11	13	11	7	9	7	7

Table 5. Manufacturing concentration ratio (ISIC Classification) comparisons between UK and China in 2003 and 2004 (%).

		UK				China				Ratio Comparison (UK/China)			
ISIC code	**Industry**	**2003 5-firm**	**2003 15-firm**	**2004 5-firm**	**2004 15-firm**	**2003 5-firm**	**2004 15-firm**	**2004 5-firm**	**2004 15-firm**	**2003 5-firm**	**2004 15-firm**	**2004 5-firm**	**2004 15-firm**
	Total manufacturing	**32.5**	**46.1**	**32.3**	**47.2**	**22.9**	**39.0**	**22.7**	**37.3**	**1.42**	**1.18**	**1.42**	**1.27**
15	Food products and beverages	48.6	64.1	46.0	64.0	21.8	36.9	20.8	35.3	2.23	1.74	2.21	1.81
16*	Tobacco products	n/a	n/a	100.0	100.0	31.8	57.2	32.5	60.7	n/a	n/a	3.08	1.65
17	Textiles	23.2	35.7	23.3	39.9	12.4	20.4	12.4	18.9	1.87	1.75	1.88	2.11
18*	Wearing apparel; dressing and dyeing of fur	n/a	n/a	10.0	18.0	7.4	14.0	6.3	12.7	n/a	n/a	1.59	1.42
19	Tanning and dressing of leather; manufacture of luggage, handbags, saddlery, harness and footwear	25.4	43.0	28.9	43.8	19.3	30.7	12.8	23.0	1.32	1.40	2.26	1.90
20*	Wood and of products of wood and cork, except furniture; manufacture of articles of straw and plaiting materials	7.0	14.0	7.0	14.0	12.2	24.0	15.5	26.4	**0.57**	**0.58**	**0.45**	**0.53**
21	Paper and paper products	24.5	55.0	21.7	36.2	17.1	29.0	16.6	28.1	1.43	1.90	1.31	1.29
22*	Publishing, printing and reproduction of recorded media	12.0	21.0	12.0	22.0	12.7	24.1	11.5	21.6	**0.94**	**0.87**	1.04	1.02
23*	Coke, refined petroleum products and nuclear fuel	75.0	95.0	67.0	94.0	28.5	55.7	29.1	54.2	2.63	1.71	2.30	1.73
24	Chemicals and chemical products	47.4	67.7	53.1	72.5	22.8	36.8	24.4	36.2	2.08	1.84	2.18	2.00
25	Rubber and plastics products	5.0	11.0	11.3	18.5	20.8	39.1	20.0	36.0	**0.24**	**0.28**	**0.57**	**0.51**

26	Other non-metallic mineral products	37.3	45.9	33.5	53.8	9.1	17.7	8.0	16.4	4.10	2.59	4.19	3.28
27	Basic metals	26.5	45.0	33.1	51.8	29.9	49.7	29.3	45.4	**0.89**	**0.91**	1.13	1.14
28	Fabricated metal products, except machinery and equipment	10.7	19.8	9.0	14.9	15.8	27.9	15.8	28.1	**0.68**	**0.71**	**0.57**	**0.53**
29	Machinery and equipment n.e.c.	26.9	36.4	23.1	35.3	23.4	38.8	22.8	36.9	1.15	**0.94**	1.01	**0.96**
30*	Office, accounting and computing machinery	n/a	n/a	61.0	76.0	24.2	50.9	24.8	47.6	n/a	n/a	2.46	1.60
31	Electrical machinery and apparatus n.e.c.	18.7	32.1	18.6	34.9	15.7	28.0	15.7	26.8	1.19	1.15	1.18	1.30
32	Radio, television and communication equipment and apparatus	34.4	n/a	33.8	54.0	26.5	46.4	27.6	44.1	1.30	n/a	1.22	1.22
33*	Medical, precision and optical instruments, watches and clocks	18.0	30.0	17.0	26.0	35.7	55.4	36.7	53.7	**0.50**	**0.54**	**0.46**	**0.48**
34	Motor vehicles, trailers and semi-trailers	27.0	46.0	34.0	50.0	30.8	45.4	25.3	39.2	**0.88**	1.01	1.34	1.28
35	Other transport equipment	60.2	72.5	53.8	75.0	26.4	48.7	25.7	47.5	2.28	1.49	2.09	1.58
36	Furniture; manufacturing n.e.c.	10.0	15.7	11.8	16.2	17.1	29.9	17.1	29.6	**0.58**	**0.53**	**0.69**	**0.55**

Notes: The UK data of industries with * are two-digit concentration ratios get directly from corresponding UK SIC code data. We use value-added as weights. The numbers before 15 in the industrial classification are for ISIC codes for non-manufacturing industries.

Table 6. Manufacturing concentration ratio (ISIC Classification) comparisons between UK and China SOE sector in 2003 and 2004 (%).

		UK				China SOE Sector				Ratio Comparison (UK/China)			
ISIC code	**Industry**	**2003 5-firm**	**2003 15-firm**	**2004 5-firm**	**2004 15-firm**	**2003 5-firm**	**2004 15-firm**	**2004 5-firm**	**2004 15-firm**	**2003 5-firm**	**2004 15-firm**	**2004 5-firm**	**2004 15-firm**
	Total manufacturing	**32.5**	**46.1**	**32.3**	**47.2**	**44.8**	**69.1**	**47.1**	**70.4**	**0.73**	**0.67**	**0.69**	**0.67**
15	Food products and beverages	48.6	64.1	46.0	64.0	49.3	70.3	58.1	76.2	**0.99**	**0.91**	**0.79**	**0.84**
16*	Tobacco products	n/a	n/a	100.0	100.0	31.9	57.5	32.7	61	n/a	n/a	3.06	1.64
17	Textiles	23.2	35.7	23.3	39.9	26.5	44.3	38.6	58.4	**0.88**	**0.81**	**0.60**	**0.68**
18*	Wearing apparel; dressing and dyeing of fur	n/a	n/a	10.0	18.0	44.1	65.6	22.4	47.9	n/a	n/a	**0.45**	**0.38**
19	Tanning and dressing of leather; manufacture of luggage, handbags, saddlery, harness and footwear	25.4	43.0	28.9	43.8	n/a	n/a	n/a	n/a	n/a	n/a	n/a	n/a
20*	Wood and of products of wood and cork, except furniture; manufacture of articles of straw and plaiting materials	7.0	14.0	7.0	14.0	39.4	70.8	41.3	76.6	**0.18**	**0.20**	**0.17**	**0.18**
21	Paper and paper products	24.5	55.0	21.7	36.2	38.4	67.4	42.8	74.4	**0.64**	**0.82**	**0.51**	**0.49**
22*	Publishing, printing and reproduction of recorded media	12.0	21.0	12.0	22.0	28.8	49.8	28.5	47.8	**0.42**	**0.42**	**0.42**	**0.46**
23*	Coke, refined petroleum products and nuclear fuel	75.0	95.0	67.0	94.0	38.0	73.4	45.5	78.4	1.97	1.29	1.47	1.20
24	Chemicals and chemical products	47.4	67.7	53.1	72.5	46.3	67.3	50.9	70.8	1.02	1.01	1.04	1.02
25	Rubber and plastics products	5.0	11.0	11.3	18.5	52.4	52.9	47.6	49.8	**0.10**	**0.21**	**0.24**	**0.37**

26	Other non-metallic mineral products	37.3	45.9	33.5	53.8	25.9	47.6	28.6	49	1.44	**0.96**	1.17	1.10
27	Basic metals	26.5	45.0	33.1	51.8	46.7	75.6	51.7	74.8	**0.57**	**0.60**	**0.64**	**0.69**
28	Fabricated metal products, except machinery and equipment	10.7	19.8	9.0	14.9	45.7	67.8	47.5	75.1	**0.23**	**0.29**	**0.19**	**0.20**
29	Machinery and equipment n.e.c.	26.9	36.4	23.1	35.3	48.0	71.0	55.5	75.4	**0.56**	**0.51**	**0.42**	**0.47**
30*	Office, accounting and computing machinery	n/a	n/a	61.0	76.0	76.0	94.0	86.7	96.1	n/a	n/a	**0.70**	**0.79**
31	Electrical machinery and apparatus n.e.c.	18.7	32.1	18.6	34.9	51.7	76.4	50	74.7	**0.36**	**0.42**	**0.37**	**0.47**
32	Radio, television and communication equipment and apparatus	34.4	n/a	33.8	54.0	72.1	88.5	64.9	81.2	**0.48**	n/a	**0.52**	**0.67**
33*	Medical, precision and optical instruments, watches and clocks	18.0	30.0	17.0	26.0	72.3	87.5	52.3	75.8	**0.25**	**0.34**	**0.33**	**0.34**
34	Motor vehicles, trailers and semi-trailers	27.0	46.0	34.0	50.0	50.7	69.5	47.4	65.7	**0.53**	**0.66**	**0.72**	**0.76**
35	Other transport equipment	60.2	72.5	53.8	75.0	38.4	67.5	41	66.2	1.57	1.07	1.31	1.13
36	Furniture; manufacturing n.e.c.	10.0	15.7	11.8	16.2	57.0	76.9	43.5	73.7	**0.18**	**0.20**	**0.27**	**0.22**

Notes: The UK data of industries with * are two-digit concentration ratios get directly from corresponding UK SIC code data. We use value-added as weights. The numbers before 15 in the industrial classification are for ISIC codes for non-manufacturing industries.

Table 7. Manufacturing concentration ratio (ISIC Classification) comparisons between UK and China POE sector in 2003 and 2004 (%).

		UK				China POE Sector				Ratio Comparison (UK/China)			
ISIC code	Industry	2003 5-firm	2003 15-firm	2004 5-firm	2004 15-firm	2003 5-firm	2004 15-firm	2004 5-firm	2004 15-firm	2003 5-firm	2004 15-firm	2004 5-firm	2004 15-firm
	Total manufacturing	**32.5**	**46.1**	**32.3**	**47.2**	**19.7**	**34.0**	**19.8**	**32.6**	**1.65**	**1.36**	**1.63**	**1.45**
15	Food products and beverages	48.6	64.1	46.0	64.0	22.0	37.8	20.6	35.4	2.21	1.70	2.23	1.81
16*	Tobacco products	n/a	n/a	100.0	100.0	63.6	63.6	27.0	27.0	n/a	n/a	3.70	3.70
17	Textiles	23.2	35.7	23.3	39.9	13.5	21.4	13.0	19.1	1.72	1.67	1.79	2.09
18*	Wearing apparel; dressing and dyeing of fur	n/a	n/a	10.0	18.0	7.6	14.2	6.4	12.9	n/a	n/a	1.56	1.40
19	Tanning and dressing of leather; manufacture of luggage, handbags, saddlery, harness and footwear	25.4	43.0	28.9	43.8	17.8	29.3	11.1	21.4	1.43	1.47	2.60	2.05
20*	Wood and of products of wood and cork, except furniture; manufacture of articles of straw and plaiting materials	7.0	14.0	7.0	14.0	13.3	25.6	14.9	26.3	**0.53**	**0.55**	**0.47**	**0.53**
21	Paper and paper products	24.5	55.0	21.7	36.2	18.9	29.0	17.3	28.2	1.30	1.90	1.25	1.28
22*	Publishing, printing and reproduction of recorded media	12.0	21.0	12.0	22.0	10.8	22.1	10.3	19.4	1.11	**0.95**	1.17	1.13
23*	Coke, refined petroleum products and nuclear fuel	75.0	95.0	67.0	94.0	15.7	34.1	26.1	40.8	4.78	2.79	2.57	2.30
24	Chemicals and chemical products	47.4	67.7	53.1	72.5	21.3	34.7	22.1	34.2	2.23	1.95	2.40	2.12
25	Rubber and plastics products	5.0	11.0	11.3	18.5	21.4	39.1	19.3	35.5	**0.23**	**0.28**	**0.59**	**0.52**

26	Other non-metallic mineral products	37.3	45.9	33.5	53.8	10.2	19.0	8.9	17.6	3.66	2.42	3.76	3.06
27	Basic metals	26.5	45.0	33.1	51.8	18.9	33.7	16.9	31.3	1.40	1.34	1.96	1.65
28	Fabricated metal products, except machinery and equipment	10.7	19.8	9.0	14.9	14.7	26.7	15.1	27.3	**0.73**	**0.74**	**0.60**	**0.55**
29	Machinery and equipment n.e.c.	26.9	36.4	23.1	35.3	23.5	39.0	21.8	35.1	1.14	**0.93**	1.06	1.01
30*	Office, accounting and computing machinery	n/a	n/a	61.0	76.0	26.5	54.1	26.0	48.2	n/a	n/a	2.35	1.58
31	Electrical machinery and apparatus n.e.c.	18.7	32.1	18.6	34.9	16.3	28.4	16.2	27.2	1.15	1.13	1.15	1.28
32	Radio, television and communication equipment and apparatus	34.4	n/a	33.8	54.0	26.2	47.1	29.1	46.1	1.31	n/a	1.16	1.17
33*	Medical, precision and optical instruments, watches and clocks	18.0	30.0	17.0	26.0	35.6	56.7	39.6	57.3	**0.51**	**0.53**	**0.43**	**0.45**
34	Motor vehicles, trailers and semi-trailers	27.0	46.0	34.0	50.0	21.6	35.3	23.1	35.5	1.25	1.30	1.47	1.41
35	Other transport equipment	60.2	72.5	53.8	75.0	25.1	40.6	28.3	41.5	2.40	1.79	1.90	1.81
36	Furniture; manufacturing n.e.c.	10.0	15.7	11.8	16.2	16.8	29.6	16.4	28.5	**0.60**	**0.53**	**0.72**	**0.57**

Notes: The UK data of industries with * are two-digit concentration ratios get directly from corresponding UK SIC code data. We use value-added as weights. The numbers before 15 in the industrial classification are for ISIC codes for non-manufacturing industries.

Each three-digit ISIC code corresponds to a group including several five-digit NAICS codes. We calculate the weighted average concentration ratio for each group as the corresponding concentration ratio using three-digit ISIC codes. Following the calculation of Chinese ratios, we also calculate the concentration ratios for both two-digit ISIC codes and the whole manufacturing industry for the US as a weighted average where industry value-added are weights. These calculations are also reported in Table 1 to compare with Chinese ratios.

2.3 UK data and concentration ratios

For the UK we use manufacturing industry concentration ratios from Mahajan's (2005, 2006) two reports giving 5 and 15 firm concentration ratios for businesses by industry in 2003 and 2004. These were published by the UK Office for National Statistics (ONS).[4] The industries are based on the Standard Industrial Classification 2003 (UK SIC (2003)), which corresponds to the United Nations classification NACE Rev. 1.1.[5] We construct a correspondence table between UK SIC and ISIC using the correspondence between UK SIC and NACE and the correspondence between ISIC Rev. 3.1 and NACE Rev. 1.1[6] to make the industrial classifications used for the UK and China comparable.

Most of the concentration ratios for the UK are for three-digit UK SIC codes. However, a few of them are for two-digit UK SIC codes. For the two-digit code concentration ratios, we list them in the tables we report as corresponding to individual industry concentration ratios for ISIC codes directly and mark corresponding industry codes with a *. For the three-digit UK SIC code concentration ratios, we first use the correspondence table between UK SIC and ISIC to transfer them to corresponding three-digit ISIC categories.

---

[4]The two reports can be available from the website. Those addresses are http://webarchive.nationalarchives.gov.uk/20160105160709/http://www.ons.gov.uk/ons/rel/elmr/economic-trends–discontinued-/no–624–november-2005/concentration-ratios-for-businesses-by-industry-in-2003.pdf and http://webarchive.nationalarchives.gov.uk/20160105160709/http://www.ons.gov.uk/ons/rel/elmr/economic-trends–discontinued-/no–635–october-2006/concentration-ratios-for-businesses-by-industry-in-2004.pdf. Unfortunately, there are no more subsequent relevant reports published. Hence, we can only use the data for 2003 and 2004 to compare with China.

[5]Explanation about the correspondence between UK SIC and NACE can be obtained in "UK Standard Industrial Classification of Economic Activities 2003", on the public website: http://webarchive.nationalarchives.gov.uk/20160105160709/http://www.ons.gov.uk/ons/guide-method/classifications/archived-standard-classifications/uk-standard-industrial-classification-1992–sic92-/uk-sic-2003.pdf.

[6]The correspondence between ISIC Rev. 3.1 and NACE Rev. 1.1 can be available at website: http://unstats.un.org/unsd/cr/registry/regso.asp?Ci= 27&Lg=1.

Using a weighted average method, we then calculate concentration ratios for two-digit ISIC codes and then for the whole of the manufacturing industry. For each year we weight industries by their value-added for the corresponding year. These calculations are also reported on in the following tables (from Tables 5 to 7) to compare with Chinese results. We mark some industry concentration ratios for 2003 as "n/a" in the relative tables, because Mahajan (2005) does not report the corresponding concentration ratios.

3 China–US–UK Pairwise Comparison of Industrial Concentration

We begin our pairwise comparisons with Table 1 which compares 4- and 8-firm concentration ratios for China and the US for 2002 and 2007. These show concentration ratios for the US as roughly double those for China and a decline in concentration over time in China and a small increase over time in the US case. This indicates a divergence in relative competitiveness of domestic markets between the US and China.

We report aggregate concentration ratios calculated on two different bases with alterative value-added weights. In the first (marked "A") we use Chinese value-added weights for China and US value-added weights for the US. In the second (marked "B") we switch the use of weights to assess robustness and use US value-added weights to aggregate Chinese ratios and Chinese value-added weights to aggregate US ratios. This alternative use of weights, however, makes little difference to results suggesting that the conclusion that Chinese ratios are roughly one half of US ratios is robust to the choice of weights.

Table 2 reports on a further pairwise comparison between the US and China where enterprise data for China is restricted to that for SOEs only. In this case, the concentration ratios in China exceed those in the US with the difference becoming larger over time. These results suggest that it is the growing private sector in China which accounts for the lower Chinese concentration ratios. This conjecture is confirmed by results in Table 3 where concentration ratios for the US exceed those for the Chinese private (non-state) sector by a factor of over 2.

Table 4 reports similarity indices in China and US comparisons in concentration ratios. A similar relationship to the mean for an industry in both countries in a pairwise comparisons we score as a +ve, dissimilarities we score as a −ve. We then sum the +ves and −ves across industries and take a predominantly positive summed index as an indicator of similarity, and hence little impact of differences in industrial structure by country on the differences in concentration ratios across countries. A picture of these differences in industrial structure is portrayed by Table 4 and it is one which is predominately positive.

Finally, Table 5 reports on China–UK comparisons for 5 and 15 firm concentration ratios for 2003 and 2004. These indicate higher concentration ratios for the UK, although the differences are not as large as in the US–China comparisons. These point towards there being a possible systemic OECD–China difference in concentration ratios rather as a specific US–China difference.

4 Concluding Remarks

The calculation we report in here points in the direction that concentration ratios seem considerably higher in the manufacturing sectors in China than in the US or the UK. The conclusions seems robust and our conjecture estimates potentially transferable to other pairwise comparisons involves the OECD and China. The hypothesis these results suggest is that domestic markets in China are significantly more competitive than in the OECD markets.

This conjecture may, however, be subject to other factors in terms of interpretation and robustness. One issue is the exclusion of many non-manufacturing industries such as banking, petroleum refining and distribution, and transportation in which large SOEs play a key role. Concentration ratios for pairwise for the whole of Chinese industry may thus be different from those for the industrial sector, but there is no data for such a broader comparison. Another issue concerns regional fragmentation in China. Regionally concentrated markets may have concentration ratios exceeding those in the US and the UK, but for the aggregate economy appear less concentrated due to the member of regions. These and other qualification would seem to provide motivation for further research.

References

Bai, C.-E., J. Lu, and Z. Tao (2009), How does Privatization Work in China, *Journal of Comparative Economics*, 37, 453–470.

Chinese National Bureau of Statistics: China Industrial Enterprises data, 2002, 2003, 2004, 2007.

Chinese National Bureau of Statistics: *National Industry Classification Comment*, China Statistics Press, 2002.

Jefferson, G.H., T.G. Rawski, and Y. Zhang (2008), Productivity Growth and Convergence across China's Industrial Economy, *Journal of Chinese Economics and Business Studies*, 6(2), 121–140.

Mahajan, S. (2005), Input–Output: Concentration ratios for businesses by industry in 2003, 624, Economic Trends (Online). Available from: http://webarchive.nationalarchives.gov.uk/20160105160709/http://www.ons.gov.uk/ons/rel/elmr/economic-trends–discontinued-/no–624–november-2005/concentration-ratios-for-businesses-by-industry-in-2003.pdf

Mahajan, S. (2006), Input–Output: Concentration ratios for businesses by industry in 2004, 624, Economic Trends (Online). Available from: http://webarchive.nationalarchives.gov.uk/20160105160709/http://www.ons.gov.uk/ons/rel/elmr/economic-trends–discontinued-/no–635–october-2006/concentration-ratios-for-businesses-by-industry-in-2004.pdf

Office for National Statistics, UK Standard Industrial Classification of Economic Activities 2003 (Online). Available from: http://webarchive.nationalarchives.gov.uk/20160105160709/http://www.ons.gov.uk/ons/guide-method/classifications/archived-standard-classifications/uk-standard-industrial-classification-1992–sic92-/uk-sic-2003.pdf.

Pryor, F.L. (2001), New Trends in U.S. Industrial Concentration, *Review of Industrial Organization*, 18, 301–326.

Pryor, F.L. (2002), New Trends in U.S. Industrial Concentration, 1992–1997, *Review of Industrial Organization*, 20, 183–185.

United Nations Statistical, Correspondence between NACE Rev. 1.1 and ISIC Rev. 3.1 (Online). Available from: http://unstats.un.org/unsd/cr/registry/regso.asp?Ci=27&Lg=1.

United Nations Statistics Division (Online). Available from: http://unstats.un.org.

US Census Bureau (Online). Available from: http://www.census.gov/econ/concentration.html.

Wang, J. and J. Whalley (2014), Are Chinese Markets for Manufactured Products More Competitive than in the US?; A Comparison of China–US Industrial Concentration Ratios, *NBER Working Paper 19898*, Cambridge.

Chapter 4

Quality Upgrading in the Chinese Manufacturing Sector*

Weili Liu

College of Economics, Shenzhen University
Nanhai Ave 3688, Shenzhen 518060, Guangdong, P. R. China

Abstract: This chapter constructs the quality of product model developed by Khandelwal (2009), Amiti and Khandelwal (2009) linking trade and quality of product. Conditional on price, imports with higher market shares are assigned higher quality. In the model with heterogeneous plants and quality differentiation, the globalization raises the quality of final goods by importing higher quality of parts and components. Developed countries export lower quality of final goods to developing countries and developing countries export higher quality of final goods to developed countries by using imported higher quality of inputs. With the measurement of quality ladders and quality ranking, we analyze the quality of imported and exported products from different countries according to both enterprise database and customs data. Empirical study supports that the quality of intermediate goods is higher than the quality of final goods exported to China. We calculate total factor productivity (TFP) with Chinese data from 2002 to 2006 and estimate the impact of quality ladder and quality ranking on productivity, skill intensity and capital intensity. These findings indicate quality upgrading is necessary for developing countries to achieve export success, upgrade technology

*Funding for the research described in this chapter is from National Social Science Fund China No. 14BJL049.

I am especially grateful to Yong Chen, Chang Yuan, Lixin Zhao, Jianzhang Wei, Qingguang Zeng, Wenjing Tan. All errors are my own.

and economic development. Processing trade can increase export, upgrade quality and increase wage.

1 Introduction

The most important element is the quality of product in the competition of product beside price and market shares. Different countries' consumers have different preferences to price and quality. Conditional on prices, the consumers will choose the higher quality product. It is difficult to measure quality of products using exact figures. The products which were made in China sell all over the world. This chapter estimates the quality of Chinese imports using Khandelwal (2009)'s model and empirical method.

Quality of product is important to importers and exporters. The quality of export product determines the competition of export product and the quality of import product affects output and employment growth. Based on Linder's (1961) Demand Decided Theory, we can obtain the conclusion: developed countries consume and export higher quality products than developing countries; the quality of the product of developing countries exported to developed country markets must be upgraded. Khandelwal (2009) argues that developed countries can insulate themselves from the South by using comparative advantage factors (e.g. skill, capital and/or technology) to specialize atop the quality ladder in long-ladder markets. However, developed countries will be directly exposed to Southern competition because quality upgrading is infeasible in short-ladder markets. Thus, the market's scope for vertical differentiation is important for understanding Leamer's notion of contestable jobs. Based on Chinese data, this chapter analyses developing countries must focus on quality upgrading in the industries where quality is more sensitive to price, or where quality is no more sensitive to price. With trade liberalization, does Quality specialization expand or reduce the imbalance in developing countries?

The values of Chinese export and import trade increase year by year in big world market share, as shown Tables 1 and 2. Table 3 shows the two-digit GB-2002 manufacture code and English comparison list. A purpose of this chapter is whether the quality of Chinese export product increases with the raising of market share. Is the quality of Chinese imported products different from different countries? Processing trade occupies a big market share in Chinese import and export trade. Intermediate trade is important to China. Intermediate goods are used to re-product instead of consumption. It is important to classify the import product. Figure 1 displays the relationship of Chinese processing trade and general trade. Chinese processing trade exceeds general trade and increases year by year. This chapter makes matching Harmonized Commodity Description and Coding

Table 1. Two-digit GB-2002 manufacture import and percentage of world import.

Year	2002		2003		2004		2005		2006	
Sector (GB-2)	Import	Percentage of World Import	Import	Percentage of World Import	Import	Percentage of World Import	Import	Percentage of World Import	Import	Percentage of World Import
13	19.45	0.12	27.08	0.15	26.23	0.12	28.71	0.12	44.12	0.17
14	797.12	0.95	926.62	0.90	1283.98	1.08	1330.41	1.01	1680.49	1.13
15	148.26	0.38	186.47	0.41	261.07	0.49	409.61	0.70	585.78	0.88
16	243.04	1.25	307.38	1.43	292.01	1.19	383.81	1.47	463.30	1.75
17	7455.41	11.48	9042.18	12.13	12027.79	13.87	12423.40	14.26	14848.75	16.20
18	1642.66	0.60	1787.19	0.58	2009.10	0.58	2184.16	0.58	2345.91	0.58
19	3537.85	6.93	4121.96	7.33	5120.22	8.01	5423.54	7.99	6274.98	8.41
20	4169.20	5.78	4666.92	5.64	5235.08	5.15	5746.16	5.36	6495.64	5.61
21	404.03	0.47	660.15	0.65	852.66	0.71	820.53	0.62	944.84	0.65
22	7036.64	6.01	8284.89	6.11	9932.22	6.41	10569.97	6.48	11355.38	6.42
23	337.11	1.37	344.73	1.21	373.70	1.16	432.92	1.25	537.66	1.44
24	457.90	0.73	544.94	0.80	613.96	0.82	736.05	0.87	893.34	0.96
25	19321.33	3.51	29247.55	3.99	48026.77	4.86	64088.96	4.67	89098.43	5.26
26	23171.46	5.96	30397.26	6.47	41030.73	7.27	48624.51	7.65	53790.15	7.63
27	1130.29	0.76	1391.57	0.75	1571.74	0.69	1958.71	0.77	2394.22	0.83
28	6327.30	14.02	6864.21	13.53	7229.16	12.58	7033.45	12.21	6622.04	11.10
29	2467.66	4.22	3715.08	5.15	4742.21	5.40	5584.95	5.61	8439.99	7.20
30	17378.44	9.12	21030.34	9.18	28055.53	9.94	33308.21	10.19	37832.89	10.16

(Continued)

Table 1. (*Continued*)

Year	2002		2003		2004		2005		2006	
Sector (GB-2)	Import	Percentage of World Import	Import	Percentage of World Import	Import	Percentage of World Import	Import	Percentage of World Import	Import	Percentage of World Import
31	2082.46	3.15	2628.33	3.35	3247.59	3.50	3383.68	3.32	3942.61	3.45
32	16011.55	7.86	25595.83	9.78	28332.70	7.48	31906.02	7.24	26980.54	5.19
33	8996.15	8.13	12016.80	9.20	17731.51	9.97	21575.41	10.44	29008.87	9.40
34	1273.62	2.34	1771.28	2.81	2484.17	3.19	3111.34	3.55	3789.95	3.84
35	52143.47	6.14	71490.88	7.18	91601.14	7.64	96283.69	7.21	109122.43	7.27
36	4.06	0.10	2.61	0.06	2.82	0.05	2.82	0.05	2.07	0.03
37	11518.96	1.63	17507.49	2.13	19471.63	2.01	19835.14	1.90	29729.00	2.51
41	14316.03	7.01	26072.40	10.51	41210.64	13.46	51060.21	14.96	59965.44	15.38
42	3690.35	2.27	4424.56	2.25	5625.96	2.34	6627.19	2.43	7982.23	2.61
39/40	73244.91	8.71	103918.39	10.57	142313.34	11.57	174835.24	12.63	218965.74	13.66

Source: Table displays the data that comes from UN Comtrade.

Table 2. Two-digit GB-2002 manufacture export and percentage of world export.

Year	2002		2003		2004		2005		2006	
Sector (GB-2)	Export	Percentage of World Export	Export	Percentage of World Export	Export	Percentage of World Export	Export	Percentage of World Export	Export	Percentage of World Export
13	2327.25	14.67	2678.84	14.66	3488.86	16.30	4364.48	17.68	5491.33	19.47
14	2935.27	3.55	3490.21	3.39	4165.99	3.49	5097.68	3.84	6139.45	4.07
15	597.21	1.51	622.38	1.31	743.00	1.37	718.41	1.22	1090.50	1.62
16	432.66	2.31	493.09	2.40	513.58	2.26	537.25	2.23	565.60	2.19
17	9602.62	14.41	11863.65	14.51	13506.00	14.51	15749.58	16.63	18698.17	18.26
18	52798.56	22.80	65819.68	23.47	78949.37	24.37	96733.55	27.30	124260.88	31.23
19	9333.37	19.80	11572.73	20.94	13667.33	21.52	15600.62	23.01	15381.44	21.05
20	3566.28	5.55	4358.74	5.93	6063.83	6.63	7569.66	7.70	9910.18	9.24
21	9854.22	12.60	12895.13	14.07	17318.60	15.86	22361.43	18.68	27955.15	20.97
22	1723.51	1.47	2327.51	1.73	2861.94	1.89	3964.51	2.51	5455.79	3.17
23	615.14	2.39	702.03	2.37	935.55	2.78	1149.13	3.20	1439.56	3.81
24	12099.55	25.45	13904.81	27.02	15901.89	28.22	20047.54	31.38	23654.04	33.43
25	8435.30	2.07	11114.25	1.95	14480.42	1.82	17622.65	1.54	17770.06	1.13
26	13824.15	3.57	17609.69	3.79	23479.37	4.21	30488.63	4.91	36220.99	5.25
27	789.98	0.54	917.57	0.51	1100.28	0.49	1364.01	0.55	1530.56	0.53
28	4949.52	11.45	6538.61	12.98	8710.37	15.23	10277.64	17.89	12131.17	20.09
29	1990.78	3.62	2553.66	3.79	3802.68	4.57	5502.76	5.82	7411.09	6.68
30	8036.05	4.24	9978.48	4.42	13105.64	4.69	17782.74	5.51	22224.40	6.04
31	5460.78	8.09	6934.18	8.72	9335.87	9.88	12256.88	12.00	15543.12	13.40
32	9569.10	4.84	12864.11	5.14	25212.88	6.97	34122.20	8.09	51915.85	10.32

(Continued)

Table 2. (*Continued*)

Year	2002		2003		2004		2005		2006	
Sector (GB-2)	Export	Percentage of World Export	Export	Percentage of World Export	Export	Percentage of World Export	Export	Percentage of World Export	Export	Percentage of World Export
33	3990.10	3.69	5430.63	4.28	8756.52	5.04	10568.31	5.18	17996.49	5.80
34	5348.28	10.11	6825.18	11.13	9771.21	13.00	12394.99	14.65	15390.99	15.84
35	50807.10	5.88	83377.29	8.29	118132.00	9.73	149694.35	11.08	186569.17	12.22
36	17.84	0.36	16.82	0.34	21.54	0.35	28.28	0.40	38.72	0.52
37	10547.69	1.35	15592.15	1.75	20998.69	2.01	28409.98	2.52	38427.62	3.01
41	9024.05	4.36	12480.04	5.12	18276.44	6.11	27473.78	8.18	34604.45	9.14
42	8648.26	5.54	10375.06	5.31	13606.12	5.74	17111.29	6.53	20783.46	6.60
39/40	65113.88	7.88	88957.09	9.38	129652.00	11.11	172313.78	13.18	227476.36	15.00

Source: Table displays the data that comes from UN Comtrade.

Table 3. Two-digit GB-2002 manufacture code and English comparison list.

Sector (GB-2)	Manufacture
13	Processing of food from agricultural products
14	Manufacture of foods
15	Manufacture of beverages
16	Manufacture of tobacco
17	Manufacture of textile
18	Manufacture of textile wearing apparel, footwear and caps
19	Manufacture of leather, fur, feather and related products
20	Processing of timber, manufacture of wood, bamboo, rattan, palm and straw products
21	Manufacture of furniture
22	Manufacture of paper and paper products
23	Printing, reproduction of recording media
24	Manufacture of articles for culture, education and sport activities
25	Processing of petroleum, coking, processing of nuclear fuel
26	Manufacture of raw chemical materials and chemical products
27	Manufacture of medicines
28	Manufacture of chemical fibers
29	Manufacture of rubber
30	Manufacture of plastics
31	Manufacture of non-metallic mineral products
32	Smelting and pressing of ferrous metals
33	Smelting and pressing of non-ferrous metals
34	Manufacture of metal products
35	Manufacture of general purpose machinery
36	Manufacture of special purpose machinery
37	Manufacture of transport equipment
39	Manufacture of electrical machinery and equipment
40	Manufacture of communication equipment, computers and other electronic equipment
41	Manufacture of measuring instruments and machinery for cultural activity and office work
42	Manufacture of artwork and other manufacturing

System categories and Classification by Broad Economic Categories necessary to distinguish the intermediate goods and final goods. If the quality of intermediate goods is higher than the quality of final goods, China will export the higher quality of final goods than sell in the domestic market.

2 Model

Based on discrete-choice models used by Berry (1994), the consumers who live in the South have discrete choice preferences. There are two regions $c, c \in \{N, S\}$,

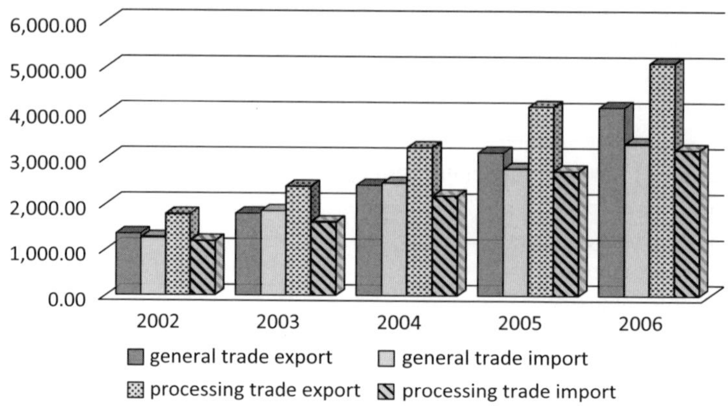

Figure 1. 2002–2006 Chinese import and export values.
Unit: 100 million dollar.

Source: The table displays the data comes from "Chinese Statistical Almanac", DRCnet and The General Administration of the People's Republic of China.

South (S) and North (N). The Northern goods are exported to the South freely. The wage is exogenous: $w_N \succ w_S$. Firm j, $(j \subset J)$ manufactures horizontally and vertically distinct varieties. Each region has J firms. Consumer n chooses the variety j which provides him with the highest indirect utility, Z_c is region c's technology, $Z_N \succ Z_S$. Following Khandelwal (2009), firm j uses technology to manufacture a variety subject to a marginal cost function that is increasing with quality λ_j. The quality λ_j is

$$\text{marginal cost} = w_c + \frac{\lambda_j^2}{2Z_c}. \tag{1}$$

If price p_j is fixed, all consumers would prefer higher quality objects. The parameter θ reflects the consumers' valuation for quality, and represents the market's quality ladder. ε_{nj} is the consumer-variety-specific term. The indirect utility is

$$V_{nj} = \theta\lambda_j - \alpha p_j + \varepsilon_{nj}. \tag{2}$$

This chapter modifies the quality ladder model used by Grossman and Helpman (1991) and Khandelwal (2009). Under this pricing rule, firms charge a markup $(\frac{1}{\alpha})$ over their marginal cost. The market's quality ladder is defined as the difference between the highest and lowest quality. The quality ladder is

$$Ladder(\theta) \equiv \theta\lambda_H^* - \theta\lambda_L^* = \frac{\theta^2}{\alpha}(Z_H - Z_L). \tag{3}$$

Denote the mean valuation for variety j as

$$\delta_j = \theta\lambda_j - \alpha p_j. \tag{4}$$

As the quality ladder increases, the market share gains are disproportionately distributed to the manufacturers of the higher quality

$$\frac{\partial \delta_N^*}{\partial \theta} \succ \frac{\partial \delta_S^*}{\partial \theta} \tag{5}$$

Khandelwal (2009) analyze is the aggregate Northern market share changes with Southern wages, and how this impact varies according to a market's quality ladder length. This chapter measures the aggregate Southern market share changes with Northern wages. As the symmetry characteristic, the first result shows that the South loses market share as Northern manufacturing wages decline:

$$\frac{\partial M_S}{\partial w_N} = -M_S M_N \frac{\partial \delta_N^*}{\partial \delta_N} > 0. \tag{6}$$

The smaller loss in markets is characterized by longer quality ladders (high θ markets):

$$\frac{\partial^2 M_S}{\partial w_N \partial \theta} = -\theta M_S M_N (M_S - M_N)(Z_S - Z_N) < 0. \tag{7}$$

The model displays that the different quality ladder can generate a different impact to North and South markets. The North can specialize in the product with long quality ladder and the South can specialize in the product with short quality ladder. Khandelwal (2009) extend product specialization to quality specialization.

3 Empirical Work

3.1 Data

This chapter contains two digit GB-2002 manufactures that have been matched with seven-digit HS products denoted by h. The seven-digit HS products are the nests. The eight-digit HS product is called a variety which is imported from country c. The data includes 7,466 eight-digit HS products, 6,990 seven-digit HS products and 223 import countries from 2002 to 2006.[1]

3.2 The quality of product

Based on Bernard *et al.* (2006), the outside variety market share is s_{ot}

$$s_{ot} = 1 - \frac{I_{mt}}{I_{mt} + Q_{mt} - X_{mt}}. \tag{8}$$

[1] *Notes*: The goods imported from China are the products manufacture inside the border, but outside the Customs Territory.

The outside variety market share (s_{ot}) is 1 minus the industry's import penetration. I_{mt} denotes the import value of t time two-digit GB-2002 industry m and X_{mt} denotes the export value of t time two-digit GB-2002 industry m. Q_{mt} denotes the industry quantity of t time two-digit GB-2002 industry m. The imported variety market share is s_{cht}

$$s_{cht} = \frac{q_{cht}}{MKT_t} \tag{9}$$

q_{cht} denotes the import quantity of variety ch. MKT_t is the total industry output:

$$MKT_t = \sum_{ch \neq 0} \frac{q_{cht}}{(1 - s_{ot})}. \tag{10}$$

According to Berry (1994), consumer n has preferences for country c's import into HS product h at time t, λ_{cht} is the quality of variety ch at time t. α, σ and γ are coefficients. p_{cht} is unit value at time t. ns_{cht} is the market share within product h. pop_{ct} is the quantity of population in country c at time t. The demand curve is

$$\ln\left(\frac{s_{cht}}{s_{ot}}\right) = \lambda_{cht} + \alpha p_{cht} + \sigma \ln(ns_{cht}) + \gamma \ln pop_{ct}. \tag{11}$$

This chapter estimates regression (11) on China's product-level import data from 2002 to 2006. The samples are 7,466 eight-digit HS products, 6,990 seven-digit HS products and 223 import countries. The data is from the National Bureau of Statistics of China Database. The results of these regressions show 1,837 products and that 40 countries are robust. There are 900 products and 40 countries for which we can calculate the quality ladder.

3.3 Quality ladders

Following Khandelwal (2009), who constructed the quality ladder as the difference between the maximum and minimum quality within a product:

$$Ladder_h = \lambda_h^{\max} - \lambda_h^{\min} \tag{12}$$

$\lambda_h^{\max}$ refers to product h's maximum quality, $\lambda_h^{\min}$ refers to product h's minimum quality, $Ladder_h$ denotes product h's maximum quality minus product h's minimum quality.

The result of regression (11) displays that the biggest quality ladder is 206,150 in 900 products and the smallest quality ladder is 0 in 900 products. There are big gap, in the quality ladder per different products of different countries. The relationship of price, market share and quality is in "Microtomes; Parts and Accessories of Instr. and App. of 90.27" (HS 9027900). Conditional on price, Figure 2 displays that the

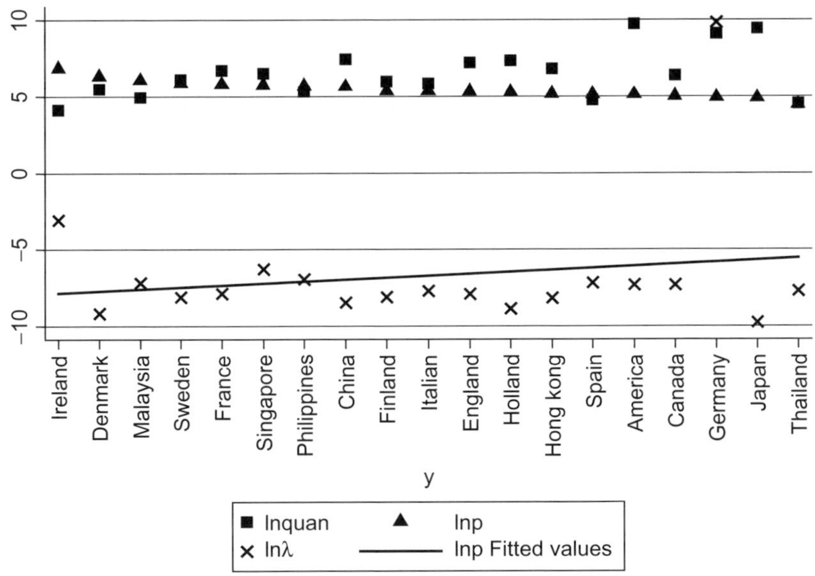

Figure 2. Price, market share and quality of microtomes; parts and accessories of Instr. and App. of 90.27 HS 9027900.

Notes: This figure displays that the quality relative to market share in the most of countries is underestimated, besides America. *p* denotes the price of import products. quan indicates the quantity of import goods. *q* means the quality of import products.

quality relative to market share in most of the countries is underestimated, besides America.

I constructed a two-digit GB-2002 industry quality ladder:

$$IndLadder_m = w_{ind} \sum_{h=1}^{H_m} Ladder_h. \tag{13}$$

$IndLadder_m$ denotes the industry m ladder which defined as the weighted average of the product ladders within the GB-2002 industry. The variable H_m refers to the product number in the two-digit GB-2002 industry m, The variable w_{ind} is the industry m's import share within GB-2002 in the industry's initial year.

The result of these regressions is summarized in Table 4. The table provides summary statistics for the two-digit GB-2002 sectors. Column 1 reports the total number of seven-digit HS products. Column 2 reports the weighted average of exporter per capita GDP. Columns 3 and 4 report skill intensity and capital intensity. Column 5 reports industrial quality ladder which is calculated by the weighted average of products quality ladder. The table displays the 32 sectors and the 20th sector has the highest quality ladder, while the 19th, 14th and the 23rd sectors are the smallest quality ladders. Column 6 reports ladder length which is calculated

Table 4. Two-digit GB-2002 sectors' summary statistics.

Sector (GB-2)	Products (HS-7) (1)	Average GDP (2)	Capital Intensity (3)	Skill Intensity (4)	Quality Ladder (5)	Ladder Length (6)
14	12	8.22	8.86	0.03	4166.13	0.95
15	15	11.22	13.66	0.02	9159.61	0.38
17	17	4.61	5.95	0.01	20894.70	11.48
19	13	3.81	2.15	0.00	5064.28	6.93
20	13	5.31	6.35	0.00	22588.65	5.78
22	34	7.32	13.95	0.01	9684.56	6.01
23	1	6.40	9.61	0.01	1409.32	1.37
25	15	24.43	37.16	0.04	10704.95	3.51
26	209	10.48	15.83	0.03	12570.44	5.96
27	5	10.67	11.74	0.04	11101.14	0.76
28	20	10.15	23.62	0.03	6022.85	14.02
29	36	6.54	8.18	0.02	13033.61	4.22
30	67	6.27	7.66	0.01	7663.65	9.12
31	26	5.74	9.24	0.01	20438.79	3.15
32	28	15.56	21.80	0.05	23136.03	7.86
33	42	12.72	16.12	0.04	10907.02	8.13
34	38	6.66	5.67	0.01	7830.04	2.34
37	19	10.15	10.39	0.06	13529.68	1.63
41	91	7.21	5.35	0.03	18730.80	7.01
39/40	187	10.62	8.05	0.04	14973.11	8.71

Notes: The table provides summary statistics for the two-digit GB-2002 sectors. Column 1 reports the total number of seven-digit HS products. Column 2 reports the weighted average of exporter per capita GDP. Columns 3 and 4 report skill intensity and capital intensity. Column 5 reports industrial quality ladder which calculates the weighted average of products quality ladder. Column 6 reports ladder length which calculates Equation (13).

from Equation (13). The ladder length of the 28th and the 17th sectors are 14.02 and 11.48 which are the longest ladder lengths in all sectors. The smallest ladder length was for the 15th, 27th and the 14th sectors.

This chapter analyses the relationship of the industry quality ladder with capital intensity, skill intensity and total factor productivity (TFP). The equation is

$$IndLadder_m = \varphi \ln(K/L_m) + \beta \ln(Skill_m) + \chi \ln(TFP_m). \tag{14}$$

Capital intensity equals the fixed asset divided by the number of employment. Skill intensity equals the technology activity employment divided by the number of employment. In this chapter, the number of employment reports labor factor inputs, the fixed asset reports capital factor input, GDP reports the output of factor inputs, and the industry added value reports the added output of factor input. These data comes from "China Industry Economy Statistical Yearbook" and the National

Table 5. 2002–2006 TFP of manufacture.

Sector (GB-2)	Effch	Techch	Pech	Sech	Tfpch
13	1.033	1.078	1.031	1.002	1.114
14	1.018	1.084	1.018	1	1.104
15	1.037	1.092	1.026	1.01	1.132
16	1	1.159	1	1	1.159
17	1.025	1.078	1.016	1.008	1.105
18	0.997	1.072	0.981	1.016	1.069
19	1	1.067	1	1	1.067
20	1.059	1.082	1.038	1.02	1.146
21	0.999	1.077	0.988	1.011	1.076
22	1.023	1.093	0.987	1.036	1.118
23	0.977	1.089	1.006	0.971	1.064
24	1.004	1.067	1.01	0.994	1.071
25	1.009	1.2	1	1.009	1.211
26	1.069	1.097	1.129	0.947	1.173
27	0.956	1.095	0.958	0.999	1.047
28	1.077	1.112	0.974	1.106	1.198
29	1.018	1.082	1.019	0.999	1.101
30	1.01	1.079	1.009	1.001	1.09
31	1.031	1.086	1.03	1.001	1.12
32	1.104	1.108	1.196	0.924	1.224
33	1.18	1.098	1.167	1.012	1.296
34	1.037	1.08	1.038	0.999	1.119
35	1.077	1.081	1.076	1.001	1.164
36	1.028	1.078	1.028	1	1.109
37	1.02	1.085	1.024	0.996	1.106
39	1.055	1.081	1.05	1.005	1.14
40	1	1.079	1	1	1.079
41	1.053	1.081	1.032	1.02	1.139
mean	1.041	1.095	1.037	1.004	1.14

Notes: Effch denotes the change of technology efficiency. Techch indicates the change of technology. Pech means the change of pure technology. Sech implies the change of scale efficiency. Tfpch signifies the change of TFP.

Source: The table displays the data comes from "China Industry Economy Statistical Yearbook" and the National Bureau of Statistics of China.

Bureau of Statistics of China. This chapter uses DEAP Version 2.1 software to get the results of the manufacture's Malmquist index and other results from 2002 to 2006 (Table 5).

This chapter calculates TFP with Chinese data 2002–2006 and estimates the impact of quality ladder on productivity, capital intensity and skill intensity. These

Table 6. The quality ladder in intermediate goods and final goods.

BEC	Primary goods	Intermediate goods		Final goods	
Quality Ladder	4977.45	12478.87		19784.89	
BEC	Primary goods	Semi-finished goods	Parts and components	Capital goods	Consumption goods
Quality Ladder	4977.45	11870.43	13087.31	23364.86	16204.93

Notes: The classification by BEC of the United Nations reclassifies the Harmonized Commodity Description and Coding System (HS) (2002 edition) headings on the basis of the principal use of the products. This result displays that the final goods of capital goods have the longest quality ladder which is 23364.86. Consumption goods' quality ladder is 16204.93.

findings indicate quality upgrading is necessary for developing countries to achieve export success, upgrade technology and economic development.

4 The Quality of Intermediate Goods

Following Lemoine and Ünal-Kesenci (2002), this chapter uses the classification by Broad Economic Categories (BEC) of the United Nations and reclassifies the Harmonized Commodity Description and Coding System (HS) (2002 edition) headings on the basis of the principal use of the products. Table 6 displays that the final import goods of capital goods have the longest quality ladder which is 23364.86. Consumption goods' quality ladder is 16204.93. The intermediate import goods have a shorter quality ladder for Semi-finished goods which is 11870.43 while for Parts and components it is 13087.31. The shortest ladder is for Primary import goods.

Empirical study show that the quality of intermediate goods is lower than the quality of final goods exported China. Processing trade in China can increase export, upgrade quality and increase wage.

5 Conclusion

This chapter calculates TFP with Chinese data from 2002 to 2006 and estimates the impact of the quality ladder on productivity, capital intensity and skill intensity. These findings indicate quality upgrading is necessary to developing countries for export success, upgrade technology and economic development. Empirical study supports the quality of intermediate goods which is higher than the quality of final goods exported China. Processing trade in China can increase export, upgrade quality and increase wage.

References

Amiti, M. and A. Khandelwal (2009), Import Competition and Quality Upgrading, *NBER Working Paper No.15503*. Available from: http://www.nber.org/papers/w15503.

Baldwin, R. and J. Harrigan (2007), Zeros, Quality and Space, Trade Theory and Trade Evidence, *NBER Working Paper No.13214*. Available from: http://www.nber.org/papers/w13214.

Bernard, A., J. Jensen, and P. Schott (2006), Survival of the Best Fit: Exposure to Low-Wage Countries and the (Uneven) Growth of U.S. manufacturing, *Journal of International Economics* 68, 219–237.

Berry, S. (1994), Estimating Discrete-Choice Models of Product Differentiation, *The RADN Journal of Economics* 25, 242–262.

Grossman, G.M. and E. Helpman (1991), *Innovation and Growth in the Global Economy*, Cambridge, MA: MIT Press, p. 85.

Khandelwal, A. (2009), The Long and Short (of) Quality Ladders, *NBER Working Paper No. 15178*. Available from: http://www.nber.org/papers/w15178.

Lemoine, F. and D. Ünal-Kesenci (2002), China in the International Segmentation of Production Processes.*CEPII, Working Paper No 2002-02*. Available from: http://www.cepii.fr/CEPII/en/publications/wp/abstract.asp?NoDoc=145.

Linders, S. (1961), *An Essay on Trade and Transformation*, Stockholm: Almqvist & Wiksell.

Sugita, Y. (2006), Matching, Quality, Upgrading and Trade between Heterogeneous Firms, *CCES Discussion Paper Series No. 20*.

Part II

External Cooperation Strategy

Chapter 5

The Impact of BITs and DTTs on FDI Inflow and Outflow: Evidence from China*

Hejing Chen

Department of Economics, Western University, Canada
hjchen.xmu@gmail.com

Chunding Li

Institute of World Economics and Politics,
Chinese Academy of Social Sciences, China
Department of Economics, Western University, Canada
chundingli@gmail.com

John Whalley

Department of Economics, Western University, Canada
Centre for International Governance Innovation (CIGI), Canada
National Bureau of Economic Research (NBER), USA
jwhalley@uwo.ca

Abstract: This chapter examines the impact of both China's bilateral investment treaties (BITs) and double tax treaties (DTTs) simultaneously on China's bilateral Foreign Direct Investment (FDI) inflows and outflows. Using China bilateral FDI flow data from 1985 to 2010, we find that the cumulative number of BITs China signed has a positive (though not always statistically significant) but minor impact

*We are grateful to the Ontario Research Fund (ORF) and Centre for International Governance Innovation (CIGI) for financial support and to ORF seminar participants for the comments.

on both China's FDI inflows and outflows. The effect of a dummy BIT using dyadic data is always significant and positive for China's FDI inflows, while negative but not always significant for China's FDI outflows. We also find evidence that the cumulative number of DTTs tends to promote China's FDI inflows and outflows in most equations with weighted cumulative BITs. However, tax treaty dummies do not reveal any robust effect on FDI flow. Generally, BITs and DTTs are more inclined to affect China's FDI inflows than to affect China's FDI outflows.

1 Introduction

China has been one of the largest recipients for global foreign direct investment (FDI) since the 21st new century. Annual realized FDI inflows have grown from $1.9 billion US dollars in 1985 to US$118.7 billion in 2013 (see Figure 1). By 2013, China had accumulated a FDI stock of US$ 1.344 trillion,[1] well ahead of other large developing and transition economies such as Brazil, India and Russia. Meanwhile, China's FDI outflows have taken off as a result of the government's adoption and promotion of a "go global" policy aimed at establishing the country's investors as international players following China's entry to the World Trade Organization

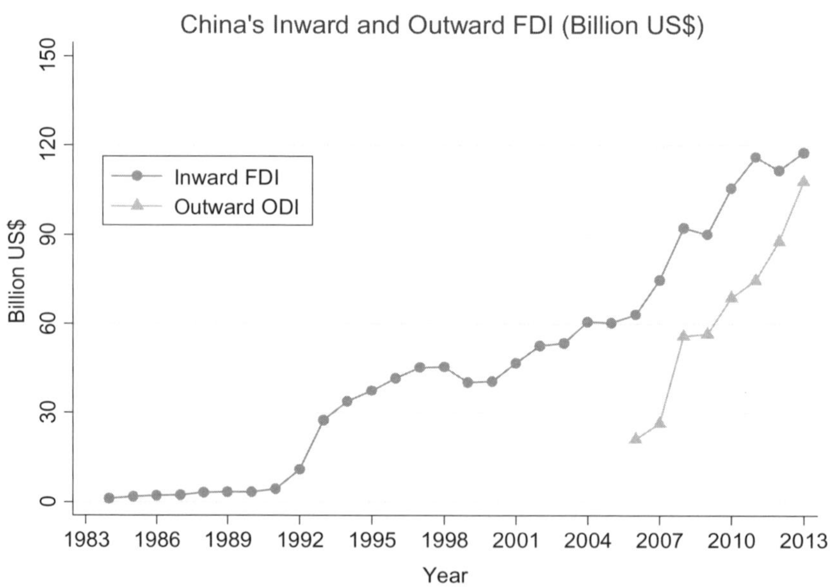

Figure 1. China's inward and outward FDI.

Source: Chinese Statistics Yearbook (CSY) (Online). Available from: http://www.stats.gov.cn/english/Statisticaldata/AnnualData/.

[1] Data got from the CSY (Online). Available from: http://www.stats.gov.cn/english/Statisticaldata/AnnualData/.

(WTO) in 2001. Although China's outward direct investment (ODI) stock is still small relative to the inward FDI stock, growth in China's outward FDI flows has become significant in recent years, growing from less than $100 million in the 1980s to $107.84 billion in 2013 (see Figure 1), and the cumulative FDI abroad (stock) had reached $660.48 billion by the end of 2013,[2] making China the fifth largest originator of ODI by value.

Bilateral investment treaties (BITs) and double tax treaties (DTTs) are the two most widely used types of international agreements for both protecting foreign investors and providing such investment non-discriminatory treatment and from double taxation. BITs are agreements between two countries for the reciprocal encouragement, promotion and protection of investments in each other's territories by companies based in either country. DTTs are aiming to avoid double taxation on income earned in any two different countries, and stimulating FDI between countries. Under a DTT agreement, a credit is usually allowed against the tax levied by the country in which the taxpayer resides for taxes levied in the other treaty country and as a result the tax payer pays no more than the higher of the two rates.

BITs and DTTs are presumed to have a positive influence on the flow of FDI between countries bound in BIT or DTT. Whether BITs and DTTs increase FDI inflows has been studied and debated for the past decades for a number of developing countries. By the end of 2014, China had already concluded 130 BITs (106 in force)[3] and 107 DTTs (including double taxation arrangement with Hong Kong and Macau), making China the largest contracting party to BITs and DTTs among developing countries. Given China's large FDI involvement, this suggests assessing separately whether China's BITs and DTTs play an important role in attracting FDI inflows, besides other determinants such as market size, labor endowment, etc. There is also an issue of whether China's BITs and DTTs have symmetrical effects on China's outward FDI.

To our knowledge, this is the first empirical study examining the impact of both China's bilateral investment and DTTs simultaneously on both China's FDI inflows and outflows. We find that the cumulative number of BITs China signed has a negative but minor impact on China's FDI inflows, but a positive (though not always statistically significant) impact on China's FDI outflows. The effect of a dummy BIT using dyadic data is always significant and positive for China's FDI inflows, while negative but not always significant for China's FDI outflows. We also find evidence that the cumulative number of DTTs tend to promote China's FDI inflows and outflows, especially when the cumulative number of BITs is weighted.

---

[2]Data got from the CSY (Online). Available from: http://www.stats.gov.cn/english/Statisticaldata/AnnualData/.

[3]The data got from UNCTAD International Investment Agreement Database (Online). Available from: http://www.unctad.org/iia.

However, tax treaty dummies do not reveal any robust effect on FDI flow. Generally, BITs and DTTs are more inclined to affect China's FDI inflows than to affect China's FDI outflows.

2 Background: BITs, DTTs and FDI

2.1 BITs and DTTs

A BIT is an agreement establishing the terms and conditions for private investment by nationals and companies of one state in another state. Treaties typically cover the following areas: scope and definition of investment, admission and establishment, national treatment, most-favored-nation treatment, fair and equitable treatment, compensation in the event of expropriation or damage to the investment, guarantees of free transfers of funds and dispute settlement mechanisms, both state–state and investor-state.

Conventionally, the declared goals of BITs include: investment protection, market and investment liberalization and investment promotion. It is the third of these goals i.e. investment promotion that this chapter evaluates. By providing that national companies of either party to the treaty may invest under the same conditions and be treated in the same way in the territory of the other, a BIT defines a symmetric relationship between the two contracting countries and provides a stable legal environment that supports foreign investment in the host country. But whether and to what extent a BIT, relative to other key determinants of FDI flows such as the market size and labor endowment of the host country, promote investment is left open (Salacuse and Sullivan, 2005).

The DTTs are bilateral agreements between two states. A primary objective is to eliminate double taxation, which is achieved by: allocating taxing rights to one or other state for specified categories of income or gains (including in some cases how much each state may tax); or if both states are entitled to tax the income or gains, specifying whether double taxation should be eliminated and, if so, which state should provide relief against double taxation (and the method by which it should do this either by exempting income or gains taxed by the other state or by giving credit for tax paid to the other state when assessing the amount of tax it will collect). DTTs will typically provide mechanisms for resolving disputes and provide a measure of protection for taxpayers against the treaty partners applying their domestic tax rules less favorably in relation to residents of the counterparty state compared with their treatment of their own residents (Clayson *et al.*, 2008).

DTTs perform four primary functions. The first is to standardize tax definitions and define the tax jurisdictions of treaty partners. The second is to reduce transfer pricing and other forms of tax avoidance. The third is linked to information exchange and the last is that they affect the actual taxation of MNEs through lowered withholding rates on interests, dividends and royalties. (Blonigen and Davies, 2004). The impacts of the last of these depends on the tax treatment in the home country; and whether a foreign credit is provided or whether taxed foreign income is exempt from domestic taxation. If the former and foreign tax rates are below domestic rates, a tax treaty has little effect via its rate reduction. Also if the MNEs engaged in FDI are more concerned with reducing their tax burdens through transfer pricing, tax treaties (with the second and third goals) may reduce incentives for FDI activity instead of increasing them. On the other hand, a tax treaty (with the first and the fourth functions) may promote investment by reducing uncertainty about the overseas tax environment. Therefore, the net effect of tax treaties on FDI is open and depends on which goal of the tax treaty dominates.

2.2 Overview of world BITs, DTTs and FDI flows

The first BIT was signed between Germany and Pakistan in 1959. Throughout the 1970s and 1980s, BITs slowly spread, with roughly 20 treaties being signed annually mainly between European and developing countries. With the decision of the US to adopt BITs as a foreign investment protection device their number started to increase sharply. When the block of developing countries decided to give up their struggle for a "New International Economic Order", including the right of host states to expropriate foreign companies' investments in the natural resource sector, the number of BITs rose even further since developing countries started to compete in capturing a share of global FDI flows, facing the dilemma of either signing BITs that privileged the contracting party exporting FDI or possibly losing FDI to other countries increasing their competitive advantage (Berger, 2008).

Worldwide, the number of BITs and DTTs has increased in recent decades. There were approximately 386 BITs in 1989, however a decade later in 1999, their number had grown to 1,857.[4] In 2010, the total stock of BITs in the world was 2,807; and at the end of 2013, world total BITs had reached 2,902.[5] The number of DTTs in force has risen from 100 in the 1960s to 2,976 by the end of 2010.[6]

During the same period, FDI has been spurred by the widespread liberalization of FDI policies, combined with advances in information and communication technologies and competition among firms. Inflows of FDI have grown at an unprecedented rate, expanding from approximately $40 billion at the beginning

[4]See M. Malik (2008), Recent Developments in Regional and BITs in the Second Annual Forum of Developing Country Investment Negotiators, November 3–4, 2008 Marrakech, Morocco.

[5]Data are from the United Nations Committee of Trade and Development (UNCTAD) International Investment Agreements database.

[6]See UNCTAD World Investment Report 2011.

of the 1980s, to $200 billion in 1990, to the historical highest $1.97 trillion in 2007 while dropping to $1.2 trillion in 2009 and reaching $1.45 trillion in 2013. The simultaneous growth in FDI and the growth of BITs and DTTs suggest a potential positive relation.

2.3 BITs, DTTs and FDI Activity in China

BITs in China began in 1982 when China and Sweden signed China's first such agreement. China signed the first income and capital type of DTT with Japan in 1983.[7] During the period 1992–1996, the number of BITs China concluded increased at a very high rate, and another 8 and 10 new BITs were signed by China in year 2001 and 2005, respectively. Year 1986, 1994–1996 saw a fast growth for the number of DTTs China signed. Figure 2 shows the fast-growing period of China's BITs and DTTs coincide with growth of China's FDI inflows and outflows, which also indicate a potential positive relationship between BITs, DTTs and FDI activity.

In terms of geographic distribution, most of China's FDI activities are concentrated in Asia and Europe, with more than 60% and nearly 20% of China's cumulative inward and outward FDI stock involving Asia and Europe, respectively. The number of the BITs China signed is more evenly distributed among continents,

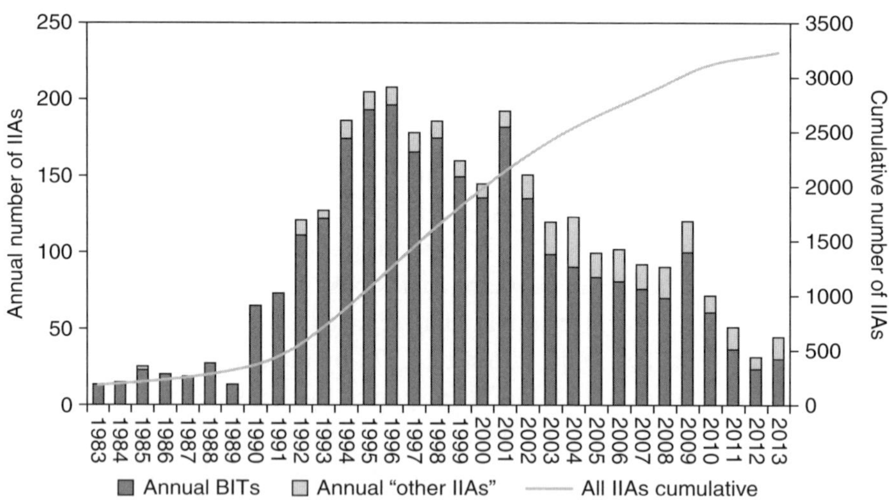

Figure 2. Trends in BITs and Other IIAs signed, 1983–2013.

Note: IIAs denotes International Investment Agreements.
Source: UNCTAD International Investment Agreement Database.

[7] There are some transportation treaties China concluded with Argentina, France, Japan, South Africa, UK and the US during the period between 1975 and 1982.

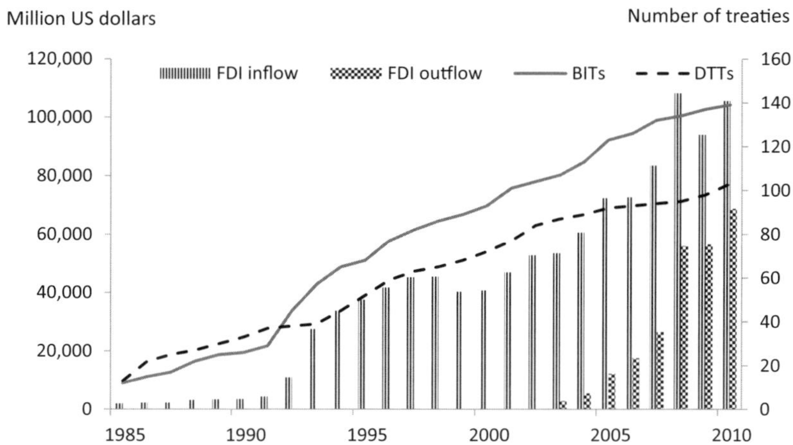

Figure 3. BITs, DTTs and FDI Flows of China, 1985–2010.

Source: Authors' calculation based on UNCTAD International Investment Agreements database (http:// www.unctad.org/iia).

except for North America, where substantial FDI actually is not covered by any existing bilateral investment protection agreement (e.g. China and the United States, China and Canada). This (large amount of FDI activity without BIT) is also the case for Cayman Islands and the British Virgin Island. For DTTs, the geographic distribution is similar to that of FDI activity, except for an expanding share for Europe. Unlike the case of BITs, both Canada and the US signed a DTT with China. As a worldwide tax haven, Cayman Islands and the British Virgin Islands are still outside of the partner list of DTTs that China has concluded (Figure 3).

2.4 Empirical Studies on the Effect of BITs and DTTs on FDI

In literature, different approaches are used empirically to model the effects of BITs and DTTs on FDI. Most are dyadic analysis taking bilateral FDI as the dependent variable in a panel setting to examine whether the existence of a BIT or DTT (in form of dummy variable) will lead to higher FDI flows, while other studies use models with the aggregate FDI inflows of individual host country as the unit of observation and examine whether the total number of BITs or DTTs affect aggregate FDI inflows into the host country (Figure 4).

Dyadic analyses have yielded mixed results as to the impacts of BITs on FDI. Most of them find little if any statistically significant increase in FDI inflows as a result of BITs. Vandervelde *et al.* (1998) found a positive coefficient for BITs in most of their statistical models, but the estimated effect was marginal and statistically not significant at conventional levels. Hallward-Driemeier (2003) raised further doubts about the effectiveness of BITs. The chapter uses bilateral FDI outflows from 20

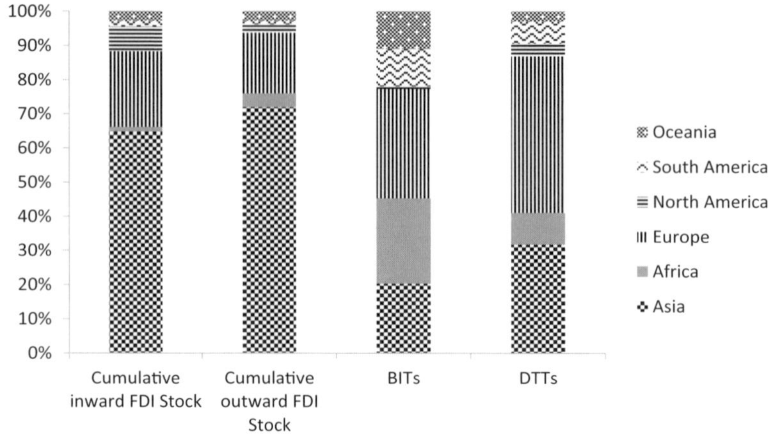

Figure 4. The geographic distribution of BITs, DTTs and FDI of China, by end 2010.

Source: Authors' calculation based on UNCTAD International Investment Agreements database (http:// www.unctad.org/iia).

OECD countries to 31 developing countries, the data covers the years of 1980–2000, capturing the surge in the number of BITs ratified, the estimated coefficient for BITs was actually negative and insignificant. This conclusion was echoed in related work by UNCTAD (2003). Similar results can also be found in Tobin and Rose-Ackerman (2005), their datasets were compiled from a variety of sources and contain a different number of observations for different variables, the data sets use panel data form the first BIT signed in 1959 through 2000 for low and middle-income countries to take into account the dynamic nature of some of the data, and to control for some of the statistical problems inherent in cross sectional analyses, the interaction term between BIT and a measure of political risk shows a conditional positive effect on FDI activity. However, Salacuse and Sullivan (2005) found that signing a BIT with the US is associated with higher FDI inflows, whereas the number of BITs signed with other OECD countries is statistically insignificant. Haftel (2008) uses a data set that includes 132 developing countries from 1977 to 2004 to perform empirical analysis, and also has provided qualified support for Salacuse and Sullivan's argument by showing that ratified (rather than merely signed) U.S. BITs boost US FDI into developing country signatories.

Empirical studies on bilateral DTTs are less, compared to BIT, and more negative in assessment of impact. Blonigen and Davies (2004) found large and statistically negative effects of treaties established in 1980s and 1990s (so called new treaties in the paper) on US FDI. Using OECD data, Blonigen and Davies (2005) also suggested that new treaties (during the 1983–1992 period) did not encourage FDI and might have actually reduced FDI activity. Egger *et al.* (2006) also found a negative effect of newly implemented DTTs in a difference-in-differences analysis of two years prior to and two years after treaty conclusion using dyadic FDI data over the period 1985–2000.

Although there are fewer empirical studies using monadic models, most of them, in contrast to dyadic analyses, find positive findings on the impact of BITs and DTTs on aggregate FDI. Gross and Trevino (2005) found the number of BITs signed by a country to be positively and statistically significantly correlated with aggregated FDI inflows into that country. Neumayer and Spess (2005) employed a larger panel data over the period 1970–2001 covering up to 119 countries and found a positive and statistically significant effect for BITs on FDI inflows. As for the effect of DTTs, Neumayer (2007) found developing countries with more DTTs with major capital-exporting developed countries have a higher overall FDI stock and share of stock and receive more FDI inflows as well as a higher share of inflows.

Most of these existing studies focus on FDI flows from developed countries to developing countries and the different approaches tend to lead to different conclusions. Most analyses using a dyadic approach find no or negative effect while most monadic studies do find an effect for BITs or DTTs on FDI.

Above mentioned researches all explore the effects of BITs or DTTs on inward or outward FDI, they are related to the topic of this chapter, especially for some of the studies include China as one of the developing host countries. But these researches are not only focused on China, and mostly explore only BITs or DTTs effects on FDI inflows to developing countries. Meanwhile, empirical research methodology in this chapter is somewhat the same as these related chapters. Therefore, there are few empirical studies on the effects of BITs and DTTs on China's FDI outflows.[8] Since China is continuously strengthening its position as a source of outward foreign investment as well as the biggest FDI recipient in the world, an analysis on the impact of BITs and DTTs on China's inbound and outbound FDI is of significance.

3 Research Design

3.1 Empirical framework

In order to examine how BITs and DTTs might affect FDI flows, a theoretical framework is required to describe the determinants of FDI. There are different frameworks used for the determinants of bilateral FDI flows, among which the gravity model and the knowledge–capital model by Carr, Markusen and Maskus (CMM) (2001) are the most widely used. The standard gravity model from empirical

[8]To our knowledge, Buckley *et al.* (2008) are the only ones evaluating the impact of BITs and DTTs on China's outbound FDI.

trade analysis (e.g. Tinbergen, 1962; Pöyhönen, 1963; Anderson, 1979; Helpman and Krugman, 1985; Deardorff, 1995; Feenstra *et al.*, 2001; Eaton and Kortum, 2002; Anderson and Wincoop, 2003) has been extended to the study on FDI flows between countries (Hejazi and Safarian, 1999, 2001; Bevan and Estrin 2004). The general idea of using a gravity model to describe determinants of FDI flows is based on the arguments that the amount of bilateral resource flow will positively depend on size of source/destination countries which reflects potential supply/demand and negatively on transportation costs.

The knowledge–capital model established by CMM is grounded in the formal theories of multi-national enterprise (MNE) model, which allows for both the horizontal and vertical FDI. Horizontal FDI is captured by the sum of two countries' real GDP and the squared difference between the two countries' real GDP in CMM model, since larger and more similar-sized markets better support the higher fixed costs associated with setting up production across countries and will lead to greater horizontal FDI activity. Vertical FDI in the CMM model is related to differences in the two countries' relative endowments of skilled and unskilled labor, and is represented by three variables, i.e. the skill difference between the home and host country, the interaction term between skill difference with the difference in GDP and the interaction term between the square of skill difference and trade openness in the host country.[9]

We use gravity model as our main regression methodology to estimate the impacts of BIT and DTT that China has signed on its FDI inflows and outflows, which is the same as most existing literatures did. In order to check the robustness of empirical results, we also use the knowledge-capital model as a comparison. Both gravity models and knowledge-capital models of FDI have precise micromodel foundations for FDI flow, and are often used methods for empirical analysis.

3.2 Variables

Our dependent variables are the annual bilateral FDI inflows into China and outflows from China between China and its investment partner economies. These are converted to constant 2005 US$ using the US GDP Deflator.[10] The measure of FDI flow is typically natural logged to capture elasticity responses (% change), but in our case, there are some observations where FDI inflows from a given country to China or opposite outflows are negative. We exclude observations for which the dependent variable takes on a zero or negative value where the log does not exist.

[9] See Carr *et al.* (2001); Blognigen and Davies (2004, 2005) for detailed explanation.

[10] See Aisbett (2009) for detailed discussion on the advantages and disadvantages of different dependent variables (e.g. FDI stocks, FDI flow, affiliate sales).

By doing this the observation number is reduced by separately 2 and 77 for China's FDI inflows and outflows. These negative observations are rare and mainly in small countries, like Angola in 2008, Argentina in 2009, Azerbaijan in 2007 and 2008, Bulgaria in 2009, Bahamas in 2003 and 2008, Belize in 2010, Bermuda in 2007 and 2008, etc. We think this treatment will not give influence to the empirical results.

Our main explanatory variables reflect the development of China's BITs and DTTs. Previous studies using the gravity or CMM model either include a BIT dummy or a DTT dummy as an explanatory variable. In our study, we include both dummies simultaneously to avoid omitted variable bias. In addition, instead of including just one DTT dummy variable as is usually done, we classify tax treaties into three dummies based on their content. The International Bureau of Fiscal Documentation categorizes tax treaties in the following manner: income/capital tax treaties; social security treaties, administrative assistance, inheritance/gift and transportation tax treaties.[11] We use two major categories from this classification, which constitute the vast majority of treaties China signed. These are (1) income and capital treaties and (2) income tax treaties. This allows for more differentiation between tax treaties since different treaties imply different degrees of integration between countries. For instance, from the point of view of foreign investors, a country with an income and capital tax treaty might be more attractive than a country with just an income tax treaty.

Furthermore, the cumulative number of China's BITs and DTTs are also included in our study due to possible positive spill-over effects from signing a BIT/DTT. In concluding a BIT/DTT, the signatory developing country explicitly commits only to protect FDI under signatory developed country law, but also implicitly signals its willingness to protect all foreign investment. A single dyadic design may therefore underestimate the effect that signing a BIT/DTT has on FDI inflows or outflows.

Our other control variables are similar to the ones used in the standard gravity and CMM model under these two frameworks. Besides the conventional determinants of FDI, such as market size (natural log of real GDP of FDI source and host country), physical distance (natural log of physical distance between the capital cities of the two countries), ethnic distance (common language dummy) and institution maturity (OECD dummy) in gravity models and five variables representing horizontal and vertical FDI in the CMM model, we also control for bilateral real effective exchange rates defined as the nominal bilateral exchange rate (calculated indirectly via the individual exchange rate with US dollar) multiplied by the major trading partner price index and divided by the Chinese price index.

[11] Coupe *et al.* (2009).

China adopted a managed floating regime of RMB exchange rate in 2005. The Chinese yuan was kept fixed to the US dollar under the dollar peg system before July 21, 2005, but fluctuated against other major trade partners' currencies. After the announcement of Chinese exchange rate system reform, it began to fluctuate against the US dollar as well as other major trade partners' currencies. By the end of 2011, the RMB/US dollar exchange rate had appreciated by 30.2%. The bilateral real exchange rate may also be an important determinant of China's FDI inflows and outflows.

Consistent with other econometric studies, data for all economic explanatory variables (GDP, exchange rate) are lagged one year to mitigate potential reverse causality problems. This treatment is also based on the argument that investors were reacting to known information from the year before. Ideally, reverse causality problems could be more comprehensively tackled by instrumental variable regressions. However, practically all economic explanatory variables are potentially subject to reverse causality and it proved too difficult to find adequate and valid instruments.

The baseline specification we use is as follows:

For the gravity model:

$$\begin{aligned} \ln FDI_{ijt} = {} & \alpha_0 + \alpha_1 \ln GDP_{it-1} + \alpha_2 \ln GDP_{jt-1} + \alpha_3 \ln DIS_{ij} \\ & + \alpha_4 COMLANG + \alpha_5 OECD + \alpha_6 BRER_{ijt-1} + \alpha_7 BITS_t \\ & + \alpha_8 DTTS_t + \alpha_9 BIT_{ijt} + \alpha_{10} ICT_{ijt} + \alpha_{11} IT_{ijt} + \varepsilon_{ijt}. \end{aligned} \tag{1}$$

For the Carr *et al.* (2001) model:

$$\begin{aligned} \ln FDI_{ijt} = {} & \beta_0 + \beta_1 \sum GDP_{ijt-1} + \beta_2 GDPDIFSQ_{ijt-1} + \beta_3 SKDIFF_{ijt-1} \\ & + \beta_4 SKDIFF_{ijt-1} * GDPDIFF_{ijt-1} + \beta_5 (SKDIFF_{ijt})^2 * T\_OPEN_{jt-1} \\ & + \beta_6 BRER_{ijt-1} + \beta_7 BITS_t + \beta_8 DTTS_t + \beta_9 BIT_{ijt} \\ & + \beta_{10} ICT_{ijt} + \beta_{11} IT_{ijt} + \varepsilon_{ijt}. \end{aligned} \tag{2}$$

3.3 Data

Our main data source is a panel dataset of bilateral FDI inflows and outflows reported by China with its 173 investment partner countries (areas) for the period 1985–2010 from the CEIC database. Data on real GDP, trade openness, official exchange rate with US dollar and inflation measured by consumer price index are from World Bank World Development Indicators 2012. We rely on the UNESCO higher education statistics for data on enrolment in tertiary education to calculate skilled labor difference. Data on the bilateral investment and taxation treaties China signed are from UNCTAD IIA Database. Distance and common language data come

Table 1. Variables description.

Variable	Description
	Dependent Variable
Ln FDI_{ij}	Logarithm of FDI flow measure in 2005 US dollar (thousand) from country i (source) to country j (host).
	Main Independent Variables
BIT	Dummy, taking 1 after the BIT between country i and j has been signed
BITS	Cumulative number of BITs China had signed by year t
ICT	Dummy, taking 1 after the income and capital tax treaty between country i and j has been signed
IT	Dummy, taking 1 after the income tax treaty between country i and j has been signed
DTTS	Cumulative number of DTTs China had signed by year t
	Gravity Control Variables
GDP	Real GDP measured in 2005 US $(thousand)
DIS	Logarithm of Physical distance in kilometers between capital cities of country i and j
COMLANG	Dummy, taking 1 for countries or areas share the same language (dialect) as China
OECD	Dummy, taking 1 for OECD members
BRER	Bilateral real exchange rate (LCU per RMB), adjusted by the price index
	Carr et al*. (2001) *Control Variables
$\sum$GDP	Logarithm of sum of GDP_i and GDP_j
GDPDIFSQ	$Ln[(gdpi-gdpj)^2]$
SKDIFF	Ln(tert.edu. $enr._i$)-Ln(tert.edu. $enr._j$)
SKDIFF*GDPDIFF	[Ln(tert.edu. $enr._i$)-Ln(tert.edu. $enr._j$)]*($lnGDP_i$-$lnGDP_j$)
T_OPEN	Trade share in GDP
$(SKDIFF)^2$*T_OPENj	$[Ln(tert.school\ enr._i)-Ln(tert.school\ enr._j)]^2$*trade share in GDP of host country j.

from CEPII gravity dataset. Table 2 provides summary descriptive information on variables. Table 3 shows the covariance matrix of Independent variables.

Figures 5 and 6 report China's inward and outward FDI data by continents in recent years. We find that Asian, Latin America and Europe are China's main inward and outward FDI source regions. The Asia is China's largest FDI source region.

Table 2. Summary statistics.

Variable	Mean	Std. Dev.	Min	Max	Observations (N)
Dependant Variables					
$\ln FDI_{ict}$	8.899192	3.023741	2.209742	17.81497	2004
$\ln FDI_{cit}$	8.890661	2.57395	2.22025	17.38747	907
Independent Variables					
$BITS_t$	77.84615	42.14702	12	139	4498
$DTTS_t$	61.53846	27.55892	13	103	4498
BIT_{ict}	0.413962	0.492597	0	1	4498
ICT_{ict}	0.258115	0.437646	0	1	4498
IT_{ict}	0.052023	0.222098	0	1	4498
Gravity controls					
$\ln GDP_{it-1}$	16.53674	2.398509	10.39391	23.30156	4040
$\ln GDP_{ct-1}$	20.80379	0.726538	19.84888	22.23811	4325
lnDIS	8.966571	0.556845	6.697034	9.867705	4446
OECD	0.196532	0.397419	0	1	4498
COMLANG	0.028902	0.167549	0	1	4498
Carr et al. (2001) controls					
$\sum GDP_{t-1}$	20.96992	0.793977	19.84888	23.64005	4482
$GDPDIFSQ_{t-1}$	41.551	1.795706	28.96584	46.11524	4482
$SKDIFF_{it-1}$	−4.35317	2.243205	−11.6661	1.494677	2642
$SKDIFF_{ct-1}$	4.353167	2.243205	−1.49468	11.66614	2642
SKDIFF* $GDPDIFF_{t-1}$	20.08008	18.11525	−1.33435	107.1482	2540
$(SKDIFF)^2$*T_ $OPEN_{ct-1}$	1083.444	1177.448	0.0065505	8471.337	2571
$(SKDIFF)^2$*T_ $OPEN_{it-1}$	2137.38	2615.445	0.0038188	26272.41	2398
Other controls					
$\ln BRER_{t-1}$	0.875151	2.827776	−8.665509	12.60468	3067

Source: By authors.

4 Empirical Results

4.1 Estimation technique

We have conducted panel data fixed effects analyses for both gravity and CMM models, as there are factors affecting bilateral FDI relationship that are not captured by our explanatory variables and that are time-invariant. A fixed country-pair and

Table 3. Covariance matrix of independent variables.

Variables	BITS	DTTS	BIT	ICT	IT
BITS	1776.37				
DTTS	1148.99	759.49			
BIT	8.95	5.80	0.24		
ICT	4.04	2.66	0.11	0.19	
IT	2.22	1.47	0.02	−0.01	0.05

Source: by authors.

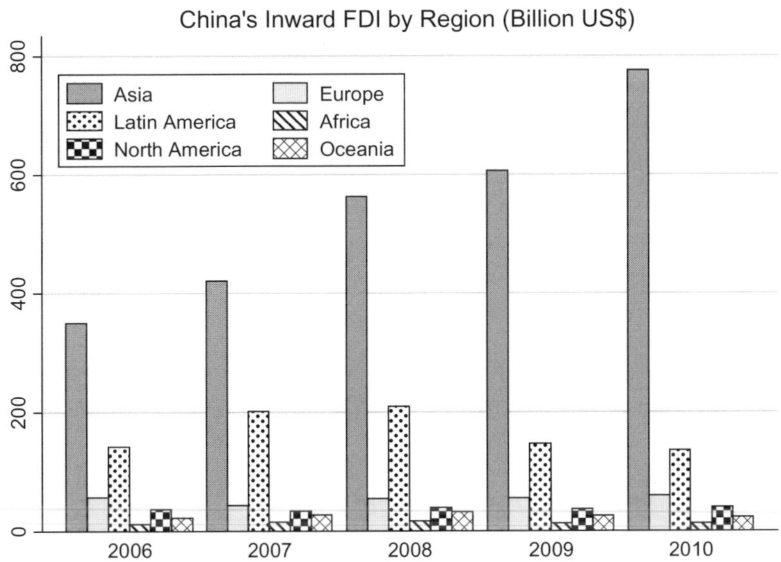

Figure 5. China's inward FDI by region.

Source: CEIC Database.

year effects specification could help to control for unobserved characteristics that affect FDI activity between China and each individual investment partner. We thus include a binary variable for each bilateral country pairing and year in addition to our control variables. The binary fixed effect country-pair variables estimate the aggregate effect of time-invariant characteristics that raise or lower FDI activity for that bilateral pairing versus average effects, and the binary fixed effect time variables are included to control for global business cycles and trends in world FDI or other omitted time-variant factors that affect all country-pairs in the same way.

Further, we create a weighted measure of BITs, which reflects the relative importance of different states as the FDI source. We calculate our measure "weighted BITs" in two ways. First, we use the ratio of lagged one year of FDI outflows of

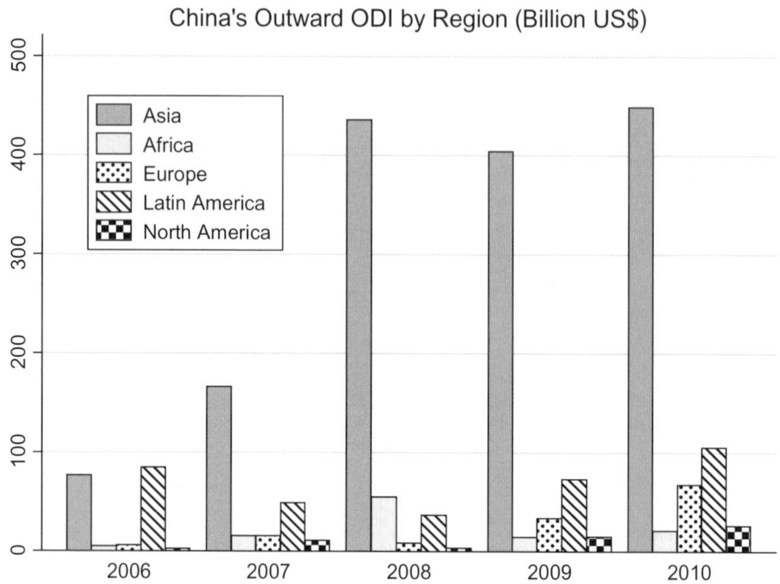

Figure 6. China's outward ODI by region.

Source: CEIC Database.

source country to that of host country as the proxy for the importance of FDI source country. Therefore, the weighted BITs variable is:

$$BITs\_OFDI = \left(\sum_{i=1}^{n-j}\left[BIT_{ijt} \times \frac{OFDI_{it-1}}{OFDI_{jt-1}}\right]\right), \quad (3)$$

where BITs_OFDI is our measure of weighted cumulative BIT, BIT is a dichotomous indicator variable coded 1 if a BIT exist between country $i$and j in year t (zero otherwise), the subscript i signifies the FDI source country as the (potential) signatory of a BIT with country j, and subscript j signifies the FDI host country for which the weighted BITs measure is recorded, while n is the universe of all sample countries in year t. The other way to calculate the weighted count of BITs is to use the ratio of lagged one year of source country GDP per capita to that of host country GDP per capita to capture the relative important position in international investment activities. Therefore the alternative weighted BITs variable is:

$$BITs\_PGDP = \left(\sum_{i=1}^{n-j}\left[BIT_{ijt} \times \frac{PGDP_{it-1}}{PGDP_{jt-1}}\right]\right). \quad (4)$$

4.2 Results of gravity model

Table 4 presents our LSDV empirical estimation results on China inbound FDI. In columns 1 and 2 cumulative BIT is unweighted while, columns 3–6 report the impact of two kinds of weighted BITs on China's FDI inflows. The country-pair and time effects always enter significantly in regressions for China's FDI

Table 4. Fixed effects results from gravity model on China's FDI inflows.

Variables	(1) lnFDIic	(2) lnFDIic	(3) lnFDIic	(4) lnFDIic	(5) lnFDIic	(6) lnFDIic
BITS	0.0546**	0.0486*				
	(0.0231)	(0.0249)				
BITs_OFDI			0.00087***	0.000414		
			(0.000243)	(0.000339)		
BITs_PGDP					0.00383***	0.000940
					(0.00100)	(0.000674)
DTTS	−0.0378	−0.0508	0.0435***	0.0196*	0.0756***	0.0288*
	(0.0306)	(0.0406)	(0.00745)	(0.0115)	(0.0152)	(0.0153)
BIT	0.606***	0.866***	0.606***	0.866***	0.606***	0.866***
	(0.200)	(0.219)	(0.152)	(0.169)	(0.152)	(0.169)
ICT	0.332	0.888***	0.332	0.888***	0.332	0.888***
	(0.327)	(0.317)	(0.227)	(0.260)	(0.227)	(0.260)
IT	0.114	0.107	0.114	0.107	0.114	0.107
	(0.235)	(0.255)	(0.184)	(0.212)	(0.184)	(0.212)
$\ln GDP_{it-1}$	0.127	0.324*	0.127	0.324*	0.127	0.324*
	(0.173)	(0.188)	(0.155)	(0.180)	(0.155)	(0.180)
$\ln GDP_{ct-1}$	0	0	0	0	0	0
	(0)	(0)	(0)	(0)	(0)	(0)
lnDIS	0.426**	0.390*	0.426	0.390	0.426	0.390
	(0.207)	(0.209)	(0.577)	(0.578)	(0.577)	(0.578)
OECD	5.096***	4.687***	5.152***	4.445***	5.152***	4.445***
	(1.392)	(1.031)	(0.763)	(0.890)	(0.763)	(0.890)
COMLANG	5.152***	4.445***	5.096***	4.687***	5.096***	4.687***
	(0.720)	(0.773)	(1.412)	(1.387)	(1.412)	(1.387)
$\ln BRER_{ict-1}$		0.0856*		0.0856*		0.0856*
		(0.0499)		(0.0474)		(0.0474)
Country effect	yes	yes	yes	yes	yes	yes
Year effect	yes	yes	yes	yes	yes	yes
Observation	1,904	1,586	1,904	1,586	1,904	1,586
R-squared	0.842	0.843	0.842	0.843	0.842	0.843

Note: Robust standard errors in parentheses, $^{***}p < 0.01$, $^{**}p < 0.05$, $^{*}p < 0.1$.

inflows. The fit of these equations increases dramatically from 47% in pooled OLS regression[12] to 84%.

When the number of cumulative BITs is not weighted, the conventional control variable for market size of source country in gravity model is a statistically significant positive factor only when the bilateral real exchange rate enters in the equation, and the GDP of China is dropped.

A surprising result is that the coefficient of distance has a positive sign and is statistically significant, which is contrary to the traditional prediction that distance may be a negative determinant for international investment. Castellani *et al.* (2011) found controlling for institutional and psychic distance,[13] in particular language and religious differences, the negative effect of geographic distance vanishes, especially in case of R&D FDI. Our LSDV results go further with the coefficient of distance having a positive sign and statistically significant. The investment cost is more related to the fixed cost of setting up branches than variable transportation cost in trade, therefore, when making the decision on approach of market entry, multinational enterprises might have a stronger incentive to invest rather than export when the distance is long enough. This might help explain the positive coefficient of distance on bilateral investment flows.

Representing institutional maturity and psychic distance, OECD and common language seem to be important factors affecting China's FDI inflows. OECD members and country (area) sharing the same language (dialect) as China on average have 4.7% and 4.4% higher annual FDI activities in China, respectively.

The cumulative number of BITs China signed has a significant positive coefficient, which is minor if compared to the coefficient of the BIT dummy. This is because cumulative BITs only have spill-over effect on bilateral investment flow, which is not as direct and explicit as a BIT between the two related parties. And when the bilateral real exchange rate is taken into account, the positive impact of BIT increases by nearly 20%. The cumulative number of DTTs China signed has non-significant and negative effect while the ICT and IT dummy has non-significant and positive effect. However, if the bilateral real exchange rate is entered in the explanatory variables, the ICT dummy becomes a significant positive factor for FDI inflows to China.

For the regression with weighted BITs, the coefficients of gravity controls and dummy treaty variables have almost the same sign and similar magnitude to those of columns 1 and 2, except that the distance now is not a significant factor.

[12]The pooled OLS regression result is available on request.

[13]Psychic distance is the sum of factors preventing the flow of information from and to the market. Examples include differences in language, education, business practices, culture and industrial development.

However, the coefficients of the cumulative number of treaties, vary a lot with those in unweighted BITs equations, where both FDI outflows weighted and GDP per capita weighted BITS have a much smaller positive impact on bilateral FDI flows, while the cumulative number of DTT now turn out to be a significant positive factor.

Table 5 reports the LSDV results on China outbound FDI. Similarly, columns 1 and 2 cumulative BIT is unweighted while columns 3–6 represents the impact of two kinds of weighted BITs on China's FDI outflows. The country-pair and time effects

Table 5. Fixed effects results from gravity model on China's FDI outflows.

Variables	(1) lnFDIic	(2) lnFDIic	(3) lnFDIic	(4) lnFDIic	(5) lnFDIic	(6) lnFDIic
BITS	0.0644***	0.0781***				
	(0.0170)	(0.0179)				
BITs_OFDI			−1.10e-08	3.54e-09		
			(2.98e-08)	(3.23e-08)		
BITs_PGDP					0.0200***	0.0220***
					(0.00598)	(0.00649)
DTTS	0.0728**	0.0281	0.194***	0.180***	−0.0137	−0.0483
	(0.0315)	(0.0336)	(0.0194)	(0.0233)	(0.0561)	(0.0603)
BIT	−0.634**	−0.486	−0.634**	−0.486	−0.634**	−0.486
	(0.306)	(0.355)	(0.306)	(0.355)	(0.306)	(0.355)
ICT	−0.0712	−0.114	−0.0712	−0.114	−0.0712	−0.114
	(0.425)	(0.426)	(0.425)	(0.426)	(0.425)	(0.426)
IT	0.653	−0.0312	0.653	−0.0312	0.653	−0.0312
	(0.489)	(0.528)	(0.489)	(0.528)	(0.489)	(0.528)
$\ln GDP_{it-1}$	0.256	0.428	0.256	0.428	0.256	0.428
	(0.337)	(0.375)	(0.337)	(0.375)	(0.337)	(0.375)
$\ln GDP_{ct-1}$	0	0	0	0	0	0
	(0)	(0)	(0)	(0)	(0)	(0)
lnDIS	−0.445***	−0.451***	−0.445***	−0.451***	−0.445***	−0.451***
	(0.110)	(0.112)	(0.110)	(0.112)	(0.110)	(0.112)
OECD	−2.191*	−2.092	−2.191*	−2.092	−2.191*	−2.092
	(1.309)	(1.483)	(1.309)	(1.483)	(1.309)	(1.483)
COMLANG	4.781***	4.456***	4.781***	4.456***	4.781***	4.456***
	(1.492)	(1.385)	(1.492)	(1.385)	(1.492)	(1.385)
$\ln BRER_{ict-1}$		0.408***		0.408***		0.408***
		(0.119)		(0.119)		(0.119)
Country effect	yes	yes	yes	yes	yes	yes
Year effect	yes	yes	yes	yes	yes	yes
Observation	879	750	879	750	879	750
R-squared	0.746	0.756	0.746	0.756	0.746	0.756

Note: Robust standard errors in parentheses, $^{***}p < 0.01$, $^{**}p < 0.05$, $^{*}p < 0.1$.

always enter significantly in regressions for China's FDI inflows. The country-pair and time fixed effects increase the fit of the equations from 33% in pooled OLS regression to 75%.

When China's FDI outflows are evaluated, common language and bilateral real exchange rate variables become positive and significant determinants of China's FDI outflows. With much greater magnitude of the coefficient than that for China's FDI inflows, a 1% increase in a bilateral real exchange rate will promotes China's FDI outflows by 0.4%, suggesting that China's outward FDI is more or less currency appreciation driven. Unlike its positive impact on China's FDI inflows, the distance and OECD dummy now deter China's FDI outflows which are consistent with the early stage of China's outward FDI (resource-acquiring and cost sensitive). Among the main explanatory treaty variables we control for, only the cumulative BITs seems to play a minor positive role in promoting China's FDI outflows.

When the cumulative BITs is weighted by the ratio of FDI outflows in the previous year, the cumulative number of BIT is not a significant factor any more, while the cumulative number of DTT turns out to have a positive impact on China's FDI outflows. If we replace the weight with the ratio of GDP per capita, things reverse as weighted cumulative BITs now is a significant though minor factor to promote FDI, and cumulative DTT has non-significant and negative impact.

4.3 Results from a CMM model

Table 6 reports the results from a CMM model specialization with China's inbound FDI as the dependent variable also using fixed effects regression techniques. In columns 1 and 2, cumulative BIT is unweighted while columns 3–6 measure the impact of two kinds of weighted BITs on China's FDI inflows. The difference between equations with the unweighted BIT and weighted BIT focuses on the coefficient of cumulative number of BITs and DTTs.

Based on the theoretical predictions and with CMM (2001) as well as Markusen and Maskus (2002), the correlation between $\sum$GDP and the FDI activity is expected to be positive, while that between GDPDIFSQ and FDI is supposed to be negative. Given the vertical FDI motives that exist in CMM knowledge–capital model, CMM predict a correlation between the three more complicated control variables and FDI activity from source to the host country. These are positive for SKDIFF, negative for SKDIFF*GDPDIFF and positive for $(\text{SKDIFF})^2$*T_OPENj, respectively.

In the fixed effects estimation results for China's FDI inflows, among treaty variables BIT dummy and ICT dummy seem to promote China's FDI inflows as expected. Two CMM variables appear to perform well as the significant positive factor. The sign and magnitude of the coefficient for skill differences indicates that difference in skilled labor abundance between investment source and host countries

Table 6. Fixed effects results from CMM model on China's FDI inflows.

Variables	(1) lnFDIic	(2) lnFDIic	(3) lnFDIic	(4) lnFDIic	(5) lnFDIic	(6) lnFDIic
BITS	0.0535**	0.0477				
BITS_OFDI	(0.0268)	(0.0316)	0.00105**	−8.53e-05		
			(0.000520)	(0.000458)		
BITS_PGDP					0.00409*	0.000316
					(0.00213)	(0.00253)
DTTS	−0.0465	−0.0245	0.0354*	0.0338*	0.0696**	0.0374
	(0.0380)	(0.0585)	(0.0181)	(0.0176)	(0.0323)	(0.0361)
BIT	0.436*	0.560**	0.436*	0.560**	0.436*	0.560**
	(0.239)	(0.255)	(0.239)	(0.255)	(0.239)	(0.255)
ICT	0.155	0.867**	0.155	0.867**	0.155	0.867**
	(0.395)	(0.394)	(0.395)	(0.394)	(0.395)	(0.394)
IT	−0.0247	0.0940	−0.0247	0.0940	−0.0247	0.0940
	(0.308)	(0.365)	(0.308)	(0.365)	(0.308)	(0.365)
$\sum GDP_{t-1}$	0.0931	−0.670	0.0931	−0.670	0.0931	−0.670
	(0.486)	(0.550)	(0.486)	(0.550)	(0.486)	(0.550)
$GDPDIFSQ_{t-1}$	0.0819***	0.0896**	0.0819***	0.0896**	0.0819***	0.0896**
	(0.0303)	(0.0446)	(0.0303)	(0.0446)	(0.0303)	(0.0446)
$SKDIFF_{it-1}$	0.225	0.783**	0.225	0.783**	0.225	0.783**
	(0.242)	(0.307)	(0.242)	(0.307)	(0.242)	(0.307)
SKDIFF*	0.0360	0.0747	0.0360	0.0747	0.0360	0.0747
$GDPDIFF_{t-1}$	(0.0426)	(0.0495)	(0.0426)	(0.0495)	(0.0426)	(0.0495)
$(SKDIFF)^2$*	0.000141	−1.88e-05	0.000141	−1.88e-05	0.000141	−1.88e-05
T_OPEN_{ct-1}	(0.000164)	(0.000254)	(0.000164)	(0.000254)	(0.000164)	(0.000254)
$lnBRER_{ict-1}$		0.244***		0.244***		0.244***
		(0.0743)		(0.0743)		(0.0743)
Country effect	yes	yes	yes	yes	yes	yes
Year effect	yes	yes	yes	yes	yes	yes
Observations	1,010	826	1,010	826	1,010	826
R-squared	0.867	0.884	0.867	0.884	0.867	0.884

Note: Robust standard errors in parentheses, *** $p < 0.01$, ** $p < 0.05$, * $p < 0.1$.

is the greatest drive for MNEs vertical FDI activities in China. The horizontal FDI incentive represented by squared difference between the host and source countries' real GDP does not follow the theoretical prediction to have a negative sign, it has a significant positive impact on China's FDI inflows instead. This also indicates the vertical FDI dominates China's inbound FDI. Besides, the bilateral real exchange rate also works as a positive determinant of China's FDI inflows. This could be explained by the continuous expectation for China's RMB appreciation.

Table 7. Fixed effects results from CMM model on China's FDI outflows.

Variables	(1) lnFDIic	(2) lnFDIic	(3) lnFDIic	(4) lnFDIic	(5) lnFDIic	(6) lnFDIic
BITS	0.0452*	0.0840***				
	(0.0244)	(0.0255)				
BITS_OFDI			−1.80e-08	4.99e-09		
			(3.46e-08)	(4.01e-08)		
BITS_PGDP					0.0102	0.0190*
					(0.0102)	(0.0111)
DTTS	0.0855	0.0348	0.180***	0.206***	0.0743	0.00882
	(0.0519)		(0.0537)	(0.0652)	(0.0782)	(0.0897)
		(0.0616)				
BIT	−0.715**	−0.500	−0.715**	−0.500	−0.715**	−0.500
	(0.356)	(0.413)	(0.356)	(0.413)	(0.356)	(0.413)
ICT	−0.210	−0.306	−0.210	−0.306	−0.210	−0.306
	(0.540)	(0.512)	(0.540)	(0.512)	(0.540)	(0.512)
IT	0.379	−0.432	0.379	−0.432	0.379	−0.432
	(0.690)	(0.740)	(0.690)	(0.740)	(0.690)	(0.740)
$\sum GDP_{t-1}$	0.491	0.195	0.491	0.195	0.491	0.195
	(0.890)	(1.001)	(0.890)	(1.001)	(0.890)	(1.001)
$GDPDIFSQ_{t-1}$	0.0370	−0.0103	0.0370	−0.0103	0.0370	−0.0103
	(0.0520)	(0.0627)	(0.0520)	(0.0627)	(0.0520)	(0.0627)
$SKDIFF_{ct-1}$	0.309	−0.282	0.309	−0.282	0.309	−0.282
	(0.589)	(0.709)	(0.589)	(0.709)	(0.589)	(0.709)
SKDIFF	−0.181	−0.125	−0.181	−0.125	−0.181	−0.125
$*GDPDIFF_{t-1}$	(0.112)	(0.106)	(0.112)	(0.106)	(0.112)	(0.106)
$(SKDIFF)^2$	0.000391*	0.000283	0.000391*	0.000283	0.000391*	0.000283
$*T\_OPEN_{it-1}$	(0.000203)	(0.000199)	(0.000203)	(0.000199)	(0.000203)	(0.000199)
$lnBRER_{ict-1}$		0.469		0.469		0.469
		(0.687)		(0.687)		(0.687)
Country effect	yes	yes	yes	yes	yes	yes
Year effect	yes	yes	yes	yes	yes	yes
Observations	590	508	590	508	590	508
R-squared	0.764	0.778	0.764	0.778	0.764	0.778

Note: Robust standard errors in parentheses, $^{***}p < 0.01$, $^{**}p < 0.05$, $^{*}p < 0.1$.

When cumulative number of BITs is weighted, the sign and magnitude of the coefficient for cumulative number of BITs and DTTs is changed if compared to those in equations with unweighted BITs. When the cumulative number of BITs takes the weight as the ratio of FDI outflows lagged 1 year, its coefficient decrease and become a non-significant factor, while the cumulative number of DTTs changes to be a significant positive determinant. The coefficient for cumulative BITs and DTTs is similar in the scenario with the ratio of GDP per capita as the weight.

The results measuring the impact of explanatory variables on China's bilateral FDI outflows suggest that neither the CMM control variables nor the bilateral real exchange rate is a significant determinant of China's bilateral FDI outflows. Although the unweighted cumulative number of BITs and cumulative number of DTTs in FDI outflows weighted equations seem to have positive impacts on China's FDI outflows, we cannot reject the null hypothesis that the impact is actually zero.

5 Conclusions

This study examines the impact of both China's bilateral investment and DTTs simultaneously on China's FDI activity, especially on China's FDI outflows. Using China bilateral FDI flow data, we find that both unweighted and weighted cumulative number of BITs China signed has a positive (though not always statistically significant) but minor impact on both China's FDI inflows and outflows. The effect of a dummy BIT using dyadic data is always significant and positive for China's FDI inflows, while negative but not always significant for China's FDI outflows. This indicates that most investment treaties China signed before 2001 aimed at attracting FDI to China, a purpose accomplished fairly well, but they do not serve to promote China's FDI outflows. We also find evidence that the cumulative number of DTTs tends to promote China's FDI inflows and outflows in most equations with weighted cumulative BITs. However, tax treaty dummies do not reveal any robust effect on FDI flow. Generally, BIT and DTT are more inclined to affect China's FDI inflows than to affect China's FDI outflows.

China has signed a lot of BITs and DTTs with other countries, and now is negotiating BITs with the United States and Europe Union. So how these BITs and DTTs influence China's inward and outward FDI is an important topic for the policy side. Our chapter uses recent data and considers the effects of BITs and DTTs at the same time. Meanwhile, we focus the discussion of BIT and DTT effects on China, which is rare in literature.

References

Bevan, A. and S. Estrin, (2004), The Determinants of Foreign Direct Investment Into European Transition Economies, *Journal of Comparative Economics*, 32(4), 775–787.

Berge, A. (2008), China's New Bilateral Investment Treaty programme: Substances, Rational and Implications for International Investment Law Making, German Development Institute (DIE),*Working Paper, November 14–15.*

Blonigen, B.A. and R.B. Davies (2004), The Effects of Bilateral Tax Treaties on U.S. FDI Activity, *International Tax and Public Finance*, 11(5), 601.

Blonigen, B.A. and R.B. Davies (2005), Do bilateral tax treaties promote foreign direct investment?, in J. Hartigan (Ed): *Handbook of International Trade, Volume II: Economic and Legal Analysis of Laws and Institutions*, Blackwell Publishers.

Buckley, P.J., J.L. Clegg, A.R. Cross, H. Voss, M. Rhodes, and P. Zheng (2008), Explaining China's Outward FDI: An Institutional Perspective, in Sauvant, K.P., K. Mendoza and I. Ince (Eds): *The Rise Of Transnational Corporations From Emerging Markets: Threat Or Opportunity*? Cheltenham, UK; Northampton, MA: Edward Elgar.

Carr, D., J.R. Markusen and K.E. Maskus (CMM) (2001), Estimating the Knowledge-Capital Model of the Multinational Enterprise, *American Economic Review*, 91, 693–708.

Castellani D., A.J. Palmero and A. Zanfei (2011), The Gravity of R&D FDIs.

Coupe, T., I. Orlova and A. Skiba (2009), The effect of tax and investment treaties on bilateral FDI flows to transition economies, in K.P. Sauvant and L.E. Sachs (Eds): *The Effect of Treaties on Foreign Direct Investment: Bilateral Investment Treaties, Double Taxation Treaties And Investment Flows*, New York, NY: Oxford University Press.

Egger, P., M. Larch, M. Pfaffermayr, and H. Winner (2006), The Impact of Endogenous Tax Treaties on Foreign Direct Investment: Theory and Empirical Evidence, *Canadian Journal of Economics*, 39(3), 901–931.

Haftel, Y.Z. (2008), The Effect of U.S. BITs on FDI Inflows to Developing Countries: Signaling or Credible Commitment?, (Unpublished manuscript, University of Illinois, Chicago).

Hallward-Driemeier, M. (2003), Do Bilateral Investment Treaties Attract FDI? Only a Bit…and they Could Bite, World Bank Policy Research, *Working Paper, No. 3121.*

Hejazi, W and E. Safarian, 1999, Trade, Foreign Direct Investment, and R & D Spillovers, *Journal of International Business Studies*, 30, 491–511.

Neumayer, E. (2007), Do Double Taxation Treaties Increase Foreign Direct Investment to Developing Countries? *The Journal of Development Studies*, 43(8), 1501–1519.

Neumayer, E. and L. Spess (2005), Do Bilateral Investment Treaties Increase Foreign Direct Investment to Developing Countries?, *World development*, 33(10), 1567–1585.

Salacuse, J.W. and N.P. Sullivan (2005), Do BITs Really Work: An Evaluation of Bilateral Investment Treaties and their Grand Bargain, *Harvard International Law Journal*, 67.

Tobin, J. and S. Rose-Ackerman (2005), Foreign Direct Investment and the Business Environment in Developing Countries: The Impact Of Bilateral Investment Treaties, *Yale Law & Economics Research Paper, No. 293.*

UNCTAD, 2003, *World Investment Report 2003*: *FDI policies for development*, New York-Geneva: United Nations.

Vandervelde, K.J.V., Aranda, and Z. Zimny (1998), Bilateral Investment Treaties in the Mid-1990s, New York-Geneva: UNCTAD.

Chapter 6

China and Global Mega Trade Deals

Chunding Li

Institute of World Economics and Politics,
Chinese Academy of Social Sciences, China
Department of Economics, Western University, Canada
chundingli@gmail.com

Jing Wang

Department of Economics, Western University, Canada
jwang624@uwo.ca

John Whalley

Department of Economics, Western University, Canada
Centre for International Governance Innovation (CIGI), Canada
National Bureau of Economic Research (NBER), USA
jwhalley@uwo.ca

Abstract: The term "mega deal" has been widely used in relation to two large prospective trade deals between the United States and Europe — the Transatlantic Trade and Investment Partnership (TTIP) — and in Asia and the Pacific — the Trans-Pacific Partnership (TPP). This chapter starts by exploring a possible description of trade mega deal, and also calculates the trade volume coverage and trade barrier coverage for potential mega deals. This chapter then explores China's situation regarding deals under current negotiation or discussion — deals that may include China as well as deals that exclude China. Descriptive analysis along with summarized general equilibrium modelling calculations on the potential impact of China's mega deals on its trade and welfare consistently show that the access benefits from mega deal negotiations maybe essential for China's security in market access. This chapter argues that were mega deals to be concluded, the pressures on those countries or blocs who were not parties to conclude their own deals will grow. A series of bilateral or plurilateral mega deals driven by large countries may also effectively replace the trade momentum multilaterally in the World Trade Organization (WTO) in the future.

1 Introduction

The term "mega deal" has been widely used in relation to large prospective trade deals between the US and Europe (the Transatlantic Trade and Investment Partnership; TTIP) and in Asia and the Pacific (Trans-Pacific Partnership; TPP) (see Felbermayr *et al.*, 2013; Plummer, 2013; Stoler, 2013; Hengel, 2013). Here we both argue that the phenomenon of mega deal is much broader than just these two (admittedly large) prospective deals, and we discuss the implication for China of the potential changes in the global trade regime spreading mega deals could imply. We include both deals from which China for now is excluded (the two above) and the mega deals that China could become involved with over the next decade. We emphasize that negotiation on these deals may be slow and may not conclude, but if the pressures for these deals to conclude accelerates as may often occur then the global trading system will be significantly changed.

Following the bilateral negotiation of the Canada–US Free Trade Agreement (FTA) in 1987, leading to the North American Free Trade Agreement (NAFTA) in 1993, the global economy has witnessed a sharp acceleration in both the number and form of regional trade agreements (RTAs). As of January 2014, 583 (RTAs) (counting goods, services and accession agreements separately) had been notified to the WTO committee on RTAs and 377 were in force (see earlier discussion in Whalley, 2008; Crawford and Fiorentino, 2005; Fiorentino *et al.*, 2007). But heavily motivated by security of access for smaller countries more so than by improved access, the vast majority of these agreements have been either between small countries or between larger and smaller countries, with a few notable exceptions, such as the China–ASEAN agreement, or NAFTA itself. Given the large country focus primarily on the WTO as a forum for substantive negotiations with other larger countries, relatively few agreements had occurred pairwise or block-wise between larger economies. However, in the last two years sparked, in part, by low expectations of future negotiation in the WTO and also by the perceived need to reinvigorate growth in the OECD through export growth, there have emerged various possibilities for a series of large/large trade negotiations covering most members of the G20.

We first explore the potential for mega deals globally and discuss how China might be involved in a medium term in a process of spreading deals. In reality many of the deals we discuss are only at early stages of discussion or negotiation and may not be concluded. We take different criteria for inclusion of agreements in the potential mega deal category, including economies with GDP greater than $1 trillion, the top 10 economies by GDP size, the top 10 by trade size and the G20. For each classification we examine deals in place, prospective deals under negotiation or in initial discussion and deals yet to be initiated. The picture emerging is that the trade room for such deals is large, and with uninitiated deals being the largest category reemphasizing the significance of all potential mega deals in the medium term.

We argue that China has a lot at stake in all these deals. Large issues between the US and the EU have already been the subject of substantial WTO negotiation and dispute settlement, unlike US–China or EU–China issues. Moreover, China with slowing growth is more in need of access improvement to repair slowing (and even receding[1]) export growth. China also needs broadened negotiations relative to its earlier largely tariff-based RTAs to address restraints of movement of capital abroad and security of access issues related to trade remedy measures against her (antidumping). In the tariff cutting component of such deals China has a significantly higher initial tariff than either the US or the EU, giving China more negotiating leverage. The present trade coverage of non-WTO trade deals in the Chinese case is more limited than for the EU or the US, and so broadening the Chinese involvement into new areas is both an opportunity and of more relative significance than for the US and the EU. Finally, the higher Chinese growth rate of GDP implies relatively more importance for Chinese trade deals in terms of future trade and growth performance.

We explore China's situation regarding deals under current negotiation or discussion, both deals which may include China and deals which exclude China. For China, there are ongoing negotiations with India, and Japan/Korea, and ASEAN+6 on a Regional Comprehensive Economic Partnership (RCEP), as well as possible future involvement in the TPP negotiation and even a possible US–China deal. For the US there are the TPP negotiations and negotiations with the EU on a TTIP for which China is not a party. For the EU there are negotiations under way with the US on TTIP, an India negotiation and an ASEAN negotiation. Again China is not party to these. In terms of trade coverage for proposed deals, calculations we report suggest that China would see a larger increment proportionally in trade coverage of RTAs than the EU, but smaller than the US were all agreements we list as under consideration to be completed. China would also see a large proportional increment of trade coverage by moving to complete coverage of all pairwise possibilities in large–large RTAs (mega deals). China would be impacted negatively by exclusion

[1]In February 2014 export growth in China was −18.1% year to year and the trade balance showed a $22.98 billion deficit. (http://finance.people.com.cn/n/2014/0310/c1004-24585749.html).

from other deals (such as US–EU), but in many cases tariff reductions in these deals are small as WTO negotiations have already reduced partner tariffs.

As far as the potential impacts of mega deals on the trade and growth performance of China, China is now targeting policy primarily to arresting falls in GDP growth and keeping growth at a minimum 7.5%. The recent stimulus package is a central element in this policy strategy, but arresting further falls in export growth is equally key. Before the financial crisis export growth rates of 25% per year prevailed. These are now sharply reduced. Improved market access and more security of access under mega deals is a key contribution mega deals involving China can make to the strategy. Mega deals of others, and from which China is excluded, can hurt the strategy. If these mega deals turn out to be predominantly tariff-based deals then China has the higher initial tariffs in several cases. This suggests more bargaining power for China. We also note in passing that while the EU–US TTIP has by far the largest trade coverage of any individual mega deals, many trade issues between the EU and US have been dealt with in the WTO, reducing the impact of an EU–US deal. If broader negotiations of substance beyond tariffs occur, then higher initial barriers, estimates in the form of trade costs (see Anderson and Wincoop, 2003; Li and Whalley, 2014) for China again suggest larger possible impacts on China. Also China's higher GDP growth rate than the EU and US suggests relatively higher medium to longer term impacts.

We use numerical general equilibrium simulation methods to explore possible mega trade deal impacts on both China and other main big countries in this chapter. The numerical structure is a 13-country Armington type global general equilibrium model. Each country produces two-goods (Tradable goods and Non-tradable goods) and has two-factors (capital and labor). The model captures trade costs and uses a monetary structure of inside money both so as to also endogenously determine trade imbalance effects from the trade initiative and also allow calibration to a base case capturing China's large trade surplus. Simulation results show that almost all mega deal member countries will gain and nearly all mega deal non-member countries will lose. The more that non-tariff barriers are eliminated by each mega deal, the more significant impacts the mega deal have on all countries. All mega deals will benefit China in terms of welfare and trade. Comparatively, RCEP and China–TPP will generate the highest welfare outcome in our model, the next highest is China–Japan–Korea FTA, and then China–US FTA. For the US, China–TPP will generate the highest welfare outcome, the next highest is China–US FTA. For the EU, all China involved mega deals will generate negative welfare outcome except China–US FTA. For Japan, RCEP will generate the highest welfare outcome and the next highest is China–TPP. For Korea, RCEP will generate the highest welfare outcome and the next highest is China–Japan–Korea FTA. For India, RCEP will generate the highest welfare outcome and the next is China–India FTA.

We conclude with remarks on mega deals and China's growth prospects. More so than the EU and the US, China's growth strategy remains outward/trade oriented, and hence the access benefits from mega deal negotiations maybe paramount in China's strategy towards them. Having said that, China's growth in trade currently lies much more with large population developing countries with more rapid growth rates (Brazil, India, Turkey and Mexico) than it does with the OECD (the US and EU) who would along with China be the focus of mega deals. As such, mega deals as currently cast may be seen as an important part of a bridging strategy for China's trade performance while higher Southern growth performance comes further on stream over the next decade.

2 Mega Deals and the Global Economy

The description of a trade deal as "mega" refers to RTAs between large countries or groups of countries. Thus, far in the global economy there are relatively few of these (EU, China–ASEAN, Japan–ASEAN). The commitment to multilateral WTO negotiation, now weakened by experience in the Doha Round, has so far largely precluded large–large bilateral or regional negotiations. Combined with a focus of restoring growth in the OECD, this picture is changed by the TPP negotiations, the EU–US TTIP, China's emerging mega trade deals (including RCEP), and deals under discussion of others including Japan and ASEAN.

Although we can then simply label all deals (promise or planned) between countries above a certain size as a mega deal, in reality, there are the "large" mega deals directly involving the EU, the US, China, and ASEAN, and deals involving the midsize economies (Japan, Canada, Brazil, Turkey, for example). In what follows, we discuss mega deals as a single category while discussing more fully on the impacts of "large" mega deals such as the EU–US TTIP. Also, large mega deals can arise from the involvement of clusters of countries (such as the ASEAN+6 (RCEP) negotiation involving China). For expositional purpose we do not explicitly discuss subsets of mega deals but refer to them as a single phenomenon which potentially collectively changes trade arrangements globally.

The mega deal category of trade deals is thus based on the size of the economies involved with the presumption being that in some sense they are large relative to others. There is, however, a degree of arbitrariness in defining inclusion in the mega grouping and we use alternative criteria in classifying deals as mega in the discussion below. One is to take all economies with GDP above $1 trillion. Another is the top 10 economies in size of GDP among global economies. Another is to take the whole of the G20, with the separate treatment of the EU bring effective size down to 16. A final one is to take the top 10 countries by size of trade (exports being chosen rather than imports), again with the EU as a single entity, as well as ASEAN as a bloc (single entity). Given EU trade negotiating authority resting in the EU Commission, we treat the EU as a single entity in all these classifications and do not separately consider member states such as Germany, the UK, France and Italy.

Our presumption is that mega deal agreements, if concluded, will, like existing smaller country agreements, cover goods, services and investment with separate chapters for a range of matters such as intellectual property, agriculture, competition rules and others. In some cases separate agreements in services might occur, and investment provisions might complement what might already exist in bilateral investment treaties (BITs), of which there are more now than RTAs. If in separate parts, the presumption is that in effect these would be an integrated into a single package. The presumption is also that the trade part of mega deals will be the most significant part, with trade opening in services being broader in scope, and investment provisions aimed to deepen the competition regime in partners.

Some of the larger mega deals (TPP, RCEP) have advanced to the working group stage where more concrete topics are discussed. In some cases there include regulatory and other issues going well beyond the topic coverage of WTO agreements. Such issues as the movement of persons across national borders are also covered in some discussion. A more major departure might occur if issues raised by the US such as regulatory coherence and state owned enterprises (SOEs) are covered by mega deals negotiations such as TPP.[2] Equally, China's incentive could be to raise trade remedy issues and specifically anti-dumping issues where they would welcome new disciplines, despite OECD opposition, as well, potentially, as restrictions on movement of capital and asset ownership abroad.

To gain a sense of the departure that might be involved for the global economy over the next several years by a package of possible mega deals, we can focus on the trade component of mega deals and explore their potential coverage from two different perspectives. One is the portion of a country's (or global) trade that might be covered by deals that are either in prospect or could be undertaken. We can also calculate the fraction of trade that might remain to be covered later were mega deals to be limited to only those under current discussion. The other coverage dimension is the trade barrier coverage of these potential agreements. The issue here is whether these agreements are effectively restricted to being largely tariff-based agreements in which mainly tariffs are substantially reduced, or whether they are broader and deal

[2]Fergusson *et al.* (2013) in a study of potential TPP negotiating issues for the Congressional Research Service itemize as negotiating issues from a US perspective as market access for goods and services; agriculture; core negotiating issues including IPR, rules of origin, technical barriers to trade, foreign investment, competition policies, trade remedies, labor, and environment; and new and cross-cutting issues such as regulatory coherence, SOEs, e-commerce, competitiveness and supply chains and SMEs.

with comparability of regulation, trade remedy measures and other barriers generally not currently covered by existing WTO discipline. There are substantial differences in the estimated size of trade barriers between tariffs on industrial products and so called "trade costs" which capture price differences between suppliers and end users across countries for a range of factors including transportation, culture, language, policy in regulation form, and others (see Anderson and Wincoop, 2003, 2004). What we term a "trade costs" targeted negotiation would be more far-reaching than tariff dominated negotiations. The approach would be to focus on such issues as regulatory consistency across countries to more sharply reduce barriers affecting trade.

A final issue in this discussion is what we count as a mega deal under negotiation or discussion, since there has been speculation of many conceivable groupings in trade or RTA deals. We begin with negotiations formally joined in that an official announcement of negotiations by all parties exists. In some cases progress beyond the start of negotiation in the form of an interim feasibility study may have been made. In other cases there may be no formal initiation of negotiation but informal discussion, such as in the research community, which points in the general direction of an eventual negotiation. We include a prospective US–China bilateral negotiation in our under discussion category, for instance, on these grounds. Negotiations thus far have produced few or no public documents on specifics of mega deals and are unlikely to do so until their conclusion and so details of negotiating issues and positions of partners remain unclear. Reliance by us in our calculations below rests heavily on press coverage and speculation.

In Table 1, we present the list of existing and prospective mega deals for China, the US and the EU using a criterion that to qualify as a deal for the mega label both partners should have GDP above $1 trillion. We report a two way classification of deals both in place (concluded) and under negotiation or discussion. There are 12 countries or blocs that meet the $1 trillion criteria. China has an existing agreement with only one of them (ASEAN). Prospective trade deals extend coverage to another five large partners. The EU has two mega deals in place (admittedly with smaller members of the group in Mexico and Korea), and prospective deals apply with five further partners. The US has deals in place with four partners, with another four appearing in the perspective deals category.

Table 2 reports on the trade coverage of these deals. Incremental trade coverage ratios for the possible mega deal category are in the 1/3 range. Incremental trade coverage for China exceeds the trade coverage of existing agreements (ASEAN + non-mega deals in place), which is not the case for the US and the EU, suggesting the added significance of potential mega deals for China.

As far as broader country coverage of mega deals globally is concerned, in Tables 3–5 we report the pairwise cases of agreements being in place (P) or under

Table 1. Existing and prospective mega trade deals for China, the EU and the US.

(Where All Partners Have GDP above $1 Trillion)

China	The EU	The US
	In Place	
ASEAN–China	EU–Mexico	US–Canada–Mexico NAFTA
	EU–Korea	US–Australia
		US–Korea
	Under Negotiation or Discussion	
RCEP	EU–ASEAN	US–EU TTIP
China–Japan–Korea	EU–US TTIP	US–Japan (under TPP)
China–India	EU–India	US–ASEAN (effectively under TPP)
China–US (Not officially started, but have been discussed in media or research papers)	EU–Japan	US–China
	EU–Canada	

Note: According to the GDP statistics (in current USD) in WDI, the countries (blocs) with GDP over 1 trillion in 2012 are the EU (Germany, France, UK, Italy, Spain), the US, ASEAN, China, Japan, Brazil, Russia, India, Canada, Australia, Mexico and Korea.

Table 2. Trade coverage of mega deals (as of 2012).

Contents	China	The EU	The US
Value of Imports (Billion USD)	1818.2	2301.1	2333.8
Value of Exports (Billion USD)	2048.8	2166.4	1545.6
% of Imports Covered by Trade Agreements in Place	21.1	25.7	34.1
% of Exports Covered by Trade Agreements in Place	31.3	29.5	46.0
% of Imports Covered by Possible Mega Deals + Agreements in Place	53.2	51.0	81.9
% of Exports Covered by Possible Mega Deals + Agreements in Place	64.3	59.6	80.2
Incremental Coverage of Imports by Possible Mega Deals (%)	32.1	25.3	47.8
Incremental Coverage of Exports by Possible Mega Deals (%)	33.1	30.1	34.2

Source: Authors' calculations using bilateral trade data from United Nations COMTRAD database.

negotiation or discussion (U) for the three alternative classifications of the 10 largest economies, the G20(16) and the 10 largest trading entities.[3]

Since most existing RTAs are either small to small deals, or large to small, the coverage of existing large to large trading relationships by arrangements in place is thus quite limited and so the potential for global mega deals is large. This is,

[3]This information is as of April 2014.

Table 3. Mega deals for the 10 largest GDP economies + ASEAN.

Country	EU	USA	CHN	IND	JPN	RUS	BRA	MEX	KOR	CAN	ASEAN
EU	—	U		U	U			P	P	U	U
USA	U	—			U			P	P	P	U
CHN		U	—	U	U				U		P
IND	U		U	—	P		P		P	U	P
JPN	U	U	U	P	—			P	U	U	P
RUS						—					
BRA				P			—	P			
MEX	P	P			P		P	—	U	P	
KOR	P	P	U	P	U			U	—	U	P
CAN	U	P		U	U			P	U	—	
ASEAN	U	U	P	P	P				P		—

Notes: U — under negotiation or discussion; P — in place.
Source: Authors' compilation based on WTO RTA database (http://www.wto.org/english/tratop_e/region_e/region_e.htm) plus press discussion.

in part, a natural outcome of WTO negotiations over 60 years which have been dominated by large countries, and in which large countries have by and large been able to pursue their trade negotiating issues with other large countries under the WTO framework and without recourse to separate RTAs, while small countries have not. As Perroni and Whalley (2000) argue, the upsurge of regional agreements following the negotiation of NAFTA has in part been driven by the insurance objectives of smaller countries seeking more secure access to larger foreign markets. Now, 20 years on and with the seeming post Doha demise of WTO negotiations, these same large countries are jointly turning to RTAs as the mechanism for negotiating directly with other large trade partners on key bilateral issues impacting both their trade access and their trade growth.

We next turn to the coverage of mega deals by trade barrier. As significant deals will inevitably vary widely in terms of potential barrier reductions that go significantly beyond what has already been achieved in WTO negotiating rounds, a critical issue here will be how far deals are able to go beyond bilateral or regional tariff elimination. At the launch of negotiations on deals, high sounding pronouncements may be made by the partners of planned major new reductions in previously WTO uncovered areas such as regulatory barriers; only to finally arrive at agreements which are largely tariff based. Research literature in recent years (see Anderson and Wincoop, 2003), however, attaches great significance to high bilateral trade costs as being indicative of much higher trade barriers than tariffs between countries (some bilaterally in the region of 50%). The issue becomes how negotiation might impact on these high trade costs, especially if much of what is involved is

Table 4. Mega deals in place/under negotiation or discussion pairwise for G20 members.

—	EU	USA	CHN	IND	JPN	RUS	BRA	MEX	KOR	CAN	ARG	AUS	IDN	SAU	TUR	ZAF
EU	—	U		U	U			P	P	U			U		P	P
USA	U	—	U		U			P	P	P		P	U			
CHN		U	—	U	U				U			U	P			
IND	U		U	—	P		P		P	U	P		P			U
JPN	U	U	U	P	—			P	U	U		U	P	U		
RUS						—										
BRA				P			—	P			P					
MEX	P	P			P		P	—	U	P		U				
KOR	P	P	U	P	U			U	—	U		U	P		P	
CAN	U	P		U	U			P	U	—		U				
AGG				P			P				—					
AUS		P	U		U			U	U	U		—	P	U		
IDN	U	U	P	P	P				P			P	—			
SAU					U							U		—		
TUR	P								P						—	
ZAF	P			U												—

Keys: U — under negotiation or discussion; P — in place.
Source: Authors compiled based on WTO RTA database (http://www.wto.org/english/tratop_e/region_e/region_e.htm) plus press discussion.

Table 5. Mega deals for 10 largest trading entities.

	EU	USA	CHN	IND	JPN	RUS	ASEAN	MEX	KOR	CAN
EU	—	U		U	U		U	P	P	U
USA	U	—	U		U		U	P	P	P
CHN		U	—	U	U		P		U	
IND	U		U	—	P		P		P	U
JPN	U	U	U	P	—		P	P	U	U
RUS						—				
ASEAN	U	U	P	P	P		—		P	
MEX	P	P			P			—	U	P
KOR	P	P	U	P	U		P	U	—	U
CAN	U	P		U	U			P	U	—

Keys: U — under negotiation or discussion; P — in place.
Source: Authors compiled based on WTO RTA database (http://www.wto.org/english/tratop_e/region_e/region_e.htm) plus press discussion.

transportation cost and language barriers. Many of the elements of high trade costs, such as language and distance seem immutable to negotiation, but others, including regulatory barriers, may be more easily lowered.

Table 6 presents 2011 MFN tariff rates for China, the EU and the US from WTO sources both as trade weighted and simple average tariff rates which can be used to gauge the potential tariff component of global liberalization that mega deal negotiations could yield. Tariff rates for China on both bases are higher than for the US and the EU, indicating both proportionately larger potential impacts for China from mega trade deals China is involved with and proportionately smaller impacts for deals China is excluded from. The relatively low trade weighted average tariff for all these countries (and especially the US and the EU at 2.1% and 2.7%) suggest relatively small incremental impacts from the tariff component of China excluded mega deals relative to the tariff reductions already achieved in the WTO and the importance of striving for something significant beyond tariffs.

Table 7 reports pairwise *ad valorem* tariff-equivalent trade cost estimates between large global trading entities produced by Li and Whalley (2014) using methods described in Chaney (2008) and Novy (2013). These use data on pairwise trade flows between countries along with a gravity model to infer price differences between domestic and partner's goods in trade between countries. The assumption implicitly made is that trade costs are borne fully by the importing country; estimates are in proportional terms for 2011.

Table 7 reveals several striking features. One is the much higher level of trade costs on average relative to tariffs in Table 6. This suggests much larger impacts for any trade negotiation focused more broadly beyond tariffs than a narrower

Table 6. 2011 MFN tariff rates for China, the EU and the US (%).

	Trade Weighted Average Tariff Import	Simple Average MFN Applied Tariff	Exports to Major Partners and Tariffs Faced (Weighted Average for 2011)	
China	4.1 (2011)	9.6 (2011)	The EU	3.5
			Japan	3.0
			The US	2.9
			HK	0
			Korea	7.5
The EU	2.7 (2011)	5.5 (2012)	The US	1.2
			Russian Fed	10.0
			Switzerland	2.3
			China	7.9
The US	2.1 (2011)	3.4 (2012)	China	5.5
			Mexico	9.6
			Canada	3.0
			Japan	4.1
			The EU	1.6

Source: World Tariff Profiles 2013, WTO. The weighted average tariffs of exports to major trading partners are calculated by the authors using data of bilateral export volumes and weighted average tariffs for agricultural products and non-agricultural products in World Tariff Profiles 2013.

Table 7. *Ad valorem* tariff-equivalent trade costs between large countries in 2011 (%).

Country	The US	The EU	China	Japan	Canada	India
The US	—	0.253	0.265	0.344	0.151	0.854
The EU	0.254	—	0.268	0.423	0.408	0.728
China	0.265	0.268	—	0.252	0.427	0.733
Japan	0.344	0.423	0.252	—	0.515	1.029
Canada	0.151	0.408	0.427	0.515	—	1.194
India	0.854	0.728	0.733	1.029	1.194	—

Source: Cited from Li and Whalley (2014).

tariff-based negotiation. A similar point is made in Felbermay and Larch (2013). A second feature is the large variation in trade costs bilaterally. They range from 1.194 in the India/Canada case to 0.151 in the Canada/US case. Trade cost estimates for China are not that different from those for the US and the EU, but are sharply smaller compared to the smaller economies of Japan, Canada and India. This suggests broadened trade cost targeted negotiations may be more significant globally but may have only limited differential impacts on China.

3 The Actual and Potential Content of China's Mega Deals

Who China's mega deals would likely be with and what they would contain at the end of potentially lengthy negotiation is at this stage no more than speculation. Few details have emerged from the negotiations thus far in progress, and if the TPP negotiations are any indication of a general trend with negotiated mega deals, few specifics will be made public prior to conclusion of any of the agreements. It is important to note that as of now China is not a party to the TPP negotiations and has neither sought to be a party nor requested to be one. Also, the time frame for mega deals seems likely to be lengthy and at minimum a number of years. The recently preliminarily concluded EU–Canada negotiation took 3 years. The China–ASEAN deal concluded with a framework agreement in 2002, but did not emerge in detailed form until around 2010. Other larger mega deals could likely be at a higher level of both complexity and potential impact and could take even longer to conclude. However, as and when deals do conclude the pressures on others who are non-parties to conclude their own deals will grow and the speed of mega deals could accelerate in the medium term.

As a potential operating guide, we can turn to the ASEAN–China agreement as China's only concluded mega deal for indications of potential content and form. This agreement which entered into force as a Free Trade Area in 2010 giving a sense of the potential time lines involved. It is, in our view, best understood as heavily a tariff cutting agreement with various provisions added regarding economic and other forms of cooperation in designated fields. There is content in services and investment, but this is limited relative to trade in goods. When compared to potential mega deals involving the EU and US, the tariff cutting component stands out as significantly more important. The agreement bilaterally between China and all ASEAN countries significantly lowers tariffs between the original six ASEAN countries and China. Bilateral tariffs go to zero for around 7,000 products or 90% of trade.[4] Tariffs on Chinese goods sold in ASEAN markets fall on average from 12.8% to 0.6%, and tariffs on ASEAN goods sold in China fall from 9.3% to 0.1%. The cooperation agreements which accompanied these tariff cutting arrangements do not deal directly with areas covered in WTO agreements, such as services, agriculture and subsides. Our expectation would be that Chinese agreements with other large developing countries or groups could follow a similar pattern. As such, the characterization of this part of China's potential mega deals with developing

---

[4] See Knowledge@Wharton (2010) "China–ASEAN Free Trade Agreement: Who's Happy, Who's Not". http://www.knowledgeatwharton.com.cn/index.cfm?fa=viewArticle&articleID=2227&languageid=1.

countries as largely tariff cutting agreements, but agreements of some consequence given higher initial tariff levels than in the EU and US, seems to us as realistic. Among these would be included a possible India–China agreement where Indian tariffs significantly exceed those in China, and an RECP agreement with ASEAN+6 other Asian countries, which would also include India.

When it comes to negotiation with developed countries, the areas outside of tariffs would potentially take on more significance. Even though China is not party to the TPP negotiations, there have been indications of a US negotiating position to focus, potentially heavily, on issues seen for a US perspective as critical for a possible eventual Chinese TPP accession. These potentially include provisions related to trade secrets and currency manipulation (although, potential discussion on this issue has remained ill specified), and also relate to trade related aspects of SOE activity. These are in addition to such non-tariff issues as services intellectual property and trade facilitation. Although no negotiations are yet scheduled for China with the EU, an eventual EU–China negotiation like other EU agreements could touch on China's competition policy regime and China's legal structure more generally. The agreement with New Zealand stands as the only developed country agreement China has concluded thus far, and in structure is different from the ASEAN agreement. Importantly New Zealand has agreed bilaterally to accord China market economy status which is potentially of significance for China's wider situation with antidumping duties.

Table 8 lists the regional agreements in place for China which could also provide part of the background precedent for prospective mega deals with other partners. Nearly all the agreements listed in each case are with smaller entities, and the China–ASEAN agreement is the only one that qualifies as being labeled as a "mega" deal. For China, only the agreement with New Zealand is a developed country agreement and this has a different structure from other Chinese developing country agreements.

As far as the specifics of prospective Chinese agreements are concerned[5] the following summarizes the state of negotiation or discussion. Two potential mega deals have gone to substantive negotiations; the others are at various stages of discussion.

3.1 Regional Comprehensive Economic Partnership (RCEP)

The RCEP is a proposed FTA between the 10 ASEAN Member countries and its FTA Partners (Australia, China, India, Japan, Korea and New Zealand). RCEP aims to be a significant step in the evolution of trade policy frameworks in East Asia. RCEP started as a study group for an FTA between ASEAN, China, Japan and

[5] Also see Li *et al.* (2014) on which this discussion draws.

Table 8. RTAs in place for China as of 2013.

RTA	Type	Date Concluded
China–Pakistan	Bilateral-with Developing Countries	November 2006
China–Chile RTA		November 2005
China–Peru FTA		April 2009
China–Costa Rica FTA		April 2010
China–New Zealand FTA	Bilateral-with Developed Countries	April 2008
China–Singapore FTA		October 2008
China–Iceland FTA		April 2013
China–Switzerland FTA		July 2013
China–ASEAN FTA	Multilateral	November 2004
CEPA	Domestic FTAs	March 2003
ECFA		June 2010
China Pilot Free-trade Zone		September 2013

Source: Compiled by authors based on information from "China FTA Network" http://fta.mofcom.gov.cn/.

Korea (known as ASEAN+3), with a parallel study process for an ASEAN+6 FTA, which included the ASEAN+3 partners plus Australia, India, and New Zealand. It has now formalized itself as a 16 country negotiation.

The participants in the RCEP FTA negotiations have a total population of over 3 billion people and a share of around 27% of global trade (based on 2012 WTO figures), covering GDP of around $US21 trillion (2012 IMF figures). China is thus one of 16 countries participating in this mega deal negotiation.

There have been two rounds of RCEP negotiations thus far in May 2013 and September 2013 respectively. Three working groups (on Goods, Services and Investment) were established in the first round. During the second round of negotiation, discussions continued on a services chapter. In goods, among other topics sessions were held on Customs Procedures, Rules of Origin and initial exchanges on tariff negotiations and on non-tariff barriers to market access. A third round negotiation was held in January 2014 and RCEP negotiations are targeted to conclude by the end of 2015.

3.2 China–Japan–South Korea FTA

The China–Japan–South Korea FTA is a proposed trilateral FTA between China, Japan and South Korea. Negotiations on the agreement were started in 2012. Three rounds of talks were held in 2013. The pace of the Japanese–Chinese element of the negotiations has, however, been slowed by the island dispute.

In the first two rounds, the three sides discussed key issues such as ways to lower tariffs and the scope of future negotiations based on terms of reference adopted at the first round of talks. The second round of negotiation included working-group meetings on goods, services and competition along with expert dialogue on intellectual property rights and e-commerce. The three Asian countries talked about the trilateral FTA's modality, such as how to draft liberalization for goods at the third round of negotiation. Working group meetings were held to discuss a wide range of topics such as indications of origin, customs, trade remedy, sanitary and phytosanitary (SPS) and technical barriers to trade (TBT) along with services, investment, competition, general rules and intellectual property rights. Discussions among experts were on e-commerce, environment, government procurement and food sectors.

Among Chinese FTA agreements under consideration the following reflects the state of discussion or negotiation.

3.3 China–India RTA

China and India have conducted a Joint Study Group which finalized a report on the feasibility of a China–India Regional Trading Agreement (RTA) in October 2007. The report supports the position that a China–India RTA would benefit each other and both sides agreed to explore the possibility of commencing discussions on a RTA but no further formal agreement to proceed further has been achieved.

In the meanwhile, economic relations between China and India have developed quickly. As two main emerging countries, China and India have most benefit to gain from an RTA, and they are near each other in geography (Antkiewicz and Whalley, 2005). These factors might suggest that China and India may take further a RTA negotiation in the reasonably near future, but with higher tariffs in India Indian manufacturing interests are cautious.

3.4 China–TPP FTA

TPP is one of the most important FTA arrangements under negotiation in the Asia Pacific region; and it has received global attention in recent years. China is, for now, not involved in the TPP negotiation, but some Chinese researchers have proposed that China should take part in the TPP negotiation (Song and Yuan, 2012). There is substantial secrecy about the possible content of TPP, with as yet no official documents released.

Despite the secrecy, there are many debates about whether China should join the TPP negotiations and they are quite lively. Not only Chinese media but also some commentators from the US and Europe have expressed interest in this topic and published comments. Newspaper commentary on one side of the debate has argued that "the unstated aim of the TPP is to create a "high level" trade agreement that exclude the world's second-biggest economy, China" and doubted such an attempt would be successful (David Pilling, Financial Times, May 22, 2013).[6] Some media in the US, however, have expressed the opposite view that the US never had any intention to exclude China and that the US would welcome China's participation in the negotiation. A Spokesman for the Chinese Commerce Ministry has claimed that China would consider positively any proposal inviting China to join the TPP negotiation.[7]

The objective of the TPP negotiations remains to develop an FTA agreement which will be able to adapt and incorporate current issues, concerns and interests of members. Since the initiation of TPP in 2010, 18 formal rounds of negotiations have been held. Working groups have been established in areas of market access, TBT, SPS measures, rules of origin, customs cooperation, investment, services, financial services, telecommunications, e-commerce, business mobility, government procurement, competition policy, intellectual property, labor, environment, capacity building, trade remedies and legal and institutional issues. A unique departure from other FTAs is the group's additional focus on cross-cutting "horizontal issues" such as regional integration, regulatory coherence, competitiveness, development and small and medium enterprises (SMEs).[8]

TPP member countries are home to more than 500 million people; one fifth of APEC's population. With Japan's recent TPP entry, the 12 participating economies will account for nearly 40% of global GDP and about one-third of all world trade. This regional FTA could have significant impacts on the global economy, and China's participation would enlarge this impact.

3.5 China–US FTA

There are as yet no official statements concerning or discussions of a China–US FTA, but at a research level, a China-US FTA has been discussed. Although there will be a lot of difficulties, as the two biggest countries in the world it may be possible to initiate a FTA negotiation in the future. Trade and investment between the U.S. and China have continued to grow at a substantial rate. As with any relationship

[6]See "It won't be easy to build an 'anyone but China' club", https://www.ft.com/content/08cf74f6-c216-11e2-8992-00144feab7de.

[7]See Yifan Ding (Deputy Director, China Development Research Center), "Should China Join the TPP Negotiation", China–US Focus, 2013-07-03, http://www.chinausfocus.com/finance-economy/should-china-join-the-tpp-negotiations.

[8]See Fergusson *et al.* (2013), "The TPP: Negotiations and Issues for Congress".

between major powers, there is friction and concern on both sides about how the trade relationship is conducted. US negotiating concerns would likely focus beyond tariff with such issues as alleged currency manipulation and its effects on the trade surplus, and SOEs and their trade impacts. Chinese objectives could potentially focus on security of access to US markets, and restrictions on foreign ownership and investment.

Across mega deals as a group of negotiations, if China focuses centrally on both her access and security of trade access for a strategy of maintaining current GDP growth and preventing future declines in export growth rates, then China would inevitably be drawn into more complex and protracted negotiations as part of a mega deal negotiation. As Li *et al.* (2014) comment on China's existing RTAs, China's strategy has been one of remaining flexible, in part, targeting each RTA to the preferences of China's partner. There is no "one size fits all" approach to RTAs as has been the case more so with the EU and the US.

Also, China may adopt a strategy of focusing more on security of access than currently in a potential US mega deal negotiation. As the largest recipient of antidumping actions worldwide, and accounting for over 28%[9] of such actions, China has a strong interest in using mega deal negotiation to improve matters. This could to be the form of proposed termination of China's non-market economy status agreed to in its WTO accession negotiation (although this is, anyway, to expire in 2015), but other possibilities exist for proposals in RTA negotiation. These include bilateral agreements to forgo the use of anti-dumping, *de minimis* arrangements, sunset provisions to ensure their removal after a time limit, and dispute settlement procedures specifically targeted at antidumping (as in NAFTA). China may also raise restrictions on their foreign investment in the US, and specifically investment activity which is claimed to have links to national security issues, as has arisen in the Hua Wei case.

To gain in areas of security of access China may have to make concessions in other areas of interest to negotiating partners. One such area is in government procurement and the extension of WTO Procurement Agreements to include SOE. This is an issue on which the EU has been especially active.

Thus, a broadening of RTA negotiations beyond tariffs maybe something China might be drawn into through mega deals to further strengthen access and security benefits from RTA negotiations, but achieving these would almost certainly imply

[9]According to WTO Antidumping database (http://www.wto.org/english/tratop_e/adp_e/adp_e.htm), China received around 40% of world total antidumping measures between 2007 and 2011, and this ratio decreased to 29% recently; Also, China received over 36% of world total antidumping initiations between 2006 and 2009, and this ratio decreased to 29% in recent years.

concessions from China. And the form these benefits and concessions might take would vary from one mega deal to the next.

4 China and the Impacts of Mega Deals on Economic Performance

4.1 Analytical analysis of mega deals influence

Both the prospect of China being involved in the negotiation of mega deals of the form discussed above and the likely emergence of more mega deals from which China is excluded clearly has potentially significant implications for China's economic performance.

As bilateral or regional deals are inherently exclusionary some of the impact of mega deals on China will come from deals of other countries to which China is not a partner. China is excluded from EU–US TTIP negotiation and thus far is not yet party to the TPP negotiation. One of the features of a mega deal world is the pressure on other parties to negotiate their own deals so as to partially compensate for their exclusion from deals among others. As such, and as the negotiation of mega deals accelerates more broadly, pressure will grow for China to conclude her own trade growth preserving mega deals.

Broadly speaking, an extensive network of mega deals negotiated by large countries should in aggregate represent a movement globally towards freer trade as with a large number of deals involving large economies the trade diverting effects of individual deals will be lessened. This should leave mega deals as in total trade liberalizing and trade growth enhancing, which for China's growth and development could be important. Whether the contribution will be significant enough to underpin a 7.5% GDP growth rate will be the issue.[10]

The impacts of trade deals stressed by traditional trade theory include both the benefits of improved and more secure access to export markets abroad, and the benefits to both consumers and producers at home of increased specialization and improved variety and quality of products imported, now made cheaper by the accompanying reduction in the Chinese tariff towards large bilateral trading partners.

[10]This is a general issue, not specific to China. General equilibrium simulation models of trade policy changes consistently show small effects of up to a few percent of GDP. As China has experienced an eight fold increase in GDP/capita since outward oriented reform began in the early 1990's (admittedly with other contributory factors such as urban–rural migration and large capital accumulation) policy practitioners are often sceptical of the results even though they are quoted extensively by negotiators to justify their negotiation. This stated difference is despite the claims of heterogeneous firm trade models producing somewhat larger welfare gains from trade liberalization (see Arkolakis *et al.*, 2012; Melitz and Redding, 2013).

There are a range of views in available literature both as to how large or modest these are potentially likely to be, and what the contribution to growth could be.

Perhaps the more significant issue from a Chinese viewpoint is the potential impact on China's growth performance that these deals could imply. On this there are also conflicting positions implied by trade literature. China's growth and development performance is, in the opinion of many, best understood as the consequence of China's integration into the world economy which began in the late 1970's and which accelerated in a major way in the early 1990s with large inflows of foreign direct investment heavily related to export platform investment. China, it is argued, had a large pool of low wage labor constrained in international mobility by visa and work permit restrictions in the OECD. The arrival of large amounts of FDI combined with access to foreign export markets since the 1990s has allowed China to transform itself into the manufacturing capital of the world and access abroad for exports has been key to this transformation. China has become the world's manufacturing workshop; and it is now the world's leading exporter with approximately 70% of Chinese exports consisting of manufactured goods,[11] and so trade is central to China's future growth also.[12] In recent years export growth rates have declined, and with them the GDP growth rate has fallen from the 11–12% range pre 2008 crisis to around 7.5%. Trade growth in the month of February 2014 was −18%, stressing the need for policy initiatives to revive trade growth, and with it GDP growth.[13]

Since the late 1990s China has also been encountering difficulties with security of market access abroad, as well as the level of access itself (see Zhang and Whalley, 2013; Bown, 2011) and further possible truncation of access in the future is a negative for growth. This has manifest itself in impacts on growth of anti-dumping actions against China by key trading partners. China is the only country who received over 40% anti-dumping actions worldwide and even today, around 30% of anti-dumping actions worldwide are against China.[14] These actions, however, are more heavily in other developing countries such as India and Brazil where penetration of Chinese

[11]See Mark Turnage, "A Mind-Blowing Number of Counterfeit Goods Come From China", Business Insider, June 25, 2013. http://www.businessinsider.com/most-counterfeit-goods-are-from-china-2013-6.

[12]More recently, the role of services trade is emphasized. Services are even larger in GDP terms than in manufactures, and service trade is faster growing than goods trade (according to China Statistics Yearbook 2013, service contributed 45.6% to total GDP in 2012, while the contribution rate of manufactures was 40.6%. Services also contributed more than manufactures in GDP terms between 2006 and 2009).

[13]In February 2014 export growth in China was −18.1% year to year and trade balance showed $22.98 billion of deficit. (http://finance.people.com.cn/n/2014/0310/c1004-24585749.html).

[14]These numbers are calculated by authors using data from the WTO Anti-dumping database.

exports has grown more rapidly than in OECD mega trade deal partners. Thus, a further dimension of Chinese bilateral trade negotiating objectives to preserve Chinese growth is to begin to find added discipline over the use of trade remedy measures against China through RTAs and mega deals. China has begun this process in the New Zealand RTA. The current non-market economy designation agreed to by China as part of China's WTO accession terms will expire in 2015 and so follow on bilateral arrangements regarding antidumping seem the likely route. China may perhaps have mega deal negotiating opportunities to push for bilateral exclusions from antidumping measures in some agreements; as well as sunset and *de minimis* provisions as part of setting the stage for the arrangements to follow in 2015.

Thus, China's objectives in mega deal negotiations could differ from those of the US and the EU in focusing more on the security of market access relative to access itself, and more on the growth enhancing benefits of trade. The size of benefits according to literature on trade liberalization is variable depending on the model and assumptions used. Tariff-based liberalization in conventional single period trade model with constant return to scale technology only yields relatively small benefits (see Shoven and Whalley, 1992), but recent literature in models with heterogeneous firms puts the gains higher (Melitz and Redding, 2013). Frankel and Romer (1999) in an econometric exercise claim a 1% increase in trade/GDP ratios increase incomes by 0.5–2%. These impacts, however, are limited to the access improvement benefits of trade liberalization not the security dimensions.

Generally speaking the rapid growth in trade worldwide since the 1990s is viewed by trade economists as the single most important catalyst to growth worldwide, and so on this argument trade growth generated by mega trade deals is a likely key element in a future Chinese strategy to maintain growth performance in the 7–8% range for the next few decades. Equally, under this view of the world mega deals could be one possible catalyst for a renewal of global growth, which is often claimed for the GATT for global performance in the 1960s and 1970s.

It is also worth stressing that China's trade is changing relatively quickly with rapid trade growth with other developing countries (Brazil, India) and slower trade growth with the OECD (see Ledyaeva and Whalley, 2014). The mega trade deals with OECD partners are thus likely to be only part of a bridging strategy while other trade with non-OECD partners comes on stream.

Overall, the effects involved for China are likely to be once and for all effects occurring over a number of years with a time limited impact on growth rates. The precise period of higher growth is hard to pin down, but China's trade with other large developing countries (India, Brazil) is growing quickly and improved trade performance with mega deal partners in the OECD and Asia can play a key role in helping to maintain the China's growth rates in the 7% range while the growing export markets of the South come on in mainstream form. Critical is the implied extension for China of trade coverage of RTAs from around 26% of trade coverage to around 60% were all mega deals under discussion or negotiation to be concluded over the next five or so years.

4.2 Numerical simulation analysis of potential impacts

One way to get a fix on the potential impacts on welfare and trade for China is with numerical general equilibrium modelling. This is a technique widely used in academic research literature. This involves the construction of a model of the global economy capturing the major regions potentially involved in China's mega deal opportunities.

We use a 13-country Armington type global general equilibrium model to numerically explore the potential impacts of mega deals on China and other countries. These 13 countries are China, the US, the EU, Japan, Korea, Canada, Mexico, India, AN (Australia plus New Zealand), CP (Chile plus Peru), BMSV (Brunei, Malaysia, Singapore plus Vietnam), CILMPT (Cambodia, Indonesia, Laos, Malaysia, Philippine plus Thailand) and the rest of the world (ROW). Each country produces two-goods (Tradable goods and Non-tradable goods) and has two-factors (capital and labor). The model captures trade costs and uses a monetary structure of inside money both so as to endogenously determine trade imbalance effects from the trade initiative and also allow calibration to a base case capturing China's large trade surplus. We use a trade cost calculation method that recognizes limitations of data by using an estimation treatment that follows Wong (2012) and Novy (2013). We capture endogenously determined trade imbalances by incorporating both current consumption and expected future incremental consumption from saving into the model using an analytical structure attributed to Patinkin (1956), also adopted in Archibald and Lipsey (1960), and use more recently in Whalley *et al.* (2011) and Li and Whalley (2014). We calibrate the model to 2011 data and use counterfactual simulations to explore mega deals effects.

For the possible China involved mega deals, we explore seven different feasible situations. The first is China–India FTA (we denote it as "C-India" later). The second is China–Japan–Korea FTA (we denote it as "CJK" later). The third is China–TPP (we denote it as "C–TPP" later). The fourth is RCEP. The fifth is China–US FTA. The sixth is a mixed situation that China–India FTA, CJK, RCEP and China–US FTA exist at the same time (we denote this as "1+2+4+5" situation). The seventh is also a mixed situation that China–Indian FTA, CJK, China–TPP, RCEP and China-US FTA exist at the same time (we denote this as "1–5" situation). Among these different situations, the former five ones are single FTAs; the latter two ones are mixed FTAs.

For the trade cost reduction level by FTAs, we separate three different situations in simulation. The first is the effects restricted to tariffs. The second is the effect of assuming FTAs eliminate tariff and 25% of non-tariff barriers. The third is the effects of assuming FTAs eliminate tariff and 50% of non-tariff barriers. We use these three different assumptions because China is involved possible mega deals which will definitely reduce both tariffs and non-tariffs among members, so if we just take account of tariff reduction effects as traditional literatures will underestimate the potential effects. But we do not know how much of non-tariff barriers can mega deals eliminate, therefore we use two different assumptions that FTAs eliminate 50% and 25% non-tariff barriers to show and compare these different influences.

4.2.1 *Impacts of mega deals on welfare*

We separately analyze the effects restricted to tariffs, and effects incorporated by trade cost to comprehensively explore mega deals effects on welfare.

On the welfare effects restricted to tariff, all FTA participation countries will gain except China in China–India FTA and China–US FTA. All FTA non-participation countries will lose. The main reason is that FTA participation countries will gain on trade, production and consumption and then increase their welfare, but the FTA non-participation countries' trade, production and consumption will decrease and then lose welfare.

For China, under only tariff elimination situation, almost all FTA arrangement can benefit China's welfare except China–India FTA and China–US FTA. The reason for negative welfare effects on China is that China's tariff level is comparatively high, meanwhile India and US are both big countries, so when China construct a FTA arrangement, tariff reduction effects and terms of trade effects jointly hurt China. Comparing all the effects of possible mega deals, China–TPP will generate the highest welfare outcome in our model for China, the next highest is RCEP, and then is China–Japan–Korea FTA. For the mixed mega deals situation, FTAs of China–India, China–Japan–Korea, RCEP and China–US exist at the same time will generate the highest welfare outcome for China in our model. For some other main countries, FTA participation countries all gain from potential mega deals but FTA non-participation countries all lose. For the separate countries, the US will generate the highest welfare outcome in our model with China-US FTA and the next highest welfare with China–TPP FTA. The EU will generate the highest welfare outcome in our model with China–US FTA and will lose with all other mega deals for she is not a mega deal participation country. Japan will generate the highest welfare outcome in our model with China–Japan–Korea FTA and the next highest welfare with China–TPP FTA. Korea will generate the highest welfare outcome with RCEP and the next

Table 9. Welfare impacts restricted to tariffs (EV as a % of GDP).

FTAs/Country	China	US	EU	Japan	Korea	India
(1) China–India FTA	−0.014	−0.013	−0.014	−0.014	−0.053	1.683
(2) China–Japan–Korea FTA	0.014	−0.008	−0.01	0.028	2.059	−1.982
(3) China–TPP	0.139	0.003	−0.04	0.009	−0.381	−0.146
(4) RCEP	0.085	−0.058	−0.054	−0.049	2.765	1.791
(5) China–US FTA	−0.029	0.009	0.001	0.012	0.039	−1.934
(6) 1+2+4+5	0.145	−0.06	−0.057	−0.050	2.767	1.787
(7) All Mega Deals 1–5	0.077	−0.043	−0.08	−0.063	2.591	1.691

Note: (1) we use the Hicks equivalent variation (EV)[15] as a % of GDP.
(2) "1+2+4+5" denotes the FTAs of China–India, China–Japan–Korea, RCEP and China–US exist at the same time.
Source: Calculated and compiled by authors.

highest welfare with CJK. India will generate the highest welfare outcome with RCEP and the next highest welfare outcome with China–India FTA (see Table 9).

We then analyze the welfare impacts incorporating trade cost variation. Actually present FTAs negotiations mainly focus on non-tariff reduction; therefore it is important to take account of the non-tariff barriers. We explore the welfare impacts by assume two situations: the first is FTAs eliminate tariff and 25% of non-tariff, the second is FTAs eliminate tariff plus 50% of non-tariff.

Under the trade cost elimination welfare effects, all FTA participation countries will gain from China's potential mega deals including China, and all FTA non-participation countries will lose by China's potential mega deals. For the welfare effects to specific countries, two characteristics are prominent. The first is all FTA participating countries' welfare gain will increase as trade cost elimination increases, but all FTA non-participation countries' welfare loss will also increase as trade cost removes more. The second is China's welfare effects will change to positive under trade cost elimination situation.

For China, China–TPP will generate the highest welfare outcome on our model, the next highest is RCEP, and then CJK. But as non-tariff barriers eliminate more (under 50% situation), RCEP will generate the highest welfare outcome and the next highest is China–TPP. In general, China–TPP and RCEP are both good choices in the perspective of welfare outcome generated by our model. For other main countries, China–TPP will generate the highest welfare outcome for the US and the next highest is China–US FTA. China–US FTA will generate the highest welfare outcome for the EU. RCEP will generate the highest welfare for Japan and the next highest is China–TPP. CJK will generate the highest welfare outcome for Korea and

[15] A widely used measure of economics welfare change in money terms.

Table 10. Welfare impacts incorporated by trade cost changes (EV as a % of GDP).

	China		US		EU	
FTAs/Country	**A**	**B**	**A**	**B**	**A**	**B**
(1) China–India FTA	0.060	0.148	−0.01	−0.017	−0.004	−0.006
(2) China–Japan–Korea FTA	0.246	0.505	−0.013	−0.019	−0.012	−0.015
(3) China–TPP	0.552	1.01	0.343	0.735	−0.062	−0.086
(4) RCEP	0.538	1.065	−0.092	−0.13	−0.079	−0.106
(5) China–US FTA	0.108	0.272	0.138	0.289	0.002	0.003
(6) 1+2+4+5	0.715	1.376	0.038	0.155	−0.078	−0.099
(7) All Mega Deals 1–5	0.596	1.378	0.279	0.712	−0.115	−0.09

	Japan		Korea		India	
	A	**B**	**A**	**B**	**A**	**B**
(1) China–India FTA	−0.014	−0.023	−0.038	−0.064	1.458	3.05
(2) China–Japan–Korea FTA	0.275	0.565	2.696	3.382	−1.686	−1.298
(3) China–TPP	0.557	1.219	−0.542	−0.719	−0.226	−0.33
(4) RCEP	0.571	1.345	4.026	5.473	4.56	8.697
(5) China–US FTA	0.018	0.025	0.084	0.138	−1.625	−1.215
(6) 1+2+4+5	0.576	1.356	4.083	5.602	4.581	8.756
(7) All Mega Deals 1–5	0.759	1.994	3.764	5.776	4.444	8.599

Notes: (1) A — Assume FTA eliminates tariff and 25% of non-tariff barriers; B — Assume FTA eliminates tariff and 50% of non-tariff barriers.
(2) We use the Hicks equivalent variation as a % of GDP.
(3) 1+2+4+5 denote the FTAs of China–India, China–Japan–Korea, RCEP and China–US exist at the same time.
Source: Calculated and compiled by authors.

the next highest is RCEP. RCEP will generate the highest welfare outcome for India and the next highest is China–India FTA (see Table 10).

4.2.2 *Impacts of mega deals on trade*

On the trade aspect, nearly all FTA participating countries' trade are positively impacted, but almost all FTA non-participation countries' trade are hurt. FTAs participation countries' trade will increase more as trade costs eliminates more, but FTAs non-participation countries' trade will decrease more.

For China, all mega deals together will generate the highest trade benefit in our model. RCEP will generate the highest trade benefit among single FTAs under only tariff elimination situation, and China–TPP will generate the highest trade benefit among single FTAs under trade cost elimination situation. Comparing trade effects of these different possible mega deals, positive impacts of China–TPP is the most significant one in the model simulation results; RCEP is the next most one, and then are sequentially China–Japan–Korea FTA, China–US FTA and China–India FTA. For other main countries, China–TPP will generate the highest trade benefit for the US in our model, trade effects to the EU are negative and China–Japan–Korea FTA will generate the lowest negative trade influence, RCEP will benefit Japan, Korea and India the most on trade side under the view of model simulation results. China–Japan–Korea FTA and China–US FTA will generate negative trade impact for India in our model. In general, FTAs participation countries will gain but non-participating countries will lose on trade (see Table 11).

5 Concluding Remarks

Because of the importance of trade and export growth to China's continued 7.5% GDP growth, our view is that China more so than any other larger country or entity will see itself as driven into her own mega trade deals by the need to compete in the system. Bilateral or RTAs are inherently exclusionary. Countries who are left out of mega deals will almost inevitably suffer from the trade creation between the regional partners, and the prospect of a world in which future trade momentum multilaterally in the WTO is effectively replaced by a series of bilateral or plurilateral mega deals is one in which most large countries will be driven to negotiate such deals in part by the actions of other countries.

As such, a critical factor in determining how far and how fast China may move down the mega deal path is the speed and coverage of an EU–US TTIP, and the prospect of a successful conclusion to a TPP negotiation in which China does not take part. The latter prospect itself may anyway draw China into the TPP negotiation, which in turn may force China into some degree of negotiation on non-tariff issues such as SOEs. The dynamic in the global economy as it absorbs other mega deals is thus key. Overall, for China it suggests ever deeper engagement and involvement in trade-based mega deals almost as an inevitability.

As we point out in the chapter, mega deals are effectively on two different levels. One includes two way deals between the large economies worldwide (the US, EU, China, ASEAN), and the other between each of these four and a number of significant middle level partners (Japan, Korea, Brazil, India, Mexico, Canada, Australia). The former set of deals between the largest four seems most likely to set the stage for the future evolution of the global trading system. China can influence the future development of the trading system by its stance towards these and other mega deals and mega deals in turn will, if concluded, seemingly likely shape the future development of the Chinese economy over the next decades.

Table 11. Trade impacts of China's potential mega deals (Unit: % Change).

FTAs/Country	China A	China B	China C	US A	US B	US C	EU A	EU B	EU C
(1) China–India FTA	0.288	0.768	1.425	−0.002	−0.015	−0.025	−0.014	−0.031	−0.055
(2) China–Japan–Korea FTA	1.357	2.516	3.819	−0.006	−0.017	−0.028	0.001	−0.015	−0.033
(3) China–TPP	3.292	6.516	10.209	3.677	6.884	10.515	−0.071	−0.321	−0.589
(4) RCEP	3.629	6.363	9.608	−0.067	−0.107	−0.15	−0.108	−0.173	−0.248
(5) China–US FTA	0.126	1.552	3.173	0.926	1.773	2.727	−0.027	−0.199	−0.397
(6) 1+2+4+5	4.619	8.615	13.277	0.831	1.628	2.521	−0.17	−0.405	−0.677
(7) All Mega Deals 1–5	4.659	8.599	13.301	3.681	6.919	10.782	−0.122	−0.396	−0.541

FTAs/Country	Japan A	Japan B	Japan C	Korea A	Korea B	Korea C	India A	India B	India C
(1) China–India FTA	0.001	−0.012	−0.02	−0.017	−0.042	−0.074	0.209	3.318	6.252
(2) China–Japan–Korea FTA	3.88	6.126	8.632	5.216	6.677	8.247	−3.885	−3.216	−2.387
(3) China–TPP	4.361	9.327	15.129	−0.277	−0.524	−0.8	−0.005	−0.007	0.022
(4) RCEP	5.183	10.456	16.806	6.83	9.909	13.442	1.272	7.009	15.356
(5) China–US FTA	−0.049	−0.171	−0.31	−0.022	−0.132	−0.258	−3.871	−3.206	−2.383
(6) 1+2+4+5	5.115	10.261	16.46	6.76	9.733	13.145	1.274	6.998	15.31
(7) All Mega Deals 1–5	6.083	13.374	22.344	6.73	9.667	12.94	1.29	7.002	15.447

Note: (1) A — Assume FTA eliminated tariff only; B — Assume FTA eliminates tariff and 25% of non-tariff barriers; C — Assume FTA eliminates tariff and 50% of non-tariff barriers.
(2) "1+2+4+5" denotes the FTAs of China–India, China–Japan–Korea, RCEP and China–US exist at the same time.
Source: Calculated and compiled by authors.

References

Anderson, J. and E.V. Wincoop (2003), Borders, Trade and Welfare, in S. Collins and D. Rodrik (eds.), Brookings Trade Forum 2001, Washington: The Brookings Institute, pp. 207–244.

Anderson, J. and E.V. Wincoop (2004), Trade Costs, *Journal of Economic Literature*, 42(3), 2004, 691–751.

Antkiewicz, A. and J. Whalley (2005), China's New Regional Trade Agreement, *The World Economy*, 28(10), 1539–1557.

Archibald, G.C. and R.G. Lipsey (1960), Monetary and Value Theory: Further Comment, *The Review of Economic Studies*, 28(1), 50–56.

Arkolakis, C., A. Costinot and A.R. Clare (2012), New Trade Models, Same Old Gains, *American Economic Review*, 102(1), 94–130.

Bown, C.P. (2011), Taking Stock of Antidumping, Safeguards and Countervailing Duties, 1990–2009, *The World Economy*, 34(12), 1955–1998.

Chaney, T. (2008), Distorted Gravity: The Intensive and Extensive Margins of International Trade, *American Economic Review*, 98(4), 1707–1721.

Crawford J.A. and R.V. Fiorentino (2005), The Changing Landscape of Regional Trade Agreements, WTO Discussion Paper No. 8, Available from: https://www.wto.org/english/res_e/publications_e/disc_paper8_e.htm.

Felbermayr, G., B. Heid, and S. Lehwald (2013), Transatlantic Trade and Investment Partnership (TTIP): Who Benefits From A Free Trade Deal?, Part 1: Macroeconomic Effects, Bertelsmann Stiftung, Gütersloh.

Felbermay, G.J. and M. Larch (2013), Transatlantic Free Trade: Questions and Answers from the Vantage Point of Trade Theory, CESifo Forum 4/2013 (December), pp. 3–17.

Fergusson, I.F., W.H. Cooper, R. Jurenas, and B.R. Williams (2013), The Trans-Pacific Partnership (TPP): Negotiations and Issues for Congress, CRS report, Congressional Research Service, pp. 7–5700.

Fiorentino, R.V., L. Verdeja and C. Toqueboeuf (2007), The Changing Landscape of Regional Trade Agreements: 2006 Update, WTO Discussion Paper No.12, Available from: https://www.wto.org/english/res_e/publications_e/disc_paper12_e.htm.

Frankel, J.A. and D. Romer (1999), Does Trade Cause Growth, *American Economic Review*, 89(3), 379–399.

Hengel, R.V.D. (2013), The Rise of Mega-FTAs, EU Centre in Singapore Fact Sheet, October (Online). Available from: http://www.eucentre.sg/wp-content/uploads/2013/10/Fact-Sheet-Mega-FTAs-October-2013.pdf.

Ledyaeva, S. and J. Whalley (2014), Trade Patterns Among the BRICs 1992–2012: Rapid Volume Growth with Growing Dissimilarity (mimeo).

Li, C. and J. Whalley (2014), China and the Trans-Pacific Partnership: A Numerical Simulation Assessment of The Effects Involved, *The World Economy*, 37(2), 169–352.

Li, C., J. Wang and J. Whalley (2014), China's Regional and Bilateral Trade Agreements, *NBER Working Paper No.19853*, Available from: http://www.nber.org/papers/w19853.

Melitz, M.J. and S.J. Redding (2013), Firm Heterogeneity and Aggregate Welfare, *NBER Working Paper 18919*, Available from: http://www.nber.org/papers/w18919.

Novy, D (2013), Gravity Redux: Measuring International Trade Costs with Panel Data, *Economic Inquiry*, 51(1), 101–121.

Patinkin, D. (1956), Money, Interests and Prices, Row, Peterson and Company.

Perroni, C. and J. Whalley (2000), The new Regionalism: Trade Liberalization or Insurance? *Canadian Journal of Economics*, 33(1), 1–24.

Plummer, M.G (2013), A Vision of Global Free Trade? The New Regionalism and the "Building Blocs" debate (Online). Available from: http://www. asiapathways-adbi.org/2013/12/a-vision-of-global-free-trade-the-new-regionalism-and-the-building-blocs-debate/.

Shoven, J.B. and J. Whalley (1992), Applying General Equilibrium, Cambridge Books, Cambridge University Press.

Stoler, A.L. (2013), Will the WTO have functional value in the mega-regional world of FTAs? (Online). Available from: http://e15initiative.org/publications/will-the-wto-have-functional-value-in-the-mega-regional-world-of-ftas/.

Whalley, J (2008), Recent Regional Agreements: Why So Many, Why So Much Variance in Form, Why Coming So Fast, and Where Are They Headed, *The World Economy*, 31(4), 517–532.

Whalley, J., J. Yu and S. Zhang (2011), Trade Retaliation in a Monetary-Trade Model, *Global Economy Journal*, 11(1), 1–28.

Wong, A (2012), Measuring Trade Barriers: An Application to China's Domestic Trade, *Job Market Paper*, University of Chicago.

WTO (2013), World Tariff Profiles.

Zhang, H. and J. Whalley (2013), China's Antidumping Problem and Use of Regional Trade Arrangements to Mitigate, Mimeo.

Chapter 7

The State-Owned Enterprises Issue in China's Prospective Trade Negotiations*

Hejing Chen
Department of Economics, Western University, Canada
hjchen.xmu@gmail.com

John Whalley
Department of Economics, Western University, Canada
Centre for International Governance Innovation (CIGI), Canada
National Bureau of Economic Research (NBER), USA
jwhalley@uwo.ca

Abstract: China in the next few years faces the prospect of major regional/bilateral trade negotiations possibly including the Trans Pacific Partnership (TPP), the Regional Comprehensive Economic Partnership (RCEP) with ASEAN+6, and separate negotiations with India, Korea/Japan, potentially the US, and even possibly the EU. A likely key element in such negotiations and one already raised by the US in the TPP negotiations[1] is that of trade arrangements involving state-owned enterprises (SOEs). China is seen from outside as having a large SOE sector, and large SOEs are seen as having a protected monopoly position in domestic Chinese markets.

*We are grateful to both the Centre for International Governance Innovation, Waterloo, Canada (CIGI) and the Ontario Research Fund for support.

[1]To which China, for now is not party.

This chapter discusses some of the key sub-issues potentially arising with SOEs in these negotiations. These include (i) arrangements for SOEs under China's anti-trust laws as well as the operation of these arrangements in practice via case law, and how trade is affected by them (ii) the potentially large increase in Chinese coverage of the World Trade Organization (WTO) government procurement code were Chinese SOEs to be included under it (iii) the implications of changing relative size of the SOE and private sectors in China for the "non-market" economy designation China consented to upon WTO accession (iv) claimed subsidization of SOEs through various devices.

These issues arise prominently in the Chinese case, but are similar to SOE issues in other negotiations, including the emerging US–EU TTIP negotiation. Reference will thus be made to similar issues and precedents elsewhere. The aim is to lay out a potential negotiating issues list for SOEs to better focus debate and outline possible approaches to accommodation rather than definitively resolve the issues.

1 Introduction

Since WTO accession in 2001, China has concluded 12 regional trade agreements. With the exception of Hong Kong and ASEAN, these are mainly with smaller trading partners, but over the next few years, the prospects are for a series of trade negotiations with larger trading partners. Bilateral negotiations have been under way for some time with Australia and Norway, and a trilateral Japan/Korea/China negotiation is also in progress. China is also negotiating with ASEAN plus five other Asian nations (Japan, Korea, India, Australia and New Zealand) on a Regional Economic Cooperation Partnership (RECP). The bilateral FTAs with India, Sri Lanka and Colombia are under consideration and joint feasibility studies are conducted. Possible future negotiations also include China's potential inclusion at some point in the ongoing Trans Pacific Partnership (TPP) negotiation which covers 12 pacific countries (including the US). Beyond these negotiations also touted are possible bilateral China–US negotiations, as well as possibly China–EU negotiations. This set of negotiations, were they to be successfully concluded, would substantially raise the trade coverage of China's trade agreements and help define a new set of arrangements reshaping China's participation in the global economy potentially for several decades.

In these negotiations, a likely central issue to be raised by China's trading partners is the treatment under these new rules of state-owned enterprises (SOEs) and special arrangements which might apply to them. These issues arise in other trade negotiations, and have been raised by the US in the TPP negotiations which, for now, China is not participating in. Recently, little has been written on these issues in published research papers, and our chapter aims to set out the key sub-issues involved.

Essentially, we aim to deal with four sub-issues under the broader heading of the trade and SOE issue for a better understanding of the general public. The first of these relates to China's anti-trust/anti-monopoly laws (AMLs). From outside, China is seen as having a large SOE sector with a number of such enterprises having protected monopoly position in key sectors. These include petroleum refining, communications, banking, transportation and others. China's AMLs date from 2008 and contain provisions under Article 7 which require the state to protect "the lawful business activities of these enterprises" while at the same time requiring SOEs to "refrain from abuse of dominant market position". We discuss the accumulation of case law under these provisions and how a new set of trade rules could evolve consistent with changed competition pricing arrangements both in China (especially in China's new economic reform agenda established in the third session of 18th CPC Plenary meeting) and in other negotiated arrangements not involving China (such as US–Singapore).

The second of these sub-issues relates to government procurement practices. The WTO government procurement code does not explicitly apply to SOEs, but were this extension to be made in the Chinese case, it would imply a significant expansion of coverage because of the size of the SOE sector. By comparing the different versions of China's original offer to the WTO Government Procurement Agreement (GPA), we address the difficulties in SOE inclusion in China's offer to the WTO GPA. Further, we present a possible RTA approach to deal with the SOE issue of government procurement in China's trade negotiation.

The third issue relates to the "non-market economy" designation in OECD anti-dumping procedures where the perception of China as having a large SOE sector was key in discussing this sub-issue as it emerged in the debate on China's WTO accession in 2001. We argue that not only has the relative size of China's SOE to private sector changed markedly since 2001, but also there are indications in 4- and 8-firm concentration ratios compared between US and China that China's domestic markets are more competitive than in the US suggesting a potential recasting of this discussion of the SOE issue.

The fourth sub-issue relates to subsidization and claims that SOEs in China, and elsewhere, often receive benefits from the state in various forms which amount to subsidization. These include special financial arrangements (non-market-based interest rates on loans, financial bailout) monopoly pricing arrangements (petroleum distribution, tobacco), and other elements of subsidization. This sub-issue involves the coverage of the WTO subsidies code and whether there should be special rules on these in China's bilateral arrangements.

In what follows, we set out each of the four sub-issues and discuss what approaches may be taken on each and in which negotiation. We suggest that given the prevalence of SOEs in Asia that in negotiations with other Asian economies the SOE issue could be raised less forcefully than in negotiations with OECD partners (the US, the EU). Also, the SOE issue need not be an area where China views itself as making all the concessions with no benefit since not only do benefits accrue to the Chinese consumer with improved competition, but also on sub-issues like the non-market economy (NME) issue China can use negotiation on the SOE issue to obtain improvements in existing arrangements through cross sub-issue bargaining.

2 China's AML and Its Application against SOEs

A potential issue in China's trade negotiation concerns SOEs and China's anti-trust regime. In that regime, special arrangements for SOEs are explicitly allowed for, and the few precedents of cases could suggest the stronger enforcement of anti-trust rules against China's SOEs at an outcome of negotiations.

2.1 China's AML: structure and the administrative regime

China's AML has been in place since August 1, 2008. Comprising three broad set of rules, the main content of the AML incorporates the model of EU and German competition law as well as the experience from the US. These rules essentially provide for three areas of regulation: the prohibition of monopoly agreements (Chapter 2), the prohibition of abuse of dominant position (Chapter 3), and merger/acquisition reporting and control (Chapter 4). Additionally, in the law, there is a special chapter on administrative monopoly (Chapter 5).

The AML comprises eight chapters and 57 articles. Chapter 1 (Article 1–12) defines the "General Provisions", i.e. the purpose and the coverage of the AML. China's AML has a very broad scope of application. It applies to all "undertakings",[2] covering any natural or legal person, or any other organization, that produces or deals in goods or provides services. "Monopolistic conduct" is defined as monopolistic agreements among business operators, abuse of dominant market position by business operators, and concentration of business operators that eliminates or restricts competition or might be eliminating or restricting of competition. Article 7 contains somewhat ambiguous language concerning the Law's application to SOEs, but the AML applies equally to all undertakings, irrespective of whether they are privately owned or owned by the State.

[2]Norton Rose Group (2012).

Chapter 2 (Articles 13–16) aims to prevent monopoly agreements. As in German law, the Chinese AML separates horizontal agreements ("among competing business operators") from vertical agreements ("among business operators and their trading parties"), and Articles 13 and 14 list the prohibited horizontal and vertical monopoly agreements.

Chapter 3 (Articles 17–19) prohibits the abuse of dominant position. Article 17 defines abusive behavior. Article 18 provides a non-exhaustive list of factors involved in verifying the existence of dominant market position. Article 19 states three presumptions of a market dominant position for business operators based entirely on market share thresholds.

Chapter 4 (Articles 20–31) provides rules on mergers to control large M&A activity and prevent mergers that restrict competition. Article 20 defines concentration and Articles 23, 24, 25 and 26 covers the procedural requirements concerning lodging concentration declarations with the anti-monopoly authorities.

China has three anti-trust enforcement authorities — the Ministry of Commerce ("MOFCOM"), the National Development and Reform Commission ("NDRC"), and the State Administration for Industry and Commerce ("SAIC") — and they perform their respective duties under the coordination and instruction of the Anti-Monopoly Commission of the State Council. Specifically, MOFCOM is responsible for merger control. NDRC enforces the price related rules of the AML, and SAIC enforces the rules against non-price monopoly agreements, abuse of dominance and administrative monopoly. The Anti-Monopoly Commission is a forum for deliberation and coordination agency of the State Council, and as such is responsible for coordinating competition policy administrative enforcement.[3]

The three AML enforcement agencies (NDRC, SAIC and MOFCOM) all take the positions that they do not afford any preferential treatment to SOEs in the application of the AML. The only economic sector that is excluded from the scope of the Law is agriculture along with the activities of rural economic organizations.

2.2 The application of China's AML to SOEs

Another issue likely to be raised regarding SOEs in Chinese negotiation on trade is enforcement and the very limited number of cases. Wang and Emch (2013) summarize the achievements of implementation of China's AML by the three administrative enforcement authorities from 2008 to the end of March 2013. MOFCOM had received 698 merger filings in total, within which 627 were registered and 588 were cleared (Wang and Emch, 2013, p. 3). SOEs have started to file notifications with MOFCOM as mostly foreign companies and other domestic

[3]Huang (2013).

companies firstly had done. Since 2008, NDRC has investigated cases against price-related anti-competitive conduct, and adopted decisions with sanctions in a number of cases, among which include: "(i) abuse of dominance through tied sales by salt companies, handled by the authorities in Jiangsu and Hubei; (ii) collusion between rice noodle manufacturers in Nanning and Liuzhou handled by the price department in *Guangxi* province; (iii) price-fixing by the Fuyang Papermaking Association, handled in Zhejiang province; (iv) the Sea sand cartel case, handled by the authorities in Guangdong province; (v) the anti-competitive practices by two pharmaceutical companies in Shandong" (Wang and Emch, 2013, p. 11). SAIC has investigated nearly 20 anti-trust cases in cooperation with its counterparts at the provincial level since the AML came into effect. The cases include: (i) cartel conduct in the concrete industry in Lianyungang, Jiangsu province; (ii) collusion between concrete enterprises in Jiangshan, Zhejiang; (iii) collusion among members of the Liaoning Provincial Cement Industry Association; (iv) monopoly agreement between LPG enterprises in Taihe, Jiangxi province; (v) cartelization in second-hand automobile market in Anyang, Henan. (Wang and Emch, 2013, p. 16).

However, due to the complex circumstances for the enactment of AML, and due to a lack of experience that the three AML administrative authorities have accumulated, there have been a few cases against big SOEs, all of which indicate weak enforcement of the AML against big SOEs. An early case was the 2009 investigation by the NDRC into suspected price-fixing by TravelSky, a SOE provider of IT solutions to the tourism industry which holds 97% share of domestic airline booking industry. In March 2009, nearly all domestic state-owned airline companies in China simultaneously increased prices. As a result, TravelSky adjusted its discounting policies and increased the air ticket price for all the airlines in TravelSky's network. The NDRC's investigation was later dropped with no prosecution of the case because soon after the investigation being set up, the Civil Aviation Administration (CAA) of China, the regulator of the aviation industry, made a public statement that such price increases were the result of independent adjustments by the airlines and the airlines had not entered into any agreement to fix the price.[4] The TravelSky case indicated that it is difficult for the young AML agencies to deal with the administrative interventions from authorities when investigating SOEs especially those controlled by central authorities at the same rank.

Another was the November 2010 case against Wuchang Salt. The NDRC's local Hubei bureau took action against state-owned salt companies for their violation of the AMLs Article 17 (prohibition on abuse of dominance) and Article 7 (which prevents

---

[4]Zhang and Zhang (2013).

SOEs from using their exclusive operation rights to jeopardise consumers' interests). This successful case, to some extent, reflected less obstacles of enactment of the AML against the SOEs at local level i.e. provincial or municipal level, compared to central SOEs.

A more recent case is the 2011 investigation into the broadband business of the telecommunications giants China Unicom and China Telecom to examine whether the two companies had abused their dominant market positions (two-thirds of domestic broadband interconnection market) by obstructing other businesses from entering the broadband and internet interconnection sector. However, following the announcement of investigation by the NDRC, in December 2011, China Telecom and China Unicom released statements on their official websites noting that they had submitted an application for "suspension of the anti-trust investigation." In addition, the two companies acknowledged the existence of inconsistencies between the value of internet connections and corresponding prices, and promised revisions and improvements in internet speed and cost. It turned out that NDRC accepts the "commitments" put forward by the two companies and the investigation was pending without any further measures. Again, for investigation against giant SOEs controlled by the central authorities, the anti-trust authorities have to be adaptive to the circumstances and pressure from various sources.

Also, in the field of merger-control MOFCOM imposed restrictive conditions concerning the establishment of a joint venture between General Electric (China) and China state-owned Shenhua Coal-to-liquids and Chemicals Group in its decision of November 10, 2011 (see Public Announcement No. 74 [2011] of MOFCOM). This was not only the first published decision of MOFCOM involving a joint venture, but also the first involving a SOE directly controlled by the central government.

Comparable cases in Europe involve much more strenuous action by anti-trust authorities, there are 2,370 anti-trust cases from 2008 to 2013 and 90 of them are related to public entities.[5] The following two examples serve to illustrate the difference. One is the Deutsche Telekom case[6] in which Deutsche Telekom charged a higher access fee at wholesale level than at the retail level to force its competitors to charge their end-users higher prices (so-called "margin squeeze"). This was found to be an abusive conduct by European Commission in 2003 and confirmed by the European Court in 2008 (Case T-271/03), and the defendant's argument was also not accepted by the European Court. Another is a June 2011 case in which the European Commission imposed a fine on a Polish telecommunications company for abusing its dominant position on the Polish broadband market.

---

[5]Base on the authors' search in the case database of European Commission Competition Forum.

[6]With case number of COMP/39523 in the case database of European Commission Competition Forum.

2.3 Changing domestic and international policy background and its impact on AML competition rule

The new economic reform agenda established in China's third session of 18th CPC plenary meeting has set up the reform directions for China's SOEs. In the report of "Decision of the Central Committee of the Communist Party of China on Some Major Issues Concerning Comprehensively Deepening the Reform" (hereafter the Decision), it is stated that SOEs are an important force for advancing national modernization and protecting the common interests of the people. Although SOEs generally have assimilated themselves into the market economy, they must adapt to new trends of marketization and internationalization, and further deepen their reform by aiming the focus at regular decision-making over operation, maintaining and appreciating the value of state assets, participation in competition on an equal footing, raising production efficiency, strengthening enterprise vitality, and bearing due social obligations. In natural monopoly industries in which state-owned capital continues to be the control shareholder, reform should be carried out, focusing on separation of government administration from enterprise management, separation of government administration from state assets management, franchise operation and government oversight. Based on the characteristics of different industries, the networks construction should be separated from operations. Competitive businesses should be decontrolled and public resources should be allocated market-orientedly. All forms of administrative monopoly should be continued to break up. Based on all these statements, a more competition neutral policy environment between SOEs and non-SOEs can be anticipated.

Aside from the change of domestic policy background, the development of the international trade negotiation system and rules also set forth higher requirements for countries, including China, in globalization. This is reflected by the incorporation of competition policy in the network of bilateral and regional trade agreements by the EU and increasingly the US and Japan. Within the EU (EC, EEA, EFTA) there have been extensive provisions on competition policy covering RBPs (vertical and horizontal agreements and abuse of market dominance), mergers, public enterprise, controls on some public monopolies and provisions on state aid/subsidies. The EU has also included provisions on competition in most bilateral agreements where the EU or its member state is a party. This is also the case for the US, Japan and even Korea. In most of bilateral and regional trade agreements the US is involved, such as US–Korea, North American Free Trade Agreement (NAFTA), US–Australia, US–Chile, US–Colombia, US–Israel, US–Peru and US–Singapore, competition policy and anti-competitive business conduct are addressed, measures to proscribe anti-competitive business conduct are required to be maintained or adopted, the effectiveness of measures undertaken is to be reviewed. A similar chapter of competition policy could also be found in most bilateral trade agreements that Japan has signed.

Among the 12 bilateral trade agreements China has signed, 10 of the early FTAs covered merely trade in goods and services. For one reason, this is because most of China's partners in China's early FTAs are developing countries or small economies, or did not urge China to incorporate competition policy in the agreements, for the other, China took a relatively conservative FTA strategy in the early stage, without touching upon complex fields such as competition policy, intellectual property rights (IPR) protection, government procurement, etc. However, the two most recent agreements of China–Iceland FTA (signed in April 2013, to be enforced in July 2014) and China–Switzerland FTA (signed in April 2014, to be enforced in July 2014) started to incorporate competition policy though under a loose regime. In the Competition Chapter of the both China–Iceland and China–Switzerland FTA, Paragraph 2 states that the application of competition chapter "shall not hinder undertakings with special and exclusive rights authorized by laws and regulations from exercising those rights", which guarantees the somewhat priority of China's SOEs. Paragraph 3 states that the provisions of this Chapter shall not be construed to create any legally binding obligations for the undertakings and are also without prejudice to the independence of the Parties' competition authorities according to their respective competition laws. However, Paragraphs 4–6 encourage cooperation between the competition authorities of two countries to deal with anti-competitive practices or abuse of a dominant market positions that may prevent or restrict competition and a joint committee not the dispute settlement provision will facilitate a resolution to anti-competitive practices concerned by the trade partner.

These two new FTAs China signed represent that China has evolved from a gradual and conservative FTA strategy to a speedy and promotional one. This trend complies with the reform directions established in China's third session of 18th CPC plenary meeting. Also in the decision, the construction of free trade zones are addressed, especially, some new fields such as environmental protection, investment protection, government procurement, e-commerce and other such new fields, are mentioned to be negotiated in the free trade zone construction from bilateral, multilateral, regional and sub-regional dimension.

Therefore, under the domestic and international policy background, a new era of China's FTA strategy, expanding from merely trade issues (both in goods and services) to a broader and more comprehensive context including investment promotion, protection of IPR, environmental protection, economic and technical cooperation as well as competition, is foreseeable. Besides, the ongoing negotiations on the China–US and China–EU bilateral investment treaties (BITs) also cover the SOE issues, as one of the most significant characteristics of Chinese outward direct investment is the close relationship between Chinese outward investors and the

Chinese state.[7] The Obama administration conducted a three-year review of the US model BIT and updated it to address SOEs and other issues. The prospecting China–US BIT is therefore expected to provide a levelled playing field by opening markets for fair competition for the investors and business from the United States. China has currently signed BIT with 26 Member States of the EU, and China is interested in a uniform EU-level agreement on investment protection. The future China–EU bilateral treaty is likely to make improvement based on the existing BITs and bear the impact of the negotiation of China–US BIT.

In short, if more bilateral FTAs that will be signed by China incorporate competition provision and if the two significant BITs China is expected to sign with EU and the US, it will place more challenges on the effectiveness of the enforcement of China's AML administrative authorities especially when China's SOEs are targeted.

3 China's SOEs and China's WTO GPA Negotiation

China's negotiations in any prospective large trade deals will likely touch upon the coverage of the WTO GPA as it involves China. China has not yet become the member of GPA, but if China does in the near future this will effectively provide a framework for bilateral negotiations. Negotiation on coverage is at the core of the GPA accession process. It decides what kind of deal will be concluded between the acceding country and existing GPA Parties. Due to China's complicated government structure and the large state sector, any negotiation on coverage poses a number of challenges and especially the difficulty in enlisting-state enterprises and ascertaining the scope of covered procurement of listed state enterprises.

3.1 Difficulties in including China's SOEs in the coverage of WTO GPA

A lack of political incentive in consideration of other industrial, environmental policy is a central difficulty with the coverage of China's GPA commitment. Enforced in 2003, China's Government Procurement Law (GPL) institutionalized in its Article 10 a "Buy Chinese" clause which gives preference to national goods, works and services, except (i) when those cannot be obtained in China or cannot be obtained in China under reasonable business conditions or (ii) are to be used outside of China. Also in China's exposure draft of GPL Enforcement Regulation, " Chinese

[7] Poulsen *et al.* (2013) points that Huawei Technologies is the only privately owned company among the 30 largest Chinese multinational corporations, the remaining 29 are all large SOEs.

products" are interpreted as commodities which are produced in China and the domestic producing cost of the final product exceeds a certain proportion, "Chinese construction and services" are defined as construction projects and services supplied by Chinese citizens, entities or organizations. Besides the above components in an active "buy national" policy, an "Indigenous Innovation Scheme" was first adopted in 2006 and further implemented in 2009, which provides a mandatory catalogue listing accredited products (while non-accredited products cannot be purchased). It includes unclear requirements relating to IPR since R&D at the origin of the IPR located in China and the absence of disputes related to the IPR. Deemed as a discriminatory policy for government procurement by many countries, in June 2011, the Ministry of Finance (MOF) of China announced the repeal of three key policies linking government procurement to indigenous innovation policy, effective the July 1, 2011. This measure was further supported by a notice issued by the State Council in November 2011, directing all government entities to remove any mention of linkage between indigenous innovation policy and government procurement incentive measures within regulatory documents and to stop such implementation by December 1, 2011.

Despite revoking the indigenous innovation policy on government procurement, the political incentive to use government procurement as a policy implementation tool to achieve other industrial, regional, environmental and even diplomatic policies exits.[8]

A fragmented institutional framework is another difficulty for China's GPA accession. WTO GPA Appendix I commitments cover three levels of government procurement entities: central government departments, provincial government organs as well as other public entities (state enterprises). Taking full charge of the GPA negotiation, the Chinese MOF does not have complete authority over procurement of all state enterprises emphasizing the problem of a fragmented institutional structure. As Wang (2009, p. 673) pointed out the procurements by the SOEs at either central or local level are significantly influenced by many national central ministries, such as the NDRC, State-Owned Assets Supervision and Administration Commission (hereinafter SASAC), line ministries such as the Ministry of Industry and Information and Ministry of Railway and provincial governments. The MOFCOM, as the chief trade negotiator, also controls procurement of imported electronic and mechanical products. Furthermore, Wang (2009) argued it is difficult

[8]The Chinese government has also used procurement of SOEs as a political/diplomatic policy instrument to ease anxiety in the US over the Sino-US trade deficit. In 2006, a delegation consisting of more than 100 Chinese state enterprises signed an array of procurement contracts worth around US$ 15 billion involving projects ranging from software, power generation equipment to automobiles and electronic products.

for MOF to coordinate the procurement behaviors of certain giant SOEs, which have ministerial, or semi-ministerial prerogatives and thus are at the same rank as MOF.[9]

A fragmented legal framework is also a difficulty. While procurement of SOEs, where public funds are used or public interests are involved, is covered by the Tendering and Bidding Law (TBL), it is outside of the scope of the GPL. The tension between these two national laws and their oversight of government ministries (namely NDRC and MOF) significantly undermines the coherence of a domestic public procurement legal framework and legal certainty. Kerckhove (2010), chairman of the Public Procurement Work Group of the European Chamber, characterized this fragmented legal framework as "the legal duality" and defined it as the most significant issue in China's GPA negotiation with the EU because market access to the projects related to energy, construction, power generation, railways and subways, water treatment and many services, which are regulated under TBL is mostly restricted to foreign bidders.

Since the GPL falls under the jurisdiction of the MOF, it only covers procurement of government organs and public institutions (such as public universities and hospitals). It will be thus difficult for MOF to include in China's GPA offer coverage of state enterprises procurement without further changes in the legal framework.

3.2 Evaluation of China's offer of accession to GPA

As a plurilateral agreement under WTO framework. the WTO GPA only regulates government procurement practices on a voluntary basis of those WTO members who choose to bind in the GPA. Based on the GPA structure, the member's commitments are reflected in the 7 Annexes in Appendix I. Annexes 1 to 3 contain lists of central level government, sub-central government and other public entities covered, while Annexes 4 and 6 specify each Party's covered goods, services and construction services, and Annex 7 stands as General Notes. Therefore, the effective coverage of commitments under the GPA is determined by the combined result of entity coverage, product coverage and threshold. For each GPA member, only those government procurement contracts falling within product list in Annexes 4 to 6 with awards above a threshold for the entities in Annexes 1 to 3 are considered and influenced by the GPA rules.

China has been accepted as a WTO GPA observer since 2002, and applied for accession to the GPA in December 2007 and submitted its initial offer in January 2008. Four revised offers were submitted on July 2010, November 2011, November 2012 and January 2014, respectively.

[9]WANG (2009).

Table 1 reports the evolution of China's GPA threshold offers. The reduced threshold indicates the concessions China has made to GPA members. However, China's latest reduced threshold offer is still much higher than that for the EU, Japan or the US.

Besides the threshold, the list of entities in Annexes 1 to 3 is a concern of the GPA members. In 2007 under China's original offer, only 50 entities at central government level were covered, and no entity was included in Annexes 2 and 3. In 2010 under the first revised offer, the number of entities in Annex 1 was increased to 61, and 14 new entities were added to Annex 3. In 2011 under the second revised offer, sub-central government entities for the first time appeared in Annex 2, which included 34 entities from Beijing Municipality, 34 entities from Tianjin Municipality, 35 entities from Shanghai Municipality, 33 entities from Jiangsu Province and 35 entities from Zhejiang Province. In 2012, under the third revised offer, the entities in Annex 2 were expanded to Fujian Province (34 entities), Shandong Province (33 entities) and Guangdong Province (33 entities). Under the recent fourth revised offer, another five provinces (Liaoning, Henan, Hebei, Hunan, Hubei) and 1 municipality (Chongqing) were added in Annex 2, while the detailed information of the newly included sub-central government entities is not yet disclosed.

There are no developments regarding SOEs inclusion in Annex 3 of China's GPA offer. So far, the 14 entities in China's Annex 3 offer are Xinhua News Agency, Chinese Academy of Sciences, Chinese Academy of Social Sciences, Chinese Academy of Engineering, Development Research Center of the State Council, China National School of Administration, China Earthquake Administration, China Meteorological Administration, China Banking Regulatory Commission, China Securities Regulatory Commission, China Insurance Regulatory Commission, State Electricity Regulatory Commission, National Council for Social Security Fund and National Natural Science Foundation.

Besides the WTO GPA, encompassing government procurement issue in free trade agreements is another trend in the internationalization of government procurement. More and more FTA or RTA negotiations include government procurement. Taking the US as the example, starting from the US–Israel FTA enforced in 1985, the US has covered government procurement issue in its FTA with Canada, NAFTA, Chile, Singapore, Australia, Morocco, Central American–Dominican Republic, Bahrain, Oman, Andean (Columbia, Peru, Ecuador), Panama, Thailand, United Arab Emirates, South African Custom Union, Korea and Malaysia. Also there is a trend in recent RTAs of incorporating elements of government procurement. Ueno (2013) highlighted 47 RTAs by OECD Members with Coverage Commitments on government procurement. This is also a possible approach for China to take to open its government procurement market.

Table 1. Threshold offer to the WTO GPA by China.

unit: thousand SDRs.

	Annex 1 Central Government Entities			Annex 2 Sub-Central Government Entities			Annex 3 Other Entities		
	Goods	**Services**	**Construction**	**Goods**	**Services**	**Construction**	**Goods**	**Services**	**Construction**
Original offer (2007)	500	4,000	200,000	N.A.	N.A.	N.A.	900	N.A.	300,000
First revised offer (2010)	500 for the 1st and 2nd year after implementation, 400 for the 3rd year, 300 for the 4th year, 200 from the 5th year	500 for the 1st and 2nd year after implementation, 400 for the 3rd year, 300 for the 4th year, 200 from the 5th year	100,000 for the 1st year after implementation, 80,000 for the 2nd year, 50,000 for the 3rd year, 30,000 for the 4th year, 15,000 from the 5th year	N.A.	N.A.	N.A.	900 for the 1st and 2nd year after implementation, 800 for the 3rd year, 700 for the 4th year, 600 from the 5th year	900 for the 1st and 2nd year after implementation, 800 for the 3rd year, 700 for the 4th year, 600 from the 5th year	200,000 for the 1st year after implementation, 180,000 for the 2nd year, 150,000 for the 3rd year, 130,000 for the 4th year, 100,000 from the 5th year
Second revised offer (2011)	Same as first revised offer	Same as first revised offer	80,000 for the 1st year and 2nd year after implementation, 50,000 for the 3rd year, 30,000 for the 4th year, 15,000 from the 5th year	750 for the 1st and 2nd year after implementation, 600 for the 3rd year, 500 for the 4th year, 400 from the 5th year	750 for the 1st and 2nd year after implementation, 600 for the 3rd year, 500 for the 4th year, 400 from the 5th year	150,000 for the 1st year after implementation, 100,000 for the 2nd year, 80,000 for the 3rd year, 50,000 for the 4th year, 30,000 from the 5th year	Same as first revised offer	Same as first revised offer	Same as first revised offer

Third revised offer (2012)	Same as first revised offer	Same as first revised offer	50,000 for the 1st year and 2nd year after implementation, 30,000 for the 3rd year, 25,000 for the 4th year, 15,000 from the 5th year	Same as the second revised offer	Same as the second revised offer	100,000 for the 1st year after implementation, 80,000 for the 2nd year, 50,000 for the 3rd year, 40,000 for the 4th year, 30,000 from the 5th year	Same as first revised offer	Same as first revised offer	Same as first revised offer
Fourth revised offer (2012)	Same as first revised offer	Same as first revised offer	Same as third revised offer	Same as the second revised offer	Same as the second revised offer	60,000 for the 1st year and 2nd year after implementation, 50,000 for the 3rd year, 40,000 for the 4th year, 20,000 from the 5th year	Same as first revised offer	Same as first revised offer	80,000 for the 1st year and 2nd year after implementation, 60,000 for the 3rd year, 50,000 for the 4th year, 40,000 from the 5th year

Source: Author's compilation based on information in http://www.ccgp.gov.cn/

4 NME and China's SOEs

Another area of trade policy where the issue of SOEs seems likely to arise in any trade negotiation that China becomes involved with developed countries concerns the issues of China's status as a market or NME. This is a matter that is involved with anti-dumping procedures in domestic law, principally in the US and the EU. At the time of China's accession to the WTO in 2001, the argument was made by US and EU negotiation that because of the extensive presence of SOEs in the Chinese economy that China should be viewed as a non-market rather than a market economy. China accepted this argument and China's accession terms explicitly allow other WTO members to treat China as a NME under their domestic laws until 2016.

In reality, there is no clear definition of what constitutes a market or an NME, but at an operational level, there is considerable impact on China, if China is being treated in this way under anti-dumping laws. By being labelled as an NME, anti-dumping procedures against Chinese exports in the US and the EU follow a different procedure both in the determination of dumping and also in the size of dumping margins, and hence rates of duty. Under the terms of the designation, China's trading partners do not need to take into account China's domestic production costs in determination of dumping. Instead, production costs in a "surrogate" third country can be used to calculate the so-called "normal value" of Chinese exports. The use of a surrogate country (often an emerging economy such as Turkey or Mexico) where material and labor which are much higher than in China typically means that Chinese exports are being sold below their "normal value". The result is that they can become subject to duties that are large and often exceed 100%.

China has repeatedly tried to change this designation to which they agreed in 2001, largely without success. In their RTA negotiation with New Zealand, New Zealand agreed to grant Chinese exports market economy status. Similar indications have been made by Australia, but no progress has been made in the larger markets of the EU and the US. Come 2016, negotiations will likely ensue as to China's designation. It could be that concession made by China on other issues, including SOEs, such as on government procurement may be needed to obtain EU and US agreement to a change in designation.

Part of the difficulty with the issue lies in the clear definition of terms. NME is a counterpart designation to market economy, and there are a diversity of economic parameters between a centrally planned and a market economy. Hence, it is difficult to legally define a market economy or a NME. Apart from the United Nations Conference on Trade and Development (UNCTAD), a detailed definition has still not been produced by influential international organizations, though there are official statements that, together, form an official structure of what is needed for a country to be considered as a market economy.

UNCTAD defines a market economy as "a national economy of a country that relies heavily upon market forces to determine levels of production, consumption, investment and savings without government intervention" Likewise, UNCTAD's definition of a NME is as follows: "A national economy in which the government seeks to determine economic activity largely through a mechanism of central planning, as in the former Soviet Union, in contrast to a market economy which depends heavily upon market forces to allocate productive resources. In a "non-market" economy, production targets, prices, costs, investment allocations, raw materials, labor, international trade and most other economic aggregates are manipulated within a national economic plan drawn up by a central planning authority. Hence, the public sector makes the major decisions affecting demand and supply within the national economy".

The WTO agreement that China entered into offers no guidance as to what constitutes an NME, nor as to how they should be treated in anti-dumping proceedings. Different users of the anti-dumping instrument use different methods for applying special rules for NMEs. We also find the origins and application of NMEs in EU's Anti-dumping law and the US anti-dumping law. These domestic laws had significant impact on China's accession to the WTO and the resulting substantial anti-dumping case involving China.

Under US domestic law and under 19 USCS §1677 (18) [Title 19. Customs Duties; Chapter 4. Tariff Act of 1930; Countervailing and Antidumping Duties; General Provisions], the term "non-market economy country" means any foreign country that the administering authority determines does not operate on market principles of cost or pricing structures, so that sales of merchandize in such country do not reflect the fair value of the merchandize.

And in making determinations whether a foreign country is a market economy or NME, the US administering authority takes six factors into account: (i) the extent to which the currency of the foreign country is convertible into the currency of other countries; (ii) the extent to which wage rates in the foreign country are determined by free bargaining between labor and management, (iii) the extent to which joint ventures or other investments by firms of other foreign countries are permitted in the foreign country, (iv) the extent of government ownership or control of the means of production, (v) the extent of government control over the allocation of resources and over the price and output decisions of enterprises and (vi) such other factors as the administering authority considers appropriate.

Come 2016, the decision as to how to treat China will remain a domestic issue under US as there will be no treaty commitments governing any US determinations since the 2001 decision by China was merely to agree to the US determination. For a 2016 change it would seemingly require a Chinese negotiation in which China makes concessions elsewhere in return for a changed designation. Meanwhile, academic research literature has stressed the rapid changes in the Chinese economy since 2001 with SOE reforms and the growth of private Chinese enterprises. Wang and Whalley (2013) have recently compared 4- and 8-firms concentration ratios for Chinese and US enterprises concluding that Chinese ratios are around 1/2 of US ratios, and a third. The implication this suggests is that the Chinese economy is more competitive than the US and has stronger market forces.

Article 15 in China's commitment to WTO agreed to the NME designation for 15 years. The Working Party Report on the Accession of China constantly refers to the Chinese economic model as in transition towards a Socialist Market Economy and it signals the fact that the Chinese economy bears characteristics of both market and NMEs. When acceding, China committed to undertake several reforms, regarding subsidies, management of SOEs, and liberalization of its banking system which would assure a level playing field between China and other economies under the WTO system. China has kept making requests to change the NME to market economy status and has taken efforts in bilateral trade negotiations to gain the market economy status. So far, there have been around 150 countries who have granted China's market economy status, while most OECD countries (e.g. EU, Japan, US) and India still label China as an NME. As Article 15 in China's commitment to WTO agreed to the NME designation for 15 years, it is all the partner country's free decision whether to grant China market economy status. And for those that have great bilateral trade volume, NME works as a strong trade protection instrument against the price competitiveness of China's manufactures. Also from the perspective of the relative bargaining power in bilateral negotiation, China has no advantages over most OECD countries.

In 2011, the World Bank published a study report arguing China still has not completed its transition process 10 years after accession. The report claims that the government continues to dominate key sectors and there are "close links between the government, big banks, and state enterprises which have created vested interests that inhibit reforms and contribute to continued ad hoc state interventions in the economy". Furthermore, the report states that "China's transition to a market economy is incomplete in many areas. A mix of market and non-market measures shapes incentives for producers and consumers, and there remains a lack of clarity in distinguishing the individual roles of government state enterprises, and the private sector". It seems, therefore that China needs to resolve these issues, accelerate structural reforms and develop a market-based system in which the state focuses on providing key public goods and services — while a private sector plays the role of driving growth.

Considering the internal opposition to further liberalization and privatization reforms, some commentators have doubted whether China could ever complete its transformation into a full market economy, given the intrinsic political links between the Party, SOEs and the means by which public policies are implemented. However, private enterprises have played a more and more important role in China's economic development and the changed competition structure indicates the smaller degree of NME character in China. The SOE issue between the US and the EU is also likely to be raised in the EU–US trade negotiation. 2016 may therefore be a watershed on this issue which will likely figure prominently in many China–OECD trade negotiations.

5 Subsidies

A final sub-issue likely connected to negotiations that touch on SOEs is the question of subsidization.

5.1 Overview of China's SOE subsidies

As a complex trade topic, government subsidization of SOEs is subject to the general WTO disciplines set out in the Agreement on subsidies and Countervailing Measures (the SCM Agreement), which supplements Articles VI and XVI of the GATT. Subsidies may take various forms, from direct transfer of funds (such as grants, loans, equity infusion and loan guarantees), to indirect benefit conferred, such as foregone government revenue otherwise due (such as tax credits), provision of goods or services other than general infrastructure, or purchase of goods by the government.[10]

From a functional perspective, all direct and indirect financial assistance from China's central and local governments to SOEs can be grouped into three general categories: (i) subsidies provided to sustain and revive loss-making SOEs; (ii) subsidies provided in order to privatize or otherwise restructure SOEs and (iii) subsidies provided to foster key SOEs.[11]

The first category of subsidies used to be the most important financial contribution of the government to China's SOEs. Between 1999 and 2001 it was estimated that one half of China's SOEs were losing money. The share of the subsidies to loss-making SOEs in China's government expenditures declined from a high of 25% in 1985 to about 2% in 2000. Subsidies to loss-making SOEs alone were 2.6% of the total profits of all SOEs in 2001 and were larger in previous years.[12] Besides the direct budgetary subsidies, China's government allowed many loss-making SOEs to stay in business and this resulted in the accumulation of a large portfolio of non-performing loans at state banks. In 2003, non-performing loans at

[10]Exceptions are provided for the agricultural sector.
[11]Qin (2004).
[12]Richard S. Eckause (2006).

Table 2. The changing share of SOEs in China's economy: 1995–2012.

	Number of state owned industrial enterprises	Share of SOEs in total number of industrial enterprises (%)	Employed persons by SOEs (10,000 persons)	Share of SOEs in employment for urban area (%)	Gross industrial output value by SOEs (100 million yuan)	Share of SOEs in Gross Industrial output Value (%)
1995	118,000	23.12	10,955.00	73.48	31,220.00	56.82
1996	113,800	22.47	10,949.00	73.76	36,173.00	57.66
1997	98,600	21.05	10,766.00	73.40	35,988.00	52.65
1998	64,700	39.19	8,809.00	71.40	33,621.00	49.63
1999	50,651	31.26	8,336.00	70.80	22,215.89	30.56
2000	42,426	26.05	7,878.00	69.97	20,156.29	23.53
2001	34,530	20.16	7,409.00	68.65	17,229.19	18.05
2002	29,449	16.22	6,923.81	65.58	17,271.09	15.59
2003	23,228	11.84	6,621.28	63.11	18,479.40	12.99
2004	23,417	8.47	6,438.21	60.88	65,971.10	32.70
2005	16,824	6.19	6,231.98	57.44	N.A.	N.A.
2006	14,555	4.82	6,170.47	55.29	30,728.16	9.71
2007	10,074	2.99	6,147.61	53.80	36,387.12	8.98
2008	9,682	2.27	6,126.12	53.20	46,856.89	9.24
2009	9,105	2.10	6,077.86	51.40	45,648.02	8.33
2010	8,726	1.93	6,145.11	50.16	57,013.00	8.16
2011	6,707	2.06	N.A.	N.A.	66,672.56	7.90
2012	6,770	1.97	6,467.24	44.90	N.A.	N.A.

Source: China data online.

the four major state banks amounted to more than 17% of China's GDP. However, data from independent sources indicated that the amount of such loans could be twice as much. China's government had taken measures to reform SOEs since the mid-1980s, one of the important measure from the mid-1990s being the closing down or restructuring the small and medium-sized loss-making SOEs and sale or consolidation SOEs into large group companies. Table 2 highlights the shrinking share of China's SOE in the economy from the mid-1990s to 2012. As a result, the number of SOEs decreased by 40% from 1995 to 2002, which in turn reduced subsidies to the loss-making SOEs. The elimination of subsidies to loss-making SOEs was also a commitment when China entered the WTO in 2001. It is difficult to estimate the size of the second category of subsidies, i.e. subsidies to help privatize or restructure SOEs. No statistics are available regarding this.

The third category of subsidies aims to foster key SOEs. Hundreds of large profit-making SOEs have been designated as State key enterprise, of which about 190 are "central enterprises" under direct supervision of the SASAC.[13] These key SOEs receive not only budgetary funding from the government, but also low-interest loans via state-owned banks.

New forms of subsidies are taken to confer the benefit to key SOEs. For example, a major state bank issued the first US dollar denominated bond in China's domestic market in 2003, and the proceeds of US$ 500 million were to be lent to SOEs to retire their existing high-cost foreign debts.[14]

5.2 The trade effects of China's SOE subsidies

These three categories of subsidies have different potential trade effects. Subsidies to loss-making SOEs merely postpone their eventual closing down, and seem to have little trade effect, because the products made by the loss-making SOEs can not easily be exported, nor can they compete with the imported products or products by foreign invested companies sold in China's domestic market.

Subsidies for restructuring and privatization of SOEs fall into the previous categories of non-actionable subsidies[15] under the SCM Agreement, as long as recipients of financial support are not specific to certain entity/industry/group of entities, and the supported SOEs are finally privatized. However, trade effects of subsidies to key SOEs are a major concern of China's trade partners, because these key profit-making SOEs are competitive rivals to large MNEs both in international markets and in China's domestic market. According to the WTO statistics on subsidies and countervailing measures, 69 investigations have been launched concerning China's export goods by the WTO members between 1995 and June 2013, 45 of them ultimately resulted in a countervailing duty to counter the effect of subsidies. Compared to 950 anti-dumping investigations and 683 measures of China's export goods for the same period, the compatible numbers for subsidies are much less. Another difference between China's anti-dumping cases and subsidies case deserving notice is the time series. As early as 1995, China was as target for 20 anti-dumping investigations and 27 anti-dumping measures, while reported subsidies and countervailing measure against China's export goods are only available from 2005. Regarding the distribution of the countries that charged

[13] Qin (2004).

[14] *Id.*

[15] The current SCM agreement defines only two categories of subsidies: prohibited and actionable. It originally contained a category of non-actionable subsidies. This category existed for five years, ending on December 31, 1999 and was not extended.

countervailing duties, the US is the country which initiated most investigations and took countervailing measures against China. In the 69 investigations and 45 measures against China, 34 investigations and 27 measures have been conducted by the US. Other important importing countries initiating countervailing investigation against China include Canada (18 investigations and 12 measures), Australia (8 investigations and 6 measures) and EU (6 investigations and 2 measures). Unlike anti-dumping investigations against China by developing countries (such as India, Argentina and Turkey), most countervailing investigations and measures against China's export goods are launched by developed countries. Therefore, in China's prospective trade negotiations with large developed economies, subsidies will surely be a major concern. The issue however is what might be negotiated beyond the existing WTO subsidies code which makes discussion between subsides to SOEs and other enterprises. Separately actionable subsidies may be discussed but the specifics of how these might work remain opaque.

6 Conclusion

Starting from the China–Iceland FTA and China–Switzerland FTA, China's prospective trade agreements, especially when negotiating with larger trade partners, are expected to use a comprehensive FTA template which expand from merely trade issues in goods and in services to a broader coverage including investment, competition policy, IPR, environment, economic and technical cooperation and even potential trade remedies and government procurement provisions. Trade negotiations on trade in goods are relatively easier to conduct as tariffs hamper market access for foreign trade, and to what extent, can be assessed in a relatively straightforward way. On that basis, countries may negotiate reciprocal concession packages of more or less similar magnitude. This procedure is unfit for trade negotiations incorporating comprehensive trade issues when non-tariff measures form the most important type of trade barriers. An integral approach with a comprehensive balancing package covering different trade issues might be the overall strategy for such trade negotiations.

As for the four sub-issues relating to China's SOEs in China's prospect trade negotiations, cross sub-issue bargaining could be a possible resolution. Based on the precedent experience of The Australian-New Zealand Closer Economic Co-operation Agreement (ANZCERTA), the potential concessions China could make might be removing the somewhat ambiguous regulation regarding SOEs in the AML (Article 7) or expanding the coverage offer of entities in the GPA. The ANZCERTA requires the Member States to revise competition law in order to address anti-competitive conduct affecting trans-Tasman trade in goods, without recourse to anti-dumping actions. This therefore offers an interesting alternative and may have lessons in the relationship between anti-dumping and competition policies for other bilateral and regional agreements or perhaps even wider international agreements on competition policy. If China's concession of revising its AML (Article 7) could, in return, grant China market economy status in the bilateral trade negotiations, the potential significant benefit of diminishing anti-dumping cases against China's exports is surely a great compensation.

References

Eckause, R.S. (2006), China's Exports, Subsidies to State Owned Enterprises and the WTO, *China Economic Review*, 17, 1–13.

Huang, Y. (2013), China's Antitrust Law Enforcement After the 18th Party Congress, Competition Policy International Antitrust Chronicle February 2013 (2) (Online). Available from: https://www.competitionpolicyinternational.com/china-s-antitrust-law-enforcement-after-the-18th-party-congress/.

Kerckhove, G.V. (2010), Are discussions around GPA missing the real issue? (Online). Available from: http://blog.strategy4china.com/wp-content/uploads/100828GPAcomments.pdf.

Norton Rose Group (2012), Antimonopoly law in China — A Norton Rose GROUP Guide, March 2012 (Online). Available from: http://www.nortonrosefulbright.com/files/download-antimonopoly-law-in-china-63824.pdf.

Poulsen, L.N. J. Bonnitcha, and J.W. Yackee (2013), Costs and Benefits of an EU-China Investment Protection Treaty, April 2013 (Online). Available from: http://www.it-alaw.com/sites/default/files/archive/costs-and-benefits-of-an-eu-china-investment-pro tection-treaty.pdf.

Qin, J.Y. (2004), WTO Regulation of Subsidies to State-Owned Enterprises (SOEs) — A Critical Appraisal of the China Accession Protocol, *Journal of International Economic Law*, 7(4), 863–910.

Ueno, A. (2013), Multilateralising Regionalism on Government Procurement, *OECD Trade Policy Papers No. 151*, OECD Publishing (Online). Available from: http://dx.doi.org/10.1787/5k46l8vvq2np-en.

Wang, P. (2009), China's Accession to the WTO Government Procurement Agreement — Challenges and the Way Forward, *Journal of International Economic Law*, 12(3), 663–706.

Wang, X. and A. Emch (2013), Five years of implementation of China's Anti-Monopoly Law-achievements and challenges, *Journal of Antitrust Enforcement*, 1(2), 247–271.

Wang, J. and J. Whalley (2013), Are Chinese Market for Manufactured Products more Competitive than in the US?: A Comparison of China–US Industrial Concentration Ratios, *NBER Working Paper W19898*.

Zhang, X. and V.Y. Zhang (2013), New Developments in China's Competition Policy against Monopolistic/Collusive Agreements, in M. Faure and G. Xu (Eds.): *Economics and Regulations in China*, Routledge.

Chapter 8

Measuring the Bilateral Trade Cost Elasticity between the BRICS: Translog Gravity*

Dan Zhou

Beijing University of Agriculture
Institute of World Economics and Politics
Chinese Academy of Social Sciences
zhoudan510@126.com

Abstract: The leading gravity models are basically based on the Constant Elasticity of Substitution (CES) utility assumption, which cannot measure the heterogeneous impact on the trade flows between different trade partners after lowering the trade cost. This chapter is on the basis of translog gravity, which Novy (2013) provides for overcoming the weak point, to measure the bilateral trade cost elasticity (TCE) between the BRICS countries (Brazil, China, India, Russia, South Africa) from 2000 to 2010. The result shows that the BRICS countries' trade costs elasticity varies within a wide range between [0.48, 245]. Russia's average TCE is on the top (36.66), followed by South Africa (29.31) and China at the lowest (1.84). The ratio of difference value of South Africa to Brazil and China is at the highest level, which demonstrates that the impact of reducing trade cost on the small countries is greater than that on the big countries.

*I am very grateful to Dennis Novy for his instructions and advice. I also appreciate Prof. Hong Song, Chunding Li, Lingyun Gao, Qingyi Su, Yan Dong, Tao Ma, Ling Zhang for their constructive comments and suggestions. The Chinese edition was published in the *Journal of Quantitative & Technical Economics*, 2013.3

1 Introduction

As the representative of the emerging economies, the BRICS countries — Brazil, China, India, Russia, and South Africa — are becoming more and more important in the world economy. Since the 2008 financial crisis, the BRICS countries have accelerated economic cooperation and reached a series of consensus in promoting trade liberalization and facilitation. In April 2011, the BRIC Bank mechanisms for cooperation and financial cooperation framework agreement was signed to expand the settlement scale of the currency in the organization of trade links for reducing trade costs between the BRIC countries. The future measures to lower trade costs will be launched soon.

However, the BRICS countries located in four continents are widely different in resource endowments, economy scale and foreign trade dependency. Thus, there will be conflicts of interest among the members in the economic and trade cooperation. The trade disputes are of frequent occurrence between the BRICS countries for the competitive trade relation. It means that a trade cost-cutting measure has heterogeneous impact on different participation, even if as for the benefit or the damage, obtained benefits or suffered losses vary. In other words, the impact of the reduction in trade costs on the different participation is non-neutral. Therefore, it is particularly important to measure the different impact of trade costs reduction on the trade volume of different countries. The impact could be denoted by the elasticity of trade cost which is helpful for analyzing the potential of the trade cooperation and separate interest demands.

Regrettably, the leading gravity models cannot measure the trade cost elasticity (TCE) for it is assumed as constant. In contrast to the leading Constant Elasticity of Substitution (CES)-based gravity models, Novy (2013) derives a micro-founded gravity model based on a translog demand system that allows for flexible substitution patterns across goods and makes it possible to measure the TCE. This chapter applies the translog gravity model (Novy, 2013) to measuring the bilateral TCE between the BRICS countries in 2000–2010 by using panel data. So far, there is no other study to measure the varying TCE except Novy (2013) measuring the TCE of the 28 OECD countries by using cross-sectional data in 2000.

On the one hand, it is of practical significance to choose BRICS countries as the research object and on the other it is more suitable to choose countries in different trade levels for the Novy (2013) method. This is because Novy (2013) particularly chooses New Zealand as an example to show the varying TCE for its trade volume in a wide range of variation with different partners. Considering the foreign trade of BRICS can be divided into three levels — as Table 1 shows China ranked second in the world in 2010, Brazil, Russia and India in the medium and South Africa smaller — the BRICS is chosen in this chapter to measure the varying TCE.

Table 1. International trade ranking of BRICS in 2010.

Country	Ranking
China	2
Russia	15
India	17
Brazil	21
South Africa	36

Source: WTO database.

The measuring result shows the TCE is all negative, which means it is beneficial to reduce the trade cost for all the member countries and the BRICS countries' trade costs elasticity in absolute value varies within a wide range between [0.48, 245]. Russia's average TCE is on the top (36.66), followed by South Africa (29.31) and China at the lowest (1.84). The ratio of difference value of South Africa to Brazil and China is at the highest level, which demonstrates that the impact of lowering trade cost on the small countries is greater than that on the big countries.

The remaining parts of the chapter are organized as follows: literature review is in Section 2. Section 3 introduces the translog gravity model and the measuring method. Estimating and measuring result is reported in Section 4. Section 5 makes an analysis. Finally it is the conclusion.

2 Literature Review

The first economic foundation for the gravity model was based on specifying the expenditure function to be a CES function (Anderson, 1979). Bergstrand (1985) derived a joint cost function that is homogeneous of degree one with Constant Elasticity of Transformation (CET). Anderson and van Wincoop (2003) decomposed the trade cost from the good price and first used the multilateral resistance. An alternative derivation of a mathematically equivalent structural gravity model was proposed by Eaton and Kortum (2002), based on Ricardian technology with heterogeneous productivity. Despite CES structure for the intermediate goods demand, the influence of σ disappears into a constant term. Chaney (2008) derives a similar supply-side gravity structure based on Ricardian productivity draws from a Pareto distribution in which the dispersion parameter of the Pareto distribution plays essentially the same role as θ in the Eaton–Kortum model (see Table 2).

The CES framework is unsuitable for describing the heterogeneous effect of lowering trade cost on trade flows. Because it means a reduction in trade cost has the same proportionate effect on bilateral trade regardless of whether tariffs were

Table 2. TCE in leading gravity models.

Leading Literature	$\left\|\frac{dln(x_{ij})}{dln(tij)}\right\|$	TCE
Deardorff (1998)	$\sigma - 1$	Constant
Eaton and Kortum (2002)	θ	Constant
Anderson and van Wincoop (2003)	$\sigma - 1$	Constant
Chaney (2008)	γ	Constant

Source: Novy (2013).

initially high or low or whether a country pair traded little or a lot. Anderson and van Wincoop (2003) summarized the existing literature and believed the elasticity seemed to be in the range [5,10]. However, it was just a speculation and cannot find a suitable method to measure the elasticity exactly.

Novy (2013) derives gravity in a highly restricted one slope parameter translog expenditure function case that allows for zeroes in demand. As Anderson pointed out "*How well does the CES do in representing the world economy? I look forward to the development of the translog case to help answer this question*".[1] In contrast to CES, translog preferences are so flexible that could break the constant link between trade flows and trade costs. The pioneering contribution of Novy (2013) generates endogenous TCE and makes it possible to measure the varying elasticity exactly.

This chapter is based on Novy (2013) to measure the bilateral TCE between the BRICS during 2000–2010.

3 Model and Measuring Method

3.1 The Translog gravity model

Novy (2013) builds on the gravity framework by Anderson and van Wincoop (2003), but instead of CES it relies on the homothetic translog demand system employed by Feenstra (2003).

Novy assumes there are J countries in the world with $j = 1, \ldots, J$ and $J \geq 2$. Each country is endowed with at least one differentiated good but may have arbitrarily many, and the number of goods may vary across countries. Let, $[Nj - 1 + 1, Nj]$ denote the range of goods of country j, with $N_{j-1} \leq N_j$ and $N_0 \equiv 0$. $N_J \equiv N$ denotes the total number of goods in the world. The translog expenditure

[1] Anderson (2011).

function is given by

$$\ln(E_j) = \ln(U_j) + \alpha_{0j} + \sum_{m=1}^{N} \alpha_m \ln(p_{mj}) + \frac{1}{2}\sum_{m=1}^{N}\sum_{k=1}^{N} \gamma_{km} \ln(p_{mj}) \ln(p_{kj}), \quad (1)$$

where U_j is the utility level of country j with m and k indexing goods and $\gamma_{km} = \gamma_{mk}$. The price of good m when delivered in country j is denoted by p_{mj}. He assumes trade frictions such that $p_{mj} = t_{mj} p_m$, where p_m denotes the net price for good m and $t_{mj} \geq 1 \forall m, j$ is the variable trade cost factor. He assumes symmetry across goods from the same origin country i in the sense that $p_m = p_i$ if $m \epsilon [N_{i-1} + 1, N_i]$, and that trade costs to country j are the same for all the goods from origin country i, $t_{mj} = t_{ij}$ if $m \epsilon [N_{i-1} + 1, N_i]$. As in Feenstra (2003), to ensure an expenditure function with homogeneity of degree one he imposes the conditions:

$$\sum_{m=1}^{N} \alpha_m = 1 \quad \text{and} \quad \sum_{k=1}^{N} \gamma_{km} = 0, \quad (2)$$

$$\gamma_{mm} = -\frac{\gamma}{N}(N-1) \;\; \forall m \quad \text{and} \quad \gamma_{km} = \frac{\gamma}{N} \;\; \forall k \neq m, \quad \text{with } \gamma > 0. \quad (3)$$

The expenditure share s_{mj} of country j for good m can be obtained by differentiating the expenditure function (1) with respect to $\ln(p_{mj})$:

$$s_{mj} = \alpha_m + \sum_{k=1}^{N} \gamma_{km} \ln(p_{kj}). \quad (4)$$

Let x_{ij} denote the value of trade from country i to country j, and y_j is the income of country j equal to expenditure E_j. The import share x_{ij}/y_j is then the sum of expenditure shares s_{mj} over the range of goods that originate from country i:

$$\frac{x_{ij}}{y_j} = \sum_{m=N_{i-1}+1}^{N_i} s_{mj} = \sum_{m=N_{i-1}+1}^{N_i} \left(\alpha_m + \sum_{k=1}^{N} \gamma_{km} \ln(p_{kj}) \right). \quad (5)$$

To close the model, he imposes market clearing:

$$y_i = \sum_{j=1}^{J} x_{ij} \quad \forall i. \quad (6)$$

As the final result, he obtain a translog "gravity" equation for import shares as

$$\frac{x_{ij}}{y_j} = \frac{y_i}{y^w} - \gamma n_i \ln(t_{ij}) + \gamma n_i \ln(T_j) + \gamma n_i \sum_{s=1}^{J} \frac{y_s}{y^w} \ln\left(\frac{t_{is}}{T_s}\right). \quad (7)$$

The variable $\ln(T_j)$ is a weighted average of trade costs over the trading partners of country j akin to inward multilateral resistance in Anderson and van Wincoop (2003).

$$\ln(T_j) = \frac{1}{N}\sum_{k=1}^{N}\ln(t_{kj}) = \sum_{s=1}^{J}\frac{n_s}{N}\ln(t_{sj}). \tag{8}$$

The trade cost function can be written as

$$\ln(t_{ij}) = \rho\ln(\text{dist}_{ij}) + \delta\text{adj}_{ij}, \tag{9}$$

where dist_{ij} denotes the bilateral great-circle distance as the trade cost proxy and adj_{ij} is the adjacency dummy.

Novy (2013) substitutes the trade cost function (9) into the multilateral resistance term (8) to obtain

$$\ln(T_j) = \rho\ln(T_j^{\text{dist}}) + \delta T_j^{\text{adj}}, \tag{10}$$

where the terms on the right-hand side are defined as

$$\ln(T_j^{\text{dist}}) \equiv \sum_{s=1}^{J}\frac{n_s}{N}\ln(\text{dist}_{sj}), \tag{11}$$

$$T_j^{\text{adj}} \equiv \sum_{s=1}^{J}\frac{n_s}{N}\text{adj}_{sj}. \tag{12}$$

The translog estimating equation follows as

$$\begin{aligned}\frac{x_{ij}}{y_j} &= -\gamma\rho n_i\ln(\text{dist}_{ij}) + \gamma\rho n_i\ln(T_j^{\text{dist}})\\ &\quad - \gamma\delta n_i\text{adj}_{ij} + \gamma\delta n_i T_j^{\text{adj}} + S_i + \varepsilon_{ij},\end{aligned} \tag{13}$$

$$S_i \equiv \frac{y_i}{y^w} + \gamma n_i\sum_{s=1}^{J}\frac{y_s}{y^w}\ln\left(\frac{t_{is}}{T_s}\right). \tag{14}$$

3.2 Measuring method

The translog TCE follows from Equation (7) as

$$\eta_{ij}^{TL} = -\gamma n_i/(x_{ij}/y_j) \tag{15}$$

γ could be obtained from Equation (13) and ρ could be obtained from

$$\ln\left(\frac{x_{ij}}{y_j}\right) = -(\sigma-1)\rho\ln(\text{dist}_{ij}) - (\sigma-1)\delta\text{adj}_{ij} + \tilde{S}_i + \tilde{S}_j + \xi_{ij}$$

$$\tilde{S}_i \equiv \ln\left(\frac{y_i}{y^w}\right) + (\sigma - 1)\ln(\Pi_i)$$
$$\tilde{S}_j \equiv (\sigma - 1)\ln(P_j). \tag{16}$$

Thus, we need to estimate the two Equations (13) and (16).

4 Estimation

4.1 Data

I chose the BRICS countries from the year 2000 to 2010 for observations, the number of which is 220 and estimated the above two equations by using the panel data of cross section weights. Table 3 shows the source of the variables in translog equation.

Table 3. Source of the variables in translog equation.

Variables	Source
x_{ij}/y_j	UN-COMTRADE database, Word Bank WDI database
n_i	As Novy (2013) I use extensive margin as a proxy for n_i Hummels and Klenow (2005)
$\ln(\text{dist}_{ij})$	CEPII Geography database
$\ln(T_j^{\text{dist}})$	CEPII Geography database, Hummels and Klenow (2005)
adj_{ij}	CEPII Geography database
T_j^{adj}	CEPII Geography database
y_i/y^w	Word Bank WDI database
$\sum_{s=1}^{J} \frac{y_s}{y^w} \ln\left(\frac{t_{is}}{T_s}\right)$	Word Bank WDI database, CEPII Geography database

4.2 Estimating results

Estimating Equation (13):

$$\frac{x_{ij}}{y_j} = -0.0022 * n_i \ln(\text{dist}_{ij}) + 0.0032 * n_i \ln(T_j^{\text{dist}}) + \varepsilon_{ij}$$
$$(-4.63)^2 \qquad (6.28)$$
$$\bar{R}^2 = 0.63 \quad F = 380.55 \tag{17}$$

[2] t-Value is reported in the brackets. Other estimating results are in Tables A.1 and A.2.

Estimating Equation (16):

$$\ln\left(\frac{x_{ij}}{y_j}\right) = -0.72 * \ln(\text{dist}_{ij}) + 0.87 * \text{adj}_{ij} + \xi_{ij}$$
$$(-113.22) \qquad (10.67)$$
$$\bar{R}^2 = 0.97 \quad F = 7215.97 \tag{18}$$

I could get $\gamma = 0.0214$ from Equations (17) and (18).

According to the translog TCE Equation (7) $\eta_{ij}^{TL} = -\gamma n_i/(x_{ij}/y_j)$

I could calculate the TCE of BIRCS countries from the year 2000 to 2010.

5 Analysis

5.1 Aggregate analysis

First of all, it can be seen from Table 4 that the TCEs of BRICS vary across broad range between [0.48, 245]. This key feature stands out in contrast to the CES-based gravity model, which is simply a constant. The constant "one-size-fits-all" TCE is

Table 4. TCE of BIRCS Countries from the Year 2000 to 2010 (in absolute value).

Country	2000	2001	2002	2003	2004	2005	2006	2007	2008	2009	2010
BC	11.08	6.99	5.79	3.63	3.56	3.31	3.24	3.26	2.77	2.48	1.93
BI	21.23	16.80	7.78	10.86	11.09	7.35	10.17	13.01	11.07	4.05	4.96
BR	6.16	2.79	2.76	2.88	3.58	2.63	2.88	3.49	3.58	4.27	3.58
BZ	4.41	2.80	2.33	2.30	2.12	1.81	1.79	1.63	1.57	2.25	2.79
CB	7.94	6.18	5.18	3.89	2.72	2.75	2.22	1.81	1.32	1.70	1.29
CI	4.44	3.80	2.86	2.70	1.83	1.41	0.98	0.78	0.58	0.70	0.64
CR	1.75	1.70	1.48	1.08	0.98	0.87	0.94	0.69	0.76	1.05	0.75
CZ	1.98	1.70	1.28	1.25	1.12	0.97	0.68	0.58	0.48	0.58	0.51
IB	32.06	22.96	13.35	13.61	11.73	8.70	6.95	6.87	4.86	8.56	5.44
IC	15.59	13.73	9.08	6.11	4.51	3.00	3.31	3.52	4.28	4.60	3.23
IR	2.90	3.49	4.47	5.91	8.95	10.35	11.19	13.45	14.56	12.12	10.18
IZ	4.13	3.47	2.26	3.44	2.35	1.68	1.19	1.28	1.06	1.38	0.96
RB	25.17	29.23	22.13	21.71	18.18	14.70	15.14	12.21	8.17	14.86	12.26
RC	2.31	2.39	2.15	2.01	1.93	1.75	1.74	2.33	2.16	3.02	3.02
RI	4.29	4.31	3.18	2.21	2.91	3.64	3.28	4.13	2.35	2.34	3.22
RZ	39.89	204.66	27.89	245.14	243.84	98.80	132.98	201.60	68.98	14.62	80.26
ZB	27.52	17.55	24.50	26.88	23.37	23.92	23.34	22.63	21.59	38.62	25.08
ZC	30.80	24.74	27.81	15.90	15.76	14.20	11.08	7.22	9.04	7.58	6.28
ZI	10.66	11.16	12.43	13.58	10.96	6.14	10.46	7.93	4.59	5.74	4.99
ZR	73.39	89.33	70.88	49.28	51.93	93.79	80.19	74.21	58.88	59.00	44.86

inconsistent with the data. However, the TCEs are heterogeneous across country pairs.

Second, the value of TCEs is negative which means all the members of BRICS could increase trade volume through the reduction in trade cost and yield trade creation effect. There will be certain potential of corporation in trade liberalization and facilitation for the BRICS in the future.

5.2 Country analysis

5.2.1 *Brazil*

Figures 1 and 2 show the TCE of Brazil to India is larger than the other three countries, which indicates there is larger space for Brazil expanding the export to India by lowering the trade cost. The TCE of Brazil to China shows a declining trend and it is limited for Brazil to increase the export to China through reducing trade cost. Thus, there is a little negative effect for China to reduce trade barriers, so

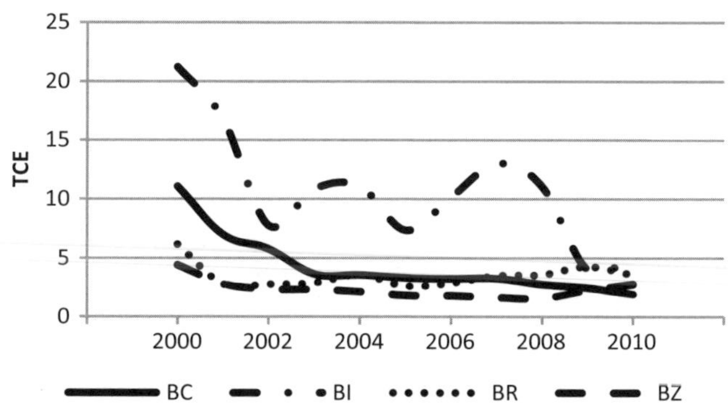

Figure 1. TCE of Brazil in 2000–2010.

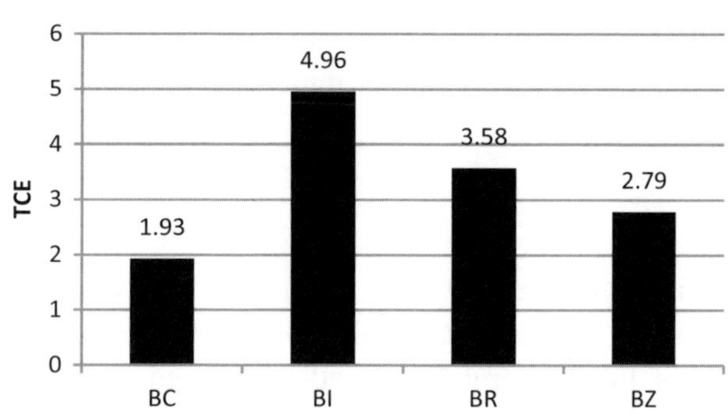

Figure 2. TCE of Brazil in 2010.

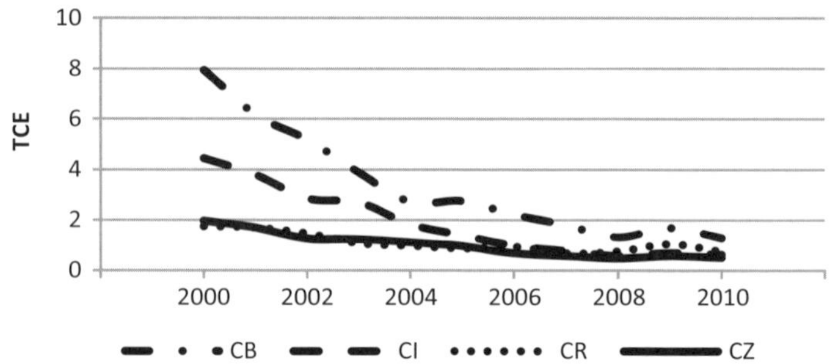

Figure 3. TCE of China in 2000–2010.

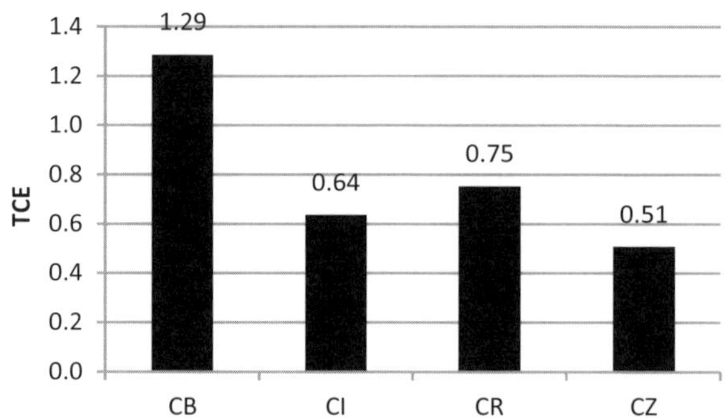

Figure 4. TCE of China in 2010.

that China could take more active part in promoting the bilateral trade liberalization and facilitation with Brazil.

5.2.2 *China*

Figure 3 shows the TCE of China to the other four countries tends to decrease year by year, which implies the room for expanding export to the other four is narrowing. It is a challenge and a bottleneck for China's foreign trade in future. In Figure 4 the TCE of China to Brazil is relatively higher than the other three and it is feasible for China to reduce trade cost to Brazil.

5.2.3 *India*

It can be seen from Figure 5 the TCE of India to Brazil, China and South Africa is in a downward trend. Russia is the only one in the upward state before 2008. It is because 90% of the bilateral trade had been used for debt refunding since Russia–India alliance ceased to exist after the collapse of the Soviet Union. The explosion of 2008 financial crisis led the two countries to enhance the collaboration

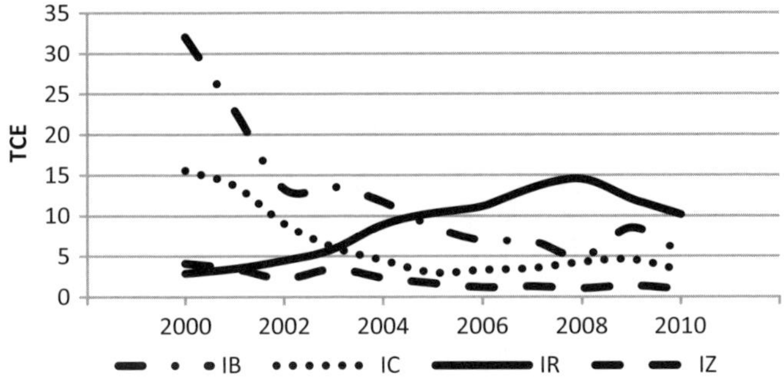

Figure 5. TCE of India in 2000–2010.

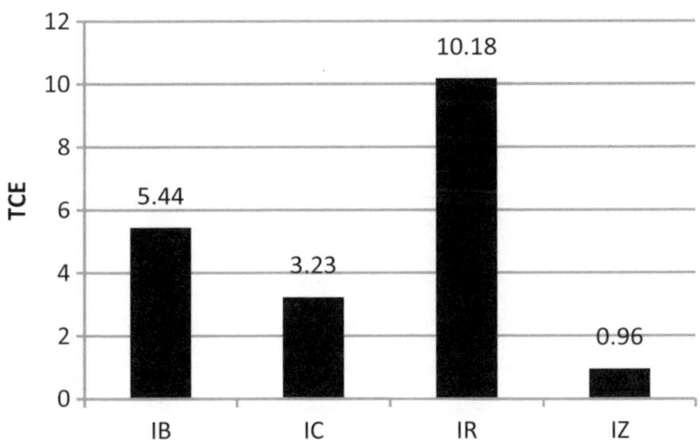

Figure 6. TCE of India in 2010.

in trade and the TCE began to decrease. In Figure 6, the TCE of India to Russia is highest (10.18) among the four countries, which means the potential of cooperation is relatively great.

5.2.4 *Russia*

As can be seen in Figure 7, the trade cost elasticity of Russia to South Africa shows a dramatic change and is higher than the other three countries. In 2010, it reached up to 80.26, which indicates the cooperation potential is great between the two countries (see Figure 8). In contrast, the elasticity of Russia to China is only 3.02 and there will be relatively little effect in expanding the export to China by lowering the trade cost.

5.2.5 *South Africa*

According to Figure 9, the TCE of South Africa to Russia is at a high level relatively and South Africa could benefit from the cooperation in reducing the bilateral trade

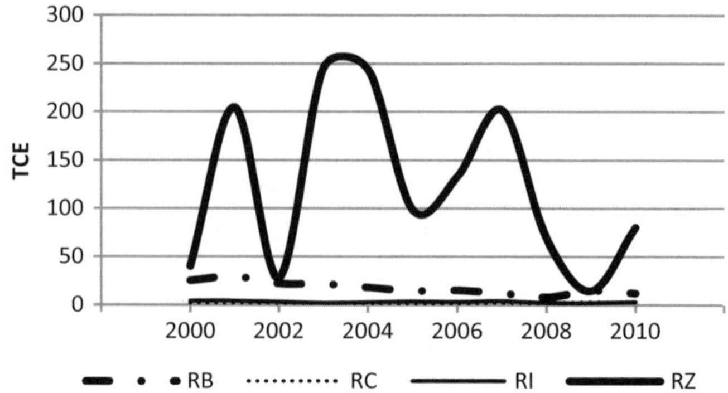

Figure 7. TCE of Russia in 2000–2010.

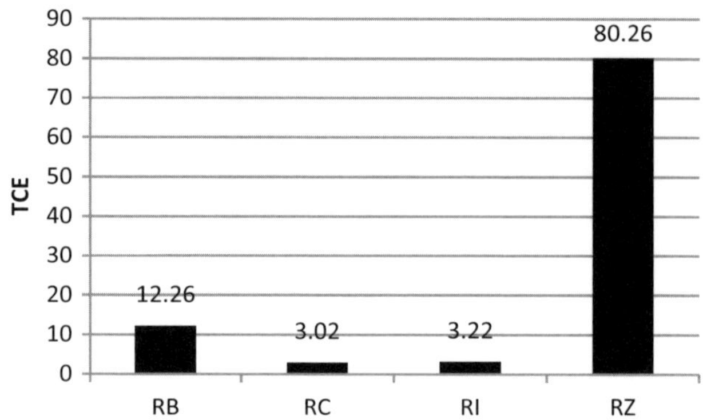

Figure 8. TCE of Russia in 2000.

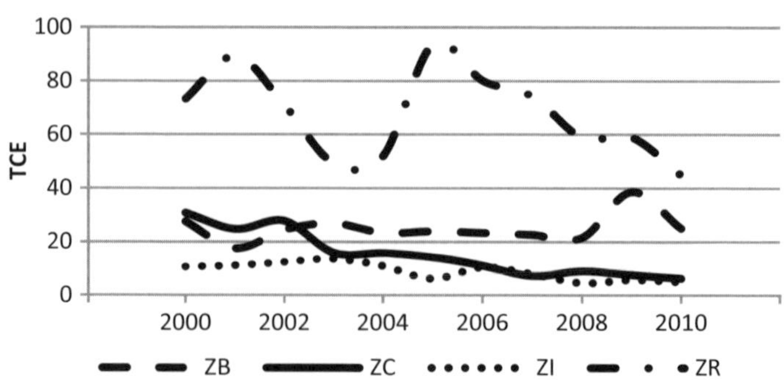

Figure 9. TCE of South Africa in 2000–2010.

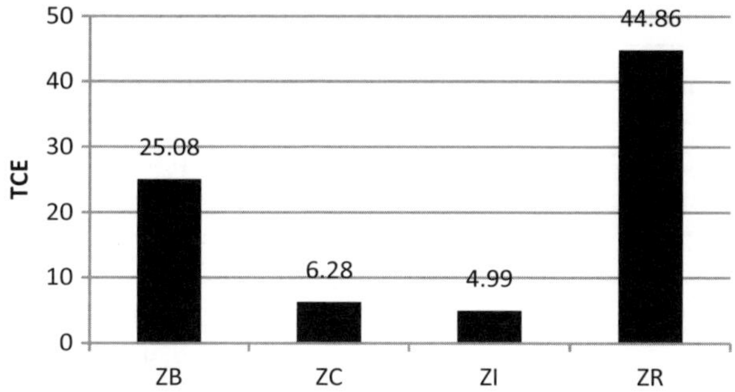

Figure 10. TCE of South Africa in 2000.

Table 5. Average TCE of BRICS in 2000–2010.

Country	Average TCE
Brazil	5.25
China	1.84
India	7.43
Russia	36.66
South Africa	29.31

cost. Similarly, it can be seen from Figure 10 that the TCE of South Africa to Brazil is 25.08 and there will be great potential in collaboration between South Africa and Brazil.

5.3 Comparative analysis

In order to make a comparison of the bilateral TCE between the BRICS, this chapter calculates the average TCE and the difference value of TCE in 2010.

As shown in Table 5, the average TCE of Russia is highest (36.66), followed by South Africa (29.31) and China at the lowest (1.84). It means Russia and South Africa could get more benefit from the reduction in trade cost than the other three.

It can be seen from the difference value in Table 6 that the TCE of India, Russia and South Africa is higher than their pair countries, which implies the three countries could benefit a great deal from lowering trade cost. The ratio of difference value of South Africa to Brazil and China is at the highest level, which demonstrates that the impact of lowering trade cost on the small countries is greater than that on the big countries.

Table 6. A comparison of TCE between BRICS in 2010.

Country	TCE	Country	TCE	Difference	Ratio
BC	1.93	CB	1.29	0.64	0.40
BI	4.96	IB	5.44	−0.48	−0.09
BR	3.58	RB	12.26	−8.69	−1.10
BZ	2.79	ZB	25.08	−22.29	−1.60
CI	0.64	IC	3.23	−2.60	−1.34
CR	0.80	RC	3.00	−2.30	−1.20
CZ	0.51	ZC	6.28	−5.77	−1.70
IR	10.18	RI	3.22	6.95	1.04
IZ	0.96	ZI	4.99	−4.04	−1.36
RZ	80.26	ZR	44.86	35.39	0.57

6 Conclusion

This chapter is on the basis of Novy (2013) translog gravity to measure the bilateral TCE between the BRICS countries (Brazil, China, India, Russia, South Africa) from 2000 to 2010. The result shows that the BRICS countries' trade costs elasticity varies within a wide range between [0.48, 245]. Russia's average TCE is on the top (36.66), followed by South Africa (29.31) and China at the lowest (1.84). On the one hand, it indicates that China stands first in the open degree among the BRICS, and on the other, it demonstrates that there will be little potential for China to expand export by reducing trade cost. This is a challenge for China's foreign trade in future. Meanwhile, there is also little potential for other four BRCIS to increase their export to China through lowering the trade cost. Therefore, China could take more active part in promoting trade liberalization and facilitation. The ratio of difference value of South Africa to Brazil and China is at the highest level, which demonstrates that trade is more sensitive to trade costs if the exporting country only provides a small share of the destination country's imports.

This chapter is based on aggregate trade flows. The future research could be an application to exploring industry-level data and analyzing the heterogeneous TCE of different industries in BRICS countries.

References

Anderson, J.E. (1979), A Theoretical Foundation for the Gravity Equation, *American Economic Review*, 69, 106–116.

Anderson, J. and E. van Wincoop, (2003), Gravity with Gravitas: A Solution to the Border Puzzle, *American Economic Review*, 93, 170–192.

Anderson, J. and E. van Wincoop, (2004), Trade Costs, *Journal of Economic Literature*, 42, 691–751.

Anderson, J.E. (2011), The Gravity Model, *Annual Review of Economics*, 3(1), 133–160.

Bergstrand, J. (1985), The Gravity Equation in International Trade: Some Microeconomic Foundations and Empirical Evidence, *Review of Economics and Statistics*, 67, 474–481.

Chaney, T. (2008), Distorted Gravity: The Intensive and Extensive Margins of International Trade, *American Economic Review*, 98, 1707–1721.

Deardorff, A. (1998), Determinants of Bilateral Trade: Does Gravity Work in a Neoclassical World? in Jeffrey A.F. (Eds.): *The Regionalization of the World Economy*, The University of Chicago Press, p7.

Eaton, J. and S. Kortum (2002), Technology, Geography and Trade, *Econometrica*, 70, 1741–1779.

Feenstra, R. (2003), A Homothetic Utility Function for Monopolistic Competition Models, without Constant Price Elasticity, *Economics Letters*, 78, 79–86.

Hummels, D. and P. Klenow (2005), The Variety and Quality of a Nation's Exports, *American Economic Review*, 95, 704–723.

Novy, D. (2013), International Trade without CES: Estimating Translog Gravity, *Journal of International Economics*, 89(2), 271–282.

Appendix

Table A.1. Translog gravity.

Dependent variable	(1)	$\frac{x_{ij}}{y_j}$ (2)	$\frac{x_{ij}}{y_j}$ (3)	$\frac{x_{ij}}{y_j}$ (4)	$\frac{x_{ij}}{y_j}$ (5)	$\frac{x_{ij}}{y_j}$ (6)
$ni \ln(\text{dist}_{ij})$	0.0009***	−0.0022***	−0.0003	0.0021**	−0.0009	−0.0011
	(0.0000)	(0.0005)	(0.0006)	(0.0009)	(0.0007)	(0.0009)
$ni \ln(T_j^{\text{dist}})$		0.0032***	0.0010*	−0.0014	0.0008	0.0009
		(0.0005)	(0.0006)	(0.0008)	(0.0007)	(0.0008)
$ni\text{adj}_{ij}$			0.0081***	0.0089***	0.0040***	0.0040***
			(0.0012)	(0.0014)	(0.0010)	(0.0010)
niT_j^{adj}				−0.0262**	0.0001	0.0021
				(0.0125)	(0.0113)	(0.0115)
$\frac{y_i}{y^w}$					0.1700***	0.1665***
					(0.0116)	(0.0125)
$n_i \sum_{s=1}^{J} \frac{y_s}{y^w} \ln\left(\frac{t_{is}}{T_s}\right)$						0.0000
						(0.0001)
Adjusted R^2	0.6335	0.6341	0.4044	0.4131	0.5175	0.5110
F-value		380.5484	75.3338	52.37637	59.7128	46.7755
Observations	220	220	220	220	220	220

Note: ***significant at 1% level, **significant at 5% level, *significant at 10% level. Standard errors are reported in parentheses.

Table A.2. Estimation of Equation (16).

Dependent variable	$\ln\frac{x_{ij}}{y_j}$ (1)	$\ln\frac{x_{ij}}{y_j}$ (2)	$\ln\frac{x_{ij}}{y_j}$ (3)	$\ln\frac{x_{ij}}{y_j}$ (4)	$\ln\frac{x_{ij}}{y_j}$ (5)	$\ln\frac{x_{ij}}{y_j}$ (6)	$\ln\frac{x_{ij}}{y_j}$ (7)	$\ln\frac{x_{ij}}{y_j}$ (8)	$\ln\frac{x_{ij}}{y_j}$ (9)	$\ln\frac{x_{ij}}{y_j}$ (10)	$\ln\frac{x_{ij}}{y_j}$ (11)	$\ln\frac{x_{ij}}{y_j}$ (12)
$\ln(\text{dist}_{ij})$	−0.69***	−0.72***	−0.72***	−0.73***	−0.73***	−0.72***	−0.04	−0.04	−0.04	−0.04	−0.04	−0.04
	0.006	0.006	0.007	0.007	0.008	0.011	0.153	0.153	0.154	0.154	0.155	0.156
adj_{ij}		0.87***	0.87***	0.87***	0.81***	0.83***	1.36***	1.36***	1.36***	1.36***	1.37***	1.37***
		0.080	0.080	0.101	0.101	0.102	0.169	0.169	0.170	0.170	0.171	0.172
$s_{\tilde{i}1}$			0.24**	0.38***	0.41**	0.32**	−6.06***	−6.06***	−6.09***	−6.08***	−6.12***	−6.14***
			0.105	0.117	0.125	0.143	1.413	1.417	1.420	1.425	1.436	1.447
$s_{\tilde{i}2}$				0.31**	0.38**	0.28*	−5.97***	−5.97***	−6.00***	−6.00***	−6.03***	−6.04***
				0.130	0.133	0.155	1.428	1.431	1.436	1.441	1.453	1.462
$s_{\tilde{i}3}$					0.20	0.10	−6.21***	−6.22***	−6.24***	−6.24***	−6.27***	−6.26***
					0.129	0.152	1.438	1.441	1.444	1.450	1.461	1.467
$s_{\tilde{i}4}$						−0.17	−6.47***	−6.47***	−6.50***	−6.50***	−6.52***	−6.54***
						0.141	1.427	1.431	1.433	1.439	1.449	1.466
$s_{\tilde{i}5}$							−6.44***	−6.44***	−6.47***	−6.46***	−6.50***	−6.50***
							1.408	1.411	1.413	1.419	1.432	1.441
$s_{\tilde{j}1}$								0.02	0.01	0.01	0.03	0.07
								0.136	0.142	0.151	0.175	0.204
$s_{\tilde{j}2}$									−0.02	−0.02	−0.004	0.05
									0.146	0.155	0.178	0.253
$s_{\tilde{j}3}$										−0.005	0.02	0.07
										0.159	0.182	0.264
$s_{\tilde{j}4}$											0.05	0.09
											0.182	0.239
$s_{\tilde{j}5}$												0.07
												0.246
Adjusted R^2	0.955	0.971	0.972	0.958	0.958	0.959	0.923	0.923	0.919	0.919	0.917	0.916
F-Value		7216.0	3844.5	1674.1	1241.6	1025.6	438.1	373.5	313.3	276.0	242.9	218.5
Observations	220	220	220	220	220	220	220	220	220	220	220	220

Note: ***significant at 1% level, **significant at 5% level, *significant at 10% level. Standard errors are reported below the coefficients.

Part III

Labor Market and Income Distribution

Chapter 9

Ownership Structure, Real Exchange Rate Movements and Labor Market Adjustment in China*

Risheng Mao

Institute of World Economics & Politics,
Chinese Academy of Social Sciences,
100732, Beijing, China
maorsh@cass.org.cn

John Whalley

Department of Economics, Western University, Canada
Centre for International Governance Innovation (CIGI), Canada
National Bureau of Economic Research (NBER), USA
jwhalley @uwo.ca

Abstract: This chapter investigates the impacts of Renminbi (RMB) real exchange rate movements on employment and wage rates. Based on the panel dataset covering 456 narrowly defined four-digit Chinese manufacturing industries and industry specific real exchange rates, we stress the links between impacts of exchange rate fluctuations on labor market with ownership structure of manufacturing industries. The empirical results show that movements of RMB real exchange rate would likely have pronounced effects on both net employment and wage rates. A 10% RMB

*We are grateful to the financial support from Ontario Research Fund (ORF) and comments from seminar participants in the department of economics, University of Western Ontario, Canada.

real appreciation (depreciation) would likely cause a net employment decline (rise) of around 3.7% and a wage rate drop of 1.9% after controlling for other factors. The impacts of real exchange rate movements on net employment and wage rates vary significantly with the ownership structure of manufacturing sectors.

1 Introduction

Recent empirical studies on the labor market implications of exchange rate change typically find a significant relationship between exchange rate fluctuations and labor market adjustments in a number of countries, but these relationships vary by industry. Several studies find significant and large impacts of real exchange rate changes on net employment. (Branson and Love, 1988; Revenga, 1992; Dekle, 1998; Leung and Yuen, 2007; Hua, 2007; Nucci and Pozzolo, 2010). Others show that wage rates are typically more responsive to real exchange rate movements than employment (Goldberg and Tracy, 2001; Campa and Goldberg, 2001). Since the reform of exchange rate regime for Renminbi (RMB) from the pegged U.S. dollar strategy to a more dynamic, flexible exchange rate regime in July, 2005, both the nominal and real exchange rates of RMB have experienced substantial appreciation. Although there have been studies investigating the overall impacts of RMB exchange rate movements on net employment using data of aggregated at provincial or specific industry level (Hua, 2007; Chen and Dao, 2011), to our best knowledge, few studies have ever investigated the different impacts of real exchange rate movements on Chinese labor market based on the narrowly defined industries and industry specific real exchange rate of RMB. Moreover, few studies for China have investigated the effects of RMB exchange rate movements on wage rates of Chinese industries, and the existing related studies only focus on investigating the significance of Balassa Samuelson effects and implied the association of RMB real exchange rate change with real wage rates adjustments (McKinnon, 2005; McKinnon and Schnabl, 2006).

In this chapter, we highlight the links between real exchange change impacts on labor market with ownership structure of manufacturing industries; this is because state-owned enterprises (SOEs), private enterprise and foreign invested enterprises (FIEs) for Chinese manufacturing industries are systematically different in trade dependence, market competitive structure, ratio of capital to labor inputs and rigidity of labor market, which all potentially play important roles in influencing the pass-through effects of exchange rate movements on labor market. We use a panel data set covering 456 four-digit industries over the period 2001–2009 to investigate the effects of exchange rate movements on labor market behavior taking into account trends of RMB real exchange rate changes by industry before and after the reform of RMB exchange rate regime in July, 2005. Instead of using an aggregate RMB real effective exchange rate (REER), we construct industry specific REERs for 163 three-digit industries over the period 2001 to 2009 which we apply to our four-digit industry data. Although the panel data covers only a short time period from 2001 to 2009, the RMB real exchange rates for almost all sectors have experienced a consistent depreciation from 2001 to 2005 and then a sharp appreciation after 2005, which provides us a very good experiment to investigate the impacts of real exchange rate movements on net employment and wage rates.

We find that real exchange rate movements for RMB have both significant effects on wage rates and net employment. A 10% change in real exchange rate will cause effects on net employment about 3.7%, and wage rates will also decline about 1.7% with a 10% real appreciation. The estimation results show that impacts of RMB real exchange rate movements on wage and employment are systematically associated with export openness, overall import penetration, profit margin and ownership structure of Chinese manufacturing industries. In contrast to the previous empirical studies (Campa and Goldberg, 2001; Nucci and Pozzolo, 2010) that highlight the different impacts of exchange rate changes on labor market through foreign sales and import input channels, we stress that a real appreciation has negative effects on net employment and wage rates both through export openness and import penetration channels.

The estimation results indicate that labor market for private enterprises is less responsive to exchange rate fluctuations than is true for SOEs. We also show that exchange rate movements generate larger effects on the labor market activity of SOEs and FIEs than private firms even after we control for the profit margins of industries and the effects of exchange rate change on labor market through trade channels. Alexandre *et al.* (2010) have earlier noted that institutional factors can substantially influence the pass-through effects of exchange rate on domestic prices and output due to rigidities and different adjustment costs in labor market. Other studies of Chinese SOEs (Buckley *et al.*, 2007; Hale and Long, 2008) generally imply that the labor market activity of SOEs is less likely to be affected by real exchange rate shocks because wage determination and hiring by SOEs is less market based and more regulated by government policy. They also argue that SOEs are more likely to obtain financial support from the government and also more likely to be immune to price and exchange rate movements. Also, and in contrast to private enterprises, most SOEs have higher hiring or firing costs due to a higher percentage of formal employment and stronger labor market regulation. However, SOEs have lower average profit margins and productivity than private enterprises and FIEs, and the ratio of capital to labor inputs for SOEs is more capital intensive than for private enterprises, which all imply that exchange rate movements can potentially have larger effects on labor market of SOEs than private firms. With lower performance and productivity, SOEs are also more likely to be driven out of the market and experience bankruptcy with increased market competition due to a real appreciation.[1] With higher capital intensive inputs, the labor input for SOEs is also more likely to be substituted by import input with a real appreciation than for private enterprises based on our theoretical framework. All the above facts suggest that it is an empirical question to investigate the links between the effects of exchange rate movements on labor market with ownership structure of Chinese manufacturing industries.

The chapter is organized as follows. In Section 2, we provide a simple theoretical framework to analyze the mechanism and channel that exchange rate movements have impacts on labor market. Section 3 describes data, summary statistics and identification strategy for wage and employment equations. Section 4 presents empirical findings and discusses their possible implications. Section 5 provides conclusions.

2 Theoretical Background and Empirical Specification

2.1 Theoretical background and framework

Exchange rate fluctuations typically affect labor demand of tradable sectors through two direct channels. Through the output channel, real exchange shocks affect relative prices between domestic and foreign sales and employment will change accordingly. They also have impacts on labor market through imported input or import competition channels. A real appreciation (depreciation) reduces (increases) cost of imported inputs and price of imported final products. Depending on the degree of substitutability between domestic output and imported goods, output and employment of domestic industries can be impacted in different ways. Exchange rate fluctuations also have ambiguous effects on labor market of non-tradable sectors through several channels indirectly; employment for non-tradable sectors tends to expand due to labor inflows from trade sectors with an appreciation of real exchange rates, while the employment for non-tradable sectors will also potentially shrink with a real appreciation due to the significant output linkage between tradable and non-tradable sectors (Chen and Dao, 2011).

The degree of responsiveness of output and employment to exchange rate shocks depends on pass-through effects of exchange rate change on prices of domestic and foreign sales. Market structure matters because, in a competitive market, firms have limited ability to set prices and firms' output is affected by changes in prices

[1]The Summary statistics for the empirical sample we use later show that the average profit to sales margins of SOEs, private enterprises and FIEs in 456 four-digit industries are −1.67%, 5.32% and 6.05%, respectively over the period 2001 to 2009. The market share of SOEs declines consistently from 18.4% in 2001 to 5.5% in 2009, while the market share of private enterprise increases from 14.5% to 39.8%. The market share of FIEs is relatively stable at around 30% over the same period.

of foreign sales. Thus in a monopolistically competitive environment and with extensive production differentiation and market power, exchange rate shocks on output and employment can be partially offset by changed price setting. Trade orientation matters because exchange rates shocks and with them pass-through on to foreign demand are proportional to export openness. The pass-through effects on output and employment of exchange rate shocks through import channel depends on the degree of import penetration, import input ratio and substitutability between domestic output and imported goods.

The regulatory environment also plays an important role. If domestic industries are protected or supported by the government policies, relative prices, costs and the market share of domestic industries may not change with an exchange rate shock. Labor market regulations also affect the speed of adjustment of employment to relative cost changes caused by exchange rate shocks. If costs of labor hiring or firing and output adjustment are large, firms are reluctant to make large changes in employment in an uncertain duration. All these factors together influence the responsiveness of employment and wage rates to real exchange shocks.

We formulate a theoretical framework that demonstrates the links between exchange rate movements and labor market adjustment. To simplify the analysis, we assume a representative firm within an industry chooses inputs and output to maximize its profit ($\pi(e)$) in every period under the condition of monopolistic competitive market, that is,

$$\pi(e) = \max_{\substack{q^d, q^x \\ L, Z, M}} \left\{ p^d(e, q^d) * q^d + \frac{p^x(e, q^x)}{e} * q^x - w * L - r * Z - \frac{s(e)}{e} * M \right\}, \tag{1}$$

where the domestic price and sales in the domestic market are p^d, q^d respectively and p^x, q^x represent price and sales in the foreign market. w and L are wage rates and labor employed, respectively; r and Z are cost of non-labor inputs and non-labor inputs employed from domestic market; $s(e)$ and M represent cost of import input and import inputs used, respectively, and the real exchange rate (e) is defined as the amount of foreign currency per unit of RMB. The maximization for Equation (1) is subject to,

$$Q = q^d + q^x = L^\alpha Z^\beta M^{1-\alpha-\beta}. \tag{2}$$

The first order conditions of outputs for the solution of the above constrained maximization problems are

$$\frac{\partial \pi(e)}{\partial q^d} = \frac{\partial p^d(e, p^d)}{\partial q^d} * q^d + p^d - \lambda = 0, \tag{3}$$

$$\frac{\partial\pi(e)}{\partial q^x}=\frac{1}{e}\left(\frac{\partial p^x(e,p^x)}{\partial q^x}*q^x+p^x\right)-\lambda=0, \tag{4}$$

$$\frac{\partial\pi(e)}{\partial L}=-w+\lambda\frac{\partial Q}{\partial L}=0, \tag{5}$$

$$\frac{\partial\pi(e)}{\partial Z}=-r+\lambda\frac{\partial Q}{\partial Z}=0, \tag{6}$$

$$\frac{\partial\pi(e)}{\partial M}=-\frac{s(e)}{e}+\lambda\frac{\partial Q}{\partial M}=0, \tag{7}$$

$$\lambda=p^d\left(1+\frac{1}{\eta^d}\right)=\frac{p^x}{e}\left(1+\frac{1}{\eta^x}\right)=\frac{s(e)}{e}\left(\frac{\partial Q}{\partial M}\right)^{-1}, \tag{8}$$

where λ is the Lagrange multiplier for the technology constraint. Combining the above first order conditions and Euler's theorem, we can derive the optimal labor demand (L_D), that is,

$$L_D=\frac{1}{w}\left\{p^d\left(1+\frac{1}{\eta^d}\right)q^d+\frac{p^x}{e}\left(1+\frac{1}{\eta^x}\right)q^x-rZ-\frac{s}{e}M\right\}, \tag{9}$$

where η^d and η^x represent the price elasticities of products demand in the domestic market and foreign market, respectively,

Differencing the optimal labor demand to real exchange rates, we derive the elasticity of labor demand to exchange rate movements, that is,

$$\frac{\partial L}{\partial e}\frac{e}{L}=\frac{1}{\alpha}\left\{\begin{array}{l}p^d\left(1+\frac{1}{\eta^d}\right)\eta^{d,e}\\ \quad+\theta\left[\frac{p^x}{e}\left(1+\frac{1}{\eta^x}\right)(\eta^{x,e}-1)-p^d\left(1+\frac{1}{\eta^d}\right)\eta^{d,e}\right]\\ \quad+\frac{s}{e}(1-\alpha-\beta)\left(\frac{\partial Q}{\partial M}\right)^{-1}(1-\eta^{s,e})\end{array}\right\}, \tag{10}$$

where the $\eta^{d,e}$, $\eta^{x,e}$, $\eta^{s,e}$ represent the pass-through effects of real exchange rate on domestic price, export price and the cost of import input, respectively. Using Equation (8), Equation (4) can be written as,

$$\begin{aligned}\frac{\partial L}{\partial e}\frac{e}{L}&=\frac{\lambda}{\alpha}\{\eta^{d,e}+\theta[(\eta^{x,e}-1)-\eta^{d,e}]+(1-\alpha-\beta)(1-\eta^{s,e})\}\\&=\frac{\bar{P}}{\alpha\bar{\mu}}\{\eta^{d,e}+\theta[(\eta^{x,e}-1)-\eta^{d,e}]+(1-\alpha-\beta)(1-\eta^{s,e})\},\end{aligned} \tag{11}$$

where $\bar{\mu}$ represents the average price over cost markup in the domestic and foreign markets, $\bar{\mu}=\frac{\bar{\eta}}{1+\bar{\eta}}$, and $\bar{\eta}$ is the average price elasticity of demand and the average price is $\bar{p}$. The above equation suggests that the response of labor demand to exchange rate will rise with an increase in labor intensity of inputs and will decline with an increase in price over cost markup, and Equation (11) also shows that the response of labor demand to exchange rate change not only depends on the export openness and import input ratio in the production, but also depends on the pass-through effects of exchange rate movements on prices in the product and factor markets. As indicated by related research (Campa and Goldberg, 1995, 1999, 2001), the pass-through effects of exchange rates are proportional to import penetration of product markets, and products of any two trade shares can be taken as very small values and assumed to be zeros, that is, $\theta * (\eta^{x,e} - \eta^{d,e}) = 0$; $(1 - \alpha - \beta)\eta^{s,e} = 0$. Hence, Equation (11) is reduced to the following form:

$$\frac{\partial L}{\partial e}\frac{e}{L} = \frac{\bar{p}}{\alpha\bar{\mu}}\{\eta^{d,e} - \theta + (1 - \alpha - \beta)\} \tag{12}$$

and the above equation shows that market competitive structure and ratio of capital to labor play important roles in influencing the response of optimal labor demand to exchange rate fluctuations, and also highlights other three important channels that exchange rate movements have effects on the optimal labor demand. As indicated by our previous analysis and the existing literature, the pass-through effects of exchange rate movements on domestic price ($\eta^{d,e}$) are not only proportional to import penetration rate, but also potentially depends on institutional factors of labor market, and in order to investigate the systematic association of exchange rate movements effects on labor market with ownership structure of Chinese manufacturing industries, we also assume that the elasticity of domestic price in product market to exchange rate movements is both proportional to import penetration (IP) and ownership structure of the firms (OWN), that is, $\eta^{d,e} \propto \delta_0 * ip + \delta_1 own$, with δ_0, δ_1 as proportionality factors, Equation (12) is written as,

$$\frac{\partial L}{\partial e}\frac{e}{L} = \frac{\bar{p}}{\alpha\bar{\mu}}\{\delta_0 * IP + \delta_1 OWN - \theta + (1 - \alpha - \beta)\}. \tag{13}$$

Combining Equations (9) and (13), the total differenced logarithm form of optimal labor demand can be expressed as,

$$\begin{aligned}\hat{L_D} = \kappa_0 + \kappa_1\hat{Y} + \{\kappa_2 IP + \kappa_3 OWN + \kappa_4\theta + \kappa_5(1 - \alpha - \beta)\}\hat{e} \\ + \kappa_6\hat{w} + \kappa_7\hat{r} + \kappa_8\hat{s},\end{aligned} \tag{14}$$

where for any variables ($\hat{Z}$) in the above equation $\hat{Z} = \Delta LnZ$, and Y is the total income generated both in domestic and foreign product market; $\kappa_0 - \kappa_8$ are coefficients for those variables. We need introduce labor supply equation to solve the equilibrium level of employment and wage in the labor market, by referring to

Klein *et al.* (2003), the labor supply for the specific firm (L_s) depends on the wage rate of the specific firm and average wage rate of other firm, that is,

$$L_s = \left(\frac{w}{W^{*\delta}}\right)^{\gamma}. \tag{15}$$

In Equation (15), W^* is the average wage rate of firms alternative to the specific firm F; δ is the cross-elasticity of labor supply between the specific firm F and firms alternative to firm F and γ is the elasticity of labor supply with respect to relative wage rates change. The total differential of logarithm of the labor supply equation is,

$$\hat{L_s} = \gamma\hat{w} - \gamma\delta\widehat{W^*}. \tag{16}$$

Combining Equations (14) and (16), the equilibrium level of employment and wage rate for the specific firm can be expressed as,

$$\begin{aligned}\hat{L} &= \vartheta_0 + \vartheta_1\hat{Y} + \{\vartheta_2 IP + \vartheta_3 OWN + \vartheta_4\theta + \vartheta_5(1-\alpha-\beta)\}\hat{e}\\ &\quad + \vartheta_6\widehat{W^*} + \vartheta_7\hat{r} + \vartheta_8\hat{s}, \qquad (17)\\ \hat{w} &= \varphi_0 + \varphi_1\hat{Y} + \{\varphi_2 IP + \varphi_3 OWN + \varphi_4\theta + \varphi_5(1-\alpha-\beta)\}\hat{e}\\ &\quad + \varphi_6\widehat{W^*} + \varphi_7\hat{r} + \varphi_8\hat{s}, \qquad (18)\end{aligned}$$

$\vartheta_0 - \vartheta_8$; $\varphi_0 - \varphi_8$ are coefficients for employment and wage equations, respectively.

2.2 Empirical Specification

Based on the theoretical background and framework in Section 2.1, we specify the dynamic estimation equations of employment and wage rates for manufacturing industries in the following form,

$$\begin{aligned}\hat{L}_{i,t} &= \chi_0 + \chi_1\hat{Y}_{i,t} + \chi_2 EXS_{i,t-1} + \chi_3 IMS_{i,t-1} + \chi_4 OWN_{i,t-1} + \chi_5 PRO_{i,t-1}\\ &\quad + (\chi_6 EXS_{i,t-1} + \chi_7 IMS_{i,t-1} + \chi_8 OWN_{i,t-1})\widehat{REER}_{i,t}\\ &\quad + \chi_9\widehat{W^*}_{i,t} + \chi_{10}\hat{L}_{i,t-1} + \upsilon_t + \epsilon_{i,t}, \qquad (19)\\ \hat{w}_{it} &= \phi_0 + \phi_1\hat{Y}_{it} + \phi_2 EXS_{i,t-1} + \phi_3 IMS_{i,t-1} + \phi_4 OWN_{i,t-1} + \phi_5 PRO_{i,t-1}\\ &\quad + (\phi_6 EXS_{i,t-2} + \phi_7 IMS_{i,t-2} + \phi_8 OWN_{i,t-2})\widehat{REER}_{it-1},\\ &\quad + \phi_9\widehat{W^*}_{i,t} + \phi_{10}\hat{L}_{i,t-1} + \pi_t + \varpi_{it}. \qquad (20)\end{aligned}$$

In the above equations of employment and wage rate, Y_{it} represents the total sales for the four-digit sector i in the year t; EXS denotes export openness at industry level measured as ratio of foreign sales to total sales.

IMS is the overall import penetration rate for different industrial sectors, which is measured as ratio of import value to total sales plus import value and minus foreign sales, due to restriction of data access, we cannot differentiate the value of import final products and the value of import input[2]; hence, the variable IMS in our study is proportional to import penetration rate plus import input rate, $IMS \propto \alpha_0 IP + \alpha_1(1 - \alpha - \beta)$, with α_0 and α_1 as proportionality factors, therefore, the interactive term of *IMS* and real exchange rate in Equations (19) and (20) investigates overall impacts of exchange rate change on the labor market though both import competition and import input channels.

OWN is the variable representing ownership structure measured as the shares of total assets for different ownership enterprises in the manufacturing industries, and *SOEs*, *PVT* and *FIEs* each represents the share of total assets for stated-owned enterprises, for private enterprises and for FIEs, respectively, in manufacturing industries, that is, $OWN = [SOEs, PVT, FIEs]$.

PRO denotes net profit margins of individual manufacturing industries measured as the ratio of net profit to total sales, which controls for the effects of domestic market competitive structure on labor market as presented in our theoretical framework in Section 2.1.

REER represents trade weighted *REER* for the specific industries disaggregated at three-digit level. As the related studies indicated, the response of employment and wage rates to an exchange rate shock not only depends on the current and the past exchange rate shocks but also depends on the expected exchange rate change in the future. Therefore, we here use the permanent component of real exchange rates in the estimation equation. To keep only the permanent component of real exchange rate changes, we apply the Butterworth time series filter[3] to remove the temporary component of real exchange rates, and the variable *REER* in our estimation equations at annual frequency is generated by the mean values of permanent component of real exchange rate at monthly frequency.

In order to investigate the impacts of exchange rate movements on labor market through different channels clearly, trade share and ownership structure variables are also controlled for individually both in wage and employment equations. To avoid the simultaneity problems for interactive terms in estimation equations, trade shares, profit margins and variables representing ownership structure are all lagged one

[2]According to the related research conducted by Campa and Goldberg (2001), Dekle (1998), Leung and Yuen (2007), Nucci and Pozzolo (2010); the import penetration rate and import input rate for industries are highly correlated variables in most cases and these two variables are not usually controlled simultaneously in the estimation equations.

[3]The decomposition of REER into permanent and cyclical components is conducted using STATA (Version 12.1) command "tsfilter bw", there are several other standard methods of decomposition time series into trend and cyclical components, such as the Beveridge–Nelson decomposition and HP filter, and the Beveridge–Nelson method require the data to be non-stationary and the HP filter requires the data to be stationary.

period in employment equation, and taking into account the possible endogenous problem between real wage rate change and real exchange rate change as indicated by Balassa–Samuelson effects, real exchange rate variable in wage equation is also lagged one period and the corresponding variables for trade share, ownership structure in interactive terms are lagged two periods.

W^* represents the average real wage rate of industries alternative to industry i, and the υ_t, π_t are time dummies in employment and wage equations respectively to control for other macroeconomics factors, such as the costs of non-labor inputs from domestic and foreign market. $\epsilon_{i,t}$, ϖ_{it} are error terms in the estimation equations.

3 Data, Summary Statistics and Model Identification

3.1 Data and summary statistics

We use industry level panel data covering 456 four-digit narrowly defined manufacturing industries over the time period of 2001 to 2009. These panel data are drawn from the Chinese industrial database provided by National Bureau of Statistics, China. The database provides over 65 financial variables for every four-digit industry, including total sales, foreign sales, total wage paid and employment, and net profits in sales. The panel dataset does not provide the import value for each industry. In order to access to the export and import values between China and its 51 bilateral trading partners corresponding to narrowly defined industries, we construct a concordance between HS (version) four-digit codes for 1,250 trade products and industry codes for 175 three-digit manufacturing industries in China.[4] Bilateral trade data disaggregated at a HS four-digit product level between China and 51 trading partners over the period of 1999–2009 are drawn from COMTRADE database of United Nations. The CPI index and nominal exchange rate for China and 51 trading partners are all drawn from International Financial Statistics, IMF.

Table 1 presents summary statistics for variables, the descriptive statistics show that comparing to private firms and FIEs, average employment size and total sales for SOEs aggregated at the narrowly defined industries are relatively smaller, while the average real wage rate for SOEs is higher than private enterprises but lower than FIEs across different percentiles. The average ratio of capital to labor inputs is substantially lower for private firms than for SOEs and FIEs; while the average net profit rate for SOEs is negative, which is also substantially lower than the profit rate of private enterprises and FIEs, but vary greatly across sectors as indicated by the larger standard deviation. Comparing SOEs and private enterprises, FIEs are highly export

[4]The concordance is constructed referring to the concordance between HS 96 codes and ISIC (Revision 4) codes and the classification codes (version 2002) for Chinese manufacturing industries.

Table 1. Summary statistics of Chinese manufacturing industries: 2001–2009.

Variables	Ownership	N	MEAN	Stand. Dev.	P25	P50	P75
Annual Average Employment (Unit:1,000 PERSON)	All	3893	139289.80	324297.2	23372	60891	147314
	SOEs	3710	21360.98	111400.3	974	3641	13557
	Private	3856	37781.46	90624.54	4540	14441.5	36488.5
	FIEs	3811	38369.72	112147.5	3303	12481	35302
Annual Average Real Wage (Unit:1,000 RMB)	All	3892	16.68	8.80	11.08	14.78	19.92
	SOEs	3535	16.21	11.01	9.16	13.35	20.04
	Private	3822	13.24	5.58	9.35	12.00	16.34
	FIEs	3741	22.48	33.93	14.11	19.06	25.75
Total Sales (Unit:1,000 RMB)	All	3893	5.49E+07	1.48E+08	5.51E+06	1.65E+07	4.60E+07
	SOEs	3710	6.40E+06	3.33E+07	1.09E+05	4.98E+05	2.39E+06
	Private	3856	1.39E+07	3.69E+07	1.10E+06	3.76E+06	1.14E+07
	FIEs	3811	1.67E+07	4.62E+07	1.19E+06	4.70E+06	1.40E+07
Ratio of Capital to Labor (Unit:1,000 RMB)	All	3892	95.30	89.07	48.39	70.32	108.97
	SOEs	3535	115.64	246.15	50.37	78.35	128.86
	Private	3822	64.30	84.79	35.16	50.99	75.47
	FIEs	3741	166.23	449.89	58.44	98.17	168.00
Net Profit Rate (Unit: Percentage of net profit to total sales)	All	3893	5.57	4.04	3.67	5.21	6.99
	SOEs	3704	−1.40	35.82	−2.42	0.69	4.18
	Private	3856	5.32	3.12	3.76	5.03	6.48
	FIEs	3811	6.09	5.81	3.21	5.39	8.39

(*Continued*)

Table 1. *(Continued)*

Variables	Ownership	N	MEAN	Stand. Dev.	P25	P50	P75
Export Openness (Unit: Ratio of foreign sales to total sales)	ALL	3892	0.21	0.21	0.06	0.14	0.33
	SOEs	3526	0.10	0.16	0.00	0.03	0.12
	Private	3821	0.13	0.16	0.02	0.06	0.18
	FIEs	3739	0.35	0.26	0.13	0.31	0.56
Import Penetration (Unit: Ratio of Import to total output plus import and minus export)	ALL	3893	0.18	0.20	0.02	0.11	0.25
REERs for three-digit Sectors (YEAR 2005 = 100)	ALL	3882	102.12	8.25	97.18	100.00	105.78

Source: The statistics in Table 1 is calculated by authors based on the dataset from National Bureau of Statistics, China and the Comtrade Database from United Nations.

oriented, and the average rate of export openness for FIEs is 0.35, while the average rates of export openness for SOEs and private firms range from 0.1 to 0.13 and are far below the corresponding statistics for FIEs in all different percentiles. The average import penetration rate across all three-digit manufacturing industries is 0.18.

Figure 1 presents the movements of RMB REERs for the selected 16 three-digit manufacturing industries of China at monthly frequency over the period of 1999 to 2011, and the real exchange rates for all specific industries are decomposed into permanent and cyclical components. Figure 1 clearly indicates that RMB real exchange rates have experienced significant fluctuations over the period of 2001

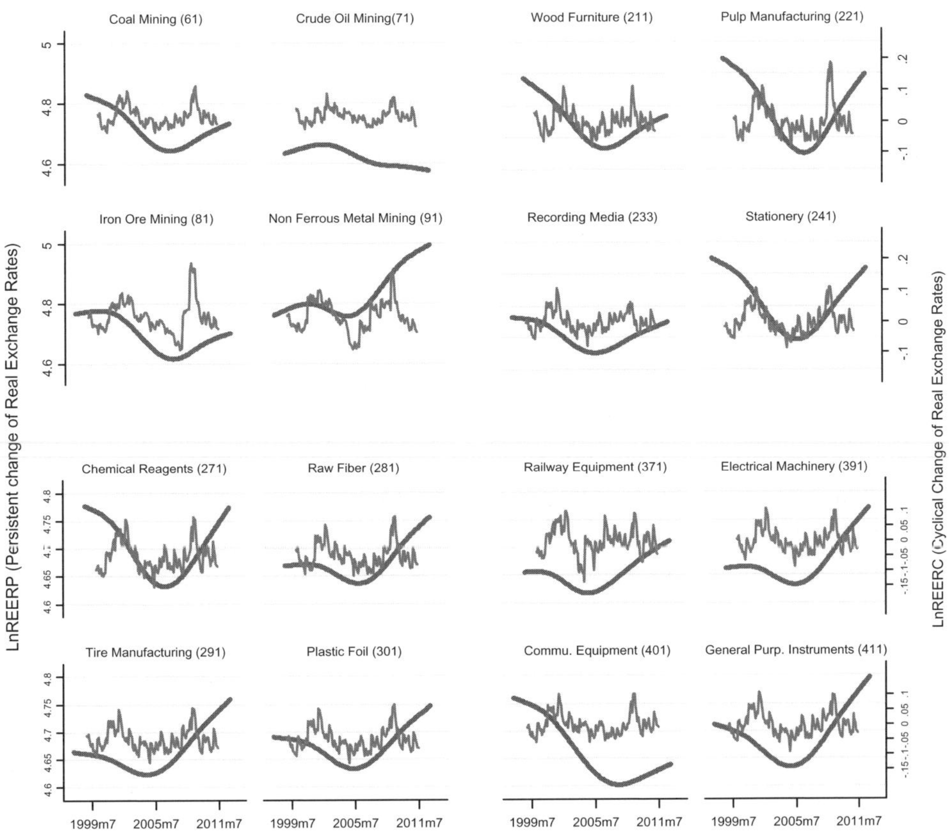

Figure 1. Monthly movements of RMB REER by industrial sectors (1999: 1–2011:6).

Notes: The smooth and thick lines in Figure 1 represent the permanent components of REER movements for different industrial sectors, while the vibrating and thin lines represent the cyclical components of real exchange rate movements; the codes for three-digit industrial sectors are in the parentheses.

to 2009, RMB real exchange rates for most sectors present consistent depreciation before the reform of exchange rate regime in July, 2005, and then demonstrate rapid real appreciation after 2005, while the magnitude of depreciation and appreciation varies significantly across sector over the period of 1999–2011. For example, the REER for crude oil mining shows consistent depreciation since 2001, and compared to other industries, the REER for communication equipment manufacturing does not show significant appreciation after the reform of exchange rate regime, which all highlight the importance of using industry specific real exchange rates instead of aggregated real exchange rate applying to all sectors. Figure 1 also shows that real exchange rate movements are mainly accounted by permanent changes and the variance of real exchange rate for 163 three-digit industries accounted by cyclical movements (temporary shocks) is only 11% on average.

3.2 Identification methods for wage and employment equations

To identify employment and wage equations specified in Section 3.1, it is not suitable to use OLS and fixed effect (FE) estimators because the endogenous variables in wage and employment equations are all potentially correlated with the error terms. The generalized moment method (GMM) and Panel IV (2SLS) FE estimators are frequently adopted measures to identify the dynamic panel data model and to control for the endogeneity problem.

To identify our dynamic employment equation appropriately, we use two-step system GMM estimators (Blundell and Bond, 1998), which provides more efficient instruments than the difference GMM estimators. Robust standard errors are reported to correct the downward bias as emphasized by Windmeijer (2005).[5] Wage equations are identified using both Panel IV (2SLS) FE estimators to control for endogeneity. As endogeneity tests of variables when applying the Panel IV-FE estimators, two variables (ΔLnY_{it} *and* ΔLnW_{it}^{*}) are set as endogenous variables both in the employment and wage equations. The lagged level and lagged difference endogenous variables and other exogenous variables are set as the instruments for those endogenous variables.

4 Empirical Results

The empirical specifications illustrated in Section 2.2 provide us a suitable framework for investigating the systematic links between the impacts of exchange

[5]The robust and two-step GMM system estimators for identifying employment equation are conducted using STATA (version 12.1) command "xtabond2", and the theoretical background and estimation details of system and difference GMM estimators in STATA are referring to Roodman (2009).

rate change on labor market with trade openness and ownership structure. In this section, we will present estimation results of those specifications and analyze factors influencing the pass-through effects of permanent exchange rate movements on labor market, and investigate the links between the effects of exchange rate changes on labor market with ownership structure of manufacturing industries.

4.1 Trade openness, ownership structure and the impacts of exchange rate movements on employment

The econometric results reported in Table 2 support the view that real exchange rate movements can have significant effect on net employment both through foreign sales channel and import penetration channel, and impacts of real exchange rate fluctuations on employment are also systematically associated with ownership structure change. In column 1 (Table 2), we investigate the effects of exchange rate variation on employment through export openness and import penetration channels respectively, the estimated coefficient for interactive variable ($\Delta LnREER_{it} * EXS_{it-1}$) measuring the effects of exchange rate change on employment through export openness is significant and negative at the 95% level, and the coefficient measuring the effects of exchange rate variation through overall import penetration ($\Delta LnREER_{it} * IMS_{it-1}$) is also significant and negative at the 90% level. Hence, an exchange rate appreciation (depreciation) will induce an employment contraction (expansion) both through foreign sales and import penetration channels, and the impact of exchange rate fluctuations on employment will increase with an increase in export openness and import penetration rate in the manufacturing industries. The above estimation results are somewhat at odds with the findings of some previous related studies (Campa and Goldberg, 2001 and Nucci and Pozzolo, 2010) that the effects of exchange rate change on employment through import input are always positive, this is because the import penetration ratio in our study measures the overall effects of exchange rate fluctuations both through import competition channel and through affecting the cost of import input. The reported estimation results also imply that the impacts on employment of exchange rate movements through import competition channel dominate those impacts on employment through affecting the cost of import input.

The estimation results for investigating the links between the effects of exchange rate change with ownership structure of manufacturing industries are reported in columns 2–7 in Table 2. The coefficient measuring the effects of exchange rate change with variation of SOEs share specified in column 2 ($\Delta LnREER_{it} * SOE_{it-1}$) is negative and insignificant after controlling for the impacts of exchange rate change through trade channels, while the coefficients for the same interactive term in columns 4 and 5 are both negative and significant if we only control for the effects of exchange rate change through export openness channel. The different

Table 2. Employment equations estimation (dependent variable: ΔLnL_{it}).

	1	2	3	4	5	6	7
ΔLnL_{it-1}	0.2901*	0.1846	0.3287**	0.1723	0.1494	0.2232	0.2075
	(0.123)	(0.130)	(0.125)	(0.133)	(0.121)	(0.130)	(0.127)
ΔLnY_{it}	0.4025***	0.4184***	0.3625***	0.4075***	0.3880***	0.4456***	0.4180***
	(0.094)	(0.095)	(0.092)	(0.082)	(0.085)	(0.098)	(0.104)
ΔLnW^*_{it}	0.1667	0.2041	0.1808	0.2191	0.2283*	0.1182	0.1271
	(0.121)	(0.126)	(0.111)	(0.121)	(0.112)	(0.106)	(0.113)
EXS_{it-1}	0.0453	0.0322	0.0325	0.036	0.0189		
	(0.026)	(0.026)	(0.026)	(0.025)	(0.024)		
IMS_{it-1}	0.022	0.0196	0.0114			−0.0186	−0.0144
	(0.021)	(0.025)	(0.017)			(0.016)	(0.016)
PRO_{it-1}	0.2668*	0.3457**	0.1988	0.3698*	0.2854*	0.3900***	0.3996***
	(0.131)	(0.129)	(0.120)	(0.145)	(0.138)	(0.103)	(0.101)
SOE_{it-1}		−0.1622***		−0.1539***	−0.2178***		
		(0.037)		(0.037)	(0.041)		
PVT_{it-1}			−0.0448		−0.0701		0.0243
			(0.035)		(0.036)		(0.038)
FIE_{it-1}						0.0926**	0.0979***
						(0.030)	(0.027)
$\Delta LnREER_{it} * EXS_{it-1}$	−0.6879**	−0.6836**	−0.8097***	−0.7266**	−0.8485**		
	(0.243)	(0.264)	(0.236)	(0.272)	(0.271)		
$\Delta LnREER_{it} * IMS_{it-1}$	−0.6189*	−0.3573	−0.6690*			−0.382	−0.4216
	(0.329)	(0.267)	(0.305)			(0.265)	(0.270)

$\Delta LnREER_{it} * SOE_{it-1}$		−0.382		−0.5495**	−0.4828**		
		(0.243)		(0.275)	(0.238)		
$\Delta LnREER_{it} * PVT_{it-1}$			0.1688		−0.0524		0.2629
			(0.256)		(0.269)		(0.193)
$\Delta LnREER_{it} * FIE_{it-1}$						−0.4736**	−0.4665**
						(0.225)	(0.218)
No.of Industries	456	456	456	456	456	452	452
Observations	2960	2836	2943	2836	2820	2895	2895
AR(2)_P	0.936	0.506	0.871	0.504	0.688	0.642	0.661
Sargan_P	0.930	0.978	0.939	0.982	0.984	0.810	0.797
Hansen J_P	0.564	0.372	0.526	0.350	0.430	0.736	0.716

Notes: The employment equations are all identified with two-step system GMM estimators (Blundell and Bond, 1998). LnL_{it-1}, LnY_{it} and LnW^*_{it} are set as endogenous variables based on the panel IV endogenous tests. The industry fixed effects and time dummies are all controlled in the above estimation equations. Robust standard errors are reported in parentheses to correct the downward bias of standard errors; ****, (**,*) indicates rejection of null hypothesis is significant at 1%, (5%, 10%).

significance for above estimation results is possibly because the effects of exchange rate changes through import penetration channel are mixed with effects of exchange rate changes with variation of SOEs shares. The coefficients measuring the effects of exchange rate change on employment with variation of FIEs share in columns 6 and 7 ($\Delta LnREER_{it} * FIE_{it-1}$) are also negative and significant at the 95% level. Due to the high correlation between FIE share and export share in Chinese manufacturing industries, the effects of exchange rate change through export openness channel are not controlled for in columns 6 and 7. The coefficients measuring the effects of exchange rate changes on employment with the variation of private enterprise share ($\Delta LnREER_{it} * PVT_{it-1}$) are all insignificant in different specifications in Table 2.

The above econometric results show that net employment for SOEs and FIEs is more responsive to exchange rate fluctuations than for private firms. Our empirical results do not support the commonly held belief that labor market of SOEs has higher rigidity and is less likely to adjust with the exchange rate shocks, while the input ratio of capital to labor for SOEs and FIEs is more capital intensive than for private enterprises as exhibited in Table 1, SOEs are less productive than private firms and have lower profit margins, and more likely to go bankrupt with the increased market competition; the trade dependence for FIEs is higher than private firms. All these facts imply SOEs and FIEs are potentially more responsive to real exchange rate shocks than private enterprises.

The coefficients for other controlled variables in our estimated equations of Table 2 also make sense. Changes in total sales (ΔLnY_{it}) and profit margins (PRO_{it-1}) both have positive and statistically significant effects on employment and the lagged dependent variables accounting for adjustment process of labor force are positive and significant in columns 1 and 3; similarly, coefficients for average real wage rate alternative to the specific industry (ΔLnW_{it}^{*}) are also positive but not significant in most specifications, which indicates that net employment for the specific industries potentially increase with an increases in average real wage rate of industries alternative to the specific industries, which fits well with the theoretical prediction. The variation of trade shares (EXS_{it-1}; IMS_{it-1}) has no significant effects on employment after we control for other variables in different specifications. An increase in SOEs share (SOE_{it-1}) has negative and statistically significant effects on employment in manufacturing industries, while an increase in FIEs share (FIE_{it-1}) has significant and positive effects on employment and changes in private enterprise share (PVT_{it-1}) have no significant effects on employment, which all imply that job loss due to restructuring of SOEs and job creation due to the fast inflows of FIEs both contribute significantly to changes in net employment. The Sargan statistics and Hansen J statistics for over identifying restrictions testing for the validity of instruments and the values of the test for absence of second order serial correlation of residuals all consistently show the validity of our specifications.

Based on the estimated coefficients for interactive variables in column 1 of Table 2 and average rates of export openness and import penetration, we can calculate the elasticity of employment to real exchange rate fluctuations. The estimation results indicate that, after taking into account the dynamic adjustment of labor demand, a 1% real appreciation (depreciation) of exchange rate will cause net employment in Chinese manufacturing industries drop (increase) 0.21% through foreign sales channel (export openness), while net employment will also drop (rise) about 0.16% through import penetration channel with a 1% real appreciation (depreciation); and the overall elasticity of net employment to RMB real exchange rate through trade channels is around 0.37 measured from our estimation results.[6]

As indicated by our theoretical framework in Section 2.1, the systematic links between the impacts of exchange rate changes and ownership structure, which possibly only reflects the different market power and input ratio of labor to capital for different ownership firms. In order to investigate the links between the impacts of exchange rate fluctuations on labor market with market structure and check the robustness of estimation results in Table 2, we use two new interactive variables, including interactions of real exchange rate change with both trade shares and market power index, and also interactions of real exchange rate change with both trade shares and ownership structure index, while the market power is positively correlated with profit margins of manufacturing industries and the impacts of exchange rate movements are negatively associated with market power of firms within an industry, so the two new interaction terms are specified to check the systematic links between impacts of exchange rate changes and market power

$$\Delta LnREER_{it} * EXS_{it-1} * (1 - PRO_{it-1}),$$
$$\Delta LnREER_{it} * IMS_{it-1} * (1 - PRO_{it-1}).$$

On the other hand, change in real exchange rate can have larger effects on SOEs and FIEs, which is possibly due to the ratio of capital to labor inputs for SOEs and FIEs being both more capital intensive than private enterprises. Compared to private enterprises, SOEs are less productive and have lower profit margins, while FIEs have higher trade shares. Hence, we also specify the following new interaction

[6]Based on the estimation coefficients in column 1 of Table 2, and taking into account the dynamic process of labor adjustment, the elasticity of employment to exchange rate movements through export openness channel is equal to $0.6879 * \left(\frac{\overline{EXS}_{it-1}}{1-0.2901}\right) = 0.21$, and the elasticity of employment to exchange rate movements through import penetration channel is equal to $0.6189 * \left(\frac{\overline{IMS}_{it-1}}{1-0.2901}\right) = 0.16$, where $\overline{EXS}_{it-1}$, $\overline{IMS}_{it-1}$ denote the average ratio of export openness and import penetration lagged one period for four-digit manufacturing industries, respectively.

terms in the new estimation equations to further check the robustness of empirical results in Table 2,

$$\Delta LnREER_{it} * EXS_{it-1} * SOE_{it-1},$$
$$\Delta LnREER_{it} * IMS_{it-1} * SOE_{it-1},$$
$$\Delta LnREER_{it} * EXS_{it-1} * (1 - PVT_{it-1}),$$
$$\Delta LnREER_{it} * IMS_{it-1} * (1 - PVT_{it-1}),$$
$$\Delta LnREER_{it} * EXS_{it-1} * FIE_{it-1},$$
$$\Delta LnREER_{it} * IMS_{it-1} * FIE_{it-1}.$$

All the above specifications are consistent with our theoretical framework and estimation results in Table 2, which indicate that the magnitude of the effects of a real appreciation on employment will increase with an increase in foreign sales rate, import penetration rate and shares of SOEs and FIEs, while the magnitude will decline with an increase in market power and share of private enterprises in manufacturing industries.

The coefficients for the above interaction terms specified in the new estimation equations are estimated and presented in Table 3, after controlling for other variables. The estimated coefficients for all interactive terms in the new specifications have the expected sign and are statistically significant and the estimation results in Table 3 also fit well with our theoretical predictions and are consistent with the empirical results reported in Table 2. The responsiveness of employment to exchange rate change depends on trade shares, market power and ownership structure simultaneously for Chinese manufacturing industries, and the implications of estimation results are opposite to the assumption that the job market for SOEs exhibits stronger rigidity and is less likely to be affected by real exchange rate movements.

4.2 Trade openness, ownership structure and the effects of exchange rate movements on wage rates

The estimation results for wage equation specified in Section 2.2 are reported in Table 4. The specifications for wage equation are all identified using IV/2SLS estimators. The coefficients for interaction terms measuring the effects of exchange rate change on wage rates through export openness and import penetration channels ($\Delta LnREER_{it-1} * EXS_{it-2}$; $\Delta LnREER_{it-1} * IMS_{it-2}$) are all negative and statistically significant in different specifications, which imply that the magnitude of the impacts on wage rates of exchange rate movements will increase significantly with a rise of foreign sales and import penetration rate. It is obvious that real exchange rate movements have similar impacts on wage rates as on employment for Chinese manufacturing industries. Based on the estimated coefficients for interactive terms

Table 3. Employment equations estimation: robustness check (dependent variable: ΔLnL_{it}).

	1	2	3	4	5	6	7
ΔLnL_{it-1}	0.2916**	0.2273**	0.2305**	0.2896**	0.2964**	0.2658**	0.2811**
	(0.124)	(0.109)	(0.113)	(0.117)	(0.122)	(0.103)	(0.106)
ΔLnY_{it}	0.4017***	0.4324***	0.4241***	0.4060***	0.3833***	0.4273***	0.4010***
	(0.094)	(0.081)	(0.087)	(0.094)	(0.089)	(0.096)	(0.099)
ΔLnW^*_{it}	0.1656	0.1619	0.1822	0.1503	0.1822	0.1428	0.158
	(0.120)	(0.119)	(0.120)	(0.122)	(0.123)	(0.110)	(0.106)
EXS_{it-1}	0.0459*	0.0573***	0.0583***	0.0635***	0.0667***	0.0283*	0.0294**
	(0.025)	(0.015)	(0.015)	(0.018)	(0.019)	(0.015)	(0.014)
IMS_{it-1}	0.0223	−0.0013	0.0007	−0.0051	−0.0002	−0.0127	−0.0083
	(0.021)	(0.014)	(0.014)	(0.015)	(0.015)	(0.014)	(0.014)
PRO_{it-1}	0.2670**	0.3888**	0.4067***	0.2866**	0.3541***	0.2958**	0.3285***
	(0.130)	(0.137)	(0.140)	(0.135)	(0.128)	(0.125)	(0.120)
SOE_{it-1}		−0.0790***	−0.0786***				
		(0.025)	(0.026)				
PVT_{it-1}				−0.0147	−0.0099		
				(0.020)	(0.021)		
FIE_{it-1}						0.0559**	0.0530**
						(0.021)	(0.021)
$\Delta LnREER_{it} * EXS_{it-1}$	−0.7037***						
$*(1 - PRO_{it-1})$	(0.252)						
$\Delta LnREER_{it} * IMS_{it-1}$	−0.7296**						
$*(1 - PRO_{it-1})$	(0.363)						

(Continued)

Table 3. (*Continued*)

	1	2	3	4	5	6	7
$\Delta LnREER_{it} * EXS_{it-1}$		−7.8174**					
$*SOE_{it-1}$		(3.273)					
$\Delta LnREER_{it} * IMS_{it-1}$			−3.084*				
$*SOE_{it-1}$			(1.772)				
$\Delta LnREER_{it} * EXS_{it-1}$				−1.1584***			
$*(1 - PVT_{it-1})$				(0.373)			
$\Delta LnREER_{it} * IMS_{it-1}$					−1.1094**		
$*(1 - PVT_{it-1})$					(0.430)		
$\Delta LnREER_{it} * EXS_{it-1}$						−1.1643**	
$*FIE_{it-1}$						(0.382)	
$\Delta LnREER_{it} * IMS_{it-1}$							−1.6341**
$*FIE_{it-1}$							(0.734)
No. of Industries	456	456	456	456	456	453	453
Observations	2960	2960	2960	2960	2960	2949	2949
AR2_P	0.941	0.927	0.920	0.845	0.925	0.718	0.709
Sargan_P	0.928	0.939	0.948	0.948	0.958	0.980	0.988
Hansen J_P	0.561	0.753	0.790	0.597	0.765	0.765	0.870

Notes: The employment equations are all identified with two-step system GMM estimators (Blundell and Bond, 1998). LnL_{it-1}, LnY_{it} and LnW^*_{it} are set as endogenous variables based on the panel IV endogenous tests. The industry fixed effects and time dummies are all controlled in the above estimation equations. Robust standard errors are computed below the coefficients to correct the downward bias of standard errors; ****, (**,*) indicates rejection of null hypothesis is significant at 1%, (5%, 10%).

Table 4. Wage equations estimation (dependent variable: ΔLnL_{it}).

	1	2	3	4	5	6
ΔLnL_{it-1}	−0.0462**	−0.0532**	−0.0447**	−0.0541**	−0.0605**	−0.0522**
	(0.017)	(0.018)	(0.017)	(0.019)	(0.019)	(0.019)
ΔLnP_{it}	0.0908***	0.1006***	0.0707**	0.0776**	0.0976***	0.0794**
	(0.027)	(0.028)	(0.027)	(0.029)	(0.029)	(0.029)
ΔLnW^*_{it}	0.4151***	0.4008***	0.4035***	0.4195***	0.4195***	0.3955***
	(0.088)	(0.088)	(0.095)	(0.094)	(0.088)	(0.095)
EXS_{it-1}	−0.0313	−0.0537	−0.0162	−0.0979	−0.0459	−0.0661
	(0.050)	(0.053)	(0.054)	(0.064)	(0.061)	(0.064)
IMS_{it-1}	0.0657	0.0545	0.0653	0.0996	0.0713	0.0839
	(0.059)	(0.060)	(0.062)	(0.062)	(0.059)	(0.062)
PRO_{it-1}	0.4293**	0.4400**	0.4508**	0.3833*	0.3728*	0.3475*
	(0.143)	(0.144)	(0.159)	(0.172)	(0.156)	(0.172)
SOE_{it-1}			0.069	0.037		0.0387
			(0.066)	(0.074)		(0.074)
PVT_{it-1}		−0.0648		−0.0596	−0.0423	−0.0674
		(0.054)		(0.058)	(0.054)	(0.058)
FIE_{it-1}				0.1132*	0.070	0.1044*
				(0.056)	(0.053)	(0.057)
$\Delta LnREER_{it-1} * EXS_{it-2}$	−0.5520***	−0.8186***	−0.5185***	−0.8721***		
	(0.182)	(0.212)	(0.183)	(0.220)		
$\Delta LnREER_{it-1} * IMS_{it-2}$	−0.3659*	−0.5489**	−0.4143		−0.4054*	−0.4047
	(0.192)	(0.201)	(0.216)		(0.193)	(0.211)

(Continued)

Table 4. (*Continued*)

	1	2	3	4	5	6
$\Delta LnREER_{it-1} * SOE_{it-2}$			0.0944	−0.0828		0.0102
			(0.236)	(0.235)		(0.256)
$\Delta LnREER_{it-1} * PVT_{it-2}$		0.6003**		0.3994*	0.4989**	0.4304**
		(0.209)		(0.203)	(0.189)	(0.192)
$\Delta LnREER_{it-1} * FIE_{it-2}$					−0.9556***	−0.9529***
					(0.197)	(0.207)
No. of Industries	452	451	447	441	446	441
Observations	2955	2937	2826	2767	2888	2767
Under Identification Test Klei.-P.rk LM statistics	234.69***	236.54***	204.41***	216.90***	244.19***	212.18***
Over Identification Test Hansen J(P.Value)	0.267	0.275	0.228	0.207	0.335	0.259
R-Squared	0.863	0.865	0.868	0.873	0.869	0.874
F_Value	949.61***	860.98***	818.50***	788.74***	848.04***	751.28***

Notes: The wage equations are identified with fixed effect/GMM2SLS estimators. ΔLnY_{it} and ΔLnW^*_{it} are set as endogenous variables based on the panel IV endogenous tests. The one and two term lagged level of endogenous variables and one term lagged and differenced endogenous variables are set as instruments for the differenced endogenous variables. The FE of industries and time dummies are all controlled in the wage estimation equations. Robust standard errors are computed below the coefficients to correct the, heteroscedasticity and autocorrelation of error terms; ****, (**,*) indicates rejection of null hypothesis is significant at 1%, (5%, 10%).

in column 1 of Table 4, we can derive that a 1% real appreciation (depreciation) will cause real wage rates to drop (increase) 0.12% through foreign sales channel, and also drop (rise) 0.07% through import penetration channel, and overall elasticity of wage rates to real exchange movements through trade shares is around 0.19%, which is relatively lower than the elasticity of employment to permanent real exchange rate change.[7]

The estimation results for interaction terms of real exchange rate with variables representing ownership structure also consistently show that the impacts on wage rates of real exchange rate change are associated with variation of ownership structures, the coefficients measuring the effects of real exchange rate with the variation of SOEs shares ($\Delta LnREER_{it-1} * SOE_{it-2}$) are all insignificant for different specifications, which suggests that the response of wage rates to real exchange rate changes is insensitive to variation of SOEs share in manufacturing industries, while the coefficients for interaction term of exchange rate change with the share of private enterprises ($\Delta LnREER_{it-1} * PVT_{it-2}$) are all positive and significant in different specifications, the estimation results in Table 4 indicate that the negative (positive) impacts on wage rate of a real appreciation (depreciation) will decrease with an increase in shares of private enterprises in manufacturing industries after controlling for other interaction terms, which also suggests that the magnitude of those impacts will decline with an increase in the share of private firms and average real wage rate for private firms are less likely to be affected by real exchange rate fluctuations. The coefficients investigating the links between the impacts of exchange rate change with variation of FIEs shares ($\Delta LnREER_{it-1} * FIE_{it-2}$) are all negative and statistically significant in different specifications, which also suggests that the response of real wage rates to exchange rate will increase with an increase in FIEs shares in manufacturing industries.

The above estimation results in Table 4 also make sense. Wage rates for FIEs and SOEs are more responsive to real exchange rate movements than the wage rates for private enterprises. As indicated in Section 2.1, industries with higher labor demand elasticity to wage rate could have smaller adjustment of wage and employment to exchange rate shocks, while industries with less elastic product demands have more responsive of wage and employment to exchange rate change, both the higher ratio of capital to labor input and lower price setting ability for SOEs indicate lower labor demand elasticity to wage and less elastic product demands, which also implies higher adjustment of labor market for SOEs to exchange rate shocks, and the higher

[7]Based on the estimated coefficients in column 1 of Table 4, the elasticity of average real wage rates to real exchange rate through foreign sales is measured as, $-0.552 * \overline{EXS}_{it-1}$, and the elasticity through import penetration channel is measured as, $-0.3659 * \overline{IMS}_{it-1}$, where $\overline{EXS}_{it-1}$ and $\overline{IMS}_{it-1}$ represent the average ratio of export openness and import penetration lagged one period, respectively.

trade dependence and higher ratio capital to labor inputs for FIEs suggest that the response of labor market for FIEs to exchange rate changes should also be larger than the labor market for private enterprises.

The coefficients for other controlled variables in wage equations also make sense; An increase in total sales and profit margins both has positively significant effects on real wage rate, and real wage rate is also positive associated with average real wage rates of industries alternative to the specific industry, which suggests there exists positively wage spillovers across different sectors. The variation of export openness and import penetration rate has no significant effects on real wage rate after controlling for other variables; the estimation results for variables representing ownership structures indicate that only the FIEs share changes have positive and significant effects on real wage rate in all specifications. The LM-statistics for under identification test and Hansen J statistics for over identification test all confirm the validity of instruments and the validity of our specifications in Table 4.

As in the previous cases, market competitive structure and ratio of capital to labor inputs also potentially affect the pass-through effects of exchange rate movements on wage rates, and our estimation results in Table 4 do not support the assumption that the wage rate for SOEs is less likely to be affected by exchange rate fluctuations possibly due to its higher rigidity of labor market, while systematic linkage of the effects of exchange rate movements with ownership structure is also possibly due to the systematic difference in profit margins and elasticity of labor demand to wage between different ownership enterprises. To investigate the linkage of the effects of exchange rate on wage rate with market power and to further check the consistency and robustness of estimation results in Table 4, we also specify new interaction terms of exchange rate with both trade shares and profit margins, and interaction terms of exchange rate with both trade shares and ownership index as specified in Section 4.1. The estimation results for different specifications with new interaction terms are reported in Table 5, the coefficients for interactive terms ($\Delta LnREER_{it-1} * EXS_{it-2} * (1 - PRO_{it-2})$; $\Delta LnREER_{it-1} * IMS_{it-2} * (1 - PRO_{it-2})$) in columns 1 and 2 of Table 5 are both negative and statistically significant, which indicates that the magnitude of the effects of exchange rate movements on wage rate through trade share channels will increase with a decrease in profit margins just as our theoretical framework predicted in Section 2.1, the coefficients for interactive terms of exchange rate with both trade shares and SOEs share ($\Delta LnREER_{it-1} * EXS_{it-2} * SOE_{it-2}$; $\Delta LnREER_{it-1} * IMS_{it-2} * SOE_{it-2}$) are all insignificant in Table 5 and consistent with the empirical results in Table 4, which all suggest that variation of SOEs shares is not significantly linked with the effects of exchange rate changes through trade channels, while the coefficients measuring the links between the impacts on wage rate of exchange rate change with the shares of FIEs ($\Delta LnREER_{it-1} * EXS_{it-2} * FIE_{it-2}$; $\Delta LnREER_{it-1} * IMS_{it-2} * FIE_{it-2}$) and one minus share of private enterprises

Table 5. Wage equations estimation: robustness check (dependent variable: ΔLnL_{it}).

	1	2	3	4	5	6	7
ΔLnL_{it-1}	−0.0463**	−0.0470**	−0.0475**	−0.0541**	−0.0559**	−0.0521*	−0.0544**
	(0.017)	(0.017)	(0.017)	(0.018)	(0.018)	(0.018)	(0.018)
ΔLnP_{it}	0.0908***	0.0772**	0.0757**	0.1045***	0.1080***	0.0830***	0.0979***
	(0.027)	(0.026)	(0.026)	(0.027)	(0.027)	(0.028)	(0.028)
ΔLnW^*_{it}	0.4151***	0.4349***	0.4330***	0.4273***	0.4293***	0.4162***	0.4309***
	(0.088)	(0.093)	(0.095)	(0.086)	(0.086)	(0.086)	(0.089)
EXS_{it-1}	−0.0312	−0.0097	−0.0075	−0.055	−0.0361	−0.0522	−0.0397
	(0.050)	(0.054)	(0.054)	(0.053)	(0.053)	(0.061)	(0.061)
IMS_{it-1}	0.065	0.0817	0.0797	0.0874	0.0509	0.0609	0.0427
	(0.059)	(0.061)	(0.061)	(0.059)	(0.060)	(0.059)	(0.059)
PRO_{it-1}	0.4290**	0.4494**	0.4533**	0.4374**	0.4348**	0.3726**	0.3653**
	(0.143)	(0.160)	(0.160)	(0.143)	(0.143)	(0.157)	(0.157)
SOE_{it-1}		0.0731	0.0696				
		(0.065)	(0.065)				
PVT_{it-1}				−0.0592	−0.0593		
				(0.053)	(0.053)		
FIE_{it-1}						0.0762	0.0745
						(0.053)	(0.053)
$\Delta LnREER_{it-1} * EXS_{it-2} * (1 - PRO_{it-2})$	−0.5705**						
	(0.190)						
$\Delta LnREER_{it-1} * IMS_{it-2} * (1 - PRO_{it-2})$	−0.3954*						
	(0.208)						

(*Continued*)

Table 5. (*Continued*)

	1	2	3	4	5	6	7
$\Delta LnREER_{it-1} * EXS_{it-2} * SOE_{it-2}$		2.0196					
		(2.391)					
$\Delta LnREER_{it-1} * IMS_{it-2} * SOE_{it-2}$			−0.5533				
			(0.897)				
$\Delta LnREER_{it-1} * EXS_{it-2} * (1 - PVT_{it-2})$				−0.9426***			
				(0.255)			
$\Delta LnREER_{it-1} * IMS_{it-2} * (1 - PVT_{it-2})$					−0.6442**		
					(0.256)		
$\Delta LnREER_{it-1} * EXS_{it-2} * FIE_{it-2}$						−1.3418**	
						(0.525)	
$\Delta LnREER_{it-1} * IMS_{it-2} * FIE_{it-2}$						−1.0694***	−2.0265***
						(0.331)	(0.500)
No.of Industries	452	447	447	451	451	449	449
Observations	2955	2826	2826	2937	2937	2927	2927
Under Identification Test Klei.-P.rk LM statistics	234.21***	211.70***	212.92***	244.39***	240.87***	245.03***	247.69***
Hansen J (P_Value)	0.267	0.215	0.226	0.279	0.403	0.255	0.311
R-Squared	0.863	0.868	0.868	0.865	0.864	0.866	0.866
*F*_Value	949.61	923.63	927.28	961.79	958.66	910.06	969.30

Notes: The wage equations are identified with fixed effects GMM2SLS estimators. ΔLnY_{it} and ΔLnW^*_{it} are set as endogenous variables based on the panel IV endogenous tests. The one and two term lagged level of endogenous variables and one term lagged and differenced endogenous variables are set as instruments for the differenced endogenous variables. The fixed effect of industries and time dummies are all controlled in the wage estimation equations. Robust standard errors are computed below the coefficients to correct the, heteroscedasticity and autocorrelation of error terms; ****, (**,*) indicates rejection of null hypothesis is significant at 1%, (5%, 10%).

$(\Delta LnREER_{it-1}*EXS_{it-2}*(1 - PVT_{it-2})$; $\Delta LnREER_{it-1}*IMS_{it-2}*(1 - PVT_{it-2}))$ are all negative and statistically significant in columns 4 to 7 of Table 5, which shows that the impacts of exchange rate movements on wage rates are systematically linked with the employment share of FIEs and private enterprises, which are consistent with estimation results in Table 4.

5 Conclusion

This study investigates the impacts on both employment and wage rates of real exchange rate movements in China, and highlights the links between the impacts on labor market of exchange rate fluctuations and ownership structure of Chinese manufacturing industries. Using a representative sample covering 456 narrowly defined four-digit manufacturing industries over the period of 2001 to 2009, we find that impacts change on labor market of exchange rate movements are systematically associated with ownership structure of Chinese manufacturing industries. The labor market behavior of SOEs and FIEs is more responsive to exchange rate movements than is true for private enterprises. This is contrary to the common belief that the less export oriented and less market-based SOEs are not responsive to real exchange rate fluctuations than private enterprises. It appears that FIEs are more likely to adjust wage and employment levels to counteract negative impacts of exchange rate appreciations on their profit margins, while private enterprises tend to adjust their price and profit margins to keep a relatively stable labor market. SOEs are more prone to be driven out of the market with a real appreciation.

We find that RMB real exchange rate movements have relatively large effects both on wage rates and net employment. A 10% real appreciation in the RMB real exchange rate will cause net employment drop of about 3.7%, and real wage rates will also decline about 1.9%, after taking in the dynamic adjustment of employment and controlling for other factors. In contrast to existing studies that stress the different impacts of exchange rate movements on labor market through foreign sales and import input channels, we stress that a real appreciation (depreciation) both have negative (positive) effects on labor market through foreign sales and overall import penetration channels, which implies that the impacts of exchange rate movements through import competition channel dominate the impacts of exchange rate movements through affecting cost of import inputs. Our estimation results also indicate that impacts of RMB real exchange rate movements on wage rates and employment are both systematically associated with export openness, overall import penetration and ownership structure of Chinese manufacturing industries.

References

Alexandre, F., P. Bacao, J. Cerejeira, and M. Portela (2010), Employment, Exchange Rate and Labor Market Rigidity, *IZA Discussion Paper No.4891*. Available from: http://ftp.iza.org/dp4891.pdf.

Blundell, R. and S. Bond (1998), Initial Conditions and Moment Restrictions in Dynamic Panel Data Models, *Journal of Econometrics*, 87, 115–143.

Branson, W. and J. Love (1988), United States Manufacturing and the Real Exchange Rate, in Marston, R. (Ed)., *Misalignment of Exchange Rates: Effects on Trade and Industry*, Chicago, Illinois: University of Chicago Press.

Buckley, P., C. Wang, and C. Jeremy (2007), The Impact of Foreign Ownership, Local Ownership and Industry Characteristics on Spillover Benefits from Foreign Direct Investment in China, International Business Review, 16(2), 142–158.

Burgess, S.M. and M.M. Knetter (1998), An International Comparison of Employment Adjustment to Exchange Rate Fluctuations, *Review of International Economics*, 6(1), 151–163.

Campa, J. and L. Goldberg (1995), Investment, Exchange Rates and External Exposure, *Journal of International Economics*, 38, 297–320.

Campa, J. and L. Goldberg (1999), Investment, Pass-Through and Exchange Rates: A Cross-Country Comparison, *International Economic Review*, 40(2), 287–314.

Campa, J. and L. Goldberg (2001), Employment Versus Wage Adjustment and the U.S. Dollar, *Review of Economics and Statistics*, 83(3), 477–489.

Chen, R. and M. Dao (2011), The Real Exchange Rate and Employment in China, *IMF Working Paper WP/11/148*. https://www.imf.org/external/pubs/ft/wp/2011/wp11148.pdf.

Dekle, R. (1998), The Yen and Japanese Manufacturing Employment, *Journal of International Money Finance*, 17, 785–801.

Goldberg, L. (2004), Industry Specific Real Exchange Rate for the United States, *Economic Policy Review*, 10(1), 1–16.

Goldberg, L. and J. Tracy (2001), Exchange Rates and Wages, *NBER Working Paper w8137*. Available from: http://www.nber.org/papers/w8137.

Hale, G. and C. Long (2008), Did Foreign Direct Investment Put an Upward Pressure on Wages in China, *Federal Reserve Bank of San Francisco Working Paper Series 2006-25*.

Hua, P. (2007), Real Exchange Rate and Manufacturing Employment in China, *China Economic Review*, 18, 335–353.

Klein, M.W., S. Schuh, and R.K. Triest (2003), Job creation, Job destruction and the Real Exchange Rate, *Journal of International Economics*, 59, 239–265.

Leung, D. and T. Yuen (2007), Labour Market Adjustments to Exchange Rate Fluctuations: Evidence from Canadian Manufacturing Industries, *Open Economies Review*, 18, 177–189.

McKinnon, R. (2005), Exchange Rate or Wage Changes in International Adjustment? Japan and China versus United States. *ZEW-Centre for European Economic Research, Discussion Paper No.05-064*. Available from: http://www-siepr.stanford.edu/papers/pdf/04-21.pdf.

McKinnon, R. and G. Schnabl (2006), China's Exchange Rate and International Adjustment in Wages, Prices and Interest Rates: Japan De'ja' *Vu*? *CESifo Economic Studies*, 52, 267–303.

Nucci, F. and A.F. Pozzolo (2010), The Exchange Rate, Employment and Hours: What Firm Level Data Say? *Journal of International Economics*, 82, 112–123.

Revenga, A. (1992), Exporting jobs? The Impact of Import Competition on Employment and Wages in U.S. Manufacturing, *Quarterly Journal of Economics* 107(1), 255–284.

Roodman, D. (2009), How to do xtabond2: An Introduction to Difference and System GMM in Stata. 2009, *The Stata Journal*, 9(1), 86–136.

Windmeijer, F. (2005), A Finite Sample Correction for the Variance of Linear Efficient Two-Step GMM Estimators, *Journal of Econometrics*, 126, 25–51.

Appendix

Referring to Goldberg (2004), the trade weighted and industry specific real exchange rate measured at monthly frequency for RMB is defined as

$$REER_{im} = \sum_{j=1}^{k} \omega^{i}_{jt} RER_{jm},$$

where the $REER_{im}$ is the trade weighted REER for industry i and at the month m, RER_{jm} represents the bilateral real exchange rate between China and its trade partner j at the month m; and the overall trade weight for the specific industry j at year t, which corresponds to the month m, is expressed as

$$\omega^{i}_{jt} = 0.54 * \frac{\sum_{c=t-2}^{t-1} ex^{i}_{jc}}{\sum_{j=1}^{k}\sum_{c=t-2}^{t-1} ex^{i}_{jc}} + 0.46\frac{\sum_{c=t-2}^{t-1} im^{i}_{jc}}{\sum_{j=1}^{k}\sum_{c=t-2}^{t-1} im^{i}_{jc}},$$

where ex^{i}_{jc} represent value of export from China to its trade partner j in the specific sector i at the year c; and im^{i}_{jc} represent the value of import by China from its trade partner j in the specific sector i at the year c. To deal with the simultaneity bias between bilateral real exchange rate movements and values of bilateral trade, we use the average values of export and import lagged one and two years measure the trade weight, while the export share of total trade for China, over the period of 1997 to 2010 is 0.54, and the import share of total trade is 0.46, and the number of trade partners for China $k = 51$, and the trade partners includes,

Austria, Australian, Belgium, Brazil, Canada, Chile, Chinese Taipei, Denmark, Egypt, Finland, France , Germany, Greece, Hong Kong, Hungary, India, Indonesia Iran, Ireland, Israel, Italy, Japan, Korea, Macro, Malaysia, Mexico, Mongolia, Morocco, Netherland, New Zealand, Norway, Pakistan, Philippines, Poland, Portugal, Romania, Russia Federation, Saudi Arab, Singapore, South Africa, Spain,

Sweden, Switzerland, Thailand, Turkey, United Arab Emirates, United Kingdom, Ukraine, United States, Venezuela, Vietnam.

The total value of export from China to the above mentioned 51 trade partners overtakes 90% of total export of China over the period of 1997 to 2010, and the total value of import by China from the 51 trade partners is over 85% of total import of China during the same periods.

Chapter 10

Labor Migration and Market Segmentation in China

Jin Song

*Department of Economic Development,
Institute of World Economics and Politics, Chinese
Academy of Social Sciences (CASS), Beijing, China
songjin511@hotmail.com*

Abstract: Rural to urban labor migration is the one of the key issues in China's urbanization and rapid developing process. It contributes to 20% of GDP growth in China, but also has largely suffered from severe market segmentation generated by Chinese hukou registration system. The system marks each individual's agricultural or non-agricultural origin, and marks their hometown which identifies migrant workers from their local resident counterpart at destination. Migrant workers consequently have to face the discriminated wage income, unequal job opportunity and limited access to social security and public service. The results of these influences are twisted migration pattern, low efficient job matching, and sacrifice of economic growth rate. Central and local governments applied a series of reforms in hukou registration and migrant population management. These efforts bring noticeable changes to Chinese labor market and influence migration behavior. The labor market has shown hierarchy feature across administrative levels and strengthened market segmentation across provinces. The recently adopted resident certificate system rewards stable migrants with more public service and social security. As a result, migration in recent years has shown preference on medium sized cities, moving within province, and migrants have incentive to stay stably in one destination. Management policy for migrant workers will consequently be changed in future. Flexibility and security are the two most important features of a good labor market, especially in face of China's "new normal" development stage.

Hukou system reform is called to be deepened. Meanwhile, it is suggested that standardized basic public services package should be designed and guaranteed by central government. Higher level of financing arrangement is also crucial.

1 Introduction

Migration scale from rural to urban area in China has reached up to 274 million in 2014. Chinese economic growth has largely benefited from this labor migration. For the economy as a whole, migration enables matching more assets to lowly asset-armed labor which definitely brings higher growth efficiency. On a micro-level, it increases income of the migrant workers who are mainly low-skilled workers, improves their living quality, decreases the occurrence of poverty and reduces income inequality. In the past 30 years, labor migration contributed to more than 20% of GDP growth in China (Yan and Li, 2007). However, at the same time, labor migration in China has suffered from severe market segmentation problem. The institution that causes the segmentation is called Chinese Hukou Registration System ("Hukou system" hereafter). Hukou system is the most distinguishing institutional feature of Chinese labor market.

Hukou system has been set up in China since the middle of 1950s. The initial purpose of the system was to register population and complete related statistics which is very important in a planned economy. The statistical system played as the supporting tool of government's management policy then in resource allocation. Urban workers were assigned rationed supporting resources such as food, coal, clothing etc. from their hukou registration place, while rural residents earned their living through public farming activities in the hukou registered "production team".[1] Population migration was strictly controlled in those days for management needs. In the absence of commodity market, free migration was not possible. From 1949 to 1985, the average migration rate from rural to urban area was 0.24% in China (Zhao, 2000). Since economic reform and opening up in the beginning of 1980s, economic development in coastal areas created a large number of job opportunities. At the same time, the implementation of rural household contract responsibility system released rural labor from farm land. Rural workers flew into townships nearby for paid work although their supporting resource had to be "self-managed". In the following years, employment induced migration from rural to urban and from central and western regions to eastern region increased sharply. The setting up of product market for food, clothing, and others also enabled migration. In 1989, migrants from rural areas were 30 million while in 1993 that scale reached up to 62 million. However, hukou

[1] It was a management unit mainly based on location of the residents.

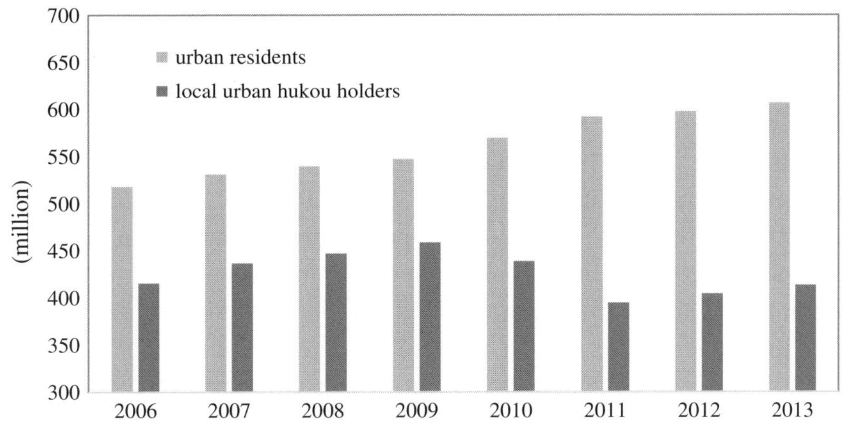

Figure 1. Trend of urban resident population and local urban Hukou holders.
Source: NBS, China Population and Employment Statistics Yearbook, various years.

conversion was not opened simultaneously with relaxing of migration restriction. Except for limited cases, most of migrants at this stage could not convert their hukou from hometown to destination. The scale of hukou registered population becomes hugely different from that of real residents. In year 2000, 31% of total urban residents are migrant population without hukou. In 2010, the percentage increased to 42%. Nowadays, in certain coastal cities, the original residents could take only a small share of real population. Figure 1 shows the statistics of urban resident and local urban hukou holders. The scale of migrants without having hukou registered to their current location is increasing.

However, the existence of large scale non-hukou migration does not mean hukou system is of no use in the labor market now. Although migration is allowed without hukou conversion, employment, social welfare, public service (including education, housing, medical service), etc. are all influenced by hukou status. Studies have shown that the influences restrict migration scale, restrain the migrant workers' wage and labor resource reallocation through migration is twisted. The twist sacrifices economic development efficiency. Henderson (2000) and Au and Henderson (2006) found that with hukou's limitation on migration, most of the cities in China have not reached its optimal scale. It causes the loss of GDP growth. If the scale of cities which are under 50% of its optimal scale can reach up to the optimum, labor productivity can increase by 40%. Yang and Chen (2000) pointed out that hukou system and labor market protection policy restricts economic development and does not really help the expansion of local residents' employment. Whalley and Zhang (2007) analyzed hukou's impact on income disparity. It is clear that labor restriction through hukou system plays a role in generating income disparity. The affect is significant with difference in labor efficiency and urban house price controlled. Chen and Lu (2008) argued that hukou system and other institutional constraints were used by cities to control rural to urban migration and limit wage of migrants. Poncet (2006) and Bao *et al.* (2009) built theoretical model and proved that hukou system significantly constrains labor migration. They indicated hukou restriction degree by variables, for example, the share of non-hukou resident to total population. It is discovered that, with releasing of hukou restriction, the scale and structure of migration will both change. DRC (2010) examined hukou's impact on the availability of public service. They measured gap of housing subsidy that government provides to urban residents and migrants and found that limited public service provided to migrant workers decreased the government's burden, but also restricted consumption of migrants and consequently lowered down the expansion of consumption and economic growth of the city. Sun *et al.* (2011) summarized the hukou reforms that took place in 16 provinces from 1998 to 2006 and compared eight of the provinces using DID method to detect the impact of the reform on rural labor migration. The paper examined total migration scale, migration scale to large and medium cities, migration length and others, and found that hukou reform does not have significant influence on short-term migration and that it plays a limited role in guiding rural to urban migration. The hukou reform in general did not help in removing market segmentation.

This chapter would like to review hukou-based labor market segmentation, and discuss the latest market change brought by hukou reform practices. The parts of this chapter are arranged as the following. The second part of this chapter describes hukou system's impact on the labor market and the several forms of market segmentation caused by hukou system. The third part analyzes the most important practices in hukou reform in the recent years and the consequence of the reforms on market segmentation. The fourth part summarizes the chapter and provides policy recommendation based on the findings.

2 Description of Hukou-Based Labor Market Segmentation

Chinese residents usually receive hukou identities at birth in terms of hukou status of their parents. Either father or mother's hukou identities can be chosen to follow. A hukou identity contains two dimensions of information. One is regarding hukou's property. That is to say, a hukou is agricultural or non-agricultural (usually being called rural or urban hukou). The other dimension is hukou's location which indicates where the individual is registered to. The location would be as detailed as the housing number of a location. With these two dimensions of information given, workers in a labor market could be easily identified as local urban/ local rural/ migrate urban/ migrate rural hukou status. For example, a local rural hukou status means the worker is from a rural area of the current prefecture he or she stays in;[2] while, a migrant urban hukou means the worker is from an urban area of other prefectures. All of local rural, migrant urban and migrant rural hukou holders are migrant workers from outside of the current labor market. According to Census 2000 and Mini Census 2005, hukou distribution of workers in the market is like the following.

Hukou status' impact on employment of migrant workers can be summarized into three aspects — wage, job opportunity and access to social security. The three aspects are also the three areas that labor market segmentation presents most.

Wage discrimination was proved to be one of the biggest pain that migrant workers suffered from the end of 1990 to around 2010. Yang and Chen (2000) and Meng and Zhang (2001) both argued that migrant workers did not share same income determination mechanism with their local resident counterpart. Hukou category and ownership of work unit were the two most important factors in wage determination. Migrant workers, unfortunately, have "bad" hukou label (which means non-local urban) and are very unlikely to get employed in state owned enterprises ("SOE" hereafter), government and party related agencies, etc. which usually offer more stable and higher payment. The discrimination that migrant workers suffered was very significant. Zhang and Meng (2007) studied the variation in income gap between migrant workers and urban residents and found that the gap has been enlarging. The main reason is that education return of rural migrant workers is decreasing. After years of residence in destination, migrant workers accumulate more working experience. Their wage generally converges to their urban counterpart, but the convergence in lower educated group is faster than in higher educated group. The

Table 1. Distribution of samples, by Hukou categories.

Proportion (%)	2005	2010
Local Urban	62.08	52.68
Local Rural	17.44	23.19
Migrate Urban	4.06	6.5
Migrate Rural	16.18	17.62
Total	100	100

Source: Calculated by author using 2000 Census Data and 2005 Mini Census micro data.

[2]Migration distance varies in different historical periods. In 1950s, moving from village to nearby township was not allowed and counted as migration. With rapid development of Chinese economy in recent decades, these years, prefecture is the lowest level administrative jurisdiction that the economy is uniformly managed and labor market is integrated.

Table 2. Migrant scale from 2010 to 2014.

	2010	2011	2012	2013	2014
Rural migrant scale	242	253	263	269	274
Increase from last year	12.45	10.55	9.8	6.33	5.01

Source: NBS, National Rural Migrant Worker Monitoring Report, 2011–2015.

finding partly reveals the new trend in migrant workers' wage determination in recent years. Wage of low skilled workers increased rapidly since 2007 in China. According to NBS, real wage growth of rural migrant workers was averagely 17.1% from 2007 to 2012. Two main factors play key roles in this growth. Firstly, Chinese economy has passed the Lewis Turning Point in around 2010 (Cai and Du, 2011). Table 2 shows the migrant scale from 2010 to 2014. Clearly, the increase of migrant scale is slowing down significantly. The era of unlimited labor supply from rural area is finished. Rapid wage increase of migrant workers is caused by changed supply demand matching situation. Secondly, minimum wage policy has been applied in China and the standard of minimum wage was largely increased. The policy was firstly set up in 2004. The primary target of the policy was to protect low income workers. In the past 10 years, the minimum wage of different places increased sharply. Researchers criticized that increasing minimum wage has been used by the governors as a tool for showing their care to residents' livelihood. Take Beijing as an example, the minimum wage increased from 495 in 2004 to 1720 in 2015. The average growth rate is 12% annually. The high standard of minimum wage leaves limited room for wage discrimination to migrant workers. As migrant workers are the ones more likely to be influenced by the increase of minimum wage, the shrinking of gap between migrant workers and local residents is significant. In 2011, the average wage of migrant workers was 43% lower than urban residents (the World Bank, 2013). However, CULS (2001, 2010) shows that, with individual characteristics controlled, wage discrimination that migrant workers suffer has decreased to 13%. If taking job characteristics into account, the discrimination has disappeared already (Giles *et al.*, 2012).

Job opportunity is another area that hukou status influences on employment, especially during 1980s–1990s. This kind of influence is a clear signal of government intervention in the labor market and the reason for intervention is the protection of the government from local workers. From 1980s, with the inflow of large scale rural workers, city governments of the destinations published a number of local regulations to restrict employers from hiring migrant workers in specific occupations and to escape migrants' crowding out local workers and guarantee local workers' privilege in employment. Taking Hebei as an example, in 1998, Labor Department of Hebei government issued a notification and clearly listed the positions that were permitted/restricted to recruit rural migrants in every industry. According to the notification, the positions that were open to rural migrants include lathe operator, manual worker, electrician, scrubber and other about 400 categories in spinning, chemical, construction and other industries. All of the positions concentrated in dirty, heavy and dangerous work while the safe, decent and well-paid positions were all forbidden to rural migrants. Such regulations obviously formed grievous obstacles in occupation access to migrant workers and restrained rural migrants' job opportunity. Wang (2005) divided jobs by ownership of the working units and occupation and found that 59% of the wage gap between migrant workers and local urban residents is caused by difference in occupation distribution. In 2004, the State Council published "The Notice on Further Improve the Employment Environment of Rural Migrant Workers". The very first statement was to ask the clearing and eliminating of the discriminatory rules and occupation restrictions against rural migrants. The institutional restriction was gradually released in the middle of first decades of 2000s. Market power plays more role in labor occupation matching.

However, central government's announcement on abolishing hukou-based occupation restriction does not mean migrants have full access to all occupations now. Table 2 compares workers' possibility of getting white collar occupation by hukou category in 2000 and 2005. Generally speaking, with native urban residents as reference group, rural migrants, especially the ones from other rural areas, are significantly less likely to get good occupation. Migrants from urban area of other places are better than rural migrants but still not as good as their native urban resident counterpart. The situation is better in 2005 than 2000. Hukou's impact on occupation accessing in both observation time is notable. Several reasons exist here. Firstly, destination governments have strong incentive in protecting employment of local residents. All kinds of informal regulation on promoting employment of local residents do exist. For example, hukou management regulation published by Beijing government announced that, private enterprise owners who do not have but want to apply for Beijing hukou have to satisfy the criterion of having employed more than 100 Beijing residents for more than three years, or having employed Beijing residents as more than 90% of total employees for more than three years. These kind of policies obviously affect job opportunity of local and migrant workers. Secondly, hukou status clearly indicates workers' origin. Discrimination against rural workers and outsiders plays an important role in job matching. Thirdly, although political restriction on occupation access through hukou is called to stop, restriction of access to social security of the migrant workers (which will be discussed soon in the following part) is still strictly adopted by the government. That affects workers' stability in destination and will consequently lower down employers' expectation and their recruitment. Song and Li (2014) examined occupation distribution of

Table 3. Occupations distribution and Hukou's impact.

	2000		2005	
Proportion (%)	**Share of having white collar occupation (%)**	**Hukou status' influence on having white collar occupation**	**Share of having white collar occupation (%)**	**Hukou status' influence on having white collar occupation**
Local urban	44.4		46.3	
Local rural	11.6	−0.12**	16.5	−0.07**
		(−31.31)		(−33.90)
Migrate urban	34.1	−0.08**	40.6	−0.06**
		(−13.32)		(−20.19)
Migrate rural	6.1	−0.20**	8.2	−0.18**
		(−42.60)		(−69.25)
Total	32.1		35.7	

Source: Calculated by author using 2005 Mini Census Data.
Note: (1) The second and fourth columns are the statistics of occupation distribution, while the third and fifth columns are the regression result of hukou status dummy variables' influence on occupation determination. Both of the results are calculated with weight applied; (2) Hukou's impact in the third and fifth columns is estimated using probit model with local urban hukou holder as reference group and individual characteristics controlled. The characteristics include gender, age group, education level, marriage status and minority status; (3) Numbers in the parentheses are z-value of the estimators. *refers to significant at 5% statistic level and **refers to significant at 1% statistic level.

migrant workers who have got their hukou converted to destination and found that with individual characteristics controlled, when migrant workers are entitled to local urban hukou, their inferiority in occupation access goes away.

More and more significantly, difference in access to social security and public service becomes the most influential impact that hukou has on migrant workers. The enrollment of social insurance in China is usually through employment. Social security include pension, medical insurance, unemployment insurance, work caused injury insurance, maternal insurance and housing public fund which are usually called "five insurances and one fund". Individual workers contribute certain share of their wage earning to the social insurance they enroll, and the work unit contributes a corresponding scale which is defined by each insurance. For urban workers' pension scheme, as an example, workers contribute 8% of his/her monthly wage, while their work unit contributes funding scaled 12% of the monthly wage. The contribution is all managed by government in a funding pool and the entitlement will be assigned when cases apply. Deng and Gustafsson (2007) examined micro data and proved that hukou status brings difference in access to social welfare, pension and others. Social security schemes open to migrant workers are different from that to local hukou registered workers. The design of the insurances is not suitable for the migrant workers. Till now, migrant workers' enrollment rate to social insurances is very low.

Regarding pension, the biggest problem in current scheme design for migrants was the poor portability of contribution and benefits. Workers had to contribute to a scheme continuously for a large number of years and be entitled finally for the benefit at the fixed place. Without contribution to one place being long enough, the workers could not get any benefit there from previous contribution. Once migrants moved to other places, their private contribution could be taken away with certain application procedure and very limited interest rate. The contribution of their work unit could not be moved at all. In 2009, Ministry of Human Resources and Social Securities of China announced the "Interim Regulation Regarding Pension Transfer and Connection for Urban Enterprise Workers". It specified the procedure of workers' transferring their pension contribution and benefit. The policy also required enterprises' pension contribution for workers to be transferred when workers migrate. Theoretically, the institutional barriers for workers' participating pension scheme has been removed. However, till 2014, pension participation rate of rural migrant workers was still as low as 16.7%. There are two main reasons hidden behind for the low participation rate. On the employer side, helping these migrant workers to participate in pension insurance only increases their labor cost. Employers tend to avoid pension contribution by not signing formal contract with migrant workers. In 2015, the share of signing contract for migrant workers was only 36.2%. A large number of migrant workers are not legally protected consequently. On the employee side, as migrant workers are usually with high mobility and low income level, their subjective discount rate of income is very low. They prefer to receive "cash" instead of pension beneficiary. In a very common case, the workers and employers negotiate not to participate in pension insurance at all. Both sides save pension contribution expenditure. Most of the migrants enroll the resident integrated pension insurance scheme in their rural hometown instead.

The problem in public service provision is very similar to this. Destination government has concern for public service induced migration and has financial constraint in providing public service to migrants. Good education is not open to non-hukou residents. College entrance examination is not open to migrant children. With education examination being largely different across provinces, the only choice for migrants is to take high school in hometown and have entrance examination there. Migrant population are not protected by destination government's housing guarantee programs. In 2013, only 10% of migrant owned housing in urban area, while that of their urban counterparts was 90% (World Bank, 2014). Social assistance such as minimum living guarantee program ("Dibao" program in China) is not open to migrants.

Regarding medical insurance, although migrant workers are entitled to medical insurance participation, employers are very likely to refuse providing rural migrant workers the insurance enrollment to save labor cost. Migrant workers have to enroll for medical insurance scheme for rural resident in their hometown and deal with complicated reimbursement procedure back home when medical expenditure occurs in urban area that they work. Similarly, maternal insurance, unemployment insurance, and housing public funding program participation is all denied from rural migrants. In case of pregnancy and unemployment, staying in their urban destination gives them no security at all. Unless employers provide dormitory for the workers to live, which is almost none with family living arrangement, migrants have to rent housing in the market without any subsidy. In 2014, share of rural migrants covered by medical insurance is around 17%, that of unemployment insurance and maternity insurance is around 10% or lower; and that of housing public fund program is as low as 5.5%.

Without access to social insurance and public services, migrant workers are living without security in the destination. It is also difficult for them to migrate with family. In 2014, the share of migrant workers with family migrating together is only 21%. These realities bring further instability of migrant workers. Migration arrangement is usually short-term arrangement instead of long-term. The workers are usually called "floating population". Ultimately, it costs the economy a bad match outcome of labor force with industry demand. At individual level, the convergence of migrant workers with their local counterparts is much slower than what it should be.

3 Hukou Reforms and New Features of Labor Market Segmentation

Since 1990s, Chinese government and local administrations attempted to reform hukou registration system. Once a while in early 1990s, local city hukou quota could even be purchased by migrant workers in the name of city expansion fees in some of small and medium cities. The main efforts that have long lasting influence so far includes township-level hukou reform in the end of 1990s, hukou uniform reform of different provinces since 2001, and, score accumulation-based hukou conversion policy of certain cities since the middle of 2000s. These reforms have profound impact on the labor market and brought new features to Chinese labor market. Migration pattern change brought by the reforms is noticeable.

Firstly, hierarchy of labor market across administrative levels and development levels has been enhanced in the past ten years. From 1997, central government began to pilot township-level hukou reform and completely liberated hukou registration in all towns in 2000. Township is grassroots level of government administration in

China. Although geographic size is usually very small and all surrounded by rural areas, residents there have non-agricultural hukou. In 1990s, a large scale of rural workers were employed by township enterprises in nearby townships of their original villages. The township-level hukou reform opened marginal opportunity of hukou conversion from agricultural to non-agricultural. According to the Small Towns Development Center of Nation Development and Reform Commission, from 1997 to 1999, 127 million rural residents got their hukou converted to urban hukou. In 2000, the reform was expanded to national wide and anybody who have stable employment, stable income source and stable residence in townships could apply for hukou there. However, the non-agricultural hukou in townships are much less attractive these years. One reason is that non-agricultural hukou no longer takes role in basic resource allocation such as food and employment, while social welfare in townships is very limited. Another reason is that jobs in townships are not comparable with jobs in the developed areas and big cities. Townships are no longer destination of migrant workers. Nevertheless, township-level urban hukou is all open since 2000. The opening up has been gradually expanded to small cities and even some middle cities especially in central and western regions. In March 2011, the State Council published the policy called "Notice on Actively and Stably Pushing Forward the Hukou System Reform". In principle, the policy called for stratified approach across administrative levels of cities for hukou management.[3] It urged more measures on liberalizing labor market in small towns and country-level cities, encouraged attempts of middle-sized cities, but for capital cities and big cities, the document asked for stricter policy in hukou population expansion control and required the continuation of hukou quota control policies. In practice, cities design and publish their hukou conversion policy accordingly. The conditions that migrant workers should meet during hukou application include the scope and years of legal and stable employment, scale of investment to the cities, minimum education degree, size of housing owned or years of housing rent, years of contribution to social insurance, etc. The conditions are designed by the governments depending on their pressure of overall carrying capacity. For some cities, a positive hukou conversion policy has been used as a tool to appeal human resources. Chan and Buckingham (2008) argued that hukou conversion conditions are usually hard to be met by rural migrant. Score-based hukou conversion policy did not benefit rural migrants in earning social welfare.

Wang and Song (2012) studied the condition that local governments required for hukou conversion application in 267 prefecture-level cities in China. The condition being compared includes requirement on education, investment, tax

[3] In 2004, the central government abolished the national-level hukou transfer quota plan and announced that the local governments could design their own hukou transfer plan.

payment, housing purchase, social security contribution or others which are most comment tunnels of hukou conversion. It used the approach of Human Development Index calculation to combine requirements in different dimensions and generated a hukou threshold index ("HTI" hereafter) to mark the strictness of hukou conversion restriction. The chapter proves that the thresholds bigger cities set are higher than that of medium cities, and thresholds set by medium cities are higher than that of small cities. Hukou strictness has a nonlinear relationship with social and economic conditions of cities such as population, population density, per capita GDP and per capita fiscal revenue. It reveals policy concerns on population management and financial capability in hukou reform. In general, the hierarchy of hukou restriction has been formed. The economic development gap and difference in industry structure across cities could be enhanced by the stratified hukou restriction policy.

The hierarchy of hukou management across cities with different development levels could bring impact on labor migration. The more developed cities show a clear sign of closing the door for migrants with less resources, lower education level, etc. to permanently settle down. The concentration of capital, human resources, techniques in big cities will be further exacerbated. Small cities and townships have opened hukou conversion, but their attraction to migrant workers could hardly increase due to their limited job opportunity and public welfare. Their absorption of migrant workers is not improved. Chan and Buckingham (2008) found that hukou reforms in small cities and towns in China did not induce large scale inflow of rural workers. The reason is that rural workers prefer large and medium-sized cities for its social welfare and public service. Secondary and middle-sized cities would be migrant workers' next destination of priority. Table 4 shows that from 2010 to 2014, the share of migrant moving to medium-sized cities increased from 54.2% to 56.6%. The growth scale is comparatively small but the trend is very stable. The city development plan could fully take labor supply potentials into account. The resources of providing social security to migrants in these cities should be considered by central government and arrange for a higher level of coordination.

Table 4. Migrant distribution across cities with different scales.

(%)	2010	2011	2012	2013	2014
Big cities	8.8	10.3	10	8.5	8.1
Medium-sized cities	54.2	54.4	55	55.4	56.6
Others	37	35.3	35	36.1	35.3
Total	100	100	100	100	100

Source: NBS, Migrant Workers Monitoring Survey Report, 2011–2015.
Note: "Big cities" indicate the centrally administrated municipals; "medium-sized cities" include capital cities and prefecture-level cities; "others" indicates counties and townships.

Secondly, segmentation across provinces has been enhanced by hukou uniform reform. Rural workers face less market segmentation within their hometown cities. It may drive migrants to find jobs within shorter distance.

From 2001, a number of provinces announced one after another to abolish the division of hukou property and adopt unified resident hukou instead. According to the policies, new hukou booklet could be applied by household from public security department (the department in-charge of issuing hukou) on which hukou property item will be deleted. The new hukou booklet declares only "resident hukou". Agricultural or non-agricultural hukou property will be no longer identified from hukou booklet. Social welfare and social administration policies that attached to original hukou property, such as family planning, veteran resettlement, social security, land contract, etc., will be maintained for a short period.[4] Taking Guangzhou as an example, the city states that they take the abolishment of agri/non-agri hukou division and adoption of the unified resident hukou as the first step. At the same time, they let the public security department mark the original hukou property in the archived file to enable social security and other related functional departments applying original policies to the according population. After an interim period, the functional departments gradually reform related policies and achieve the "both residents, same treatment" outcome between urban and rural population. Finally, public security department removes the marking of the original hukou property and the real hukou unification is achieved. Although difference in social welfare entitlement will be maintained temporarily, in the job market, since local urban and rural residents could not be distinguished, the institutional limitation that rural workers face goes away. In this sense, hukou uniform reform becomes a milestone in urban/rural labor market integration. Song and Li (2014) examined hukou uniform reform's impact on job opportunity. Especially, the paper separately evaluated the impact across workers with different hukou property origins. It is discovered that hukou uniform reform improved job opportunity of workers from local rural area. As local rural workers share same resident hukou with their urban counterparts now, their job opportunity is significantly improved. However, these local rural workers to some extent crowed the migrants from other places out. Workers holding urban and rural workers from other places have to face worse job opportunity in places that implement hukou uniform reform. Local urban workers' job opportunity

[4] According to one child policy in China, each couple is encouraged to have only one child; however, in many provinces, rural families are applied with looser birth control regulations. Detailed regulation could be found in each province's specified one child policy. For example, in Xinjiang, the Population and Family Planning Regulations announced that a couple of Han urban residents are entitled to have only one child while their rural counterparts are entitled to have two; a couple of minority urban residents are entitled to have two children while their rural counterpart are entitled to have three.

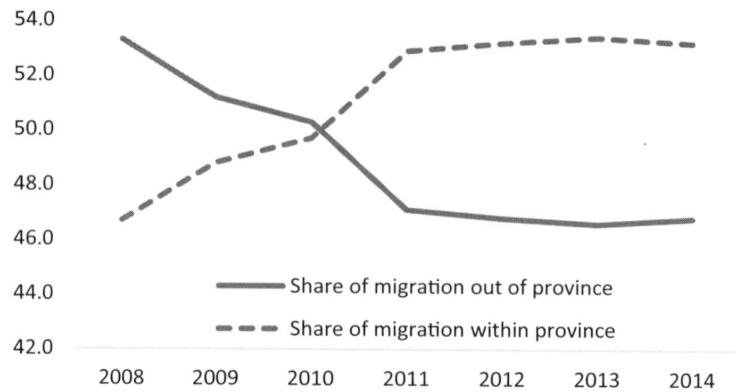

Figure 2. Trend of migration distance distribution in recent years.
Source: NBS, Migrant Workers Monitoring Survey Report, 2011–2015.

actually is worse off from the reform too, but the effect is very limited. In general, the employment segmentation between rural and urban hukou is weakened by the reform, but the segmentation between local and outside hukou is strengthened. The hukou uniform reform brings a concentration of employment resources in the reformed region to local urban and local rural workers.

Migration responds to the reform too. Figure 2 shows migration trend in recent years. National Statistical Bureau classified migration type into "within province" and "out of province". It is clear that migration out of provinces has been significantly decreased. The share in 2008 was 53.3% and has declined to 46.8% in 2014. The trend is quite stable and could be largely explained by inter-province segmentation caused by hukou uniform reform. Hukou uniform reform opens up job market to local rural workers but sacrifices outside workers in the middle. The ultimate impact on labor supply in terms of scale and quality should be further tested and may differ across provincial context. But clearly a province's hukou policy will significantly influence its labor supply. It should be well-designed and coordinated at a higher administrative level.

Thirdly, a number of cities have set up the resident certificate system in recent years for population management and basic public service provision. The system encourages migrants to live stably in their destination. The impact on migration distribution in a longer run should not be ignored.

To date, the resident certificate system has been adopted in Shanghai, Guangdong, Chongqing, Chengdu, Zhejiang, Jiangsu and most recently in Beijing. In big cities like Shanghai and Beijing, the resident certificate is mainly used as an account for score accumulation for hukou conversion. Resident certificate does not ensure much substantial benefit to the migrants. However, in lower-level cities, migrant population does get certain degree of public welfare through a resident identity.

Taking Guangdong as an example, resident certificate system was firstly built up in 2009. According to government's policy, migrants who have stable employment and resident place can apply for resident certificate. Compared to migrants without resident certificate, migrants with resident certificate are entitled to certain extra services.[5] More importantly, as long as resident certificate holders have contributed to social insurance at one place for more than five years, their children can be included into pre-school and compulsory education as children with local hukou. When the length of social insurance contribution reaches up to seven years, the certificate holders are entitled to apply for local resident hukou.[6] In Chengdu, as another example, resident certificates are classified into short-termed and long-termed. Migrant workers from local rural area who stay in city for a period longer than one month and shorter than one year can apply for short-term certificate. The ones who stay in the city for more than one year can apply for long-term certificate. Public service and social security entitled to different resident certificates holders are different. The ones with long-term certificate can enjoy much more service and welfare and are eligible to apply for hukou conversion in future. Comparing cases of Guangdong and Chengdu, it is easy to find out that public service and social security are gradually assigned to migrants through resident certificate system; and, the migrants with higher stability are rewarded with more social welfare. In 2011, Chinese central government published the announcement that resident certificate system should be expanded throughout the country; all provinces should work on improving the migrant population registration; resident place, instead of hukou registered place which is usually the birth place, should be the basis for public service provision; public service allocation should be relieved from hukou identification.

The resident certificate system is of great importance in migration management of contemporary China. Hukou system has been used in public resource allocation. To local governments with large migration population, assigning public resources to the new entrants without hukou registration is against local residents' interest and brings public expenditure pressure to their budget. Despite these, two detailed information have to be collected for arranging public resource to migrants, statistics of migrant scale for funding arrangement and statistics of migration stability for public service entitlement design. Taking Guangdong as an example, from 2005 to 2011, students in Guangdong without local hukou increased from 1.8

[5]First, migrants could apply for driver's license and register automobile to the resident place; second, apply for Hong Kong and Macao entrance approval at resident place; third, participate in community organization and related social administration activities at registration place; fourth, other public service that the government provides.

[6]The approval of hukou application will be determined on score rank of all the candidates and have total amount control each year.

million to 3.4 million. The average growth rate of these students is 13%. To accommodate these students, local governments need resources to build up new public schools, increase the accommodation capability of current public schools, and encourage the development of private schools.[7] To achieve the target that more than 75% of migrant student could be accepted by public schools, demand for public budgetary funding is estimated to be 38.5 billion RMB.[8] Financial transfer payment on education from Central government is currently all based on hukou resident statistics. Educational allocation to migrant students consequently is all given to their hometown governments instead of destination governments. Reforming financing arrangement of public service is necessary and needs reliable statistics of migration population. Resident certificate system could serve in this process. Besides, it should be noticed that migrant workers' residence at destination is all induced by job opportunity. Public resource allocation should take the workers' stability and corresponding demand for public service into account. Sequence of policy priority should be identified and the arrangement should be designed with adjustment flexibility. Settling down the migrants who have stably lived at destination for a long period is government's unavoidable choice, with least policy risk, and lowest social integration cost. Current resident certificate system design and entitlement assignment practice reflects the policy consideration.

So far, there is no empirical work that compares the stability of migrants in the places before and after adopting resident certificate system. But according to Migration Population Dynamic Monitoring Survey Data in 2010, the migration population have averagely stayed in current destination for five years. That includes 79.5% who have lived for over a year, 53.2% who have lived for over three years, 36.7% who have lived for over five years and 14.1% who have lived for over 10 years. It is reasonable to assume that with the gradual adoption of resident certificate system, a large number of them have the intensity to settle down at destination and migration population could generally reach better social welfare and public service. With corresponding financial and other necessary reforms implemented, large proportion of migrants could be absorbed by certain urban areas. Migration trend and related management will enter into a new stage by that time.

---

[7]Public schools in China usually have higher education quality and enrollment into public school will be exempted of tuition for compulsory education. Comparatively, private schools charge tuition and related fees. Their education quality is generally lower than their public counterparts.

[8]That includes 20 billion RMB for school construction, 4.9 billion for student budgetary allocation if it guarantees these students with equal per student budgetary allocation as their local counterpart and 13.6 billion for teachers' salary and welfare. Compared to this, subsidy allocated by central government is only 517 million. Huge gap exists between funding demand and central government allocation.

4 Conclusion and Policy Recommendation

Rural to urban population migration is the biggest issue on Chinese labor market at current development stage. However, the labor market has severe segmentation based on hukou registration system. The segmentation exists in wage determination, occupation opportunity and access to social insurance and public welfare. Until the latter half of the first decades of 2000s, the level of wages paid was much lower to migrant workers than their local urban hukou registered counterparts. By gradually intensifying low skilled labor supply, wage discrimination has been adjusted. Job opportunity of migrant workers was largely restricted by destination governments. The main concern there was the crowd out effect of labor inflow to local resident labor. The institutional limitation is removed by central government now. But destination governments still have informal regulations there on protecting local residents' employment job. Opportunity gap still exists between migrant workers and local residents. Nowadays, hukou status' impact on migrant workers more and more takes the form of limited access to social security and public service in the destination. The problem was not strongly concerned by migrant workers who mainly wanted to improve household income through short-term migration and non-agricultural work in urban area. Nowadays, it has become the biggest obstacle that migrant workers meet with in settling down at destination. Excluding migrant workers from social security and public service provision saves local governments' public budget expenditure, but it also sacrifices economic efficiency as a whole. In very recent years, Chinese government implemented a series of reforms in migration management. These practices include the full opening of hukou registration in townships and small cities, stratified population control policy according to administrative levels, score accumulation-based hukou conversion policy, canceling urban and rural hukou classification within certain provinces, and the adoption of resident certificate system. These policies bring noticeable change to Chinese labor market and migration behavior. Firstly, hukou restriction across cities has shown a clear hierarchy feature. Big cities have very conservative attitude to migrant workers and only welcome high skilled workers and financial investment through its hukou management. Medium-sized cities show a more open attitude to migrants and are gradually accommodating more and more migrants. Small cities and towns completely liberate hukou registration but their attraction to migrants is very limited. Migration responds to the policy change. More migrants concentrate in medium-sized cities instead of gathering in big cities nowadays. Secondly, segmentation across provinces has been enhanced by hukou uniform reform. A number of provinces canceled their agricultural and non-agricultural hukou property classification. The policy increased the competitive power of local rural workers, but to some extent excluded workers from other places. Migration across provinces has been decreased in recent years. Thirdly, the resident certificate system that has been gradually set up promotes migrants to live stably at one destination. The system helps building up better statistics of migration population and entitles migrants with higher stability more public service and social security. Considering the migration composition reality that a large share of migrants is quite stable, the resident certificate system sorts migrants to be absorbed by their destination.

Flexibility and security are the two most important features of a good labor market. In general, hukou system in China has been playing a negative role in both the aspects. However, pressure of improving flexibility and security nowadays comes from both of the development stage of Chinese economy and the appeals of current migration management situation. Chinese government has been dealing with the "new normal" of economy growth. GDP growth rate dropped to under 10% for five years. To improve resource allocation is of great policy priority at current stage, during which releasing restriction in labor migration is an important action. The old generation migrants in China value much in wage income and can accept temporary residency in urban area without social security. However, the new generation (usually refer to the ones born after 1980s), who account for higher than 60% of total migrant population, has changed. Survey has proved that only 18% of new generation migrants migrate "to earn money".[9] They have high aspiration in settling down in urban area and as low as 1.4% of them plan to go back to hometown to do farm work (Baogaowang, 2015). Getting social security and public service is the problem to be solved in front of them and also the problem that needs increased consideration of governments. Different entitlement in public service and social security, such as education, medical service, pension, etc. will further accelerate difference in job opportunity, productivities and incomes. Ultimately, to provide quality guaranteed social security and public service to all population groups across all geographic locations should be the country's development goal. From an economic point of view, as long as disparity in social security and public service level exists, welfare induced migration will occur. It will disturb the smoothing of productivity difference through migration and sacrifice the efficiency of the whole economy. Reforming hukou registration system in China and gradually removing its resource allocation function without doubt are the directions of Chinese government's effort. In the process, the following two aspects are the most important areas that the government should work on.

[9]Comparatively, the share of "migrating to earn money" in migrants who were born in 1960s is 76%, and the share in migrants who were born in 1970s is 35%.

Firstly, standardized basic public services package should be designed and guaranteed by central government. The services covered by the package should include education, medical service, elderly care, social assistance, housing, etc. Difference of public service across places is allowed but only be supported by local financial resources. Social security benefit should also be generally coordinated by central government. The standard should be unified with regional living cost adjusted. The balance of the contribution account should be conveniently carried over across places. An efficient labor migration should be migration of workers from places with lower productivity to places with higher productivity, instead of being from places with lower public service and social welfare to places with higher public service and social welfare. The provision of generally guaranteed public service and equalized social security benefit could reduce occurrence of public service induced migration. It improves the flexibility of workers across different jobs and different places and further increases productivity.

Secondly, to support the public service design and equalized and portable social security, higher level of financing arrangement would be crucial. Providing standardized basic public service package and social security needs integrated financial planning. At the primary stage of settling down migrants, to provide services to the long-term stable migrants, subsidy from central government to destination place is not avoidable. Detailed estimation of unit cost of integrating the migrants should be the ground of division of central and local governments' responsibility. In a long run, public service funding pool should be built up with the design of a flexible allocation rule according to workers' location, that relies on concrete statistics of migrant population. Information platform should be built up. Aggregate data should be publicly and regularly exchanged to monitor and evaluate migration trend. The system will also release concern of destination government on service provision.

References

Au, C.-C. and J.V. Henderson, (2006), How Migration Restrictions Limit Agglomeration and Productivity in China, *Journal of Development Economics*, 80(2), 350–388.

Bao, S., O.B. Bodvarsson, J.W. Hou and Y. Zhao, (2009), The Regulation of Migration in a Transition Economy: China's Hukou System, *IZA* DP No.4493.

Baogaowang, New Generation Rural Migration Survey Report 2015. Available at http://bg.yjbys.com/diaochabaogao/12517.html.

Cai, F. and Y. Du (2011), Wage increase, wage convergence and Lewis turning point, *China Economic Review*, 22, 601–610.

Chan, K.W. and W. Buckingham (2008), Is China abolishing the Hukou system?, *The China Quarterly*, 195.

Chen, Z. and M. Lu (2008), From segmentation to integration: The political economy of urban-rural economic growth and social harmony, *Economic Research Journal*, 1, 21–32.

Deng, Q. and B. Gustafsson (2007), Permanent migrant workers in China, *Economic Study*, 4, 137–148.

DRC (Develop Research Center of State Council of China) (2010), The Impact of Citizenlizing Rural Migrants on Enlarging Domestic Demand and Economic Growth, *Economic Study*, 6, 4–16.

Giles, J., P. Albert, F. Cai, *et al.* (2012), "Weathering a storm: Survey-Based Perspectives on Employment in China in the Aftermath of the Global Financial Crisis", *World Bank Policy Research Working Paper*, No. 5984.

Henderson, J.V. (2000), "How Urban Concentration Affects Economic Growth", *The World Bank Policy Research Working Paper*, No. 2326, Washington D.C.

Meng, X. and J. Zhang (2001), The two-tier labor market in urban China: occupational, segregation and wage differentials between urban residents and rural migrants in Shanghai, *Journal of Comparative Economics*, 29, 485–504.

Poncet, S. (2006), Provincial migration dynamics in China: Borders, costs and economic motivations, *Regional Science and Urban Economics*, (36), 385–398.

Song, J. and S. Li (2014a), Hukou's impact on labor occupation segmentation, *China Agricultural Economic Review*, 10, 4–16.

Song, J. and S. Li (2014b), Township level Hukou reform and its impact on labor market occupation segmentation, *Chinese Rural Economy*, 10, 4–16.

Sun, W., C. Bai and P. Xie (2011), The impact of Hukou system reform on rural labor migration in China, *Economic Study*, 1.

Wang, D. and J. Song (2012), Understanding the Hukou System through Quantifying Hukou Thresholds: Methodology and Empirical Findings, *Background report for World Development Report 2013*, the World Bank.

Wang, M. (2005), Employment opportunities and wage gaps in the urban labor market: A study of the employment and wages of migrant laborers, *Social Sciences in China*, 5, 36–46.

Whalley, J. and S. Zhang (2007), A numerical simulation analysis of (Hukou) labour mobility restrictions in China, *Journal of Development Economics*, 83(2), 392–410.

Yan, Y. and X. Li (2007), Quantified measurement of migrants' contribution to economic growth and its result, *Statistics Study*, 1, 22–26.

Yang, Yunyan and Jinyong Chen (2000), Segmentation and competition in the labor market during the transformation — Based on an empirical analysis of investigations in Wuhan, *Social Sciences in China*, 5.

Zhang, D. and Xin Meng (2007), Assimilation or Disassimilation? The Labour Market Performance of Rural Migrants in Chinese Cities, Paper presented at the 6th conference on Chinese economy, CERDI-IDREC, Clermont Ferrand, France.

Zhao, Y. (2000), Rural-to-urban labor migration in China: the past and the present. *Rural Labor Flows in China*, Loraine, A. West and Yaohui, Zhao (eds.), Institute of East Asian Studies, University of California, Berkeley.

Chapter 11

The Causal Effect of Father's Schooling on Children's Schooling: An Estimation Based on Cultural Revolution Instrument

Juan Yang* and Tingting He†

School of Economics and Business Administration
Beijing Normal University, China
**yangjuan@bnu.edu.cn*
†126lavender@163.com

Abstract: Because paternal ability is unobservable, OLS estimation cannot tell us whether paternal schooling attainment has a causal impact on an individual's schooling attainment, and simple inclusion of this variable on the right-hand side of a regression will generate a downward-biased coefficient. This chapter treats the Cultural Revolution as an instrument to study how human capital is transferred from parent to child using the Chinese Household Income Project 2002. The data show that education of the cohort that was affected by the Cultural Revolution is 2.5 years less than that of cohorts that were not affected by the Cultural Revolution. The Cultural Revolution is an exogenous event and can be a good instrument to solve the endogenity problem. Since most individuals who live with their parents and are under 22 years old have not finished their education, the data will be analyzed using a Cox proportional hazard model to control for censoring. The results of Cox proportional hazard model using the instrument show that father's schooling has a causal effect on children's schooling.

1 Introduction

With the enlarged income inequality in China, the role of education and intergenerational mobility has attracted the attention of researchers. It is a stylized fact that education plays quite an important role to individuals' income and individuals' education is largely dependent on their parental socio-economic status. That is to say, intergenerational transmission concerns whether the income inequality will be sustainable and stable. Therefore, it is quite meaningful to examine this classical topic of impact of family background on their children's educational attainment in China, i.e. education transmission across generations. In addition, recent researches in China found the average socio-economic background of college students is much higher than the national average level. The probability of children from families in management class to attend higher education is five times of children from rural families (Wen, 2005). It is interesting to study the phenomenon whether the genes of college students inherited from educated parents are better or whether educated parents have higher education productivity to their children.

The causation or correlation relationship between family background and individuals' education is also quite an important issue concerning the public fiscal policy. If the father's education has a causal effect on their children's schooling, that is to say, father's knowledge and schooling will provide a higher productivity for their children, then increasing public educational investment and expanding educational system will benefit the next generation's educational level. Funds aim at providing educational aid or enlarging government educational expenditure will be reasonable. On the contrary, if it is an association relation, any educational funds' influence on reducing social mobility may be neglected.

In addition, the involvement of Chinese parents in their children's education may be "better" than the parents' in other countries. In China's traditional culture, schooling or degree is the only benchmark for one's success so Chinese parents push hard their children in order to secure a good university for them. It is interesting to investigate, compared to other countries, whether the impact of father's schooling will have a causal effect or not.

According to a general equilibrium model, individuals' educational attainment is determined on three factors: government's educational resources, families' educational endowment and individuals' educational choice. Government's educational fund will affect school's and teacher's quality; families' educational endowment may influence children's school choice, leisure time and classmates and the most important factor, children's educational choice will determine their study motivation, study time and effectiveness. While in empirical studies, researchers mainly consider the impact of family background on individuals' schooling from one dimension based on three identification strategies, twins approach, adoption strategy or instrumental variables methods.

Twins approach (Haveman and Wolfe, 1995; Behrman and Rosenzweig, 2002; Antonovics and Goldberger, 2005) assumes that unobserved differences, such as ability could be removed within twins, and therefore in estimating results one could avoid the bias generated from OLS regression. However, the small sample size and within-pair differences lead to varied estimating findings among studies. Haveman and Wolfe (1995) and Holmlund *et al.* (2008) showed higher parental education is associated with more years of investment on their children's education and the impact of the mother's education is larger than that of the father. While the findings by Behrman and Rosenzweig (2002) (henceforth, BR) indicate father's schooling is the most important. Antonovics and Goldberger (2005) reexamine the results provided by BR by recoding the schools and restricting the twins' age to 18 years or older. They found similar findings as BR that father has significant positive influence on children's schooling and mother's effect is much smaller and insignificant. The insignificant effect of mother's schooling is also confirmed by Bingley *et al.* (2009) using a Scandinavian register data.

Adoption strategy (Dearden *et al.*, 1997; Sacerdote, 2000, 2002, 2007; Plug, 2004; Björklund *et al.*, 2004, 2006) is to exploit the genetic effects by regressing the schooling of adopted children on schooling of the adoptive parents. Since the adopted children did not share the same genes with their parents, the relation between adoptees and their adoptive parents can be treated as "nurture" or environment effect. Holmlund *et al.* (2008) argues if the adoptees are not randomly selected, there is a selection bias in the estimation, especially those who are from better background families and may investigate children's original parents. The research by Sacerdote (2007) controls the selective placement problems by using Korean American adoptees and finds that adoptive mother's education has an impact on the education of the children. However, Oreopoulos *et al.* (2006) argues that observed correlation could still be driven by parental characteristics that are not genetically transmitted to children and thus affect children's education. In addition, such kind of studies are still restricted by small samples.

Studies on instrumental variables method generally employ compulsory schooling reform to be an instrument for parental education and estimate the effect of the parents' schooling on their children's education. This method tries to control the unobserved differences by introducing an independent instrument. Black *et al.* (2005) answer the causal or associated effect of parents' education on own children's schooling by using a unique dataset from Norway. The reform of the educational system implemented across municipalities from 1959 to 1973 was treated as an instrument for parental education and they find weak evidence of a causal relationship between parents' education and children's education. They do find a statistically significant effect of mother schooling on their children. Oreopoulos *et al.* (2006) reexamine the intergenerational mobility of compulsory schooling by using a comparatively large census data in 1960, 1970 and 1980 and minimum number of years of schooling required as instruments. In their regression, they use the sum of mother's and father's schooling years as the indicators and find that mother's and father's schooling have significant impacts on their children's grade repetition and those who live with their parents, parental compulsory schooling may affect their off-spring's drop-out probability. The study by Maurin and McNally (2008) treat the events in May 1968 of students' turmoil in France as a natural experiment to analyze the intergenerational transmission of human capital. Their regression results suggest fathers' education has a significant impact on children's grade repetition.

The research on the impact of family background on their offspring's education in China is limited. Knight *et al.* (2009) analyzes the impact of family income and parental schooling to children's middle school dropout and high school attainment through CHIP-2002 rural sample. The results suggest the higher the household income and the greater the parental schooling, the probability to dropouts is smaller and the continuation to high school is greater. Knight *et al.* (2011), employing CHIP-2007, researched the educational inequality from intergenerational mobility prospect. They found education had risen across generations in the aggregate levels, but the impact of parental schooling for each cohort was varied due to different educational expansion policies in different periods. Connelly and Zheng (2003) analyzes the affected factors of school enrollment and graduation rate using 1990 census data and they found parental education to have a strong impact on their children's education. Sato and Li (2007) used the rural sample of the CHIP 2002 survey to examine the influence of class background (chengfen) on offspring's education. They found that the offsprings of landlord or rich peasant families (as officially classified) are likely to have more education than those of other families, even after accounting for parents' education, family wealth and other household characteristics. All of these researches are based on simple OLS regressions and cannot figure out whether parental schooling has a causal effect on children's schooling or not.

Institutional and cultural differences across countries may lead to differences in estimating results. In this chapter, we would like to examine the causal effect of China's intergenerational mobility in education by employing cultural revolution as an instrument. The rest of the chapter is organized as follows: the second part explains the estimating methods. Section 3 provides the data and descriptive statistics. Section 4 presents the empirical estimating results and the conclusion is summarized in Section 5.

2 Methodology

Ten years of Cultural Revolution (CR) from 1966 to 1976 in China resulted in a series of loss to the whole society and one of the key effects is that it interrupted a generation's education. In late 1950s, Chairman Mao encouraged students in middle school to go to the rural areas and learn from peasants by eating, living and working with them together, called "three together". The encouragement transformed into an administrative order after "May, 16" notice in 1966. In other words, most of the educational institutions were closed after 1966 for a few years, including universities, middle schools and primary schools. Since then, students' normal school life was interrupted and most of the junior students went to the countryside. Although some primary and secondary schools re-opened in 1968 or 1969 and university enrollment began to recover in 1972, teachers were not allowed to teach as usual and students were only allowed to study Mao Zedong's quotations or learn farming and manual crafts from farmers and workers (Zhang *et al.*, 2007). From 1972, universities began small-scale recruitment, based upon political attitudes or family background (social identity) rather than on academic (social identity) rather than on academic performance. The measuring standard of the family background during the CR period was different when compared to the current period, the poorest rural families were treated as "good families". In other words, children from wealthy families (capitalist) or educated families had few opportunities to attend universities.

The interruption of ordinary education did not affect the cohorts to acquire middle school qualifications. Those who were in junior or senior high school during the period of Cultural Revolution were given qualifications at the ordinary graduation age even though they had missed various years of standard schooling (Meng and Gregory, 2002).

CR interrupted the whole educational system, but its effect among different cohorts was quite different. Those who were in middle school during CR period got the most serious shock. They were reluctant to accept higher education during their later life since the qualification they got was much below the required standard (Meng and Gregory, 2002). However, the impact of CR on cohorts who were born before 1945 or after 1960 was very weak. Therefore, CR can be a good external instrument to estimate the impact of father's education on their children's education.

The turmoil of the education system suggests the real meaning of qualification in terms of human capitals and is quite different for different cohorts. The human capital stock will be higher for those who got junior or senior school qualification before or after the CR period. One group of cohort that needs to be specified is *Lao Sanjie high school graduates* and *Lao Sanjie junior school graduates,* who graduated from junior school or studied in junior school in 1966. Since they received normal education at school before CR, their human capital stock was comparatively higher than other cohorts. That is to say, compared to other cohorts, their qualification was undervalued. Therefore, in order to estimate the impact of father's schooling accurately, we need to adjust human capital according to the year of starting school.

First, consider a simple relationship between parents' schooling and children's access to higher education. Holmlund *et al.* (2008) argue that by adding spousal education in the equation, the coefficient explains the effect of an increase in a parent's schooling on the schooling of his or her child, without spousal education in the equation, the coefficient measures both the direct transfer from a given parent and the indirect transfer from the other parent. Knight *et al.* (2011) shows education-matched parents may deliver a larger impact on their children than from father or mother only. While in China, most of the scholars think the impact of parental education is mainly from father's schooling (Liu, 2008; Sun, 2011). Therefore, we will estimate the impact of father's schooling on children' education.

In the first step of simple regression, the impact of father's education on their children's education can be represented as

$$H_i = \alpha + \beta_1 F_i + \beta_2 X_i + \beta_3 Z_i + \varepsilon_i, \qquad (1)$$

where H_i represents child i's educational attainment, F_i denotes individual i's father's schooling. X_i is individual i's demographic characteristics, such as gender, age, located province, minority. Z_i represents father's other characteristics, such as his age, minority, province dummy, etc. Considering the impact of higher education implemented in 1999, later born cohort may find it easier to attain higher education. Similarly, children's schooling is also affected by their father's age. The younger the father, the younger their children will be and the probability to attend higher education will be greater. Thus, father's age, father's age square, children's age and children's age square were added into the regression to control age trend.

In order to match parents with their children, we have to use the children's sample that live with their parents. While those who live with their parents are generally quite young and may not have finished their studies. This generates the data censoring problem. Cox proportional hazard model could solve the problem of unobserved final schooling with some observations. We assume individuals face the risk of dropping out of school and this risk is determined by age, family background and other individuals' characteristics. When the data is collected, some individuals' dropping out risks have occurred, i.e. they have already left school. While others are still in school and face the risk of drop-off. We can use this method to estimate the impact of father's schooling on individuals' probability to survive until higher education is achieved (i.e. attain higher education).[1]

[1] In China, the drop-off rate in higher education is very low (less than 3%). Once youngsters attended the universities, most of them could graduate from the universities.

Individual i's drop-off probability in time t can be represented as

$$h(t) = h_0(t)\exp(\beta_1 X_{ij} + \beta_2 F_i + \beta_3 X_j), \quad (2)$$

where $h_0(t)$ represents baseline hazard in time t and baseline hazard means the hazard of all the independent variables equal to zero. $\exp(\beta)$ is the reported results from Cox model, which represents the proportional risk compared to baseline hazard.

Since father's ability is unobservable and has to be reflected in the residual items, the estimation on $\beta_2$is biased. We could introduce instrument variable into Cox proportional model to solve this problem. As we mentioned in the previous section, CR is an external event interrupting a generation's education. Those affected groups' education is shortened and the education quality has deteriorated. In the first step, we could estimate father's schooling and treat CR as an instrument

$$F_i = \delta_0 + \delta_1 C_{iA}^f + \delta_2 X_{ij} + \delta_3 X_j + u_i^f, \quad (3)$$

where C_i^f shows individual i's father's cohort, the subscript A represents the group whose education are affected by the culture revolution. u captures other non-observable variables. After combining Equations (2) and (3), we can conclude, the impact of parent's education on their children's higher educational attainment.

3 Data and Statistics Description

Chinese Household Income Project 2002 (hereafter designated CHIP-2002) urban survey will be used to estimate the impact of father's schooling on their children's educational achievement. The questionnaires are designed by Chinese and foreign scholars and contain a wide range of aspects including individuals' basic characteristics, education, school performance, career and parents' background providing comprehensive information for us to conduct the current research. There are 12 provinces included in CHIP-2002 covering the West, East and Middle part of China. Approximately 7,000 households and more than 20,000 individuals took part in the survey.

CHIP data was composed by three parts, urban, rural and immigration survey. However in China, if individuals attended the college or university, his household registration (*hukou*) will move to the college (university) location. There are no colleges or universities in rural areas in China, which means all the students with tertiary education will come under city registration, no matter what their previous statuses are. In addition, CR only interrupts urban children's education, therefore we only selected urban observations as our research sample.

This chapter intends to employ CR as an exogenous instrument to estimate the impact of parental education on their children's higher education attainment. Therefore, the target objects are the individuals whose education is affected by CR and the before and after cohort. According to Figure 1, those mostly affected groups are born between 1946 and 1960, we could treat those born between 1940 and 1945 as well as those born between 1961 and 1965 as the contrast group. In other words, we would like to analyze the children of those who are born between 1940 and 1965 as our research sample.

As shown in Figure 1, the average schooling of the affected cohorts (i.e. individuals born between 1946 and 1960) is a little bit lower than the before-cohort (i.e. born between 1940–1945 group) and significantly lower than the after-cohort. The results suggest CR indeed shortens a cohort's education and can be a good external instrument for father's education. After matching the fathers with their children, we got 3,203 observations including 1,636 men and 1,567 women. The descriptive statistics of matched CHIP-2002 is show in Table 1.

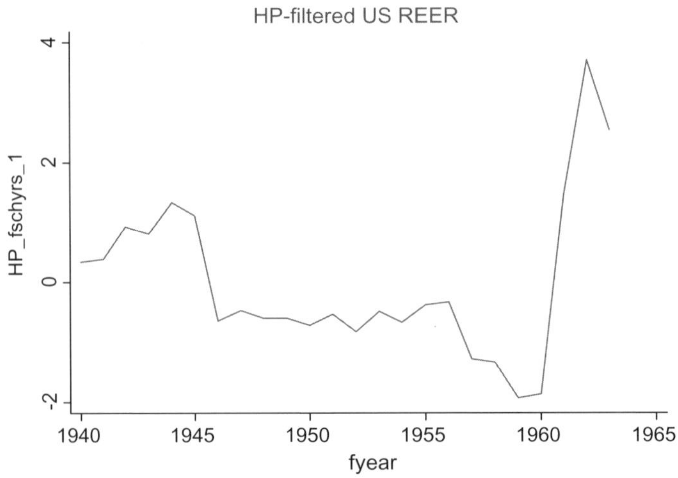

Figure 1. Average schooling of individuals born between 1943 and 1964.

Table 1. Variables' definition and descriptive statistics.

Variables	Definition	Mean	Std. dev.	Min	Max	Obs
fschyrs	father's schooling	10.85	3.076	0	23	3203
fage	father's age	44.67	5.278	30	69	3203
fminority	Father's minority	0.0428	0.202	0	1	3203
cmale	Children's gender, if boy = 1	0.511	0.500	0	1	3203
cage	Children's age	16.06	3.542	10	22	3203

4 The Impact of Father's Schooling to Children's Higher Education Attainment

4.1 The results from Cox proportional hazard model

First, we estimate the impact of father's schooling on their children's higher education attainment by Cox proportional hazard model for full samples, males and females separately. In order to let the survey sample reflect the whole population, we weighed the sample based on 2000 census data. The regression results in Table 2 show when father's schooling increase by one year, the risk of children not attending higher education will decrease 10.21% and the results are statistically significant. The findings comply with most of the results in China and other developed countries (Behrman and Rosenzweig, 2002 and Plug, 2004). The results are different for boys and girls: the hazard ratio may reduce 12.09% for girls, while only 8.54% for boys by increasing the father's education by one year. This suggests father's schooling has a strong relationship with children's higher educational attainment in China and girls from well-educated families are more likely to accept more education.

Other factors may also affect individuals' college enrollment. The hazard ratio of gender variable shows girls are more likely to survive in schools. The probability of not attending universities for boys is 32.23% higher than girls and statistically significant in 1% level. This is probably because boys can do some manual work after graduating from high schools, while girls prefer to do some office work and have to receive more education or partly reflecting Chiappori *et al.* (2009)'s marriage matching opinions. They suggest girls are more likely to attend higher education

Table 2. The impact of father's schooling on Children's higher education attainment by Cox proportional model.

	Full sample		Male		Female	
	Haz. ratio	**Std. err.**	**Haz. ratio**	**Std. err.**	**Haz. ratio**	**Std. err.**
cmale	1.3223***	0.0288				
fschyrs	0.8979***	0.0033	0.9146***	0.0049	0.8791***	0.0043
fage	0.9715	0.0298	0.8754***	0.0341	0.9274	0.0462
fage2	0.9998	0.000303	1.0006	0.000384	1.0005	0.000493
fminority	1.1405**	0.0667	1.1643**	0.0877	1.0778	0.1006
cage	0.0980***	0.0041	0.0467***	0.0029	0.1833***	0.0119
cage2	1.0700***	0.001247	1.0924***	0.001852	1.0511***	0.001857
N	58358		29663		28695	
pesudo R^2	0.251		0.381		0.198	

Note: t-statistics in parentheses. $^{*}p < 0.05$, $^{**}p < 0.01$, $^{***}p < 0.001$. 58,358 observations are the weighted sample size.

to match boys better in order to get better life-time rewards. Though the Chinese government provides some preferential policies for minorities, the regression results by Cox model still show the children from minority families are less likely to attend higher education compared to "han" children, especially for boys. The sign for children's age is within expectations that older girls are more likely to attend higher education since we censored age at 20.

From basic Cox proportional hazard model, we can only conclude there is a positive correlation between father's education and children's education. However, we cannot figure out whether the correlation is due to genes inherited from father or nature and environment. Fathers with high educational achievements are more likely to possess high abilities and to transfer high IQ genes to their children. Since father's IQ is unobservable in empirical studies, it is included in the error term thus the estimating result shows a downward bias. In order to investigate the whether there is a causal effect between father's schooling and children's schooling, we include instrument variables into the Cox proportional hazard model to solve the endogenous problem.

4.2 The results from IV Cox proportional hazard model

4.2.1 *The validity of IV*

We add CR instrument in the Cox proportional hazard model in order to solve the endogenous problem of father's schooling. Before we estimate model IV, we need to examine whether CR is a valid instrument. Since the number of IV is equal to the number of endogenous variable, the equation belongs to an exactly identified regression and we can do weak-instrument robust inference tests. After the first stage regression, the F statistic is 28.9 and $P < 0.01$, which suggests CR is not a weak instrument. In other words, we can use CR as an external instrument to estimate father's schooling.

4.2.2 *Regression results*

The first stage regression results in Table 3 show the coefficient of fCR is −0.242, which implies affected cohorts (1949–1958 born cohort) may have 0.242 year less than the contrast cohorts controlling all the other affected factors. Since the result is statistically significant, it means Cultural Revolution did have a negative impact on individuals' education. And the numbers for female and male cohort are −0.263 and −0.217 separately. In other words, Cultural Revolution has a comparatively larger negative impact on women's education than men's education.

The IV results show father's schooling does have a causal effect on children's schooling, especially for girls. However, the impact on boys is insignificant. The

Table 3. The regression results by IV Cox proportional hazard model.

	Full sample		**Male**		**Female**	
	Coeff/Haz. ratio	**Std. err**	**Coeff/Haz. ratio**	**Std. err**	**Coeff/Haz. ratio**	**Std. err**
	First stage (OLS regression: coefficients)					
cmale	0.0934***	0.0242				
fCR	−0.2418***	0.0450	−0.2169***	0.0630	−0.2632***	0.0644
fage	−0.0958	0.0659	−0.0590	0.0886	−0.1567	0.0985
fage2	0.0003	0.000695	−0.0001	0.000934	0.0010	0.001042
fminority	−0.0366	0.0701	−0.3200***	0.0985	0.2539**	0.0998
cage	−0.2355***	0.0360	−0.1525***	0.0515	−0.3067***	0.0505
cage2	0.0052***	0.001104	0.0024	0.001582	0.0077***	0.001548
_cons	16.9235***	1.4689	15.5947***	1.9947	18.7957***	2.1785
adjusted R^2	0.179		0.0897		0.0663	
	Second stage (Cox regression: hazard ratio)					
cmale	1.3317***	0.0389				
fschyrs	0.6955*	0.1501	1.6220	.5352	0.4575***	0.1363
fage	0.5249***	0.0513	0.6012***	0.0704	0.5242***	0.0925
fage 2	1.0058***	0.000894	1.0049***	0.001031	1.0057***	0.001670
fminority	1.1728***	0.0687	1.4765***	0.1782	1.3105**	0.1596
cage	0.0730***	0.0047	0.0550***	0.0042	0.1031***	0.0111
cage 2	1.0785***	0.001733	1.0892***	0.002013	1.0674***	0.002975
N	55809		28315		27494	
pesudo R^2	0.281		0.383		0.222	

Note: t-statistics in parentheses. $^{*}p < 0.05$, $^{**}p < 0.01$, $^{***}p < 0.001$. 58,358 observations are the weighted sample size.

hazard ratio for children not attending higher education will decrease 30.45% with one year's increase of father's schooling, while it may reduce 54.25% for girls. This complies with the research in America (e.g. Oreopoulos *et al.*, 2006; Plug, 2004). The conclusion implies well educated fathers do have an important effect on children's educational attainment and the policy aims to increase the national educational level could benefit the next generation's education. The results from IV estimation is a little bit higher than the ordinary Cox regression, which overcome the downward bias resulted by missing variables.

5 Conclusions and Policy Suggestions

This chapter researches the impact of father's schooling on children's higher education attainment using Cox proportional model with CR as an instrument according to CHIP-2002 data. The first stage IV regression shows Cultural Revolution does interrupt a generation's education and the affected cohort's education is 0.242 year less than the unaffected group. The results of Cox proportional hazard model with instrument shows father's education does have an impact on children's education, especially for girls and the impacts for boys are insignificant. The hazard ratio for Children not attending higher education will decrease 30.45% with one year's increase of father's schooling, while it may reduce 54.25% for girls.

If father's education does have a causal effect on children's education, it implies the government's allocation system of education opportunity will affect the equality of next generation. China began to expand the education system at the end of 90s, which could improve the next generation's education level. However, the expansion system of education is learning towards families in cities and high socio-economic classes, which will enlarge the inequality of education in the next generation. This kind of allocation system is still developing and only children coming from better family backgrounds are benefiting from this education expansion (Li, 2003). This system prevents the education improvement in rural and poor families resulting insignificant gaps among children, especially between rural and urban areas. Policy makers should consider how to make an effective allocation system for education in order to let children from different social classes and different areas have equal educational opportunities.

References

Antonovics, K.L. and A.S. Goldberger (2005), Do Educated Women Make Bad Mothers? Twin Studies and the Intergenerational Transmission of Human Capital, *American Economic Review*, 95(5), 1738–1744.

Behrman, J.R. and M.R. Rosenzweig (2002), Does Increasing Women's Schooling Raise the Schooling of the Next Generation?, *American Economic Review*, 91(1), 323–334.

Bingley, P., K. Christensen, and V. M. Jensen (2009), Parental Schooling and Child Development: Learning from Twin Parents, The Danish National Centre for Social Research Working Paper 07.

Björklund, A., M. Lindahl, and E. Plug (2004), Intergenerational Effects in Sweden: What Can We Learn from Adoption Data, *IZA Discussion Papers 1194*, Institute for the Study of Labor (IZA).

Björklund, A., M. Lindahl, and E. Plug (2006), The Origins of Intergenerational Associations: Lessons from Swedish Adoption Data, *Quarterly Journal of Economics*, 121(3), 999–1028.

Black, S.E., P.J. Devereux, and K.G. Salvanes (2005), Why the Apple Doesn't Fall Far: Understanding Intergenerational Transmission of Human Capital, *American Economic Review*, 95(1), 437–449.

Chiappori, P.A., M. Iyigun, and Y. Weiss (2009), Investment in Schooling and the Marriage Market, *American Economic Review*, 99(5), 1689–1713.

Connelly, R., and Z. Zheng (2003), Determinants of School Enrollment and Completion of 10 to 18 Year Olds in China, *Economics of Education Review*, 22(4), 379–388.

Dearden, L., S. Machin, and H. Reed (1997), Intergenerational Mobility in Britain, *Economic Journal*, 107, 47–66.

Haveman, R. and B. Wolfe (1995), The Determinants of Children's Attainments: A Review of Methods and Findings, *Journal of Economic Literature*, 33(4), 1829–1878.

Holmlund, H., M. Lindahl, and E. Plug (2008), The Causal Effect of Parent's Schooling on Children's Schooling: A Comparison of Estimation Methods, *IZA Discussion Papers 3630*, Institute for the Study of Labor (IZA).

Knight, J., S. Li, and Q. Deng (2009), Education and the Poverty Trap in Rural China: Setting the Trap, *Oxford Development Studies*, 37(4), 311–332.

Knight, J., T. Sicular, and X. Yue (2011), Educational Inequality in China: The Intergenerational Dimension, *University of Western Ontario, CIBC Centre for Human Capital and Productivity Working Papers 201113*.

Li, C. (2003), Social Political Changes and Inequality of Educational Opportunity. *Social Sciences in China*, 3, 86–98.

Liu, J. (2008), Changing Patterns of Inequality of Educational Opportunity in Basic Education in China, *Social Sciences in China*, 5, 101–116.

Maurin, E. and S. McNally (2008), *Vive la* Revolution! Long-term Educational Returns of 1968 to Angry Students, *Journal of Labor Economics*, 26, 1–33.

Meng, X. and R.G. Gregory (2002), The Impact of Interrupted Education on Subsequent Educational Attainment: A Cost of the Chinese Cultural Revolution, *Economic Development and Cultural Change*, 50(4), 935–959.

Oreopoulos, P., M.E. Page, and A.H. Stevens (2006), Does Human Capital Transfer from Parent to Child? The Intergenerational Effects of Compulsory Schooling, *Journal of Labor Economics*, 24(4), 729–760.

Plug, E. (2004), Estimating the Effect of Mother's Schooling on Children's Schooling Using a Sample of Adoptees, *American Economic Review*, 94(1), 358–368.

Sacerdote, B. (2000), The Nature and Nurture of Economic Outcomes, *NBER Working Paper 7949*, National Bureau of Economic Research Inc.

Sacerdote, B. (2002), The Nature and Nurture of Economic Outcomes, *American Economic Review*, 92(2): 344–348.

Sacerdote, B. (2007), How Large are the Effects from Changes in Family Environment? A Study of Korean American Adoptees, *Quarterly Journal of Economics*, 122(1), 119–157.

Sato, H. and S. Li (2007), Class Origin, Family Culture, and Intergenerational Correlation of Education in Rural China, *IZA Discussion Papers 2642*, Institute for the Study of Labor (IZA).

Sun, Z. (2011), Family background, public expenditure an high school's enrollment opportunity, *Renmin University Education Review*, 1.

Wen, D. (2005), The Impacts of SES on Higher Education Opportunity and Graduate Employment in China, *Peking University Education Review*, 3(3).

Zhang, J., P. W. Liu, and L. Yung, 2007, The Cultural Revolution and returns to schooling in China: Estimates based on twins, *Journal of Development Economics*, 84(2), 631–639.

Part IV

Other Issues

Chapter 12

Conditions of Maternal Healthcare Services and Exploration on Improving it in Poor Ethnic-minority Areas of China

Min Du, Hongyan Liu, Hui Wan, Shuangyan Gong, Dongmei Liu and Yi Shi

China Population & Development Research Center, China

Abstract: Low level of maternal and child health care is a channel of inter-generational poverty transfer. The United Nations Fund for Population Activities (UNFPA) has worked with China Family Planning Association to implement the maternal healthcare project in the ethnic minority areas of Longlin County of Guangxi Province since 2012. This paper summarized the major factors preventing pregnant and lying-in women from accessing the maternal healthcare services and assessed the effect and experiences of UNFPA project based on a survey conducted by the China Population and Development Research Center (CPDRC) in two poor counties in China. By identifying support targets precisely and diverting resources to the poorest areas, developing community-level service network, and carrying out publicity, mobilization and support activities relating to maternal healthcare, the project effectively improved the accessibility of healthcare service in mountainous communities, significantly strengthened the maternal healthcare knowledge gained by peasant households, and significantly improved the proportion of women receiving maternal services in this area.

Maternal healthcare is an important measure to reduce maternal and child mortality and improve the birth quality of infants. The importance of maternal healthcare is that it not only provides safety for women, but also enhances human capital of the family, and is of important significance for preventing inter-generational transmission of poverty. Therefore, maternal healthcare has become a fundamental component of government's public services. However, inadequate maternal healthcare services are being provided for women from poverty-stricken and remote areas of China. According to a survey launched by The United Nations Fund for Population Activities (UNFPA) and China Family Planning Association in Longlin County of Guangxi Province in 2011, the prenatal examination rate and institutional delivery rate only reached 57% and 37%, respectively in the mountainous areas of this county. The above survey indicates that major factors preventing pregnant and lying-in women from accessing the maternal healthcare services include: subjective perception of the importance of healthcare services; quality and quantity of available services; convenience in service access; affordability of service costs. The quantity and quality of available services and the convenience in service access well reflect the service accessibility, while the affordability of service costs also implies service availability. In order to improve the level of fundamental public services, we cannot afford to neglect factors such as accessibility, availability and perception. With regard to government's practices in public service provision, at least the following problems remain unresolved: inadequate attention paid to those poverty-stricken and remote areas resulting in significant regional differences; underdeveloped service network preventing effective expansion of services to the community level; lack of concern for perception and lack of necessary education to transform perception.

Ever since 2012, UNFPA has been working with China Family Planning Association to implement the maternal healthcare project in the ethnic minority areas of Longlin County of Guangxi Province. By focusing on removing poverty-stricken areas, mobilizing social resources and public participation, improving the MCH network (Maternal and Child Health Network), and strengthening publicity and mobilization, this project has played a positive role in improving the MCH level in mountainous areas, eliminating regional differences and covering the shortages of government services; it also helps accumulate the experience for promoting MCH services in other poverty-stricken areas. In July 2015, as entrusted by China Family Planning Association and UNFPA, China Population and Development Research Center (CPDRC) launched a survey on the local maternal healthcare project in Xinzhou Town (excluding neighborhood committee) and De'e Town of Longlin County, and analyzed and summed up the project implementation status, effects and experience upon interviews and questionnaire survey.

1 General Information about Surveyed Areas and Sample Characteristics

1.1 General information about surveyed areas

Longlin Ethnic Minority Autonomous County is at the Northwest of Guangxi Autonomous Region. Located at the Southeastern edge of Yunnan-Guizhou Plateau, it is a mountainous county covering a total area of 3,551 square kilometers. Longlin County governs 16 townships (towns) and 179 administrative villages (communities), and is inhabited by five ethnic groups (Miao, Yi, Gelao, Zhuang, and Han). By the end of 2014, the total population of the county reached 420,000, with ethnic minority population accounting for 81.2% of gross population. Among the parents involved in the questionnaire survey, Miao people accounted for 68.1% and Zhuang people accounted for 22.7%. The mountainous areas are mainly inhabited by Miao people (77%), while the urban areas are mainly inhabited by Zhuang people (91.3%).

1.2 Survey method

This survey covered eight administrative villages of De'e Town and Xinzhou Town, with Minqiang Village being an urban village located at the rural–urban fringe zone and the other seven being mountainous villages. Meji, Neme, Shuidong and Sanchong are key intervened villages of this project. The survey covered sample questionnaire survey and qualitative survey. The questionnaire survey mainly targeted women with 0–3 child(ren), and samples were selected using the multistage random sampling method (Table 1). Specifically:

Stage 1: Identify the sampling ratio of pregnant and lying-in woman in two towns. During implementation, this project has rendered maternal healthcare services for 1,150 and 1,858 clients, respectively in Xinzhou Town and De'e Town (ratio of 2:3). Based on this ratio, the project team selected 120 clients in Xinzhou Town and 180 clients in De'e Town, with the total number of samples being 300.

Stage 2: Determine the sample village. The randomly selected 4 administrative villages from two towns accounts for 30.8% of the 13 administrative villages of Xinzhou Town and 26.7% of the 15 administrative villages of De'e Town respectively.

Stage 3: Determine sample pregnant and lying-in women in the sample villages. Random sampling selected 30 persons from each of the 4 administrative villages of Xinzhou Town, and 45 persons from each of the 4 administrative villages of De'e Town.

If the spouse of respondent is at home, the research team would also complete the questionnaire survey of spouse at the same time. This survey eventually

Table 1. Sampling design and actual sampling results.

	Number of women with 0–3 child(ren) (1)	Proposed samples (2)	Proposed proportion n (%) (3)	Weight (%) (4)	Actual samples (5)	Proportion n (%) (6)
Xinzhou Town						
Hanshan Village	204	30	14.71	165.58	21	6.80
Minqiang Village	203	30	14.78	164.77	40	12.90
Neme Village	71	30	42.25	57.63	26	8.40
Shuidong Village	94	30	31.91	76.30	34	11.00
De'e Town						
Bake Village	193	45	23.32	120.50	45	14.50
De'e Village	115	45	39.13	71.80	45	14.50
Meji Village	138	45	32.61	86.16	54	17.40
Sanchong Village	126	45	35.71	78.67	45	14.50

completed 310 questionnaires for women and 193 questionnaires for spouse. During qualitative survey, group discussions and individual interviews were organized with women, their spouses, government officials, doctors, FP association staff members, village cadres, village doctors, ethnic minority doctors, etc.

1.3 Sample Characteristics

1. Education

Local villagers are generally less educated, and most of the women are illiterate or semiliterate. For the 310 respondents, 48.1% have received elementary education and 16.2% have never been to school, while 18.7% of respondents from mountainous areas have never been to school. For their spouses, those having received junior high education account for 45.3%. Only 34.5% of respondents can listen, speak and read Mandarin; 10% can understand but cannot speak and read Mandarin; 4.2% cannot understand, speak and read Mandarin. Limited education and poor Mandarin are inhibiting local women from accessing healthcare knowledge and fostering health awareness, thus preventing them from improving the level of maternal health.

2. Current age and the age at first marriage and first birth

The average age of respondents is 25.5, with women aged 21–25 accounting for 41.9%. The average age is 27.6 among urban respondents and 25.2 among mountainous respondents, and 27.7 among their spouses, with those aged 26–30 accounting for 41.6%.

Local women are prone to get married and have child(ren) early. 60% of respondents didn't reach the legal marriage age of 20 at their first marriage (the lowest age at first marriage is 15), with age 15–17 accounting for 8.4% and age 18–20 accounting for 51%. 8.28% of respondents gave birth to their first child at the age less than 18, and 26.8% at the age of 18–20. Low age at first birth is inhibiting them from understanding the maternal health knowledge and compromising the protection of pregnant and lying-in women and their children.

3. Incomes of peasants

Longlin County is a national-level poverty-stricken county,[1] with per capita net income of peasants reaching only RMB 5,120 in 2014, equivalent to 51.8% of the nationwide average per capita net income of peasants. The per capita net income only reaches RMB 3649.7 among the sample peasant households covered by this survey, or RMB 3285.3 only among the sample households living in mountainous areas (only one half of the per capita net income among the sample households living in urban areas). Peasant households from four key intervened villages mainly earn their incomes from crop production, resulting in even lower income level. Among others, the per capita net income among the sample peasant households only reaches RMB 3,600 in Sanchong Village, RMB 2000 in Meji Village, RMB 1,700–1,800 in Shuidong Village and RMB 1,500–1,600 in Neme Village. Poverty has blocked their access to medical and health services and is posing challenges to project intervention.

4. Transportation conditions

For a long time, scattered residence and poor transportation conditions have been the leading causes of low accessibility to maternal healthcare services. The average distance from sample households living in mountainous areas to the township is 9.6 km, while it is only 2.3 km for sample households living in urban areas.

[1]According to the Outline for Development-oriented Poverty Reduction for China's Rural Areas (2011–2020) as promulgated in December 2011, the poverty line is raised to RMB 2300 based on the prices of 2010. According to this poverty line, there were 122.38 million poor population in China, accounting for 13% of rural population. In this Outline, key poverty reduction areas to be supported by the government in the new stage shall include the contiguous poor areas with special difficulties like Liupan Mountain area, Qinba Mountain area, Wuling Mountain area, rocky desertification areas in Yunnan, Guizhou and Guangxi provinces and Tibet where special policies are being implemented. Longlin County is located in the rocky desertification areas in Yunnan, Guizhou and Guangxi provinces.

Table 2. Distribution of distances from sample households to township (%).

Distance (km)	Mountainous area	Urban area	Overall
Less than 2.5	10.7	87.5	20.7
2.5–5	12.6		11.0
5–7.5	17.0	2.5	14.8
7.5–10	23.3		20.7
10–12.5	11.5	2.5	10.3
12.5 and more	24.8	7.5	22.6

Among sample households living in mountainous areas, those whose distance to the township exceeding 12.5 km account for 24.8%, and those reaching 7.5–10 km account for 23.3% (Table 2). In recent years, due to the considerate investment made by Longlin County in transportation infrastructures, the transportation conditions have improved significantly which facilitated the antenatal care and institutional delivery of pregnant and lying-in women, however, the road conditions in remote villages are still inadequate to meet the travel needs. For example, the distance from Shuidong Village to the county reaches about 15 km, and the mountain road is rugged and narrow. By the end of this survey, 50% of the road remains unpaved. Meanwhile, given the backward public transportation in many villages, women are still faced with many inconveniences in travel.

2 Scope of Project Work

Based on the results of the baseline survey carried out in 2011, this project selected mountainous areas as intervention targets in order to explore the effective way to improve the level of maternal healthcare in remote areas. The objective of this project is to improve the level of maternal healthcare by improving the accessibility of MCH services and promote the use of MCH services among women.

2.1 To identify support targets precisely and divert resources to the poorest areas

Low level of maternal healthcare service utilization is mainly observed in poverty-stricken and remote mountainous areas. Long distance and poor transportation conditions are inhibiting the service access of peasant households and preventing medical workers (including village doctors) from delivering door-to-door services. Therefore, this project has diverted its resources to 27 mountainous villages and employed the precise support strategy to ensure effective utilization of limited resources. Under proper guidance, these villages have developed the information map of community resources and pregnant and lying-in women to mark the geographic location, distance, road conditions and available means of transport of each village, and to provide information about gross population and pregnant and lying-in women. Through the community map, we could have a clear understanding of the most underdeveloped and the remotest communities dominated by home birth. Furthermore, a regular meeting is held once every month in the pilot town so that each village can report the information about local pregnant and lying-in women, identify those in dire need of support and discuss the support plan. In the early phase, this project covered 452 villagers' groups of 28 administrative villages, well increasing the institutional delivery rate in the short run. In the medium phase, the project resources were concentrated in four villages (Sanchong, Shuidong, Neme and Meji) which are underdeveloped in economy and backward in the MCH service level in order to carry out focused interventions. In the final phase, the institutional delivery rate of all administrative villages was improved significantly, yet there was a big gap between the antenatal care rate and the stipulated 5-time antenatal care. Project resources were further concentrated in the most backward 10 administrative villages to carry out community support activities.

2.2 To develop community-level service network

Currently, China implements a three-tier (county, township, and village) healthcare service network system, with village-level healthcare service being the most vulnerable part. The government investment in public health is always made from top to bottom, with county-level and township-level medical institutions being the key targets of community-level investment, particularly the county-level medical institutions. Such a model is undoubtedly the most efficient choice in regions with well-developed transport system and concentrated population, yet for those scattered peasant households living in mountainous areas with underdeveloped infrastructures, this model means poor accessibility and availability of healthcare services (Ling, 2001). The chronic absence of healthcare services in these areas will in turn suppress their attempts to access medical services. This is exactly the case in Longlin County. Before the implementation of this project, Longlin County was attempting to improve the maternal healthcare level through the three-tier healthcare service network. Still, due to inadequate medical resources and weak technical forces at the community level and the absence of a mechanism to kindle the enthusiasm of medical workers, the operating efficiency of three-tier service network is not very high. This problem is especially severe in mountainous villages. Given the vast area, excess number of villagers' groups[2] and scattered

[2]For instance, among the 15 administrative villages of De'e Town, 9 villages have more than 20 villagers' groups each, and one village has even 28 villagers' groups.

residence of villagers, the village-level service network, with an excess service radius, cannot provide convenient and instant service for remote communities. To address the problem of "first one kilometer" faced by pregnant and lying-in women seeking and using the maternal healthcare services, this project has mobilized community forces to add community-level into the three-tier service network. Under the support of this project, a community-level health group has been set up in all administrative villages, with village head or secretary-general serving as the leader and members including village cadres, family planning association members, village doctors, head of women's affairs, special family planning cadre, leader of villagers' group and volunteers. The health groups leverage the model of dividing up the work and assigning a part to each group to establish one-to-one connection between the community and individuals, and carry out MCH publicity and support among pregnant and lying-in women in the remote mountainous areas. In the four-tier service network, the community becomes a tie connecting individuals and households with medical institutions, thus avoiding the problem of remote peasant households being marginalized in the traditional three-tier service network. By mobilizing and utilizing community resources, the practice of bottoming the service network at the community level in remote mountainous areas is of important enlightening significance and demonstration effect for China to strengthen the MCH work in the poverty-stricken remote areas.

2.3 To carry out publicity, mobilization and support activities relating to maternal healthcare

Ever since its implementation, the project has been relying on the community health group to carry out the publicity, education and mobilization of maternal and child healthcare. Specific tasks included: (1) to calculate the number of pregnant and lying-in women; (2) to distribute "China-UNFPA CP7 Ethnic Minority Reproductive Health Component: Maternal Healthcare Manual" and "Key Information for Mothers-to-be"; (3) to disseminate maternal healthcare knowledge to every household with pregnant or lying-in woman, such as signs of pregnancy, how to calculate the expected date of childbirth, frequency, timing and contents of prenatal examinations, dangerous signs in the pregnant and puerperal period, prenatal nutrition and use of drugs, signs of labor, benefits of institutional delivery, essential conditions for home birth, etc; (4) to mobilize and urge pregnant and lying-in women to receive antenatal care and institutional delivery service; (5) to pay postnatal visits; (6) to provide necessary assistance for underprivileged households with pregnant and lying-in women.

Yang Yachun (Miao ethnic group, aged 32) from Baobao Community, Neme Village, Xinzhou Town said: *"My husband wasn't at home to help me when I was in labor, and nobody would help me out. So I sought help from the head of village (member of Health Group), and he managed to find me a car."*

The contact person of health group will report the collected information to the village doctor and the FP cadre, and such information is further reported to the township health center and FP office after collation. The township health center will establish the maternal health records based on such information and include them into the maternal healthcare system. This model has offset the current limitations confronted by medical institutions, namely the medical workers can only come into contact with visiting patients and know nothing about the situations of those pregnant and lying-in women who have never been to the hospital. In addition, once a pregnant woman has been mobilized to attend antenatal care, the doctor can immediately learn about her information and have the opportunity to carry out follow-up publicity, mobilization and service. The township FP offices and FP service stations are also directly carrying out maternal healthcare publicity, mobilization and support in the villages, during which they need to cooperate with the community-level health group. Such a model has effectively addressed such problems as blocked information dissemination and poor accessibility of public health services due to the scattered distribution of ethnic minority villages.

3 Project Outcomes

3.1 Effectively improved the accessibility of healthcare service in mountainous communities

By setting up the community health groups, the project was able to take care of every pregnant woman, change their inherent attitude and encourage and urge them to make full use of the medical service resources.

Head of Shuidong Village (leader of the health group) said: *"Since the launch of the 'Project to reduce maternal mortality rate and eliminate neonatal tetanus', the order of publicity has been issued by the county government. The village has over 40 pregnant and lying-in women every year, and the publicity work used to be undertaken by the village doctor who was too busy to do the job. After the establishment of the health group in 2012, we divided up the work and started to mobilize these women to go to the hospital. Now villagers start to attach importance to prenatal examination."*

Leader of the community health group of Meji Village said: *"Every month we report the information about pregnant and lying-in women (including name, number of prenatal examinations, postnatal visits, etc.) to the health center and urge them to go get examined. At first they refused to go because they have no idea about the prenatal examination. Later they all know about the prenatal examination." "At first we go to every household to do the publicity, advising them to examine whether the position of fetus is normal and to deliver the baby in the hospital in case of massive hemorrhage after the delivery. From mouth to mouth, they all go to attend the prenatal examination eventually."*

Villager Yang Zhengfu has two children. The first child was born in 2010 and the second was born in 2015. He said: *"We didn't attend the prenatal examination when we had the first child, but we attended 10 prenatal examinations for the second child. We knew nothing about the prenatal examination when we had the first child. We know this now because we were told by the head and secretary of the village. According to the publicity, prenatal examination helps you determine whether the baby is OK."*

Through the community health group, the project has also expanded publicity and mobilization into every household with pregnant or lying-in woman. In the hospital, the doctor can only meet the pregnant or lying-in woman alone, who might have difficulties in Mandarin communication due to low level of education. By advising and mobilizing the whole family, the community health group manages to persuade the family to urge the pregnant woman to attend prenatal examination and deliver the baby at the hospital. A woman from Sanchong Village mentioned that the notice is usually delivered by the community leader, and will be pasted onto the door if no one is at home. If no family member can read, the community leader will explain to the whole family. Under our persistent publicity and mobilization, the inherent attitude of all family members has been transformed. With a better understanding of knowledge and information about the prenatal and postnatal periods, all family members will proactively support and assist pregnant and lying-in women to accept the services.

You Yaren from Shuidong Village is 22 years old. She only finished the 3rd Grade of elementary education and has given birth to one child. She was pregnant when the survey was carried out. She told the surveyor that she had attended two prenatal examinations, upon insistance from her husband and the village head (her contact person in the health group). The first child of You Yaren was born in 2011 at home, and the second child will be delivered at the hospital. She said: *"My mother told me to deliver the child at the hospital as home birth could be dangerous."*

3.2 Significant improvement in the maternal healthcare knowledge gained by peasant households

3.2.1 *Increasing proportion of knowledge access*

Ever since the implementation of this project, the proportion of pregnant and lying-in women gaining MCH knowledge has been significantly increased, and the gap

Table 3. Proportion of women and their spouses gaining varied knowledge in the past three years (%).

	Woman	Man
Importance of prenatal examination	88.9	91.9
Importance of institutional delivery	87.5	97.3
Childhood immunization	86.2	77.7
Benefits of breast feeding	82.4	84.8
Dangerous signs of pregnant woman and child	75.3	59.2
Nutrition for pregnant/lying-in woman and child	74.3	63.6
Expected date of childbirth	56.1	46.2
Maternal health	55.1	48.6

between urban areas and mountainous areas is narrowing rapidly. During the period from the baseline survey in 2011 and the end-line survey in 2015, the proportion of women having gained MCH knowledge in the past 3 years have increased from 55.2% to 96.3% (from 72.2% to 100% for women from urban areas and from 46.7% to 95.7% for women from mountainous areas). The gap between them has been reduced from 26% to 5%.

One major outcome of this project in its family-based interventions is the evident improvement in knowledge access among males. During this period, the proportion of spouses gaining relevant knowledge has also increased from 49.6% to 93.8%, and the urban–rural gap has dropped from 30% to around 7%.

3.2.2 *Richer knowledge gained and key knowledge enhanced*

Among the MCH knowledge, the knowledge on the importance of prenatal examination and institutional delivery is best disseminated, followed by the knowledge on the importance of childhood immunization and the benefits of breast feeding (Table 3).

The awareness of two critical indicators of project interventions, namely the required times of prenatal examinations and the dangerous signs in the gestational period, has also been significantly improved. During the period from baseline survey to end-line survey, the proportion of women knowing that at least 5 prenatal examinations are needed has went up from 37% to 62.8%. This proportion has increased from 22% to 62.8% among women living in the mountainous areas, and the urban–rural gap has dropped from 43% to 22%. The same transition also applies to their awareness of the dangerous signs in the gestational period. The proportion of respondents who know more than 3 dangerous signs in the gestational period has

Table 4. Variations of two critical intervention indicators by area (rural and urban) and by gender (%).

		2011		2015	
		Urban	Rural	Urban	Rural
Female	Knowing that pregnant women must attend at least 5 prenatal examinations	65.6	22	85	62.8
	Knowing at least 3 dangerous signs in the gestational period	68.9	32.4	80	75.9
Male	Knowing that pregnant women must attend at least 5 prenatal examinations	38.5	12.2	71	61
	Knowing at least 3 dangerous signs in the gestational period	56.4	28.4	60	48.9

increased from 44.5% to 76.4%, or from 32.4% to 75.9% among women living the mountainous areas. This proportion has gone up from 38.1% to 50.3% among males (Table 4). The proportion of spouses who know that pregnant women must attend at least 5 prenatal examinations and the proportion of spouses who know more than 3 dangerous signs in the gestational period are all lower than same proportions among women, yet the gap is narrowing significantly, especially in the mountainous areas.

3.2.3 *More diversified measures of gaining knowledge and information*

During the baseline survey, MCH knowledge was mainly passed down from generation to generation inside the family. During the end-line survey, extensive and standardized publicity, education and mobilization have become the primary means for women to gain relevant knowledge and information. About 94.1% of respondents have received the manual for mother and child; 84.1% believe that "Key Information for Mothers-to-be" is extremely helpful for maternal healthcare. Among persons who advise pregnant women of the importance of prenatal examination and mobilize them to attend prenatal examination, health group contact person, village cadres, doctors and FP cadres account for 84.5%, 82.1%, 81.5% and 81.4% respectively, while husband, parents and parents-in-law, sisters and other relatives only account for 71.5%, 57.8%, 38.9% and 26.8%. Among persons who advise pregnant women of the importance of institutional delivery and mobilize them to have institutional delivery, prenatal examination doctors, health group contact person and FP cadres account for 86.9%, 82.3% and 74.5% respectively, far higher than the proportions of other family members, relatives and friends.

Table 5. Arrangements made by the father during the gestational and lying-in period of the youngest child (%).

	Overall	Rural	Urban
Gain knowledge on the gestational and lying-in period	65.48	66.3	61.3
Gain knowledge on child rearing	58.16	62.4	35.5
Advise wife of the MCH knowledge	57.14	61.2	35.4
Improve the nutrition of wife	91.84	90.3	100
Urge the wife to attend prenatal examinations	67.35	69.7	54.8
Contact the hospital and prepare for delivery	64.29	66.7	51.6
Accompany the wife to attend prenatal examinations	86.73	85.5	93.6
Do the housework proactively	87.24	87.9	83.9

3.2.4 *Significant changes in the attitude toward maternal healthcare*

The publicity and mobilization of maternal healthcare have also transformed the attitude of pregnant and lying-in women and their families. During the end-line survey, 99.5% of spouses opted for institutional delivery; this proportion is 16% higher from the 83.6% during the baseline survey; 82.5% of pregnant women were accompanied by family member(s) during each prenatal examination, and only 3.4% had no company. The spouses now attach reat importance to nurturing their pregnant wives. Only 11.3% of spouses were still working outside during the gestational period of their wives, and 80.8% accompanied their wives during the lying-in period. During the gestational and lying-in period, certain spouses also managed to improve the nutrition of their wives and do household work in an active manner. It is noteworthy that in regard to finding child rearing knowledge, reading MCH manual, advising the wife of MCH knowledge, urging the wife to attend prenatal examinations and contact the hospital, the spouses of women from mountainous areas did better than those from urban areas (Table 5). It could be attributed to the project influence on the awareness of spouses living in mountainous areas. On the other hand, it is more difficult for women living in the mountainous areas to attend prenatal examinations and have institutional delivery, and thus it is more necessary for the husband to urge and provide help.

3.3 Significant improvement in the proportion of women receiving maternal services

3.3.1 *Evident improvement in the indicator of prenatal examination service*

Major indicators for measuring the prenatal examination service include prenatal examination coverage, 5-time prenatal examination coverage, etc. Generally

Table 6. Receipt of prenatal examination service (%).

	Baseline			End-line		
	Longlin	Rural	Urban	Longlin	Rural	Urban
Attending prenatal examinations	69.9	57.1	95.6	98.7	98.5	100
Attending 5-time or more prenatal examinations	29.4	8.8	71.1	69.2	67.4	82.5
On-schedule prenatal examinations	18.8	3.9	48.9	47.1	43.7	70
Prenatal examinations covering at least four items	39.3	9.3	71.1	94.2	93.3	100

speaking, all relevant indicators improved significantly during project implementation, with the urban–rural gap narrowing apparently. During the end-line survey, the prenatal examination coverage reached 98.7%, up by 29% from the baseline survey; the 5-time prenatal examination rate reached 69.2%, up by 40%; the on-schedule prenatal examination rate[3] reached 47.1%, up by 28%; the proportion of prenatal examinations covering at least four items reached 94.2%, up by 55% (Table 6).

The prenatal examination coverage reached 98.5% among women living in the mountainous areas, up by 31% from the baseline survey, and the urban–rural gap reduced from 38.5% to 15%. The urban–rural gaps with regard to 5-time prenatal examination rate, on-schedule prenatal examination rate and the proportion of prenatal examinations covering at least 4 items have also dropped from 62.3% to 15.%, from 45% to 26.3% and from 61.8% to 6.7% respectively.

3.3.2 *Significant improvement in the proportion of institutional deliveries*

According to the end-line survey, the proportion of institutional delivery of last child among respondents was 92.6% (which is lower than the official institutional delivery rate of 98.5% obtained in 2015), and the proportion of institutional delivery of the penultimate child was 60%, up by 35% and 23% respectively from the baseline survey. During the baseline survey, the urban–rural gap with regard to institutional delivery rate reached as high as 61%, and when it came to the end-line survey, the urban–rural gap dropped to 8.5%. Increased emphasis is now being put on

[3]On-schedule prenatal examination means that the respondent can attend the prenatal examinations required in all four stages of the gestational period (first 12 weeks, weeks 13–27, weeks 28–36, week 37 to labor), namely, the total number of prenatal examinations meet the 5-time requirement and were attended on schedule.

institutional delivery, which has become a fashion even in the villages. People may feel losing face if the baby was not born in the hospital.

4 Experience and Implications

The maternal healthcare project carried out in ethnic minority areas gave full play to the institutional innovation advantage and resource mobilization capacity of NGOs and well reflected the complementary roles of the government and non-government organizations in the poverty reduction actions. The characteristics of the project in its practices and explorations have also provided helpful experience for reducing the health risks of women and children in broader poverty-stricken areas.

4.1 Focusing on remote poverty-stricken areas and addressing the imbalanced MCH service level

Low level of maternal and child heal is a major cause of inter-generational poverty transfer. Providing maternal healthcare service aid for pregnant and lying-in women from underprivileged families will not only ensure the physical safety of the mother and the child, but also contribute significantly to the improvement in the future human resources situations of these families and the elimination of poverty. The poverty-stricken remote areas are characterized by the weakest MCH services. The low usage of maternal healthcare service by women living in the poverty-stricken remote areas is not because they do not need such services. Some of them do have such a need but cannot have access to the corresponding services due to the financial conditions, traffic conditions, etc. Others have no idea of the presence or the benefits of such public services due to the remoteness of their residence or their limited knowledge and education. This project, by concentrating the limited resources and sticking to the principle of adjusting measures to local conditions and helping the poor precisely, invested the resources in pregnant and lying-in women living in poverty-stricken mountainous areas and their families. This accurate targeting strategy has instantly eliminated the regional difference with regard to the MCH service level. Given its helpful role in improving the population quality and accelerating poverty reduction, this strategy shall become the basic rule for allocating government and non-government resources in MCH service construction.

4.2 Strengthening the construction of embedded organizations and facilitating service decentralization

This project started with the weakest part of maternal healthcare service network and facilitated the decentralization of maternal healthcare services into the poverty-stricken rural communities, thus improving service accessibility at low costs. The model of dedicating the community health group to its responsible district well caters to the scattered residences of peasant households in the remote areas. By exploiting the community resources and uniting the community forces, this project has effectively strengthened the functionality of rural MCH network. Under the circumstance of limited public expenditures and limited NGO resources, only by allocating resources to targets well facilitating the effective prevention of the health risks of mothers and children can we achieve the expected results at low costs. As stressed by UNFPA, "money is an important resource, but resource doesn't necessarily mean money." Although the community health group might look shabby from the view of healthcare service provision and institutional construction, it has effectively improved the public awareness of the basic public health services, and has leveraged its own authority to encourage and urge the general public to accept the maternal healthcare services, thus developing the fashion and habit eventually. In addition, the community health group can also help solve many realistic difficulties, such as arranging a car to drive the pregnant/lying-in woman to the hospital, helping take care of the livestock and the family when the woman is in hospital, and providing financial support by borrowing money. Promoting such embedded community-level new organization like the community health group and building the four-tier (county, township, village, community) MCH service network in greater scope should be the essential requirements for comprehensively improving the MCH service level. During this process, the newly established community-level organization shall recruit more female members to facilitate communication, publicity and mobilization.

Reference

Ling, Z. (2001), Improving Village-level Social Service Capacity and Reducing the Maternal and Child Health Risks of Underprivileged Households, *Chinese Journal of Population Science*, 6.

Chapter 13

Empirical Analysis on Competition among Railway, Highway and Civil Aviation in the Passenger Market in China — From the Perspective of Railway Industry Regulatory Reform

Qing Guo* and Yongchao Li†

Economics School,
Shandong University of Finance and Economics, China
**gq1992@163.com*
†*liyongchao87130@163.com*

Abstract: The empirical analysis of competition patterns among railway, highway and civil aviation shows the following: The competition between railway and highway in short — distance market focuses on price and network scale; The competition among railway, highway and civil aviation in medium — long distance market mainly focuses on price, and network; in long — distance market, the competition between railway and civil aviation focuses on price and speed. This chapter suggests that the intermodal competition should be highly valued, and the new regulation agency of railway should design the regulatory policies based on intermodal competition.

1 Introduction

Railway in China is traditionally a state-owned organisation, regulated and operated by the Ministry of Railway (MoR). For regulation, MoR acts as a division of the government, and for operation it acts like an enterprise (Zhang and Dominique, 2005). State Railway Administration and China Railway Corporation were set up in the institutional reform of the State Council of 2013 in China, the former is a component department of Ministry of Transport of the People's Republic of China, and the latter is an enterprise. Although the isolated roles of the government from enterprise were achieved through reform by creating an independent regulatory agency, the industry is still monopolised by one operator. It is necessary to introduce competitive mechanisms in Chinese railways.

There are four ways to introduce competitive mechanisms in railways. The first way is on-track competition which separates infrastructure management from transport operation. The common opinion about the natural monopoly industries is that deregulation is needed in the fields of competitive business, but business in networks still has the natural monopoly so long as the economies of scale or scope exist. (Yu and Yu, 2004; Hausman and Stewart, 2002). Therefore, establishing new enterprise structure for railway transport by separating infrastructure management from transport operation may be a useful way to increase competition. However, whether to opt for a market structure that vertically integrates infrastructure and operations, or for one that separates them depends on whether infrastructure costs and operating costs are related, i.e. if there are complementary or substitute effects between infrastructure and operations (Cantos, 2001).

The second way is parallel competition. If the network could provide the possibility of different routes between the main traffic generators, there aren't any large cost distortions between the routes and with effective regulations, parallel competition could improve welfare.

The third one is competition for the market. If monopoly is the optimal market structure, in other words, the industry is a natural monopoly industry, competitive tendering for the operating right will put sufficient competitive pressure on the monopoly operator. But to do so, there should be no large-scale sunk cost and collusion between the bidders (Morrison and Clifford, 1987).

The fourth one is yardstick competition. By splitting a monopoly railway company horizontally into several regional companies, the yardstick competition regulation would induce them to compete with each other and improve their efficiency. To perform yardstick competition, the regional companies should have similar cost structure and there should be no collusion between them.

In regulation practice, the US opted for parallel competition; the EU countries mostly adopted on-track competition; yardstick competition was used in Japanese railway regulation (Ou, 2004). In China, sizeable literatures suggested to separate infrastructure management from transport operation (Rong, 2000; Liu, 2003; Xiao, 2004). Some studies suggested setting up regional companies and implementing yardstick competition regulation (Yu, 2003; Zhao, 2005). Considering the restriction of some economic or political factors, insignificant literatures suggested to implement parallel competition or competition for the market reform. In fact, two plans were made out respectively in Chinese railways reform, one was based on the on-track competition theory, and the other was based on the yardstick competition theory, but none was actually implemented.

With the large scale construction of highway and the development of low-cost airlines, more and more evidences show that railways are facing considerable external competition (Severin, 1992; Frank and Kopplelmann, 2002; Preston, 2002; Clever *et al.*, 2008; Peter, 2009; Dobruszkes, 2011). Some empirical studies show that intermodal competitions exist in Chinese passenger transport market (Luo and Yan, 2000). Although more and more papers focus on intermodal competitions, there are still no regulatory policies based on this kind of competition in China.

This chapter will focus on the introduction of competition in Chinese railways by analyzing intermodal competition in China. The second part will examine the competition among railway, highway and civil aviation in the passenger market in China. The third part will get some conclusions based on the empirical studies.

2 Pattern of Intermodal Competition

2.1 Change of mode share

When choosing transport mode, passengers mainly consider the following characteristics: safety, price, time for the shipment, comfort and convenience. Each transportation mode has characteristics distinguishing it from others. It implies that competition will not exist in all ranges, and the competition pattern will vary with distance. To analyse the change of modal share of each mode from 1987 to 2010, this chapter found that the participants of mode competition are different in different distances. Table 1 provides the changes of modal share.

Highway has predominance over railway and civil aviation within 100 km. The highest mode share of railway was 11.7% in 1987 and declined sharply to only 0.6% in 2010. While civil aviation never offered service in this distance.

From 101 to 500 km, the competition of railway and highway is fierce. The mode share of highway gradually increased in the range of 101–200 km and 201–500 km, ascending from 37.5% and 22.5% in 1987 to 88.1% and 58.3% in 2010, respectively. In the corresponding period, railway declined from 57.6% and 70.7% to 20.5% and 40.7%. Civil aviation has never been involved in the market of less than 200 km. The highest mode share of civil aviation was only 0.8% in 201–500 km, and then reduced after 2000 and finally withdrawn from this market.

Within the range of 501–1000 km, mode share of highway increased from 6.4% (1987) to 12.5% (2010) gradually, and civil aviation ascended from 2.4% (1987) to

Table 1. Changes of modal share (%).

	Year	100^{-1} km	101 to 200 km	201 to 500 km	501 to 1000 km	1001 to 2000 km	2001^{+} km
Highway	1987	83.3	37.5	22.5	6.4	—	—
	1990	89.5	52.5	30.2	7.3	1.6	—
	1995	93.8	64.8	43.3	7.1	3.5	—
	2000	96.5	73.8	50.6	9.0	4.0	—
	2005	97.7	82.4	53.8	11.4	5.6	1.2
	2010	98.6	88.1	58.3	12.5	6.9	2.0
Railway	1987	11.7	57.6	70.7	89.5	93.0	90.0
	1990	7.0	43.8	64.2	84.2	84.6	82.3
	1995	4.2	32.7	53.3	81.9	68.9	84.7
	2000	2.1	25.1	48.1	78.4	71.1	80.8
	2005	1.4	22.8	45.4	73.1	66.5	71.2
	2010	0.6	20.5	40.7	70.3	62.7	66.3
Civil Aviation	1987	—	—	0.3	2.4	7.0	10.0
	1990	—	—	0.6	5.2	13.8	17.7
	1995	—	—	0.8	9.3	27.6	15.3
	2000	—	—	0.4	9.5	24.8	19.2
	2005	—	—	0.2	12.3	27.9	27.6
	2010	—	—	—	16.9	30.4	31.7

Data source: Website of the ministry of railways, civil aviation administration and the ministry of transport.

16.9% (2010). Accordingly, railways decreased from 89.5% in 1987 to 70.3% in 2010. So, in this distance there are competitions among highway, railways and civil aviation.

Over 1001 kilometers, mode share of highway was only 6.9% and 2.0% in 1001–2000 km and over 2001 km till 2010. So the main participants of mode competition in this distance are railways and civil aviation.

2.2 Model and data

The following model was set up to test the pattern of intermodal competition.

$$Y_t = r_0 + r_1 \ln TE_t + r_2 \ln RM_t + r_3 RS_t + r_4 RP_t + r_5 \ln HM_t + r_6 HP_t + r_7 \ln AM_t + r_8 AP_t + u_t,$$

where Y stands for output of railways which was measured by 1,000 passenger trip per unit mileage; t stands for years; TE stands for economic development level measured by Per capita expenditures on traffic; *RP*, *HP* and *AP* stand for price of railway, highway and civil aviation respectively; *RM*, *HM* and *AM* stand for mileage of railway line, highway and civil aviation domestic routes respectively; *RS* stands for speed of passenger train.

It is worth noting that marketization reform of civil aviation was introduced in 1997 in China. Price of civil aviation has come down with the deregulation reform. Accordingly, railways have raised speed six times after 1997.

Therefore, considering the effect of distance and reform process, this chapter extends the basic model to the following models.

$$Y_{st} = r_0 + r_1 \ln TE_{st} + r_2 \ln RM_{st} + r_3 RS_{st} + r_4 RP_{st} + r_5 \ln HM_{st} + r_6 HP_{st} + u_t \quad , \qquad \text{(Model I)}$$

$$Y_{t1} = r_0 + r_1 \ln TE_{t1} + r_2 \ln RM_{t1} + r_3 RS_{t1} + r_4 RP_{t1} + r_5 \ln HM_{t1} + r_6 HP_{t1} + r_7 \ln AM_{t1} + r_8 AP_{t1} + u_{t1}, \qquad \text{(Model II}_1\text{)}$$

$$Y_{t2} = r_0 + r_1 \ln TE_{t2} + r_2 \ln RM_{t2} + r_3 RS_{t2} + r_4 RP_{t2} + r_5 \ln HM_{t2} + r_6 HP_{t2} + r_7 \ln AM_{t2} + r_8 AP_{t2} + u_{t2}, \qquad \text{(Model II}_2\text{)}$$

$$Y_{lt1} = r_0 + r_1 \ln TE_{lt1} + r_2 \ln RM_{lt1} + r_3 RS_{lt1} + r_4 RP_{lt1} + r_7 \ln AM_{lt1} + r_8 AP_{lt1} + u_{t1} \quad , \qquad \text{(Model III}_1\text{)}$$

$$Y_{lt2} = r_0 + r_1 \ln TE_{lt2} + r_2 \ln RM_{lt2} + r_3 RS_{lt2} + r_4 RP_{lt2} + r_7 \ln AM_{lt2} + r_8 AP_{lt2} + u_{t2} \quad . \qquad \text{(Model III}_2\text{)}$$

Model I is applied to analyse the competition between railways and highway in the short-distance market (101–500 km). Models II_1 and II_2 are applied to analyse the competition among railways, highway and civil aviation in the medium – long distance market (501–1000 km). Among the two, the former is used for the period of 1987–1997, and the latter is used for the period of 1997–2010. Models III_1 and III_2 are applied to analyse the competition between railways and civil aviation in the long-distance market (over 1001 km), and were used for the period of 1987–1997 and 1997–2010 respectively.

This chapter uses the time series data from 1988 to 2011. The data is available in *China Statistical Yearbook*, *China Transportation Yearbook*, *The Analysis Report of Chinese Railway Industry* (*from 2005 to 2011*) and website of the National Bureau of Statistics, the Former Ministry of Railways, the Former Ministry of Transport, Civil Aviation Administration of China and the China Economic Information Network. The prices are calculated at constant prices based on 1987. All of the data passed the Augmented Dickey–Fuller stationary test. Table 2 provides summary statistics.

Table 2. Descriptive statistics.

Variable	Mean	Maximum	Minimum	Standard deviation
Expenditures on traffic (Ln *TE*)	4.311	5.749	3.021	0.881
Railways mileage (Ln *RM*)	1.908	2.21	1.723	0.141
Speed of passenger train (*RS*)	66.129	80.6	56.2	8.939
Price of railways (*RP*)	0.078	0.13	0.02	0.033
Highway mileage (Ln *HM*)	5.082	5.994	4.448	0.528
Price of highway (*HP*)	2.469	2.941	2.175	0.205
Mileage of Civil Aviation domestic routes (Ln *AM*)	4.815	5.622	3.621	0.607
Price of civil aviation (*AP*)	0.429	0.71	0.11	0.191

Table 3. Time series data regression estimates.

Variable	Model I	Model II_1	Model II_2	Model III_1	Model III_2
C	10.56368	−3.00066	−6.655223	−0.129026	−8.63538
	(2.863508)***	(−1.671017)*	(−1.866261)*	(−10.96496)***	(−18.03411)***
Ln *TE*	2.990670				
	(4.587540)***				
Ln *RM*		4.215503	4.655447		
		(2.620029)**	(2.735947)**		
RS				0.012039	0.165292
				(1.626089)*	(3.551501)**
RP				−3.151287	−18.83400
				(−2.355294)**	(−1.769771)**
Ln *HM*	−2.256193				
	(−2.069493)**				
HP	0.893697	0.169993	0.274055		
	(1.089529)**	(0.834151)**	(1.749469)*		
Ln *AM*		−1.089154			
		(−5.162247)***			
AP			0.981007	0.424826	4.340271
			(0.637797)**	(1.331683)	(3.052963)**
R^2	0.750202	0.946121	0.895930	0.665198	0.932450
Corrected R^2	0.712732	0.923030	0.861239	0.521712	0.907119
D. W. Value	1.572296	1.771300	1.731532	2.267388	2.352946
F statistic	20.02160	40.97337	25.82662	4.635966	36.81046

Note: Among the Dependent variables, the first line is the coefficient estimates, the parentheses in the second line is *t*-statistics. "***, **, *" Represent 1%, 5%, 10% significance level, respectively.

2.3 Empirical results

Since there is no any given hypotheses about the competition pattern from the existing papers, this chapter tries to disclose the pattern by stepwise regression. Table 3 provides the results of the regression.

2.3.1 *Short-distance market*

Competition between railways and highway in short-distance market (101–500 km) mainly focuses on price. Per unit fall of the relative price of highway will cause a reduction of 0.894 in 1,000 passenger trip. This implies that railways and highway can be substituted in this market, and the factors influencing the relative price such as tolls, price of petrol will influence the competition between railways and highway.

The competition not only focuses on price but also infrastructure construction. One percent increase of highway mileage will cause a decline of 2.256 in 1,000 passenger trip of railways. Actually, the construction of highway network is the main reason for the decline of railways mode share.

Although raising speed is seen as an important means for railways to compete with highway, the regression shows that the impact of raising speed is not significant. There are two causes for this result. First, owing to the large scale construction of highway network and the improvement of coach's performance, it is comfortable and convenient to travel by coach in short distance. Railways cannot obtain any significant advantage only by raising speed. Second, up to a certain extent, the time saved by raising speed is traded off by traffic congestion.

2.3.2 *Medium–long distance market*

The regulatory policies on relative industries determine the choice of competition pattern. Competition among railways, highway and civil aviation focuses on price and scale of network.

The competition pattern before and after 1997 is different. In the first stage (1987–1997), RM, HP and AM can explain 90% of the output variation of railways. It implies that the competition between railways and highway focuses on price, and that between railways and civil aviation focuses on network construction. In the second stage (1998–2010), after the regulatory reform in civil aviation, RM, HP and AP can explain 90% of the output variation of railways. It implies that railways and civil aviation concentrated on competition via price instead of network construction. In other words, the change of regulatory policies results in the change of competition pattern.

Price competition is important for railways in medium — long distance market. Whatever competes with highway or civil aviation, price is the focus of competition for railways. Particularly, civil aviation price has a greater influence on output of railways than relative price of highway. That is to say, civil aviation is the main competitor of railways in price competition.

The scale of railways network has positive impacts on railways output. In the two stages, 1% raise in railways mileage will result in an increase of 4.215 and 4.655 in 1,000 passenger trip respectively. Therefore network construction would enhance railways competitiveness in medium — long distance passenger market.

2.3.3 *Long-distance market*

Railways and civil aviation concentrated on competition via price and speed in long — distance market. The competition has undergone two main stages.

In the first stage (1987–1997), most of the coefficients were non-significant. RS, RP and AP can only explain 66.5% of the output variation of railways. Actually, the brands' measure of differentiation δ[1] is only 0.11 in this stage. Railways and civil aviation cannot be substituted under the strict price regulation and with the significant speed difference.

In the second stage (1998–2010), RS, RP and AP can explain 93.2% of the output variation of railways. All of the coefficients passed the T test. The brands' measure of differentiation δ has increased five times compared with the first stage. The competition between railways and civil aviation mainly focuses on price. Since the own-price elasticity of railways is bigger than cross-price elasticity, price reduction is a useful way for railways to enhance competitiveness. Another way to enhance competitiveness is by raising speed. The regression shows that the raising of 1 km/h in passenger train speed will cause an increase of 0.165 in 1,000 passenger trip.

3 Conclusions

Although four ways to introduce competitive mechanisms in railways have been suggested, none has been used in Chinese railways reforms. With the large scale construction of highway and the development of low-cost airlines, more and more evidences show that railways are facing considerable external competition.

Empirical study shows that competition between railways and highway in short-distance market (101–500 km) focuses not only on price, but also on network construction. In medium — long distance market (501–1000 km), competition focuses on price and civil aviation is the main competitor of railways in price

[1] See Oz (1995). Assume the demand structure for the two products: $p_1 = \alpha - \beta q_1 - \gamma q_2$ and $p_2 = \alpha - \gamma q_1 - \beta q_2$, where $\beta > 0$, $\beta^2 > \gamma^2$, then the brands' measure of differentiation, denoted by δ is: $\delta = \gamma^2/\beta^2$.

competition. While, railways and civil aviation concentrated on competition via price and speed in long — distance market (over 1001 km).

Although railways have raised speed six times after 1997, this chapter shows that raising speed only can enhance railways competitiveness in long-distance market, not in short-distance and medium-long distance market.

Regulatory policies on relative industries determine the choice of competition pattern. Regulatory reforms of civil aviation in 1997 have changed the competition pattern of railways and civil aviation. Railways reform in 2013 achieved to separate the functions of the government from enterprise by creating an independent regulatory agency, but the industry is still monopolized by one operator. Since it's difficult to introduce competition in railway industry, it is important to consider the intermodal competition while designing the new regulatory policies.

Acknowledgments

We would like to acknowledge and sincerely pay special thanks and regards to Professor John Whalley (Department of Economics, Western University of Ontario) for his comments and suggestions. We thank the ORF for its financial support. All remaining errors are our own.

References

Cantos P.S. (2001), Vertical Relationships for the European Railway Industry, *Transport Policy*, 8, 77–83.

Clever R., M. Mark and Hansen (2008), Interaction of Air and High-Speed Rail in Japan, *Transportation Research Record: Journal of the Transportation Research Board*, 2043, 1–12.

Dobruszkes F. (2011), High-Speed Rail and Air Transport Competition in Western Europe: A Supply-Oriented Perspective, *Transport Policy*, 18, 870–879.

Frank S. and Kopplelmann (2002), Multidimensional Model System for Intercity Travel Choice Behavior, *Transportation Research Record*, 1241, 1–4.

Hausman J. and M. Stewart (2002), Regulating the United States Railroads: The Effects of Sunk Costs and Asymmetric Risk, *Journal of Regulatory Economics*, 22(3), 287–310.

Liu Sh.J. (2003), Reform and Restructure Models of China's Railway Industry: The Third Selection, *China Industrial Economy*, 3, 28–33.

Luo X.Y. and Y.S. Yan (2000), The Investigation and Analysis on the Passenger Transportation Market Between Railways and Highways, *Journal of Southwest Jiaotong University*, 3, 239–241.

Morrison S.A. and W. Clifford (1987), Empirical Implications and Tests of the Contestability Hypothesis, *Journal of Law and Economics*, 30(1), 53–66.

Ou G.L. (2004), Feasibility Analysis and Theoretical Foundation of Competition in Chinese Railways, *The Journal of World Economy*, 6, 46–50.

Oz S. (1995), Industrial Organization Theory and Applications, p. 136.

Peter J. (2009), Substitution Opportunities of High Speed Train for Air Transport, *AerLines E-Zine Edition*, 43, 1–4.

Preston J. (2002), The Transaction Cost Economics of Railways, *Trasporti Europei*, VII (20–21), 6–15.

Rong Ch.H. (2000), On the Relationship between the "Separating Infrastructure Management from Transport Operation" and Railway Reorganization, *Journal of Northern Jiaotong University*, 3, 35–40.

Severin B. (1992), The Evolution of U.S. Airline Competition, *Journal of Economic Perspectives*, 6(2), 45–73.

Xiao X.Zh. (2004), Systematic Analysis of Vertical Separation, *Economic Management*, 12, 4–11.

Yu J. (2003), *Railway Reorganization*: *Theory and Practise*. Economic Science Press.

Yu, L.Ch. and H.Y. Yu (2004), How "Natural" is the Monopoly of Natural Monopolies? *China Industrial Economy*, 11, 32–39.

Zhao J. (2005). Boundary Problem of Firm in Restructuring China Rail, *China Industrial Economy*, 1, 63–70.

Zhang, R. and B. Dominique (2005), How Can Competition be Introduced into Chinese Railways? *Transport Policy*, 12, 345–352.

Chapter 14

Water Availability as a Constraint on China's Future Growth

Dana Medianu[*,§] and John Whalley[*,†,‡,¶]

[*]*Department of Economics, Western University, Canada*

[†]*Centre for International Governance Innovation, Canada*

[‡]*National Bureau of Economic Research, USA*

[§]*dmedianu@gmail.com*

[¶]*jwhalley@uwo.ca*

Abstract: Recent writings on China's water situation often portray China's water problems as severe, and suggest that water availability could threaten the sustainability of China's future growth. However, China's high growth in the last 20 years or more has been obtained with relatively little increase in the physical volume of water. In this chapter, we use a growth accounting approach to investigate both the contribution provided in the past by water availability in constraining China's growth performance, and what would be involved in the future. We use a modified version of Solow growth accounting, in which, water in efficiency units enters the production technology, and investment in water management assets raises efficiency of water use. Our results suggest that if investments in water assets in the future were lower than they were in the past, growth might slightly increase by about 0.1 percentage points if non-water capital and water in efficiency units are close substitutes, but growth rates could decrease by as much as 0.2–3.9 percentage points, if investments in water assets were small, and if the elasticities of substitution were low.

On the other hand, our experiments suggest that with faster growth of investments in water assets than in the past, a low elasticity of substitution growth rates could increase. But if non-water capital and water in efficiency units are close substitutes, growth rates could even decrease, as in other cases.

1 Introduction

There has been considerable discussion in popular writings on China's potential to continue high growth performance at rates comparable to those prevailing before the 2008 financial crisis of water availability as a constraint on future growth prospects (Gleick, 2009; Jiang, 2009; Naughton, 2007; Shalizi, 2008; World Bank, 2009). In agriculture, growing consumption of grains, the grain requirements of sharply increased meat consumption, falling water tables in the North China plain and rising water demands from increased agricultural output have all attracted attention, and in urban areas sharply increasing water demand from rapid urbanization and industrialization are thought to play a similar role.

Over the past 20 years, however, China has been able to experience continued high growth with relatively small increase in the physical volume of water used. Since 1990 China's GDP growth has been around 10% per year, while water use increased by only 14.8% in total, between 1993 and 2009. Agricultural water use, which is the largest user of water in 2009 accounting for about 63% of total water use, decreased by 8% between 1993 and 2009. Agricultural water use increased until the mid-1990s, but decreased later as agricultural water use efficiency increased (Jin and Young, 2001; Shalizi, 2006). This has been achieved through increased investment in water treatment plants, improved irrigation and water management, and water diversion and other infrastructure projects. The throughput of water volume in the economy has grown much more slowly than the economy in general, since through investment in water management assets, the speed and ease of reuse has increased. Thus, water use per capita in China differs by only small amounts from much higher income per capita economies in Europe and North America, and has changed far less over time than GDP, suggesting water availability need not be a serious impediment to future higher growth.

Here we investigate water availability as a potential constraint on Chinese growth using a growth accounting framework in which water enters the aggregate production function along with capital and labor, but in efficiency terms reflecting speed and quality of water treatment. The efficiency of water use can be raised through investment in water management and so Chinese investment is differentiated between water management assets and all other assets. Using calibration procedures we calibrate a water efficiency function which relates increments in efficiency units of water to investment in water assets in each period, using a power function. We then perform growth accounting analysis for the period 1998–2009 using this structure, and forward project growth rates using various assumed investment rates in water and other assets over a 10-year period.

Our results suggest that if water asset investment occurs at similar rates as for other assets, water availability need not constrain future high growth in China. The extent of any such constraint depends on the elasticity of substitution in technology. Water constraints also depend on elasticities of substitution between water and other inputs in production.

2 China's Water Situation

Recent literature on China's water situation often pictures China's water availability as severe and suggests this could threathen the sustainability of China's growth (Gleick, 2009; Jiang, 2009; Shalizi, 2008; World Bank, 2009). Gleick (2009) reports that China's water problems are poor water quality, water-related environmental disasters, water availability and quantity, groundwater overdraft, floods and droughts, climate change and water, water and politics and growing regional conflicts over water. Since 1980, China's water quality[1] decreased due to rapid industrialization, urbanization and intensive use of agricultural pesticides and fertilizers. Water in China is severely contaminated with pollutants from untreated industrial and municipal wastewater and from agricultural pesticides and fertilizers. It is estimated that 40% of surface water can be used only for industrial or agricultural purpose (Gleick, 2009) and that water quality in 20.7% of China's river length is below Class V, which means that it is not safe for human consumption, or appropriate even for irrigation (Naughton, 2007). The World Bank (2009) estimates that water that is below Class V is used to irrigate about 7.4% of China's irrigated land, especially in North China plain. This type of water is essentially wastewater that lowers harvests and reduces the quality of crops.

In addition to water quality deterioration, water shortage is another major source of concern. Water is unevenly distributed between Southern and Northern China, with Northern China having far less water per capita than Southern China. This uneven distribution of water has led to reliance on groundwater in the North China Plain which is unsustainable. Water is extracted from underground faster than the natural capability of reload and this has caused the water table to fall, especially in Hebei province. In the Hai River basin water tables fall by 0.5 m per year, and in Beijing groundwater tables fall by 100–300 m (Jiang, 2009).

Climate change compounds China's water problems, because rising temperatures accelerate the melting of glaciers (Gleick, 2009). China is one of the largest countries in the world covered by glaciers. However, due to climate change it is estimated that glaciers decreased by about a third in the past century. In many

[1]As measured by biological oxygen demand and chemical oxygen demand, water quality decreases as it is depleted of oxygen and the increasing presence of heavy metals, and chlorinated hydrocarbons in the water also decreases its quality (see Naughton, 2007).

regions in China, water is obtained from melting of glaciers and the loss of glaciers leads to fewer water resources.

Another recent study by Jiang (2009) suggests that the severity of China's water problems could threaten China's food security and extends China's water problems to a global scale. If China had to rely on global markets to feed its population, it could have major impacts on the global economy through increasing demand of food and increasing prices for food products. Brown (1996) goes even further and says that "China's water scarcity will become the world's water scarcity". He suggests that China's rapid industrialization and increasing incomes will increase the demand for food and combined with water scarcity could lead China to rely heavily on food imports.

Despite all of the problems related to water availability, China's economic growth over the last two decades was high and this growth was achieved with little increase in physical water use. Table 1 reports data on China's water use and real GDP growth from 1997 to 2009. The data show that water use increased very little. In 1997 water use (measured in 100 million cubic meter) was 5,566 and it increased to 5,965 in 2009, a 7.2% increase. In contrast, real GDP (measured in 100 million 1995 yuan) increased from 72,493 to 204,251, a 181% increase, over the same period.

The slow growth in water use over the last decade was achieved by increased investment in water treatment plants, improved irrigation and water management, and water diversion and other infrastructure projects. Table 1 reports growth rates of investments in non-water assets and growth rates of investments in water assets. Investments in water assets grew 3–4 times faster than investments in non-water assets in the period 1997–2000. In 2001, the growth rate of investments in water assets was almost zero and picked up again in 2002–2004 when it was almost the same at the growth of investments in non-water assets. In 2009, the growth rate of investment in water assets reached 58%, the highest since 1997.

Table 2 shows that nominal investments in water assets increased 17-fold in the last 14 years from 29 to 503 billion yuan (nominal investments in non-water assets increased 7.5-fold over the same period). Investments in the period 2006–2009 totaled 1,314 billion yuan and surpassed the investments for the period 1995–2005 which totaled 1,168 billion yuan. Moreover, the Chinese government announced that investments in water assets would amount to 4 trillion renminbi over the next 10 years[2] which is twice as high as investments made in the last 10 years. The largest investments are in management of water conservancy, which account on average, for 53% of total investments and investments in production, and supply of water which

---

[2]See Xinhua (2012).

Table 1. Water use, real GDP, growth rates of water use, growth rates of real GDP, growth rates of investments in non-water assets and growth rates of investments in water assets, China, 1997–2009.

Year	Water use (in 100 million cubic meter)	Real GDP (in 100 million 1995 Yuan)	Growth rates of water use (%)	Growth rates of real GDP (%)	Real growth rates of investments in non-water assets (%)	Real growth rates of investments in water assets (%)
1997	5,566.03	72,493.33	n/a	8.80	6.02	14.97
1998	5,435.39	78,147.81	−2.35	7.80	9.70	41.01
1999	5,590.88	83,696.30	2.86	7.10	6.76	30.02
2000	5,497.59	90,392.00	−1.67	8.00	9.18	26.68
2001	5,567.43	96,990.62	1.27	7.30	11.44	0.89
2002	5,497.28	104,749.87	−1.26	8.00	15.21	19.56
2003	5,320.40	114,491.61	−3.22	9.30	20.07	16.11
2004	5,547.80	125,368.31	4.27	9.50	15.16	19.48
2005	5,633.00	138,155.88	1.54	10.20	12.32	8.54
2006	5,795.00	153,491.18	2.88	11.10	17.12	3.64
2007	5,818.70	171,756.63	0.41	11.90	13.79	12.30
2008	5,910.00	187,214.73	1.57	9.00	13.14	13.43
2009	5,965.20	204,251.27	0.93	9.10	24.46	58.85

Source: Authors' calculations based on China Statistical Yearbook (1996–2009).

account for 27% of total investments. Data on investments in drainage works and treatment in wastewater are not available before 2000 or there were no investments in these, but after 2000 investments in drainage works account for 17% of total investments, and investments in treatment of wastewater account for 6.5%.

Even though water quality is still below national standards in many rivers, China made significant progress at improving the treatment rate of wastewater through investments in wastewater treatment facilities. Wastewater treatment is a relatively recent phenomenon, as can be seen from the data. In 1980, China had only about 20 wastewater treatment plants which were small with low capacity of water treatment. Through increased investment, in 2000, the number of wastewater treatment facilities increased to 400. The urban wastewater treatment rate increased from 16.2% to 35% in 2000.[3] In 2005, the municipal wastewater treatment rate was 45%. The 11th Five Year Plan set a target to increase the municipal wastewater treatment rate to 70% by 2010. However, in small cities, towns and rural areas, the wastewater treatment rate is still much lower and overall in China it seems

[3]See OECD (2004).

Table 2. Nominal investments in water assets by sector (in 100 million Yuan), China, 1995–2009.

		Nominal investment in water assets by sector				
Year	**Nominal investment in water assets**	**Production and supply of water**	**Geologic prospecting**	**Management of water conservancy**	**Drainage works**	**Treatment of wastewater**
1995	297.16	123.10	25.30	148.70	n/a	n/a
1996	391.32	152.50	23.20	215.70	n/a	n/a
1997	457.53	155.00	19.70	282.80	n/a	n/a
1998	643.86	177.20	23.80	442.80	n/a	n/a
1999	833.82	177.90	20.90	566.20	n/a	68.80
2000	1,067.90	187.50	18.20	603.40	149.30	109.60
2001	1,081.71	188.80	11.60	583.90	224.50	72.90
2002	1,295.89	197.90	18.20	733.40	275.00	71.50
2003	1,537.77	337.20	25.70	712.30	375.20	87.40
2004	1,940.18	460.90	25.30	996.00	352.30	105.60
2005	2,139.52	508.70	61.50	1,067.60	368.00	133.70
2006	2,250.59	654.90	59.80	1,053.20	331.50	151.10
2007	2,625.96	835.70	78.60	1,105.60	410.00	196.10
2008	3,243.71	1,045.40	87.30	1,420.40	496.00	194.60
2009	5,028.92	1,755.70	176.00	2,217.90	729.80	149.50

Source: China Statistical Yearbook (1996–2009).

that wastewater treatment rate is as low as 20%. In 2002, 500 municipal treatment facilities operated in 310 of the 660 cities, but 17,000 towns had no municipal wastewater treatment facilities (OECD, 2007). Compared to the OECD, the share of China's urban population connected to wastewater treatment plants in the early 2000s was about 33%, while in the OECD on average it was 64%, and in some countries such as Germany and UK it was as high as 90–95%.

Industrial wastewater treatment has also improved in the last 10–15 years. According to the OECD (2007), there were more than 60,000 industrial wastewater treatment plants built in China and about 90% of industrial discharge complies with national standards. The building of so many wastewater treatment plants came as a result of a Chinese policy that required industries that are heavy polluters to treat the water, or to close the enterprise if water treatment was not feasible.

In the agricultural sector, which is the largest user of water, water saving technologies have also been expanded in recent years (see Blanke *et al.*, 2007) which increases the efficiency of water use.[4] Blanke *et al.* conducted two surveys in

[4]Water use efficiency is defined as crop production at the field level per unit of water input (see Blanke *et al.*, 2007).

Northern China provinces covering more than 400 villages and found that most benefits in water saving came from water saving technologies adopted at the household level. In the early 1990s, the rates of use of household water saving technologies accelerated. In 1995 surface pipe use was 23% and in 2004 it increased to 48%. The use of other water saving technologies at household level have also increased, such as drought resistant technologies, plastic sheeting and retaining stubble. On the other hand, traditional technologies (such as border irrigation, furrow irrigation, level fields) and saving technologies at community level (such as underground pipe, lined canal and sprinkler) grew more slowly. For example, the adoption rate of lined canals increased between the early 1990s and 2004, but the adoption is still low at only 25% in Northern China. The water saving technologies that expanded more slowly require high fixed investments. Even though water saving technologies in agriculture expanded in recent years in China increasing water use efficiency, the efficiency of irrigation is still low (40–50% in China and 55–65% in North China Plain) (see Blanke *et al.*, 2007; Hubacek and Sun, 2007).

China has also undertaken major investments in projects to transfer water from the South to water scarce Northern China. A South–North water transfer project is being built to transfer 45 billion cubic meters per year to the North China Plain from the Yangtze River basin by 2020, and it was approved in 2002 (OECD, 2007; Gleick, 2009). The construction of a western route was expected to begin in 2010 and will transfer 17 billion cubic meters per year at a cost of around $37 billion. The central route will transfer 14.6 billion cubic meters by 2020. The eastern route already transfers 9 billion cubic meters, and this will increase by 2020 to 13 billion cubic meters. The costs for the eastern and central routes will be $14.5 billion, and $3 billion in resettlement costs. However, even all this may not be enough to meet China's growing demands for water. According to the Ministry of Water Resources (2007), additional investments in key water projects were 96 billion yuan to harness 717 large rivers and lakes which were under construction in 2007, 63 billion yuan accumulative investment in reservoir projects including completion of Phase-III of the Three Gorges Project, investments in irrigation, drainage and rural water supply, rural hydropower and electrification, soil and water conservation and ecology restoration and capacity building.

3 China's Growth and Water Constraints: A Growth Accounting Approach

We use a growth accounting framework to assess both the past and potential future effects of water availability on China's real output growth. Unlike in traditional growth accounting exercises which use only two factors of production (capital and labor) and total factor productivity (TFP) , here we add a third factor of production, water. This, however, enters the production function in efficiency units to also reflect water treatment and recycling, as well as physical volume. Thus, if investment in recycling occurs, water in physical volume terms need not expand for water in efficiency units to increase. We distinguish between Chinese investments in water assets and investments in all other assets. Investments in water assets increase the efficiency of water use, but the resources shifted to improve water use efficiency cannot be used in other productive activities.

Growth accounting exercises decompose the growth rate of output into a growth rate of factors of production (capital, labor and water) and a growth rate of TFP. Thus, it is possible to find what portion of China's growth is attributable to the growth in capital stock, labor and improved water use efficiency. TFP in the growth accounting exercise is a "residual" and it accounts for the growth in output that is not explained by the growth in factor inputs weighted by their respective shares in national output. Essentially, the growth of TFP accounts for the efficiency change in the combined use of capital and labor but because it is "residual" TFP can embody many other things in addition to efficiency change such as technological progress and omitted variables.

Growth accounting originates with Solow (1957) who ran an experiment on the US economy for the period 1909–1949 using two factor inputs (capital and labor). Solow wanted to find out how much of the increase in output per man hour was attributable to technical change (shifts in the production function), and how much was attributable to the increase in capital per man hour (movements along the production function). His results showed that 87.5% of the increase in output per man hour in the US was due to technical change, and 12.5% of the increase was due to an increase of capital per man hour. His initial calculations were modified and extended in various ways in Denison (1962), Kendrick (1961), and Jorgenson and Griliches (1967).

More recently, Wang and Yao (2003) and Whalley and Zhao (2010) have used a growth accounting framework to find the contribution of TFP and factor input growth to China's economic growth. They also incorporate human capital accumulation into the growth accounting exercise. They find that human capital accumulation played an important role in the growth of Chinese economy. They use a Cobb–Douglas production function.

Here, we assume that China's production function can be characterized by the following three factor input function, with capital, labor and water as inputs

$$Y_t = A_t F(K_t, L_t, e_t \bar{W}), \tag{1}$$

where Y is the output, A TFP, K the capital stock in non-water assets, L the quantity of labor, $\bar{W}$ the quantity of water used and e the efficiency of water use. The quantity of water use changes little over time, which is represented by the bar sign on $\bar{W}$. The

e_t that we use in the production function allows for water management-augmenting technological progress which is the result of investments in water assets; that is, even though the growth of water use remains constant, if water-augmenting technological progress through investments in water assets increases, it is as if water inputs would grow with unchanged technology.[5] Thus, water use does not have to increase in order to increase output; water use could remain constant and if China invests in more water management assets, water is used more efficiently and water is not a constraint.

Here, we use a two-level, three factor Constant Elasticity of Substitution (CES) production function with non-water capital and water in efficiency units in the nested function and labor as a substitute[6] to the composite of non-water capital plus water in efficiency units (see Kemfert, 1998[7]):

$$Y_t = A_t\Big[a\Big\{(bK_t^{(\gamma-1)/\gamma} + (1-b)(e_t W_t)^{(\gamma-1)/\gamma})^{\gamma/(\gamma-1)}\Big\}^{(\sigma-1)/\sigma} + (1-a)L_t^{(\sigma-1)/\sigma}\Big]^{\sigma/(\sigma-1)}, \tag{2}$$

where A_t is Hicksian neutral technological progress, γ the elasticity of substitution between non-water capital and water, σ the elasticity of substitution between labor and the composite of capital and water, and a and b are share parameters.

The elasticity of substitution, γ, shows how easily water and non-water capital can be substituted for each other, and the elasticity of substitution, σ, shows how easily labor and the composite of non-water capital and water can be substituted for each other. With an aggregate production function that has an elasticity of substitution less than one, the diminishing returns to the faster growing factor occur faster than otherwise. For given water-augmenting technological progress, and a given elasticity of substitution between water and non-water capital, as the implicit price of water increases, the share of water in the production also increases.

Taking natural logarithms, Equation (1) becomes:

$$\ln(Y_t) = \ln(A_t) + \frac{\sigma}{\sigma-1}\ln\Big[a\Big\{(bK_t^{(\gamma-1)/\gamma} + (1-b)(e_t W_t)^{(\gamma-1)/\gamma})^{\gamma/(\gamma-1)}\Big\}^{(\sigma-1)/\sigma} + (1-a)L_t^{(\sigma-1)/\sigma}\Big]. \tag{3}$$

[5] See Solow (1978) for discussion on resources and economic growth.

[6] It is common to argue that water and capital are pairwise complements. In this function, substitutability only occurs between the composite of capital and water and labor, and so there is no calibration for the pairwise capital–water substitution possibilities. Kemfert (1998) discusses this also.

[7] Kemfert (1998) investigates the substitution elasticities between capital, energy and labor for West Germany industry using three approaches of a two-level CES production function.

From Equation (3) we can estimate $\ln(A_t)$, the value of TFP as:

$$\ln(A_t) = \ln(Y_t) - \frac{\sigma}{\sigma - 1}\ln\left[a\left\{(bK_t^{(\gamma-1)/\gamma} + (1-b)(e_t W_t)^{(\gamma-1)/\gamma)\gamma/(\gamma-1)}\right\}^{(\sigma-1)/\sigma} + (1-a)L_t^{(\sigma-1)/\sigma}\right], \quad (4)$$

where $(1 - a)$ is the share of national income attributed to labor, a the share of national income attributed to a composite of non-water capital and water, $(1 - b)$ the share attributed to water and b the share attributed to non-water capital.[8] The shares of factors of production in output are the factor social marginal products multiplied by factor inputs and divided by output. We assume that factors are paid their marginal products with the exception of water. The production function is a constant return to scale production function.

Using calibration procedures we next calibrate a water efficiency function which relates increments in efficiency units of water to investment in water assets in each period using a power function of the following form:

$$\hat{e} = g(I^w) = a(I^w)^b, \quad b < 1, \quad (5)$$

where $\hat{e}$ is the increment in the period in efficiency units of water use, I^w investment in water assets and a and b are positive numbers with $b < 1$. The expectation is that b will be a positive number but less than 1 due to diminishing incremental efficiency returns to investments in water assets.

Here, we investigate the degree to which water availability could constrain China's growth under the different assumptions on elasticities of substitution. The elastictiey of substitution between labor and the composite of non-water capital and water in efficiency units is held constant at unity. The assumptions on the elasticity of substitution between non-water capital and water in efficiency units are 1.1 (strong substitutes), 0.75, 0.5 and 0.025 (when they become almost perfect complements).[9]

---

[8]If the elasticties of substitution are unity, the production function is Cobb–Douglas and factor shares are constant. If the elasticity of substitution between non-water capital and water in efficiency units is greater or less than 1, non-water capital and water shares will change over time if the non-water capital–water in efficiency units ratio changes. For example, if the elasticity of substitution is less than 1, an increase in non-water capital–water in efficiency units ratio will result in an increase in the water share over time.

[9]Grebenstein and Field (1979) argue that water and labor inputs are substitutes, and that water and capital are complements.

4 Data Sources

4.1 Output

GDP data is from China Statistical Yearbook access various years and covers the period 1995–2009. Because GDP data reported in China Statistical Yearbooks is in nominal terms (at current prices), we construct a GDP deflator to convert nominal GDP data into the real terms which are actually used in our growth accounting exercise. We choose 1995 as the base year. Following Zheng *et al.* (2009), we first calculate a year-on-year GDP deflator and calculate the GDP deflator and real GDP using the following:

$$P_t = \frac{\text{GDP}_t^{\text{Nominal}}}{(\text{GDP}_{t-1}^{\text{Nominal}} \times \text{GDP}_t^{\text{Growth}})/100} \times 100, \tag{6}$$

$$(\text{GDP}_{\text{deflator}})_t = \frac{(\text{GDP}_{\text{deflator}})_{t-1} \times P_t}{100}, \tag{7}$$

$$\text{GDP}_t^{\text{Real}} = \frac{\text{GDP}_t^{\text{Nominal}}}{(\text{GDP}_{\text{deflator}})_t}, \tag{8}$$

where P_t is the year-on-year GDP deflator and $\text{GDP}_t^{\text{Growth}}$ the index of GDP in year t. Indices of GDP that are reported in China Statistical Yearbook are calculated at comparable constant prices with the previous year as the base year (i.e. 100). Table 3 reports our calculation of real GDP and real GDP growth for the period 1995–2009.

4.2 Capital stock data

Capital stock data for non-water assets is not directly available in the China Statistical Yearbook. To construct capital stock data we use an initial real capital stock for the year 1995 calculated by Wang and Yao (2003) (from which we deduct the initial capital stock in water assets) and gross fixed capital formation from the Chinese Statistical Yearbook (2010). Wang and Yao (2003) estimate capital stock based on investment data from Hsueh-Li for the period 1952–1995 and from CSY for 1996–1999. They use total social fixed investment to measure gross fixed capital formation.

Our chosen series to construct the capital stock is gross fixed capital formation because this is a more accurate measure of the change in reproducible capital stock (see Bai *et al.*, 2006). We observed that investment in fixed assets to GDP ratio increased from 32% of GDP in 1995 to 65% in 2009. NBS includes investment in fixed assets, the value of land purchases and expenditure on used machinery and pre-existing structures. These should not be included in the calculation of the capital

Table 3. Nominal and real Chinese GDP 1995–2009 (in 100 million yuan).

Year	Nominal Nominal GDP	Indices of GDP	Year-on-year GDP deflator	GDP deflator	Real GDP	Real GDP Growth (%)
1995	60,793.7	110.5	100.00	100.00	60,793.70	n/a
1996	71,176.6	109.6	106.82	106.82	66,629.90	9.60
1997	78,973.0	108.8	101.98	108.94	72,493.33	8.80
1998	84,402.3	107.8	99.14	108.00	78,147.81	7.80
1999	89,677.1	107.1	99.21	107.15	83,696.30	7.10
2000	99,214.6	108.0	102.44	109.76	90,392.00	8.00
2001	109,655.2	107.3	103.00	113.06	96,990.62	7.30
2002	120,332.7	108.0	101.61	114.88	104,749.87	8.00
2003	135,822.8	109.3	103.27	118.63	114,491.61	9.30
2004	159,878.3	109.5	107.50	127.53	125,368.31	9.50
2005	184,937.4	110.2	104.97	133.86	138,155.88	10.20
2006	216,314.4	111.1	105.28	140.93	153,491.18	11.10
2007	265,810.3	111.9	109.81	154.76	171,756.63	11.90
2008	314,045.4	109.0	108.39	167.75	187,214.73	9.00
2009	340,902.8	109.1	99.50	166.90	204,251.27	9.10

Source: Authors' calculations based on China Statistical Yearbook (1996–2009).

stock. On the other hand, NBS does not count expenditures on small-scale investment projects. Liang (2006) note that China's real estate development expanded fast in recent years which led to an overstatement of investment if land purchases are included in investment spending.

For gross fixed capital formation we rely on Table 2–18 (CSY, 2010) from national accounts which provides data on components of GDP by expenditure approach for the period 1978–2009 at current prices. Gross fixed capital formation is defined by (CSY, 2010) as "the value of acquisitions less those disposals of fixed assets during a given period. Fixed assets are the assets produced through production activities with unit value above a specified amount and which could be used for over one year.... Total tangible fixed capital formation includes the value of the construction projects and installation projects completed and the equipment, apparatus and instruments purchased (less those disposed) as well as the value of land improved...Total intangible fixed capital formation includes the prospecting of minerals and the acquisition of computer software minus the disposal of them".

Therefore, this series does not include the land purchases and the expenditure on used machinery and pre-existing structures, but it includes the expenditures on small-scale investment projects. Gross fixed capital formation (in nominal terms) grew at a much slower rate after 2003 compared to investment in fixed assets, and its share in GDP in 2009 was 45% as opposed to 65% for investment in fixed assets.

Table 4. Real investment in non-water assets and real capital stock in non-water assets 1995–2009 (in 100 million yuan).

Year	Nominal investment in non-water assets*	Price index of investment in fixed assets	Investment deflator at time t	Real investment in non-water assets	Growth Rate of real investment in non-water assets (%)	Real capital stock in non-water assets	Growth rate of real capital stock in non-water assets (%)
1995	20,587.84		100.00	20,587.84		124,823.53	
1996	23,656.78	104.00	104.00	22,746.90	10.49	141,329.26	13.22
1997	25,507.47	101.70	105.77	24,116.43	6.02	158,379.23	12.06
1998	27,925.14	99.80	105.56	26,455.17	9.70	176,915.44	11.70
1999	29,693.48	99.60	105.13	28,243.40	6.76	196,313.06	10.96
2000	32,776.50	101.10	106.29	30,836.65	9.18	217,334.06	10.71
2001	36,672.79	100.40	106.72	34,364.89	11.44	240,832.25	10.81
2002	42,336.21	100.20	106.93	39,592.71	15.21	268,383.34	11.44
2003	51,952.93	102.20	109.28	47,540.35	20.07	302,504.53	12.71
2004	63,177.52	105.60	115.40	54,745.82	15.16	342,125.12	13.10
2005	72,093.38	101.60	117.25	61,487.96	12.32	386,506.83	12.97
2006	85,703.51	101.50	119.01	72,015.72	17.12	439,197.20	13.63
2007	101,322.64	103.90	123.65	81,944.46	13.79	499,181.81	13.66
2008	124,840.69	108.90	134.65	92,713.16	13.14	566,935.88	13.57
2009	151,650.88	97.60	131.42	115,393.24	24.46	653,982.33	15.35

Source: Authors' calculations based on China Statistical Yearbook (1996–2009).
*Nominal investment is based on Gross Fixed Capital Formation data.

Between 2003 and 2009 gross fixed capital formation grew at 20% per year while investment in fixed assets grew at 26.4% per year. Between 1995 and 2002 the levels and growth rates for both series were almost the same.

We use the price index for investment in fixed assets reported in Table 9-1 (CSY, 2010) to calculate the real investment in fixed assets (see Table 4) and the real capital stock is then calculated via a perpetual inventory method using

$$K_t = I_t + (1 - \delta)K_{t-1}, \tag{9}$$

where the real capital stock at time t is equal to the sum of investment in fixed assets at time t and the balance of the depreciated capital stock from the previous period; and δ is the depreciation rate. Here we use a depreciation rate of 5% as in Wang and Yao (2003) and Zheng *et al.* (2009).

The price index is important in the calculation of the growth of real output, the growth of real capital stock in non-water assets and the growth of real capital stock in water assets. Literature on China argues that the rate of inflation is often underestimated and therefore, real output growth is overestimated (Bosworth and Collins, 2007). The same argument also applies to the calculation of the growth rate of the real capital stock. If the price index is underestimated, the growth rate of real capital stock is overestimated. As a result of this problem with the data, alternative price indexes have been constructed by Young (2003) and other researchers.

Here, we calculate the real variables based on Chinese price indices. These Chinese indices show that the inflation rate was faster for GDP in general than for investments in fixed assets. Indices of GDP are higher than the price indices of investment in fixed assets. These calculations show that the growth in real capital stock in non-water assets accelerated especially after 2002 from 10–11% per year to 13–15% per year in 2008–2009 (see Table 4).

In our calculations, we assume that there is no idle capacity for the capital stock. If there is idle capacity the calculation needs adjustments for the capital stock that is not in use. Because there is a lack of data on the utilization of capital, this could be approximated by the labor force unemployed. Capital stock in use in each year would be equal to the capital in place multiplied by the percentage of the labor force unemployed under the assumption that, idle capital stock and labor unemployed are equal with the same percentage (Solow, 1957). China's unemployment rates are not high; in 2008–2009 these were in the range of 3–4% depending on the region. Thus, taking into calculation the idle capacity of the capital stock would thus likely not significantly change our calculations.

Investments in water assets refer to investments in the production and supply of water, investments in geologic prospecting, investments in management of water conservancy, investments in drainage works and investments in treatment of wastewater. The data is denominated in 100 million yuan and is taken from CSY over various years and covers the period 1995–2009. In 2004, the National Bureau of Statistics of China changed the format for reporting these investments. Between 1995 and 2003, investments in fixed assets were reported as investment in capital construction and investment in innovation, by type of construction and sector. Since 2004, data on investments in fixed assets is being reported as investments in fixed assets, in both urban and rural areas. CSY reports data by sector only for investments in urban areas. For nominal investment in fixed assets in production and supply of water, geologic prospecting and management of water conservancy (investment in capital construction and investment in innovation) we rely on Tables 5-14 and 5-19 (CSY, 1996), Tables 5-16 and 5-21 (CSY, 1997), Tables 6-16 and 6-21 (CSY, 1998, 1999), Tables 6-16 and 6-20 (CSY, 2000, 2001, 2002), Tables 6-9 and 6-22 (CSY, 2004), Table 6-13 (CSY, 2005–2007) and Table 5-13 (CSY, 2008–2010).

Investments in drainage works and treatment of wastewater data is taken from Table 12-47 (CSY, 2010) "Investment in the Treatment of Environmental Pollution" and Table 12-49 (CSY, 2010) "Investment Completed in the Treatment of Industrial Pollution" from the Resources and Environment section of the China Statistical Yearbook. Table 12-47 "Investment in the Treatment of Environmental Pollution" reports data on Investment in Urban Environmental Infrastructure (Gas Supply, Centralized Heating, Drainage Works, Gardening and Greening, Environmental Sanitation), Investment in the Treatment of Industrial Pollution (Treatment of

Waste Water, Treatment of Waste Gas, Treatment of Solid Waste, Treatment of Noise Pollution and Treatment of Other Pollution) and the "Three Simultaneities" Environmental Investment for New Projects. Here we use only data that is related directly to water treatment such as drainage works and treatment of waste water. The data on investment in drainage works is available starting in the year 2000 and investment in treatment of wastewater is available starting in the year 1999.

The initial capital stock in water assets in the year 1995 is not directly available in the China Statistical Yearbook, nor is it calculated in previous research studies. Thus, we rely on a method of calculation of the initial capital stock reported by Nehru and Dhareshwar (1993). We calculate the capital stock in water assets each year via a perpetual inventory method initially assuming that the initial capital stock in water assets is zero. Then we calculate the average of the capital–output ratio for the years 2005–2009, and apply this ratio to find the initial capital stock in the year 1995. The average capital–output ratio in the last 5 years is 0.071, and the initial water asset capital stock in the year 1995 is 4,338.13 (100 million yuan).

When the initial capital stock is estimated, the real capital stock calculated in the first 2–3 years is sensitive to the initial capital stock estimate (Barro and Sala-i-Martin, 2004). This can be seen from Table 5 where the growth rates of the real water capital stock between 1996 and 1998 are lower (3–7% per year) than in the subsequent years, suggesting that the initial capital stock could be overestimated and real investments are low relative to the real capital stock in water assets. As the real capital stock in water assets depreciates, the capital stock becomes more accurate, especially from 1999, when growth rates remain in the range of 10–13% per year.

4.3 Labor data

Labor force data is from World Bank Development Indicators database and is for the years 1995–2009. The total labor force consists of economically active population of age 15 or older as reported by the International Labour Organization criteria. We assume that average hours per worker do not change over the period.[10]

4.4 Factor shares

The shares of factors of production in output are the factor social marginal products multiplied by factor inputs and divided by output. In order to compute factor shares, we need to have estimates for the social marginal products of labor, capital and water. These are not directly available from the data, but the assumption used in the

[10] We take the labor input in production as the number of hours worked in a year under the assumption that each worker worked 2,080 hours per year.

Table 5. Real investment in water assets and real water capital stock, China, 1995–2009 (in 100 million yuan).

Year	Nominal investment in non-water assets*	Price index of investment in fixed assets	Investment deflator at time *t*	Real investment in non-water assets	Growth Rate of real investment in non-water assets (%)	Real capital stock in non-water assets	Growth rate of real capital stock in non-water assets (%)
1995	297.16		100.00	297.16		4,338.13	
1996	391.32	104.00	104.00	376.27	26.62	4,497.49	3.67
1997	457.53	101.70	105.77	432.58	14.97	4,705.20	4.62
1998	643.86	99.80	105.56	609.97	41.01	5,079.90	7.96
1999	833.82	99.60	105.13	793.10	30.02	5,619.01	10.61
2000	1,067.90	101.10	106.29	1,004.70	26.68	6,342.76	12.88
2001	1,081.71	100.40	106.72	1,013.64	0.89	7,039.25	10.98
2002	1,295.89	100.20	106.93	1,211.91	19.56	7,899.20	12.22
2003	1,537.77	102.20	109.28	1,407.16	16.11	8,911.40	12.81
2004	1,940.18	105.60	115.40	1,681.24	19.48	10,147.08	13.87
2005	2,139.52	101.60	117.25	1,824.78	8.54	11,464.51	12.98
2006	2,250.59	101.50	119.01	1,891.15	3.64	12,782.43	11.50
2007	2,625.96	103.90	123.65	2,123.74	12.30	14,267.04	11.61
2008	3,243.71	108.90	134.65	2,408.95	13.43	15,962.64	11.88
2009	5,028.92	97.60	131.42	3,826.57	58.85	18,991.08	18.97

Source: Authors' calculations based on China Statistical Yearbook (1996–2009).

research literature is that the social marginal products are equal to their input prices (Barro and Sala-i-Martin, 2004). Therefore, the social marginal product of capital is equal to the rental rate of capital, and the social marginal product of labor is equal to the wage rate.

Labor factor shares are calculated using data from China's National Accounts. We use Table 2-16 (CSY, 2008–2010), Table 3-10 (CSY, 1998–2003, 2006), Table 3-12 (CSY, 2004, 2005), Table 2-17 (CSY, 1997) and Table 2-18 (CSY, 1996) which report data for 31 regions based on an income approach to components of gross regional product. The data is calculated at current prices. We obtain labor shares as the ratio of compensation of employees to the sum of gross regional product. The NBS defines the compensation of employees as "the total payment of various forms to employees for the productive activities they are engaged in…includes wages, bonuses and allowances, which the employees earn in cash or in kind…includes the free medical services provided to the employees and the medicine expenses, transport subsidies and social insurance, and housing fund paid by the employers". Between 1995 and 2004 the labor share is stable in the range of 0.50–0.53. In 2005, it decreased to 0.41 and remained at this value until 2008. In 2009, the labor share increased again to 0.47. On average for the entire period labor share was 0.48. This is almost the same as the labor share used by Wang and Yao (2003), but is smaller than the labor share computed by Young (2003) who found an average labor share of 0.6 for the period 1978–1997.

In the case of China, the assumption that social marginal product of water is equal to the water price is not realistic. It is common in developing countries that water prices are usually significantly lower than their marginal product. Wang and Lall (2002) estimated the marginal productivity of water using a production function for the industrial sector with five inputs (capital, labor, water, energy and other raw materials), and data for about 2,000 Chinese industrial firms. They obtained data from China's State Environmental Protection Administration (SEPA) for 1993, and found that the industry average marginal productivity of water was 2.45 yuan per cubic meter of water while the price of water in 1996 was in the range of 0.70 and 1.20 yuan in cities in Hebei Province. This suggests that the water price was about 2–3.5 times lower than the marginal product. Giving that the comparison data is for the year 1996 and the study uses data for the year 1993, the gap between water price and marginal product could be even larger. The authors also note that their sample consists of large- and medium-sized enterprises and that the marginal value product of water could be as high as 3.92 yuan per cubic meter of water if small-scale industries were included.

Also, World Bank (1997) noted that the willingness to pay was about 1.8 yuan per cubic meter in some coastal cities, and 4.3 yuan per cubic meter in a representative city for water-scarce Hai River Basin. The industries' economic value of water in Shanxi and Hai River Basin was about 24 yuan per cubic meter, in sharp contrast with the average price in the region which was in the range of 0.5–0.9 yuan per cubic meter.

Because the marginal product of water is higher than the price charged for water, we calculate the share parameter of water $(1-b)$ under different assumptions. These are if the marginal product of water is four times higher than the average price of water reported by the Ministry of Water Resources 2006 and 2007, and if the marginal product of water is eight times higher and 12 times higher. The implied values for distribution parameters in the aggregate production function are reported in Table 6.

4.5 *e*-function

To calibrate the e function, we find the values for the positive parameters a and b by constructing a system of two equations and solving for the two parameters. Our system of equations takes the efficiency of water use at time t, denoted by e_t as equal to the efficiency of water use at time $t-1$, denoted by e_{t-1} plus the water efficiency increment function, denoted by $\hat{e}$.

$$e_t = e_{t-1} + \hat{e} = e_{t-1} + a(I_t^w)^b. \tag{10}$$

Using data for 1998 and 2008 in Table 7, and assuming that the efficiency of water use at time t is equal to real GDP at time t divided by water use at time t, we

Table 6. Distribution parameters in production for different water pricing assumptions.

	Distribution parameter	Assumed ratio of water marginal product to price		
		$\lambda = 4$	$\lambda = 8$	$\lambda = 12$
Non-water capital	b	0.9867	0.9734	0.9601
Water in efficiency units	$1 - b$	0.0133	0.0266	0.0399
Composite of Non-water capital and water in efficiency units	a	0.5173	0.5173	0.5173
Labor	$1 - a$	0.4827	0.4827	0.4827

Source: Authors' calculations based on Ministry of Water Resources (2006–2007) and China Statistical Yearbook (1996–2009).

can solve for the values of parameters in Equations (4) and (5) as

$$14.38 = 13.02 + a(609.97)^b,$$
$$31.68 = 29.52 + a(2,408.95)^b.$$

Solving these equations for the parameters a and b yields values 0.1526648 and 0.3402391, and substituting these values into the water efficiency function yields

$$\hat{e} = 0.1526648(I^w)^{0.3402391}. \tag{11}$$

Equation (11) implies that the function $\hat{e}$ exhibits positive and diminishing returns to investment in water assets. For $I^w > 0$, $\frac{\partial \hat{e}}{\partial I^w} > 0$ suggesting that there are positive marginal products with respect to investments in water assets and $\frac{\partial^2 \hat{e}}{\partial^2 I^w} < 0$ suggesting that the marginal product is diminishing. Each additional unit of investment in water assets increases $\hat{e}$, but the increase falls as investment in water assets increases.

Table 7 reports in column D, the actual efficiency of water use (Real GDP/Water Use) and in column G, the calculation of efficiency of water use (e_t) using the calibrated e-function. Using the calibrated function yields slightly higher efficiency of water use (column G) than in reality (column D) in most of the years.

We perform sensitivity analysis on the parameters used in the e-function. Table 8 reports our calculations for the calibration of e-function using data for seven different pairs of years which are taken randomly. The calculations show that there are significant differences for the values of parameters a and b suggesting that the results of the counterfactuals could change if the calculations are performed using the values from other rows (the values from row 6 are used in our counterfactual analysis). For all pairs of years reported (see Table 8, rows 1, 2, 3, 4, 5, 6, 7) the value of parameter b is less than 1 and greater than 0; the e-function exhibits positive and diminishing marginal products with respect to investment in water assets.

Table 7. Efficiency of water use China, 1998–2009.

A	B	C	D	E	F	G	H
Year	Real GDP (in 100 mill 1995 yuan)	Water Use (in 100 mill cu.m)	Efficiency of water use (Real GDP/ Water Use)	Real Investment in Water Capital	$\hat{e}$	e_t	$e_t W$
1995	60,793.70	n/a	n/a	297.16	1.06	n/a	n/a
1996	66,629.90	n/a	n/a	376.27	1.15	n/a	n/a
1997	72,493.33	5,566.03	13.02	432.58	1.20	13.02	72,493.33
1998	78,147.81	5,435.39	14.38	609.97	1.35	14.38	78,147.81
1999	83,696.30	5,590.88	14.97	793.10	1.48	15.86	88,656.77
2000	90,392.00	5,497.59	16.44	1,004.70	1.60	17.46	95,994.44
2001	96,990.62	5,567.43	17.42	1,013.64	1.61	19.07	106,169.89
2002	104,749.87	5,497.28	19.05	1,211.91	1.71	20.78	114,229.46
2003	114,491.61	5,320.40	21.52	1,407.16	1.80	22.58	120,123.16
2004	125,368.31	5,547.80	22.60	1,681.24	1.91	24.49	135,858.32
2005	138,155.88	5,633.00	24.53	1,824.78	1.96	26.45	149,012.78
2006	153,491.18	5,795.00	26.49	1,891.15	1.99	28.44	164,823.82
2007	171,756.63	5,818.70	29.52	2,123.74	2.07	30.51	177,536.47
2008	187,214.73	5,910.00	31.68	2,408.95	2.16	32.67	193,085.26
2009	204,251.27	5,965.20	34.24	3,826.57	2.53	35.20	209,967.81

Source: Authors' calculations based on China Statistical Yearbook (1996–2009).

Table 8. Sensitivity analysis for *e*-function.

Row #	Data for years	a	b	$\hat{e}$	$\frac{\partial \hat{e}}{\partial I^w}$	$\frac{\partial^2 \hat{e}}{\partial^2 I^w}$
1	1998/2003	0.0136196	0.7170643	$= 0.0136196(I^w)^{0.7170643}$	>0	<0
2	2005/2008	0.0901988	0.4078173	$= 0.0901988(I^w)^{0.4078173}$	>0	<0
3	2002/2009	0.1013375	0.3915791	$= 0.1013375(I^w)^{0.3915791}$	>0	<0
4	2000/2007	0.0018649	0.9650913	$= 0.0018649(I^w)^{0.9650913}$	>0	<0
5	1999/2009	0.0011881	0.9305185	$= 0.0011881(I^w)^{0.9305185}$	>0	<0
6	1998/2008	0.1526648	0.3402391	$= 0.1526648(I^w)^{0.3402391}$	>0	<0
7	2005/2006	0.0584134	0.4656757	$= 0.0584134(I^w)^{0.4656757}$	>0	<0

Source: Authors' calculations based on China Statistical Yearbook (1996–2009)

5 Results

Here we report the results of growth accounting calculations on the significance of water availability for China's growth for a number of counterfactual cases. We use values for parameters a and b as reported in row 6 from the Table 8 for the e-function. The marginal product of water is calculated as the average price of water reported by

Ministry of Water Resources for the years 2006 and 2007 and multiplied by a factor λ which can take the alternative values of 4, 8 and 12. The elasticity of substitution between the composite of non-water capital and water, and labor is assumed to be unity and this value does not change during the experiments.

Table 9 reports the results of change in growth rates under the hypothesis that investments in water assets grew at zero after 1997 and under the assumption of different elasticities of substitution between water and non-water capital and different marginal products for water. The results show that if there was no growth in investments in water assets, output growth rates would have been changed only a little when compared to actual output growth rates if elasticity of substitution between water and non-water capital was 1.1 or 0.75.

Larger changes in output growth rates occur if the elasticity of substitution approaches zero and water and non-water capital become almost perfect complements. If elasticity of substitution was 0.25 or 0.025, output growth rates would have been decreased in 2009 by as much as 1.3–1.8 percentage points. In the first years of the experiment, the magnitude of growth decrease when compared to actual growth rates is not so large, but as diminishing returns to non-water capital, the faster growing factor, occurs faster than, otherwise, the decrease in output growth rates becomes larger and larger. When the elasticity of substitution is 0.025 the diminishing returns sets in much faster and growth rates fall earlier than when the elasticity of substitution is 0.25 (see Table 9).

The actual average growth rate of real non-water capital for the period 1998–2009 was around 12.5% per year and the growth rate of water in efficiency units was 9.29%. If there was no growth in investments in water assets, the efficiency of water use would have increased from 13.02 in 1997 to 27.09 in 2009 (20.8% lower than the actual efficiency of water use) and water efficiency increments would have been around 1.17 unit per year. The growth rate of water in efficiency units falls from 9.29% to 6.93% per year (around 25% lower), and because there is more investment available for non-water capital assets, the growth rate of real non-water capital raises a little to 12.7% per year. Therefore, with a very low elasticity of substitution, a faster growth of non-water capital input relative to water in efficiency units indicates that the implicit share of non-water capital would decrease, and the share of water would increase over time. As a result, the growth rate of output would decrease, because of the larger share on the growth rate of water in efficiency units which was lower than the growth rate of non-water capital.

Table 10 reports the results of change in growth rates under the strong hypothesis that there were no investments in water assets (they were set at zero) between 1997 and 2009. We assume that the savings rate in the economy was the same between 1997 and 2009 and instead of investing in water assets, investments took place in non-water assets. Under these assumptions, the change in growth rates is negative.

Table 9. **Change in growth rates under the hypothesis that there was no growth in investments in water assets 1998–2009 (percentage point change).**

	$\gamma = 1.1$			$\gamma = 0.75$			$\gamma = 0.25$			$\gamma = 0.025$		
	Marginal Product of Water = $P_W \times \lambda$											
Year	$\lambda = 4$	$\lambda = 8$	$\lambda = 12$	$\lambda = 4$	$\lambda = 8$	$\lambda = 12$	$\lambda = 4$	$\lambda = 8$	$\lambda = 12$	$\lambda = 4$	$\lambda = 8$	$\lambda = 12$
1998	0.05	0.04	0.03	0.04	0.03	0.02	−0.03	−0.10	−0.15	−0.58	−0.58	−0.58
1999	0.08	0.07	0.06	0.08	0.06	0.04	−0.04	−0.14	−0.23	−0.91	−0.91	−0.91
2000	0.11	0.09	0.08	0.10	0.08	0.06	−0.09	−0.24	−0.36	−1.19	−1.19	−1.19
2001	0.08	0.07	0.05	0.08	0.06	0.04	−0.09	−0.22	−0.32	−1.02	−1.02	−1.02
2002	0.09	0.08	0.06	0.08	0.06	0.04	−0.18	−0.38	−0.51	−1.15	−1.15	−1.15
2003	0.09	0.07	0.06	0.08	0.05	0.02	−0.38	−0.65	−0.82	−1.26	−1.26	−1.26
2004	0.10	0.08	0.06	0.09	0.06	0.03	−0.26	−0.49	−0.65	−1.41	−1.41	−1.41
2005	0.08	0.06	0.04	0.07	0.04	0.01	−0.44	−0.72	−0.88	−1.38	−1.38	−1.38
2006	0.05	0.03	0.01	0.03	0.01	−0.02	−0.50	−0.77	−0.92	−1.29	−1.29	−1.29
2007	0.04	0.02	0.01	0.02	−0.01	−0.04	−0.81	−1.13	−1.28	−1.33	−1.33	−1.33
2008	0.04	0.02	0.00	0.02	−0.01	−0.04	−0.88	−1.18	−1.31	−1.39	−1.39	−1.39
2009	0.10	0.08	0.06	0.08	0.03	−0.01	−1.35	−1.73	−1.87	−1.81	−1.81	−1.81

Source: Authors' calculations based on China Statistical Yearbook (1996–2009).

Table 10. Change in growth rates under the hypothesis that there were no investments in water assets 1998–2009 (percentage point change).

	$\gamma = 1.1$			$\gamma = 0.75$			$\gamma = 0.25$			$\gamma = 0.025$		
	Marginal Product of Water $= P_W \times \lambda$											
Year	$\lambda = 4$	$\lambda = 8$	$\lambda = 12$	$\lambda = 4$	$\lambda = 8$	$\lambda = 12$	$\lambda = 4$	$\lambda = 8$	$\lambda = 12$	$\lambda = 4$	$\lambda = 8$	$\lambda = 12$
1998	0.10	0.03	−0.04	0.07	−0.03	−0.13	−0.71	−1.37	−1.87	−5.37	−5.37	−5.37
1999	0.11	0.04	−0.03	0.08	−0.02	−0.12	−0.83	−1.54	−2.06	−5.29	−5.29	−5.29
2000	0.12	0.05	−0.02	0.08	−0.03	−0.13	−1.32	−2.21	−2.80	−5.25	−5.25	−5.25
2001	0.07	0.01	−0.05	0.04	−0.06	−0.16	−1.43	−2.26	−2.77	−4.78	−4.78	−4.78
2002	0.07	0.01	−0.04	0.02	−0.08	−0.18	−2.21	−3.17	−3.67	−4.69	−4.69	−4.69
2003	0.05	0.00	−0.05	−0.01	−0.12	−0.23	−3.43	−4.41	−4.80	−4.59	−4.59	−4.59
2004	0.05	−0.01	−0.06	0.00	−0.10	−0.20	−2.56	−3.29	−3.62	−4.51	−4.51	−4.51
2005	0.03	−0.02	−0.07	−0.03	−0.14	−0.24	−3.51	−4.14	−4.36	−4.31	−4.31	−4.31
2006	−0.01	−0.06	−0.10	−0.07	−0.17	−0.28	−3.68	−4.15	−4.29	−4.09	−4.09	−4.09
2007	−0.02	−0.06	−0.10	−0.09	−0.20	−0.32	−4.77	−5.03	−5.00	−3.99	−3.99	−3.99
2008	−0.02	−0.06	−0.10	−0.09	−0.20	−0.31	−4.53	−4.65	−4.59	−3.79	−3.79	−3.79
2009	0.05	0.00	−0.04	−0.05	−0.18	−0.31	−5.54	−5.46	−5.29	−4.13	−4.13	−4.13

Source: Authors' calculations based on China Statistical Yearbook (1996–2009).

When elasticity of substitution is 1.1 or 0.75, the change in output growth rates is small (but larger than in the case of no growth of investments in water assets). As the elasticity of substitution decreases, growth is lowered to a larger extent.

The major changes in output growth occur when the elasticity of substitution is 0.25 and 0.025. In 2009 growth rates would be reduced by 4.1–5.5 percentage points. This is because with no investments in water assets the efficiency of water use remains constant at 13.02 and water in efficiency units changes very little (grows at 0.6% per year). On the other hand, the capital stock in non-water assets grows at the rate of 12.7% per year. With a higher growth rate of the capital stock and almost no growth in water in efficiency units and an elasticity of substitution less than 1, the share of water (the slow growth factor) increases and the share of the faster growing input decreases leading to a fall in output growth which gets larger every year.

Table 11 reports our results under the hypothesis that investments in water assets grew twice the rate actually observed between 1997 and 2009. In this case, investments in non-water assets would have been smaller than they were in the period considered. In this case, growth rates would have decreased by 0.03–1.38 percentage points if the elasticity of substitution was 1.1 or 0.75. But output and growth rates would increase if elasticity of substitution was 0.25 or 0.025. The biggest increase in output and growth rates occurs if the elasticity of substitution was 0.025. With double the growth rate for investments in water assets the efficiency of water use increases from 13.02 in 1997 to 45.87 in 2009, 33.9% higher in 2009 when compared to the actual efficiency of water use of 34 in 2009. Along with this increase in efficiency, water use in efficiency units also increases at an average rate of about 11.73% per year. On the other hand, the growth rate of the real capital stock falls a little to 11.7% per year. Therefore, water in efficiency units contributes positively to growth of output in this case.

In Table 12 we also report a sensitivity analysis of the change in growth rates using a Cobb–Douglas production function, where the elasticity of substitution is unity and factors shares are constant over time. The results obtained are close to the results reported in Tables 8, 10 and 11 under the hypothesis that the elasticity of substitution is 1.1.

We also report sensitivity analysis of change in growth rates using the CES production function under different assumptions of values of parameters a and b that are calculated in Table 8. The sensitivity analysis shows that the results of the counterfactual experiments are almost the same in all cases if non-water capital and water are close substitutes. On the other hand, the results show larger variations in counterfactual experiments if non-water capital and water are poor substitutes. If the power of e-function, parameter b, takes higher values closer to 1, a one unit increase in investments in water assets increases the efficiency of water use by larger amounts if the parameter b is closer to 0.

Table 11. Change in growth rates under the hypothesis that there was double the growth rate of investments in water assets 1998–2009 (percentage point change).

	$\gamma = 1.1$			$\gamma = 0.75$			$\gamma = 0.25$			$(\gamma = 0.025)$		
	Marginal Product of Water = $P_W \times \lambda$											
Year	$\lambda = 4$	$\lambda = 8$	$\lambda = 12$	$\lambda = 4$	$\lambda = 8$	$\lambda = 12$	$\lambda = 4$	$\lambda = 8$	$\lambda = 12$	$\lambda = 4$	$\lambda = 8$	$\lambda = 12$
1998	−0.05	−0.04	−0.04	−0.05	−0.04	−0.03	0.01	0.07	0.11	0.47	0.47	0.47
1999	−0.11	−0.10	−0.09	−0.11	−0.09	−0.07	−0.01	0.08	0.15	0.82	0.82	0.82
2000	−0.20	−0.18	−0.17	−0.19	−0.17	−0.15	−0.04	0.10	0.21	1.13	1.13	1.13
2001	−0.15	−0.14	−0.13	−0.15	−0.13	−0.11	−0.04	0.07	0.15	0.95	0.95	0.95
2002	−0.23	−0.21	−0.19	−0.22	−0.19	−0.17	−0.03	0.13	0.25	1.12	1.12	1.12
2003	−0.29	−0.27	−0.25	−0.28	−0.25	−0.22	0.04	0.28	0.45	1.27	1.27	1.27
2004	−0.41	−0.39	−0.37	−0.41	−0.37	−0.34	−0.20	−0.01	0.14	1.48	1.48	1.48
2005	−0.41	−0.39	−0.36	−0.40	−0.37	−0.33	−0.10	0.13	0.31	1.45	1.45	1.45
2006	−0.32	−0.30	−0.28	−0.31	−0.28	−0.25	−0.02	0.20	0.36	1.33	1.33	1.33
2007	−0.39	−0.37	−0.35	−0.38	−0.34	−0.31	0.10	0.42	0.63	1.41	1.41	1.41
2008	−0.52	−0.49	−0.47	−0.50	−0.46	−0.43	0.00	0.33	0.55	1.52	1.52	1.52
2009	−1.38	−1.34	−1.29	−1.35	−1.29	−1.22	−0.50	0.05	0.41	2.10	2.10	2.10

Source: Authors' calculations based on China Statistical Yearbook (1996–2009).

Table 12. Sensitivity analysis of change in growth rates using Cobb–Douglas production function under different hypotheses (percentage point change).

	No growth of investments in water assets			No investments in water assets			Double growth of investments in water assets		
	Marginal Product of Water = $P_W \times \lambda$								
Year	$\lambda = 4$	$\lambda = 8$	$\lambda = 12$	$\lambda = 4$	$\lambda = 8$	$\lambda = 12$	$\lambda = 4$	$\lambda = 8$	$\lambda = 12$
1998	0.04	0.03	0.01	0.04	−0.10	−0.24	−0.04	−0.03	−0.02
1999	0.07	0.04	0.01	0.04	−0.11	−0.25	−0.10	−0.08	−0.05
2000	0.10	0.06	0.03	0.05	−0.08	−0.22	−0.19	−0.15	−0.12
2001	0.07	0.04	0.01	0.01	−0.12	−0.24	−0.14	−0.11	−0.08
2002	0.08	0.05	0.01	0.01	−0.11	−0.23	−0.21	−0.18	−0.14
2003	0.08	0.04	0.01	0.00	−0.12	−0.23	−0.28	−0.24	−0.20
2004	0.08	0.04	0.00	−0.01	−0.13	−0.25	−0.40	−0.35	−0.30
2005	0.06	0.02	−0.01	−0.03	−0.14	−0.25	−0.39	−0.35	−0.30
2006	0.03	−0.01	−0.04	−0.07	−0.17	−0.27	−0.31	−0.26	−0.22
2007	0.02	−0.01	−0.05	−0.07	−0.17	−0.27	−0.37	−0.33	−0.28
2008	0.02	−0.02	−0.05	−0.07	−0.17	−0.26	−0.51	−0.46	−0.40
2009	0.08	0.03	−0.02	−0.01	−0.12	−0.22	−1.40	−1.31	−1.21

Source: Authors' calculations based on China Statistical Yearbook (1996–2009).

Given the results obtained under the assumption of different elasticities of substitution and investments in water assets, one could also ask what would be the optimal value of investments in water assets which minimize the reduction in output in the year? The response to this question depends on the elasticity of substitution between non-water capital and water in efficiency units. If the elasticity of substitution is high and the share of water in production is low, then it is optimal to invest more in non-water capital assets, instead of water assets, because the share in production is higher. The growth in output is about 0.1 if there would be no growth of investments in water assets. If the elasticity of substitution between non-water capital and water in efficiency units is low, then investing more in water assets would also benefit growth (see Table 14).

Table 14 reports some projections of future changes in real GDP growth rates for the period 2010–2022 if there is no growth of investments in water assets, no investments in water assets and double the growth rate of investments in water assets. We compare the growth rates of real GDP under counterfactual analyses with projected growth rates of real GDP if real GDP, real investments in non-water assets and real investments in water assets continue to grow at the average annual growth rates from the last 10 years. If the elasticity of substitution between non-water capital and water in efficiency units, γ, is 1.1 then GDP growth rates would slightly increase by 0.1 percentage points per year if there is no growth of investments in

Table 13. Sensitivity analysis of change in growth rates using CES production functions under different parameterizations (percentage point change).

	No growth of investments in water assets													
	$\gamma = 1.1$							$\gamma = 0.025$						
Year	$a = 0.013$ $b = 0.717$	$a = 0.090$ $b = 0.407$	$a = 0.101$ $b = 0.391$	$a = 0.001$ $b = 0.965$	$a = 0.001$ $b = 0.930$	$a = 0.152$ $b = 0.340$	$a = 0.058$ $b = 0.465$	$a = 0.013$ $b = 0.717$	$a = 0.090$ $b = 0.407$	$a = 0.101$ $b = 0.391$	$a = 0.001$ $b = 0.965$	$a = 0.001$ $b = 0.930$	$a = 0.152$ $b = 0.340$	$a = 0.058$ $b = 0.465$
1998	0.03	0.04	0.04	0.03	0.04	0.04	0.04	−1.15	−0.63	−0.61	−1.03	−0.52	−0.58	−0.67
1999	0.04	0.07	0.07	0.04	0.07	0.07	0.06	−1.92	−1.02	−0.99	−1.86	−0.99	−0.91	−1.10
2000	0.06	0.09	0.09	0.06	0.09	0.09	0.09	−2.59	−1.34	−1.30	−2.69	−1.49	−1.19	−1.47
2001	0.04	0.06	0.07	0.03	0.06	0.07	0.06	−2.21	−1.17	−1.13	−2.39	−1.41	−1.02	−1.29
2002	0.04	0.07	0.07	0.03	0.06	0.08	0.07	−2.57	−1.33	−1.29	−2.90	−1.77	−1.15	−1.48
2003	0.04	0.07	0.07	0.03	0.06	0.07	0.07	−2.83	−1.46	−1.41	−3.32	−2.11	−1.26	−1.64
2004	0.03	0.07	0.07	0.02	0.05	0.08	0.07	−3.22	−1.65	−1.59	−3.90	−2.55	−1.41	−1.86
2005	0.02	0.06	0.06	0.00	0.03	0.06	0.05	−3.13	−1.62	−1.56	−3.88	−2.65	−1.38	−1.83
2006	−0.01	0.02	0.03	−0.03	0.00	0.03	0.02	−2.90	−1.52	−1.46	−3.64	−2.58	−1.29	−1.72
2007	−0.02	0.02	0.02	−0.04	−0.01	0.02	0.01	−3.02	−1.58	−1.52	−3.86	−2.82	−1.33	−1.80
2008	−0.02	0.01	0.02	−0.04	−0.02	0.02	0.01	−3.14	−1.65	−1.58	−4.05	−3.02	−1.39	−1.87
2009	0.02	0.07	0.07	−0.02	0.02	0.08	0.06	−4.48	−2.19	−2.09	−6.14	−4.60	−1.81	−2.52

Source: Authors' calculations based on China Statistical Yearbook (1996–2009).

*Marginal Product of Water = $P_W \times \lambda$; $\lambda = 8$.

Table 14. Future projections of change in growth rates under different hypotheses of growth in investments in water assets 2009–2022 (percentage point change).

	No growth of investments in water assets				No investments in water assets				Double growth of investments in water assets			
	$\lambda = 8$*				$\lambda = 8$*				$\lambda = 8$*			
Year	$\gamma = 1.1$	$\gamma = 0.75$	$\gamma = 0.25$	$\gamma = 0.025$	$\gamma = 1.1$	$\gamma = 0.75$	$\gamma = 0.25$	$\gamma = 0.025$	$\gamma = 1.1$	$\gamma = 0.75$	$\gamma = 0.25$	$\gamma = 0.025$
2010	0.05	0.04	−0.10	−0.24	0.23	0.16	−2.16	−4.18	−0.05	−0.04	0.08	0.21
2011	0.08	0.07	−0.22	−0.44	0.19	0.10	−2.78	−4.11	−0.10	−0.09	0.19	0.41
2012	0.11	0.09	−0.37	−0.61	0.15	0.05	−3.29	−4.06	−0.16	−0.14	0.31	0.60
2013	0.12	0.10	−0.53	−0.76	0.12	0.01	−3.68	−4.00	−0.23	−0.21	0.45	0.77
2014	0.13	0.11	−0.70	−0.89	0.10	−0.02	−3.95	−3.95	−0.31	−0.28	0.60	0.94
2015	0.14	0.11	−0.86	−1.01	0.09	−0.05	−4.11	−3.91	−0.40	−0.37	0.74	1.09
2016	0.14	0.11	−1.02	−1.12	0.08	−0.07	−4.19	−3.87	−0.52	−0.48	0.88	1.23
2017	0.14	0.10	−1.16	−1.21	0.07	−0.10	−4.21	−3.83	−0.66	−0.61	1.01	1.37
2018	0.14	0.10	−1.29	−1.29	0.06	−0.12	−4.19	−3.79	−0.84	−0.78	1.13	1.49
2019	0.14	0.09	−1.41	−1.37	0.06	−0.13	−4.15	−3.76	−1.06	−0.99	1.23	1.60
2020	0.14	0.08	−1.50	−1.44	0.05	−0.15	−4.10	−3.73	−1.33	−1.25	1.30	1.71
2021	0.14	0.07	−1.59	−1.50	0.05	−0.17	−4.04	−3.70	−1.68	−1.59	1.35	1.80
2022	0.13	0.06	−1.66	−1.56	0.05	−0.19	−3.98	−3.68	−2.13	−2.03	1.34	1.89

Source: Authors' calculations based on China Statistical Yearbook (1996–2009).

*Marginal Product of Water = $P_W \times \lambda$.

water assets. If the growth rates of investments in water assets were twice the growth rate from the past, the GDP growth rates would decrease by 0.05–2.13 percentage points per year between 2010 and 2022.

If non-water capital and water in efficiency units are poor substitutes, γ is 0.025, GDP growth rates would increase by 0.2–1.89 percentage points per year if investments in water assets would increase at twice the rate from the past. The growth would decrease by 0.2–1.5 percentage points per year if there would be no growth of investments in water assets and by 3.6–4.1 if there would be no investments in water assets.

6 Concluding Remarks

In this paper, we use a growth accounting approach to investigate both the contribution played in the past by water availability in constraining China's growth performance, and what would be involved in the future. We use a modified version of Solow growth accounting in which water in efficiency units enters the production technology, and investment in water management assets raises efficiency of water use. We note that China's high growth in the last 20 years or more has been obtained with relatively little increase in the physical volume of water. We adopt various assumptions on the relationship between the price of water and marginal product, and on substitution elasticities in making our calculations.

Our counterfactual experiments suggest that water affects China's growth rates and will affect growth in the future but at uncertain rates. The degree depends on the elasticity of substitution between non-water capital and water in efficiency units and on the size of investments in water assets. If investments in water assets in the future were lower than they were in the past, growth might slightly increase by about 0.1 percentage points if non-water capital and water in efficiency units are close substitutes, but growth rates could decrease by as much as 0.2–3.9 percentage points if investments in water assets were very small, and if the elasticities of substitution were low.

On the other hand, our experiments suggest that with faster growth of investments in water assets than in the past, low elasticity of substitution growth could increase. If non-water capital and water in efficiency units are close substitutes growth rates could even decrease.

Acknowledgment

The authors are grateful to the Ontario Research Fund for financial support.

References

Bai, C.E., C.T. Hsieh and Y. Qian (2006), The Return to Capital in China. *NBER Working Paper* 12755, Massachusetts: NBER.

Barro, R.J. and X. Sala-i-Martin (2004), *Economic Growth*, Second Edition, Institute of Technology, Massachusetts.

Blanke, A., S. Rozelle, B. Lohmar, J. Wang and J. Huang (2007), Water Saving Technology and Saving Water in China, *Agricultural Water Management*, 87, 139–150.

Bosworth, B. and S.M. Collins (2007), Accounting for Growth: Comparing China and India, *Working Paper* 12943, Massachusetts: NBER.

Brown, L. (1996), Who will feed China?, *Futurist*, January/February, 30(1), p. 14.

Denison, E. (1962), Sources of Growth in the United States and the Alternatives Before Us, *Supplement Paper 13*, Committee for Economic Development, New York.

Gleick, P.H. (2009), China and Water in *The World's Water 2008–2009*, The Biennial Report of Freshwater Resources, Washington, DC: Island Press.

Grebenstein, C. and B. Field (1979), Substituting for Water Inputs in U.S. Manufacturing, *Water Resources Research*, 15(2).

Hubacek, K. and L. Sun (2007), Economic and Societal Changes in China and their Effects on Water Use, *Journal of Industrial Ecology*, 9(1–2), 187–200.

Jiang, Y. (2009), China's Water Scarcity, *Journal of Environmental Management*, 90, 3185–3196.

Jin, L. and W. Young (2001), Water Use in Agriculture in China: Importance, Challenges, and Implications for Policy, *Water Policy*, 3, 215–228.

Jorgenson, D.W. and Z. Griliches (1967), The Explanation of Productivity Change, *Review of Economic Studies*, 34, 249–280.

Kemfert, C. (1998), Estimated Substitution Elasticities of a Nested CES Production Function Approach for Germany, *Energy Economics*, 20, 249–264.

Kendrick, J.W. (1961), *Productivity Trends in the United States*, Princeton University Press, Princeton, NJ.

Liang, H. (2006), China's Investment Strength is Sustainable, *Goldman Sachs Global Economics Paper no. 146*.

Ministry of Water Resources, P.R. China (2006), 2006 Statistic Bulletin on China Water Activities. Available from http://www.mwr.gov.cn/english/200601.pdf. Accessed on April 15th 2012.

Ministry of Water Resources, P.R. China (2007), 2007 Statistic Bulletin on China Water Activities. Available from: http://www.mwr.gov.cn/english/200701.pdf. Accessed on April 15th 2012.

National Bureau of Statistics (NBS), China Statistical Yearbook CSY, various years. Available from: http://www.stats.gov.cn/english/Statisticaldata/AnnualData/.

Naughton, B. (2007), Environmental Quality and the Sustainability of Growth, in *The Chinese Economy, Transitions and Growth*, The MIT Press, Cambridge, Massachusetts, London, England.

Nehru, V. and A. Dhareshwar (1993), A New Database on Physical Capital Stock: Sources, Methodology and Results, *Revista de Analisis Economico*, 8(1), 37–59.

OECD (2004), Financing Strategy of the Urban Wastewater Sector in Selected Municipalities of the Sichuan Province in China. Available from: http://www.oecd.org/dataoecd/44/23/2408767.pdf. Accessed on February 10th 2012.

OECD (2007), OECD Environmental Performance Reviews CHINA, OECD Publishing.

Shalizi, Z. (2006), Addressing China's Growing Water Shortages and Associated Social and Environmental Consequences. *World Bank Policy Research Working Paper 3895*.

Shalizi, Z. (2008), Water and Urbanization, in Yusuf, S. and T. Saich (Eds.): *China Urbanizes Consequences, Strategies, and Policies*, The World Bank, Washington, DC.

Solow, R.M. (1957), Technical Change and the Aggregate Production Function, *The Review of Economics and Statistics*, 39(3), 312–320.

Solow, R.M. (1978), Resources and Economic Growth, *American Economist*, 22(2), 5–11.

Wang, H. and S. Lall (2002), Valuing Water for Chinese Industries: A Marginal Productivity Analysis, *Applied Economics*, 34(6), 759–765.

Wang, Y. and Y. Yao (2003), Sources of China's Economic Growth 1952–1999: Incorporating Human Capital Accumulation, *China Economic Review*, 14, 32–52.

Whalley, J. and X. Zhao (2010), The Contribution of Human Capital to China's Economic Growth, *NBER Working Paper 16592*, Massachusetts: NBER.

World Bank (1997), Clear Water, Blue Skies: China's Environment in the New Century, The World Bank, Washington, DC.

World Bank (2009), Addressing China's Water Scarcity, Recommendations for Selected Water Resource Management Issues, The International Bank for Reconstruction and Development, The World Bank.

World Bank (2012), WDI (World Development Indicators). Available from: http://data.worldbank.org/data-catalog. Accessed on February 20th 2012.

Xinhua (2012), Water shortage, pollution threaten China's growth: Official. Available from: http://news.xinhuanet.com/english/china/2012-02/16/c_131414176.htm. Accessed on March 3rd 2012.

Young, A. (2003), Gold into Base Metals: Productivity Growth in the People's Republic of China during the Reform Period, *Journal of Political Economy*, 111(6).

Zheng, J., A. Bigsten and A. Hu (2009), Can China's Growth be Sustained? A Productivity Perspective, *World Development*, 37(4), 874–888.

Index